A COMMITMENT TO THE WORLD'S WOMEN

PERSPECTIVES ON DEVELOPMENT FOR BEIJING AND BEYOND

EDITED BY NOELEEN HEYZER

WITH SUSHMA KAPOOR & JOANNE SANDLER

UNIFEM

The United Nations Development Fund for Women (UNIFEM) was created as a result of the energetic advocacy of women at the 1975 International Women's Year (IWY) Tribune in Mexico City. Established by the United Nations in 1976 as the Voluntary Fund for the UN Decade for Women, UNIFEM became an autonomous organization within the UN family in 1985. UNIFEM provides direct technical and financial support to programmes that promote women. By supporting the full participation of women in the developing world to achieve their objectives of sustainable economic and social development and equality, UNIFEM works to improve the quality of life for all.

This book was published by UNIFEM's Advocacy Facility which prepares and disseminates state of the art information on women and development. The views expressed in this book are those of the authors and do not necessarily represent the views of UNIFEM, the United Nations or any of its affiliated organizations.

© 1995 UNIFEM
United Nations Development Fund for Women
304 East 45th Street, New York, NY 10017 USA

A Commitment to the World's Women: Perspectives on Development for Beijing and Beyond
Edited by Noeleen Heyzer
with Sushma Kapoor and Joanne Sandler
ISBN 0-912917-38-5

All UNIFEM publications are distributed by Women, Ink.
777 UN Plaza, New York, NY 10017 USA
Phone: (212) 687 8633 Fax: (212) 661 2704

Photos: (top to bottom) UNICEF, UNICEF/M. Murray-Lee, UNICEF/ J. Horner, U.N./ J.K. Issac, (middle) UNHCR/M. van Strien

Cover & book design by a. piccolo graphics

CONTENTS

ACKNOWLEDGEMENTS

As an organization that links the priorities and practices of the United Nations, governments, NGOs and the women's movement, UNIFEM's programme is dependent on close and synergistic working relationships with all of these actors. This anthology has benefited enormously from our history of bridging these worlds.

Our deepest appreciation must first be conveyed to the authors who so generously contributed their time and, most importantly, their thinking to the compilation of this book. The lives and work of these authors offer indisputable proof of their commitment to the ongoing project of putting women on the development agenda. Their willingness to take time out of their hectic schedules to revise or create articles for this book is a testimony to their unfailing commitment to women and to the work of UNIFEM. In this regard, special thanks must also go to the many individuals who work with them — secretaries, assistants and others — who necessarily became involved in transmitting, correcting and communicating about most of these contributions.

We want to acknowledge the work of the many individuals who were involved in the production of the final manuscript. Jane Garland Katz and Avis Lang tirelessly worked on copyediting and proofreading. Eleni Alemayehu also assisted throughout with typing, faxing and so many other critical tasks.

Our colleagues at UNIFEM are a constant source of support and inspiration in all of the publications work undertaken. For this anthology, they suggested authors and offered valuable editorial feedback.

Finally, this book would never have been conceived were it not for the realities and lives of the world's women. The courage and commitment with which so many women have confronted the challenge of making the world better now and for the next generation is awe-inspiring. Our partnerships with these women underpin all efforts to articulate and achieve a transformative development agenda for the 21st century.

PREFACE

BOUTROS BOUTROS-GHALI
SECRETARY-GENERAL, UNITED NATIONS

In September, 1995, in Beijing, the world community will gather at the invitation of the United Nations to discuss how to remove obstacles to the full participation of women in all spheres of public and private life, including economic and political decision-making.

The Beijing Conference is the fifth in the cycle of global conferences, all of which have stressed the vital role of women in the development process. At Beijing, Governments will build on work and institutional standard-setting from previous conferences. They will move towards a vision for the twenty-first century; that vision will include a much-needed gender perspective.

UNIFEM's publication of this book, *A Commitment to the World's Women,* comes, therefore, at an opportune moment. It raises for discussion, in an interesting and thought-provoking way, some of the crucial issues involving women and development. It provides useful guidance to the international community as we seek to build consensus on the concrete actions and commitments which Member States can undertake to ensure that women can be full and active participants in development.

A Commitment to the World's Women is a significant contribution to the process of formulating a new and compelling collective vision for the international community. I congratulate UNIFEM for bringing together in this volume so many leading thinkers, actors and advocates for women's advancement.

A Women's Development Agenda for the 21st Century

Noeleen Heyzer

As women and their Governments prepare for the Fourth World Conference on Women (WCW) in Beijing, September 1995, there seems to be agreement on one idea: This conference must develop a specific and realistic list of imperatives and commitments for advancing women's status and ensuring women's empowerment. In fact the Government of Australia made the plea to "ensure that the Fourth World Conference on Women is a Conference of Commitments."

Based on various levels of consultation and consensus during the preparatory process, the decades of work put in by women's groups toward understanding the grounded realities of women's lives at local levels, and the recommendations and strategies emanating from the five major UN conferences of this decade, there is a convergence of efforts at a multiplicity of levels to shape common directions and convert words into concrete outcomes.

In Beijing there has to be a forceful call to action, since the normal workings of economic and political processes will not automatically bring about the advancement of women. Women must have the commitment of their governments and the international community to pursue the following:

• the strong foundations and gains that have been made at the different world conferences and summits. From Rio to Vienna, Cairo and Copenhagen, Governments have acknowledged that the equality and empowerment of women are prerequisites for sustainable human development. In Beijing, the Platform for Action must be confirmed as the Agenda for Equality;

• gender-responsive development that will empower people, build on women's realities and rights, eradicate poverty and create sustainable livelihoods, build stable lives in healthy communities, and promote peace on a long term basis;

• an agreement by governments to eliminate the remaining gender gaps in basic needs, especially in education and health, over the next decade through an accelerated investment in a human development agenda at the country level;

• new partnerships between governments and civil society so that common problems can be addressed collectively and more effectively;

• a worldwide campaign for the elimination of violence against women;

• the ratification of the Convention on the Elimination of All Forms of Discrimination Against Women (CEDAW) to provide the legal framework for equality;

• adequate resources, mechanisms and processes for the implementation of the Beijing Platform for Action.

1

To assist in bringing clarity and understanding to the nature of these commitments, UNIFEM has brought together a collection of articles representing a diversity of insights. The book is organized into four parts: the first is on the economic empowerment of women: women's entitlement to, access and control over economic resources, assets, opportunities and benefits on a sustainable and long-term basis. The second part is on women's political empowerment: women's power to control their own lives within and outside the home, and their power to influence the direction of social change toward the creation of an equitable and sustainable society nationally and internationally. In both these sections, the different authors deal with issues in ways that provide guidance for policy and practice from the micro to the macro level. The empowerment of women economically and politically and the creation of an enabling environment through good governance based on the promotion of participatory decision-making and the development of human capacities are seen as mutually reinforcing processes for the sustainable eradication of poverty and the shift to gender equality and equity.

The third section of the book deals with the analysis of this decade's UN conferences. The key themes and threads at these conferences and women's action in the shaping of the international development agenda have focused on priority objectives and essential components for sustainable human development and women's empowerment: social services for all; access to productive assets, livelihoods and full employment; an enabling environment for poverty eradication and social development; gender equity and women's advancement; ecologically sustainable development. These issues are further developed in this section as part of the women's development agenda — an agenda for change shaped from the synthesis of women's contributions on economic and political empowerment at major UN conferences and the regional preparations for the WCW in Beijing.

Finally, in part four, a symphony of different voices provide reflections on how to move from recommendations to actions that will empower women in the 21st century. The best practices of the last decade that have brought about changes, lessons learned, old problems that need new solutions, and the new problems seeking solutions can all be translated into a guiding vision for the future and a call to action. A shaping of the women's development agenda is hence our attempt, in a small way, to make visible analysis, synthesis, and some solutions that can convert the commitment to the world's women into concrete improvement in the lives of women.

SHAPING A WOMEN'S DEVELOPMENT AGENDA

Although much progress has been made since the First World Conference on Women in Mexico City 20 years ago, gender inequality still exists in many areas of life. There has been improvement in women's health and education. Women's life expectancy has increased 20 per cent faster than male life expectancy and maternal mortality rates have been nearly halved. In primary and secondary school education, the gender gap was halved in the last 20 years. In developing countries, female enrolment at the tertiary level increased to over 70 per cent of the male rate from less than 50 per cent in the 1970s. Despite such progress through investment in social development and human capacity building, we are preparing for the Fourth World Conference on Women and entering the 21st century with the following situation of women:

- Women earn 1/10 of the world's income, own less than 1/10 of the world's property and hold 1 per cent of chief executive positions worldwide.
- While progress has been made in terms of women's access to education, women still comprise two-thirds of people who cannot read or write. Women still represent

60 per cent of more than 1 billion adults who have no access to basic education. Girls constitute the majority of the 130 million children with no access to primary school; worldwide, girls currently attend school 55 per cent as much as boys do.

• Although economic progress has benefited many, a fifth of the world's people today live in absolute poverty. Poverty has a female face. Women are 70 per cent of the world's 1.3 billion absolute poor. Women within poor countries and communities are more impoverished than men. In African countries, for example, women account for more than 60 per cent of the agricultural labour force, contribute up to 80 per cent of the total food production and receive less than 10 per cent of the credit to small farmers and 1 per cent of the total credit to agriculture.

• In many ecologically fragile zones, especially those in war-torn areas and in communities undergoing economic and social disintegration, women and children comprise 75 per cent of affected and displaced people.

• Only 10 per cent of parliamentary seats and 6 per cent of cabinet positions are occupied by women.

These existing inequalities may be further deepened and new inequalities may emerge in the current development context where integration into the global market directs development, where there is accelerating technological change, where national economies are destabilized by transnational processes and where the ecological crisis facing humanity is at its worst. In many cases the structural collapse of some centrally planned economies and nation states, the casualization of work, cuts in social security, childcare and revenue for human development as countries undergo transition or structural adjustment to compete in the international market — all these have affected the livelihood and life-chances of women in the nineties more explicitly than the period preceding the World Conference to mark the end of the Decade for Women (Nairobi) in 1985. As a consequence, many of the gains made over the last twenty years may not be sustained in the next decade: women work longer hours, maintaining households on reduced resources; there are threats of increased transmission of intergenerational poverty along gender lines as girls are deprived of scarce household resources, held back from school, and expected to be the family's secondary nurturer.

These trends are not acceptable. We need to change the processes that have brought about a world of inequality, instability, and conflict. Today, given the ecological and social crisis and our endangered future there is an urgent need for humanity to renew the effort in visioning, commitment, and action as we enter a new century. This is, hence, a time for women to be bold, to explore new ideas, and to develop new visions and strategies.

In this era of increasing globalization, United Nations conferences are assuming ever greater significance in setting standards and directions for policy planning and practice at national, regional and global levels. At the UN Conference on Environment and Development in Rio (1992), world leaders accepted women's vital role in achieving sustainable development. At the World Conference on Human Rights in Vienna (1993), governments acknowledged that women's rights are human rights and paid attention to violence against women. At the International Conference on Population and Development in Cairo (1994), women's empowerment was recognized as a cornerstone of effective population policies. At the World Summit on Social Development in Copenhagen (1995), gender equality was recognized as a prerequisite for the achievement of productive employment, social integration and poverty eradication.

The Fourth World Conference on Women is a particularly crucial time for women to build on the achievements of the previous UN Conferences. To sustain this momentum, it is necessary to bring together issues of environment, human rights, population, development and women's empowerment, as interlinked phenomena. These are related, not isolated and unconnected topics.

At Beijing, women want to affirm the kind of world we want to live in. This world is one where development processes will empower people and women in particular. It has to be one where we can create sustainable livelihoods, build stable lives in healthy communities, where we can build peace and resolve conflict on a long-term basis. For this to happen, we need a new development ethics and morality to be placed at the core of development thinking and practices. This has to include the perspectives and realities of women's lives. The objective is to keep pulling together opposing strands of thought, so that differences can be negotiated on an ongoing basis, resulting in the firm establishment of common ground. Therefore, the WCW is a particularly crucial time for women all over the world to add their voices to the strengthening of a Women's Development Agenda for the 21st Century.

What then is the substance of this Women's Development Agenda? The Women's Development Agenda addresses the key challenges of our time in four ways:

- *Through finding new pathways of development that will eliminate the feminization of poverty, provide equitable benefits for all and cease to generate new patterns of poverty in the wake of economic restructuring and globalization.* This requires a fundamental shift in development thinking, planning and practice. The move towards a shift in the development process has already been initiated by those who are focusing on the basic needs and entitlements of the poor and who are pushing for direct and systematic social development that would secure livelihoods and eradicate poverty. It is important that in the search for alternative development processes, women's perspectives and realities are not lost, for then one development mistake would be replaced by another. The Women's Development Agenda places gender equity as the central principle of a new development process that would benefit women and men equally.

- *The creation of new modes of environmental and social sustainability that take into account the everyday processes of how people produce, consume, survive and reproduce in specific societal contexts.* The Women's Development Agenda emphasizes women's livelihood needs and the key role that women play in maintaining the ecological sustainability and renewability of finite natural resources. Women's livelihood needs and realities must therefore be the primary basis on which resource use and allocation is decided.

- *The social reintegration and rebuilding of stable lives for women affected by war, and economic and social disintegration.* In this context, it is vital to ensure the daily security and well-being of ordinary people whose lives are disrupted by massive and sudden changes that have been dictated by both global and local events. But apart from analysing the causes and consequences of these processes — environmental degradation, land loss, war, and poverty — the Women's Development Agenda seeks to provide possible directions and solutions. As peace is a vital foundation for the sustainable livelihoods and secure lives of all persons, women seek constructive ways of actively mediating for global peace.

- *Through the promotion of development ethics and good governance based on equity, sustainability, and social justice.* Policies emerging from a system of good governance would be responsive to the livelihood needs and realities of women and communities instead of serving powerful private interests and threatening livelihoods through the appropriation of development resources. The Women's Development Agenda thus calls for the capacity to deal with global economic forces without sacrificing the sustainabililty of the lives of women and communities. Women's transformative role is crucial now, when the human race is facing what is perhaps our most decisive challenge of collective survival.

The Women's Development Agenda is thus based on the principle of social justice that addresses women's livelihood needs in terms of their access to and control over resources. It seeks to engender new development thinking and practice, a new ethics of governance, and new processes of leadership. This innovative agenda looks forward to the creation of new institutions, new social values and new community structures. This agenda aims to empower women to reorient and reshape the policies and decisions visited on them.

NEW PATHWAYS OF DEVELOPMENT

Understanding the Causes of Women's Poverty

The challenge of finding new pathways of development that will provide gender-equitable benefits is the first priority, given that the "feminization of poverty" has become a global phenomenon. Currently more than 564 million women live in absolute poverty in rural areas (60 per cent of the world's 1 billion rural poor). This is a 50 per cent increase for women since 1970 compared to a 30 per cent increase for men over the same period.

The impoverishment of women has been exacerbated by the transformations taking place in the world economic system through trade deregulation, rapid technological changes, changes in industrial production, the transition to a market economy, structural adjustment programmes, and the power of global financial markets. These processes of global economic restructuring are uneven. While some sectors of society enjoy the benefits of rapid growth, others experience stagnation or even a deterioration in living standards. These processes have created new patterns of wealth and poverty. They have simultaneously provided new opportunities and intensified existing inequalities or even created new ones. Indeed, these processes have gender-differentiated consequences for men and women, due to the constraints of the gender hierarchy imposed on women's ownership of assets, educational and employment opportunities, and physical and social mobility.

It is clear from existing evidence that:

- the recession of the 1980s and the cutback of state welfare programmes have impacted more severely on women than on men;
- female wage labour has been displaced by certain forms of agro-technology without new forms of employment being generated;
- new opportunities for the creation of women's employment are primarily in the low-waged, casual segment of the labour market, such that increased employment does not lead to increased quality of life.

The process of impoverishment through a weakening or loss of the household resource base brings about poverty for both women and men. However, women experience poverty more profoundly than men do through impoverishment in three ways:

- *First, through more limited access to scarce and valued resources.* Women, in many

5

societies, have fewer entitlements not just to economic resources but also to the physical, legal, social, and cultural entitlements that are the basis of well-being and a sense of self-worth: less food, less health care, less education, less leisure and lower economic returns for their labour. Women have less command over labour, both their own and that of men. In crisis situations, women's assets are often sold before men's assets. There is also a tendency for households headed by females to be poor, especially those maintained entirely by female earnings and those with dependent children, due to the gender inequalities that disadvantage women in the labour market.

• *Second, through the disintegration of support systems.* With the breakdown of systems of reciprocity and support, women's burden becomes even heavier than men's, because women have to struggle not just to keep themselves alive but also to ensure the survival of those dependent on their care and nurture — the young, the old, the sick and the disabled. In cases where a working woman is able to transfer her domestic workload, it is shifted to other women — usually those who are older, dependent, or poorer. The burden of housework, child care and other dimensions of the domestic workload is seen as the sole responsibility of women rather than the shared responsibility of both men and women.

• *Third, through the intergenerational transfer of poverty along gender lines.* The family's scarce resources are bestowed on sons so that they can escape from the poverty trap. Daughters, on the other hand, are deprived of these scarce resources, held back from school and expected to be the family's secondary nurturers, assisting in the care of siblings and other needy members of the family. This has severe consequences for the intergenerational transmission of poverty, as girls born into poverty are brought up to be women who will remain in poverty. It also results in the transmission of gender injustice, where the girl child's rights to life and her own person are not assured. Girl children born into poverty are more likely to suffer early deaths — either through deliberate infanticide or through less deliberate but no less fatal deprivation of food, clothes and health care. If a girl child is allowed to live, she is often vulnerable to abuse, condemned to remain illiterate, or reduced to being a family resource to be sold into bondage, whether as child-bride, prostitute or debt-slave.

These tendencies are exacerbated in times of internal crisis (such as the illness or death of the main breadwinner), or external crisis (such as the rising prices of basic foodstuff and other necessities, or environmental disasters including floods and earthquakes).

For these reasons, policies and programmes to reduce poverty need to be sensitive to gender issues within and among households. Within households, efforts to provide the fulfilment of basic needs must take into account the intra-house dynamics which affect use of income and decisions over resource allocation along gender lines. Policies geared to the abstract category of women without considering their current responsibilities within the household and how these are going to be substituted for, run the risk of merely sharing certain burdens differently among each group. When new demands are made on women's time something has to give and that something is, more often than not, another woman's time. Very often macro-level data on poverty conceals these differences and overlooks reality at the micro-level.

Possible Solutions Poverty elimination cannot be a piecemeal effort directed on a case-by-case basis at local communities, as if poverty itself were a problem intrinsic to these communities. Over and beyond these communities, the processes of impoverishment through dispossession, dislocation and de-skilling, are occurring nationally and globally.

Since the two main obstacles to the improvement of the condition of women in poverty are their positions of powerlessness and time constraints, development policies should empower women, alleviate the "double burden" of women in poverty and increase the economic returns to the time they spend working.

The transformative poverty agenda needs to begin from a recognition of women's achievements, not their neediness. It should aim at enhancing women's capabilities, not their dependence. It starts by building economically on what assets poor women have. The skills and knowledge of women are of special importance in ensuring not only their own survival but indeed the survival of whole families and communities. Unfortunately, the poor have generally been stereotyped as the unskilled and uneducated, capable only of lowly-paid manual labour. Such a stereotype has been used particularly on women, who are disadvantaged in education and employment opportunities, and who are therefore often regarded as fit only for domestic work, factory work or other forms of menial labour. While it may be the case that the poor, especially poor women, have not significantly acquired an urban-biased, middle-class form of school education, they are nevertheless in possession of their own tried and tested survival skills and environmental knowledge. But unfortunately, such skills and knowledge are either ignored, under-valued, or commercially exploited by others. We need to install macro-economic social policies that allow women to exercise and build on their existing skills.

Ensuring an increase in women's rights and entitlements over resources and their own labour has emerged as an important policy objective for which a variety of measures can be advocated. These measures may be roughly summarized as follows:

- *The protection of women's existing sources of livelihood.* Governments and planners must not promote development that actually results in the loss of female control over earnings that were traditionally theirs. There are numerous examples of displacement of female labour and consequent loss of income in agriculture, manufacturing, and trading. This is an area where measures to provide women with the necessary training, organizational skills and credit resources so that they can retain activities over which they already have some control has particular pertinence.
- *The elimination of discriminatory laws on the ownership and control of productive assets.* The elimination of legislation barring women from access to productive assets in terms of rights of inheritance, ownership and control of property and the adoption of positive measures to ensure their equitable access to land, livestock, and other productive resources is essential. However, legal access to resources does not, in and of itself, ensure control.
- *The promotion of equitable access to agricultural inputs, credit, extension services, and education.* The inequality of women's access to agricultural inputs, credit and services as well as to extension and education have been well documented. Access to credits and to favourable terms is problematic for all economically and politically disadvantaged groups. In the case of rural women, these problems are compounded by the fact that their recognition as legal adults has in many places yet to be established. The measures proposed to enhance rural women's access to credit range from the support of grass roots self-help networks to the founding of cooperatives and the introduction of supportive government legal systems.
- *The support of extra-household forms of organization of women's labour.* There is strong advocacy for extra- or supra-family institutions to organize rural women's

7

work. A strong case is made, for instance, for separate women's organizations, such as women-only cooperatives. The choice is justified on several grounds, such as building on already existing female networks or modes of cooperation, avoiding confrontation with cultural patterns which oppose the mixing of unrelated men and women, and avoiding a submergence of women's interests and loss of leadership to men which occurs all too frequently in cooperatives with household membership.

• *Reducing women's double burden.* There is growing awareness that measures designed to enhance women's options as producers must be matched with parallel efforts to reduce their domestic responsibilities. An important factor to consider in this respect is that the creation of new opportunities for one category of women in a household should not work to the detriment of others. It is essential to look at the household as a total system and to evaluate the impact of changes in the life options of any member in terms of the effects it has on others. For example, opportunities to earn and control cash income for certain women should not result in their daughters being withdrawn from school to take care of household tasks and their younger siblings.

• *Eliminating violence against women and increasing their well-being.* There may still be an act of faith involved in the notion that providing women with a cash income will automatically ensure a significant improvement in their standing within the household. A factor that needs further investigation with direct implications for women's welfare has to do with changes in household dynamics following the creation of employment opportunities for women, especially in the context of male unemployment or underemployment. It may be worth exploring whether in situations of male dominance and where cultural systems emphasize male responsibilities there are short-term or long-term increases in domestic violence as well as other manifestations of stress and conflict. Conversely, where men's opportunities for earning wages are far ahead of those of women and where women are perceived as an economic liability, they may suffer great abuse, as in the case of India where soaring dowry rates have been related to the increasing incidence of dowry deaths and even to female infanticide. In some situations, there is the rise of religious fundamentalism as a means of curtailing women's autonomy. Conscious efforts must be directed to eliminate all forms of violence against women through legal and other means. On the whole there is relatively little detailed information about how changes in women's options affect sexual dynamics in the household and the workplace in different cultural settings. These effects should not be expected to be uniform or unilateral but should be explored in their own right, since they may spell the difference between increasing levels of harassment and abuse or, on the contrary, greater autonomy and well-being.

• *The encouragement of increased capacity for political empowerment, decision-making, and organization.* It is important to build rural women's organizational capacity to achieve significant advances in women's rights, entitlement, and access to resources, services, and even their own persons. Measures for women's political empowerment, decision-making and participation are crucial to any attempt to reduce poverty. There are now numerous women's organizations and solidarity networks outside the home in many cultures. The extent to which women's networks have been used and supported to help women survive, maintain existing privileges, resist unfair treatment or as political tools to create change is also being increasingly documented. Several studies, however, alert us to the fact that class, caste, and ethnic divisions may introduce strong competing loyalties as well as genuine differences of interests.

While the package or target-group approach to women in poverty might produce effects in the short term it can be no substitute for development strategies with a serious commitment to tackle the mechanisms that reproduce inequality and poverty. These strategies need to be informed by an acute awareness of the culturally and historically specific forms that women's subordination takes.

Strengthening Women's Livelihoods

Balancing ecological sustainability with economic viability The global environmental crisis cannot be addressed nor can there be sustainable development if the livelihoods of local communities are at risk. Yet there is a seeming contradiction between shorter-term economic needs and longer-term ecological imperatives. On the one hand, shorter-term economic needs have to be met without destroying long-term concerns for sustainability. On the other hand, longer-term ecological imperatives have to be addressed without neglecting the immediate livelihood needs of local communities. There is thus an urgent need to balance economic viability with ecological sustainability in an increasingly globalized world economy, where the social crisis of poverty converges with the environmental crisis.

Women in many societies mediate between these dualities. Women's reproductive labour, both biological and social, underwrites the entire process of human development. Not only do women bear and rear children, they are usually the managers of local resources on which everyday life depends. They attend to the long-term ecological imperatives of sustainability and renewability while also attending to the short-term livelihood needs of families and communities. In conditions of rapid change — including environmental deterioration, the outmigration of men, changing economic activities and aspirations, and government interventions — women play an even more crucial role in the maintenance of livelihoods, cultural continuity and community cohesiveness.

The crisis of resource depletion The ongoing degradation of the environment has put at risk many communities whose livelihoods depend on the sustainable use of natural resources. It has led to the massive displacement and disintegration of communities. The environmental changes that have adversely affected sustainable livelihoods include:

- the loss of land, topsoil, water quality, air quality, marine and other natural resources necessary for sustainable livelihoods;
- widespread deforestation and the loss of flora and fauna, including valuable food and medicinal resources; and
- the mismanagement of pollutants and wastes, including toxic- waste dumping in ecologically fragile zones

The degradation of nature has a negative impact on the whole population, especially the vulnerable members of the community. Women, in particular, are affected by the crisis of resource depletion faced by so many endangered local communities. As community care-givers and resource managers, women's daily lives are undermined by environmental degradation and the contamination of the raw materials they handle. Their problems and those of the environment are interrelated as both are marginalized by existing development policies.

The challenge of maintaining sustainable livelihoods in a degrading environment is

9

hence, a gender-differentiated challenge. Women are the ones who feel the immediate effects of environmental degradation and community disintegration, because of their responsibility for social reproduction and everyday livelihoods. Women are the main subsistence farmers of Africa, Asia and South America. Daily these women farmers are facing the challenge of maintaining sustainable livelihoods for themselves, their families and their communities, as their resource base of fuel, water, and food becomes increasingly depleted.

Furthermore, research on environmental health shows that as the level of contaminants rises in the environment, women's health declines in inverse relation, for women's bodies absorb more toxins than men's bodies do. There is thus a direct correlation between the state of environmental health and the state of women's health. These consequences of environmental degradation affect not just women themselves, but also the children they bear, the communities they nurture, and the resources they manage.

In the process of economic change, as resource-extractive industries penetrate the rural sector, men's livelihoods become based increasingly on wage work while women's livelihoods remain resource-based. This can lead to gender-differentiated conflicts of interest, even within a community, over the use and management of environmental resources. For these women, environmental conservation and sustainable development are not just philosophies but livelihood necessities.

Community disintegration and women's loss of status Environmental degradation leads inevitably to social and cultural disintegration, including the loss of indigenous knowledge relating to the management of the natural environment. As "people without papers" in a bureaucratic nation-state, many rural and indigenous communities face the loss of land and resource ownership through the absence of title deeds. Rural and indigenous communities are thus very vulnerable to the encroachment of the outside world, a vulnerability compounded by their naiveté about commercial dealings.

The loss of land and resources has often resulted in the massive movement of peoples within and between countries, often to areas that are also arid and infertile, making the question of everyday livelihoods a matter of serious concern. For rural and indigenous communities who live in close interdependency with the natural environment, the habitat itself constitutes the ecological context of indigenous knowledge of the environment. Loss of land, resources, and home means that such knowledge survives only as memories in the minds of the older generation.

These communal crises have serious consequences for women. The loss of indigenous identity and communal integrity often entails the loss of economic and social status for women, through:

- the loss of women's ownership or usufruct rights over land and resources that are often equal to men's rights in the indigenous land tenure systems but tend to be ignored by the state in the process of determining resource use;
- loss of the natural resources themselves, since women, more so than men, base their livelihoods on natural resources as a result of the gender-biased restrictions placed on their access to other economic opportunities;
- the increasing shortage and contamination of essential natural resources, causing longer hours of work and heavier workloads for women;
- a consequent decline in women's nutritional status and income as resources become more scarce;
- increased vulnerability to environmentally-related health problems;

- increasing isolation and lack of social support as traditional social structures and resource management systems break down; and
- sexual exploitation by men from outside the community taking advantage of women's naiveté, resulting in the risk of HIV infection and sexually transmitted diseases.

Where their very habitat and resource base are disappearing, many rural and indigenous communities are becoming environmental refugees experiencing dispossession and dislocation. If they enter the waged labour market, they tend to do so through the bottom, where they become proletarianized and impoverished recruits to the ranks of the urban poor.

Possible solutions: empowering women, sustaining livelihoods Women play a crucial role in the maintenance of livelihoods, cultural continuity, and community cohesiveness. Yet women's perspectives, which may differ significantly from those of men, have been invisible in the processes of change. These perspectives need to be integrated into the formulation of new modes of sustainability that would be viable and relevant in a modern world system. Hence, there is a need to make visible women's knowledge, particularly in relation to the maintenance of sustainable livelihoods for communities under threat and to the search for alternatives.

Given their crucial ecological and social role, the empowerment of women and the strengthening of communities actually form one single process. This process must address the affirmation of community-centred identities that prioritize their own needs and realities and the protection of communal rights over land and resources. The rights of the most vulnerable members, including women, must be taken into account throughout the process.

Development planning and practice must be needs-and-rights-based, with accountability to the poorest, the most powerless and the indigenous in society. Infusing development thinking and practice should be a morality which puts respect for life and the intrinsic worth of all human beings at the core. In the future, solutions to allow sustainable livelihoods to evolve will require that:

- there is active learning of the mistakes of past development processes in both industrialized and developing states;
- governments and international agencies facilitate the democratization of decision-making, and the articulation of people's voices (especially women's voices) at all levels and within all structures of civil society. Governments should facilitate the fullest participation of the people in both conceptualizing their development needs and goals and in development decision-making;
- governments undertake effective pro-active measures to safeguard environments that support the sustainable livelihoods of people, especially in the context of increasing environmental degradation due to industrial and military activities;
- monitoring organizations (both national and international) be created and strengthened to assess the social, gender and environmental impact of all policies and programmes;
- there is a rejection of conspicuous consumption as an expression of affluence and "growth." Instead there should be a serious re-thinking of development in terms of the enhancement of human worth, sustainability of livelihoods, and a framework for enhancing and building capacities towards goals of human development (such as those defined in the UNDP *Human Development Report*).
- there is an affirmation of the human right for all people to have sustainable

11

livelihoods in self-renewing ecosystems. There should thus be an increase in national budget allocations for the promotion of sustainable livelihoods and self-renewing environments;

• there is an emphasis on prevention of investments by the private sector and international capital that result in the further degradation of resources and the forced eviction of women and local communities;

• the vital role of women in maintaining inter-generational sustainability in a self-renewing environment is acknowledged.

In the context of structural adjustment programmes and new economic policies, governments and international agencies must undertake pro-active measures to develop and promote sustainable livelihoods for women, by: enhancing women's capacities for human development; ensuring women's rights to land entitlement; ensuring women's access to common land and wasteland for water, food, fodder, and fuel; providing shelter and security of tenure as a basis for the sustainable livelihoods of women in both urban and rural areas; introducing deliberate policies of providing credit without gender discrimination; recognizing and including women as co-heads of households in the formulation and implementation of policies and programmes and in the allocation of resources (including access to assets and technologies); creating and strengthening legal mechanisms to ensure accountablity of the state to women and the environment; evolving legislation for priority access to resources for sustainable livelihoods to be allotted to local producers, especially women.

In addition, it is important to build strong transnational alliances of women's networks with other organizations of major social groups in society, so as to engage in advocacy and lobbying across the international economic order and across national boundaries.

Building Stable Lives in Healthy Communities

When social disintegration has occurred in families, communities and countries, women are relied upon to reconstruct social relationships and the social fabric of human living through care and nurturing. The emotional and psychological costs are high as women try to build stable lives in the flux of the massive population movements that are now occurring both within and between nation-states. These population movements have become very significant processes affecting millions of people, with particular impact on women. On the one hand, there is population displacement as a result of changes that are beyond the control of the people themselves, such as deforestation, industrial zoning, and war. Such displacements have resulted in environmental refugees, developmental refugees and war refugees. On the other hand, there is also labour migration that has arisen as a result of the asymmetry between population and economic development, leading to the over-supply or under-supply of labour in different sectors and different countries.

Both types of population movement have very different consequences for men and women. Though women may be displaced as refugees, they are nevertheless still care-givers of other, even more vulnerable, members of their community — namely, children, the old and the sick. Consequently, women refugees are often less mobile and less able to grasp economic opportunities in their new locations. They are thus caught in a double bind of being exposed to new vulnerabilities and dependencies while still being obliged to fulfill existing responsibilities as care-givers of the community.

Women labour migrants too continue to be the care-givers of their community, faithfully remitting wages home to support families, often for work that involves considerable personal risks and costs. Women labour migrants tend to fill gender-segregated jobs that are underpaid, undervalued and under-protected — such as domestic work in the employer's home or non-unionized factory work. Moreover, the overseas employment of these women workers may not necessarily enhance their status when they return home, as their own community may expect them to revert to a subordinate position in the traditional gender hierarchy.

Another form of gender-specific migration that is even more problematic is the sexual trafficking of girls and women by organized prostitution rings. This is often forced migration for girls sold off by poor parents and for women who may be tricked into these situations. Their very lives are in danger from violence, sexually transmitted diseases, and AIDS. For women in all these situations of uncertain transition, the quest for stable lives is a survival issue and not a distant goal that can be left to remote policy makers.

A major challenge that is increasingly faced by women in the process of building stable lives is the rise of conflicts in the power vacuums left by the collapse of old political structures. With the end of the Cold War, the hope for peace exploded onto the world stage, offering real opportunity to create a more just and humane future. Yet, profound struggles remain. Yugoslavia, Somalia, and Rwanda remind us of the post-Cold War legacy.

This situation of uncertainty and danger has particular impact on women. War is definitely a gender-differentiated activity where there is no victory for women, no matter which side wins. The challenge of securing peace and social integration is therefore a matter of crucial concern for women, who can no longer accept their passive fate as victims of war.

Violence against women is common not just in war but in the street, in the workplace, and, most commonly, in the home. Domestic violence not only causes women and their children profound physical and psychological suffering but is also a major obstacle to women's individual growth, their sense of self-worth, and their participation in the development of their societies.

Women setting a peace agenda Women want peace in their societies and in their homes. They are at the centre of peace movements because they know the effects of militarism, genderized violence in war-torn societies, and conflict-prone families. The violation of women has been a time honoured method of destroying a country's morale. From the case of the trafficking in "comfort women" during World War II to the use of rape as a systematic weapon of war in the former Yugoslavia, women have been treated as legitimate booty.

Women are the worst victims of war and hence the highest stakeholders of peace. People who have to fight to protect even their own bodies from abuse are the ones who understand the full potential of what destruction means.

What women are asking for is not just the destruction of arms but the creation of new institutions and new mind-sets, and this has to start from an evaluation of ourselves, of our social relationships, and of the kind of development we want. We need a new development paradigm that puts ethics and social justice at its core. We need a new understanding of ethics, governance and power. We need to convince governments that high levels of arms are not necessary to ensure peace, justice, and security for the people of this planet.

Peace-building as defined by women means any activity directed toward the replacement of armed violence and coercion in situations of conflict by nonviolent, justice-seeking behaviour. Peace-building is seen as creating new kinds of social space in society for new behaviours and social relations.

The women and development movement has chosen the theme of Equality, Development, and Peace for the Fourth World Conference on Women. These are not separate,

13

compartmentalized issues; they are interconnected. The type of development that is desirable needs peace as a motivating and creative force. At the same time, there can be no peace in a situation of inequality, force, fear, and unfulfilled basic needs and rights.

Peace according to women's perspective is not simply the absence of war. It is a way of life that is compassionate. It is the creation of a certain mind-set of sharing, of reciprocity, of love, of care, and of happiness that should be at the centre of our development paradigm, our societies, and families. Unfortunately, few people talk of human happiness and love as a motivating force. Yet these are the ethical values that can be used to change institutions and the world.

Engendering Ethical Governance and Leadership

Ethical governance refers to the collective power of people to shape, through consensus, a future that is more peaceful, equitable, and sustainable. It requires new vision and leadership that can galvanize people to achieve higher levels of cooperation in areas of common concerns and shared destiny.

The urgent need for global governance has presented the United Nations with new and urgent challenges. The UN is the only forum with near-universal membership and with policies, practices, and systems designed by Member States. With the celebration of its 50th anniversary occurring just after the Fourth World Conference on Women, there are calls for institutional strengthening, especially in its developmental role. The Commission on Global Governance and the Secretary-General's Agenda for Development try to build on the best in international cooperation. Both emphasize the need to translate a substantial global consensus into the reality of "doing."

It is increasingly clear to many that if we did not have a UN system, we would have had to create one. There are many roles that the UN plays. The first is to establish universal norms, including the framework of the global rule of law. The second role is to resolve conflict and build peace. The third is to develop strategies for economic and social progress. The fourth is to build human capacity for sustainable development. The fifth is to give voice to those who have been historically silenced. In the UN, governments collectively express and set global priorities. Therefore, despite its many problems, we need to find ways to increase its effectiveness and credibility, so that it can deal with an increasingly complex world where many problems cut across national boundaries.

Whatever the dimension of global governance, whatever its content, its quality ultimately depends on enlightened leadership. At this moment of so many world crises, we cannot afford another one — a crisis of leadership. There is an urgent need for new concepts of leadership and new ethics of governance that deal seriously with issues of poverty, equity, peace and sustainability. Old styles of leadership cannot adequately address our new world situation, our new world problems. We need a style of leadership that does not exercise power over people, resources, and territories. It exercises power with them. It is leadership that does not dominate or coerce, but rather facilitates and empowers. It leads by allowing people to grow.

The challenge to promote ethical principles of good governance must recognize women's leadership and decision-making roles. These principles must include the indisputable assertion of the universality of human rights, including women's human rights. These ethical principles cross national, cultural, and racial boundaries and should be universal guarantees of the right to human dignity for all.

Women's potential to participate in and transform development depends on respect for women's right to speak and participate in the public world, to control their bodies and lives in the private sphere, and to obtain food, shelter, education, a healthy environment, and employment. Women are not waiting to have these rights recognized but are making them a cornerstone of the Women's Development Agenda for the 21st Century. These rights have been consistently agreed to in plans and programmes of action coming out of Rio, Vienna, Cairo, Copenhagen, and in the Convention on the Elimination of All Forms of Discrimination Against Women (CEDAW).

Central to making these principles a reality is enhancing and enabling leadership in the policy-making process. Women must be part of the discussions of UN reform, of global governance, of the Secretary-General's Agenda for Development, and of setting up world trade regulatory bodies. There is an urgent need to generate new thinking and to review the world's changing political and economic situation in light of what it means for the people caught in changes beyond their control. In particular, women need to address each of the four key challenges of the Women's Development Agenda as a gender issue, because it is the prevailing gender hierarchy that critically disadvantages and even endangers women's lives and chances.

There is also an urgent need for women to articulate their own agenda for change; to not only address their specific needs and concerns but, more fundamentally, to transform the very processes that have generated such problematic consequences. These critical challenges are reaching disaster proportions on a global scale. In such a situation, the temptation is to lapse into a state of constant crisis management that reacts to catastrophes as they arise, without a more pro-active rethinking of the root causes of these problems. "Fire-fighting" techniques can, at best, put out flames, but they do not prevent them from blazing up again. By building the institutions and practices that contain ethical principles in their governance, women can counter the narrow fundamentalism and ethnic and nationalistic chauvinism that are polarizing the world. The promotion of these principles is critical to development, democracy and human rights in the 21st century.

Also crucial to the promotion of good governance is the monitoring of accountability and the strengthening of civil society. At the major international conferences of the last five years, elected officials made numerous promises and commitments to the world's women. Strategies have been devised, action plans have been formulated, and target dates have been set. But by and large, adequate resources have not been committed to the implementation of these plans, particularly those that affect women's lives. Good governance is by definition accountable to its constituents, half of whom are women. Women now have to play a leading role not only in building a new vision of development, but in the implementation of systems and processes that will create a sustainable future for all. Women are asking for greater commitment, accountability, and resources for the implementation of what has come out of the various world summits and conferences. It is crucial at this time to build on our collective gains and to respond to women's demand that substantial resources be invested to translate words into meaningful actions.

Through their international networks, women have showed new leadership and have become a global force that cannot be ignored. Women have worked extremely hard to create new political spaces where their voices have been heard, and consensus has been forged. In so doing, they have reshaped the international political process and contributed to the building of a global civil society. These hard-won gains have to be the foundation stones on which we build the document coming out of Beijing.

Yet because this global force embraces such diversity, there is a need to find new bases of solidarity, and to build on lessons learned through women's empowerment as part of social capacity building. We need to find ways to strengthen consensus that weaves together the

15

different realities of women at all levels of society. We need to build solidarity not by finding the lowest common denominator but through a collective vision of hope that inspires. There is much that can be learned from women's efforts in bringing about change, reform and tranformation in development practice. Elizabeth Reid, in her essay in this collection reflecting on the achievements of the women's movement, recounts the learnings that we can extract from women's organizing in the 1970s. She includes the development of a collective sense of purpose; the valuing of all women's voices; stronger connection between theory and practice based on concrete realities; the creation of spaces for reflection and sharing of fears, pains, hopes, dreams and "how-to" that created a growing connectedness with others; creating sites of consensus-building, collective problem-solving, and creativity, rather than sites for the imposition of the politically correct.

Social capacity-building and the way we shape our future can only evolve in the context of meaningful human relations and interactions. There need to be more opportunities for collective thinking within the UN system. At present, UN representatives, governments and civil societies are limited to talking at each other through formal speeches or with each other on a one-to-one basis. Opportunities for collective thinking rarely occur. A new synergy needs to be created.

The UN must also recognize the growing worldwide emergence of citizen groups. This requires a reassessment of the relationship between the UN and civil society. At this critical juncture of human history, we need to pull together evey effort, large and small, that is headed in the right direction. For it is only through the global convergence of energies that we can build a sustainable and equitable world, not just for ourselves but for future generations.

THE DIRECTION AND ROLE OF UNIFEM

UNIFEM evolved out of women's hopes and aspirations while at the same time being part of the UN system. It is the voice and conscience of women within the United Nations. UNIFEM has a long history — in fact, 20 years — of building women's empowerment and partnerships among governments, the UN and civil society. Our role now is to bring the key lessons and best practices learned from working with women into the development agenda of mainstream organizations. In so doing, UNIFEM will facilitate women's inputs into the formulation of sound social and economic policies and practices, and the creation of an enabling environment based on good governance, greater accountability and secure livelihoods. This is especially important as we follow up on the commitments made by the international community at various UN conferences. In all these conferences the empowerment of women and the strengthening of governance with respect to partnership with civil society and accountability were recognized as central to the creation of a sustainable world.

There is indeed a very special relationship between UNIFEM and the UN Conferences on Women, for the idea of UNIFEM itself was born out of the first of these conferences in 1975. As a result of a "call to action" by women around the world, a Voluntary Fund was constituted with the aim of bringing women's concerns onto the UN's development agenda. By 1985, at the end of the Decade for Women, there was a decision to expand the mandate of this Fund and to reconstitute it as UNIFEM, the United Nations Development Fund for Women. This was a clear affirmation by the international community that the Fund had a special role to play in contributing to the advancement of women and should therefore be strengthened. UNIFEM's growth and development record since the time of its inception is testimony to the confidence of the women's movement and the unwavering support of the international community.

UNIFEM is mandated to use its resources in three priority areas:

- to serve as a catalyst with the goal of ensuring the appropriate involvement of women in mainstream development activities (A/RES/39/125)
- to support innovative and experimental activities benefiting women in line with national and regional priorities (A/RES/39/125)
- to play an innovative and catalytic role in relation to the United Nations overall system of development cooperation (A/RES/39/125).

Within the framework of its original mandate, UNIFEM's directions and strategies to meet its current challenges and the priorities of women in the 21st century are contained in its women's development agenda. UNIFEM's priority is founded on two key concerns:

- the economic empowerment of women
- the political empowerment of women

UNIFEM is an innovative Fund that puts resources directly in the hands of women in developing countries to support their livelihoods and to build their leadership and capacity so that they can take advantage of new economic opportunities. Another aspect of work is assisting in the formulation of gender-sensitive macro-economic policies and practices in key areas that have different impact on the lives of men and women such as trade, structural adjustment and transitional economies. Of special importance is the examination of development models, best practices, principle constraints and lessons learned for widening choices and opportunities for women's economic participation and decision making at all levels of society.

For the political empowerment of women, UNIFEM must be an effective advocate in promoting gender equity in decision-making structures from the household to the community, national and international levels. It has to advocate for the engendering of legal and policy frameworks, codes and instruments that deal with issues such as property rights, and inheritance laws. It has to generate new development thinking and practice, new ethics of governance, and new processes of leadership that will be more responsive to women's realities. UNIFEM must design strategies for advocacy and action that will improve women's status, eliminate violence against women, and support the advancement of women's rights. It has to strengthen women's organization and their capacity to participate in the decision-making process at all levels.

For all this to happen, we have to build upon our micro-level, small-scale projects, to gather wider momentum for change. We need to draw lessons from past experiences and use these to guide our new directions. UNIFEM's projects are being re-conceptualized and implemented in more strategic ways so that there is greater impact at the macro level. In this process of connecting micro and macro levels, UNIFEM is developing fresh approaches and new knowledge centred on women's experiences and needs, and will bring these to the attention of mainstream agencies. This will keep women's issues high on the agendas of mainstream organizations and will ensure more gender-sensitive development planning and implementation.

UNIFEM's comparative advantage vis-à-vis other development agencies lies in its wealth of knowledge and experience in gender and development, particularly in the following areas:

17

- identifying emerging gender issues, such as trade, structural adjustment, population displacement;
- developing innovative approaches and strategies to address critical issues affecting women;
- applying a gender perspective in development interventions;
- supporting innovative operational programmes and projects directly benefiting women; and
- acting as a catalyst within the UN system and at the regional and national levels to bring about women's empowerment.

Another area of strength is UNIFEM's partnership with NGOs in development initiatives. UNIFEM has the most extensive experience in the UN system in mobilizing and working with women's organizations at all levels — grassroots, national, regional, and global. UNIFEM can be the nexus of multiple networks, drawing in international and regional agencies, governments and NGOs, policy makers and local communities, as well as any other relevant grouping engaged in innovative development thinking and practice. Through these multiple linkages extended globally, UNIFEM can be the effective advocate of women, articulating and amplifying the realities of the different regions.

UNIFEM thus seeks to contribute to systems and processes that will strengthen women's agenda for change. In the process, UNIFEM will aim to provide women with the analytical and practical tools and information that would empower them and enhance their life chances. In this capacity, UNIFEM seeks to empower women by training them to negotiate effectively in international conferences on policy decisions that will have a direct impact on their livelihoods and their lives.

UNIFEM keeps women's issues high on the agendas of mainstream UN organizations. It does this by playing a mediating role between women and the UN system. It interfaces and builds partnerships with other UN agencies in bringing about sustainable and gender-equitable development. Its experiences at previous UN Conferences have demonstrated the importance of creating new political spaces where women's voices can be heard and consensus can be forged.

At this juncture, UNIFEM serves as the much needed base within the UN system that is synthesizing these critical issues and ensuring that the key recommendations of the various UN Conferences are translated into catalytic and innovative programmes that will empower women in the developing world. Without such a base, the gains women achieve at these conferences will fragment and dissipate into the periphery of mainstream discourse, and women's concerns will once again be neglected in development planning and implementation.

Hence, to summarize, we see UNIFEM playing the following roles:

- establish itself as a key institution within the UN system that has expertise on gender and development and is a source of technical expertise based on the lessons learned;
- develop and test cutting-edge interventions that address gender issues through innovative approaches;
- be a leader in bringing about gender-sensitive development planning and practice;
- play a mediating role, creating synergy by building new partnerships to address key issues;
- pilot selected key projects at the micro level; and

- strengthen women's organizations and build women's capacities by finding effective ways of responding to women's needs.

The Fourth World Conference on Women is an important landmark for UNIFEM. Our mandate provides a firm and strong basis for us to respond to the WCW. And the WCW provides a strong endorsement of our mission, policy framework and strategies. We have an overall policy framework based on the Women's Development Agenda that guides the organization's programmes and operations at all levels. This will involve focusing on key areas and strategies that will bring about the economic and political empowerment of women at the micro and macro levels. Within this context, our concerns are to assist in creating sustainable environments for women and men to lead economically and socially stable lives in healthy communities, advance women's rights and capacities for leadership, address women's concerns in peace-building and conflict resolution, and bring women's perspectives into decision-making and the practice of good governance based on equity and sustainability. Our regional staff will work to integrate global commitments with regional and national priorities as articulated in the various regional platforms. Most important of all, based on our relationships with both governments and women's networks and organizations, we will facilitate dialogues, partnerships and assist in the generation of the political will necessary for a commitment to the world's women.

PART 1

BALANCING THE SCALES: THE ECONOMIC EMPOWERMENT OF WOMEN

"As women are generally the poorest of the poor and at the same time key actors in the development process, eliminating social, cultural, political and economic discrimination against women is a prerequisite of eradicating poverty, and promoting sustained economic growth in the context of sustainable development."

— *Programme of Action, International Conference on Population and Development, Chapter III, para. 3.16.*

THE FEMINIZATION OF POVERTY

MARTHA ALTER CHEN

When the international women's movement was officially launched two decades ago at the historic Mexico City meeting for International Women's Year in 1975, the promise that continued economic growth would lead to development for all seemed reasonably assured. A related belief in feminist circles was that if women could obtain jobs for wages outside the home or otherwise earn independent incomes, they would come to exercise increased bargaining power within their households as well as enjoy improvements in their well-being and that of their families. Twenty years later, these beliefs have been widely assailed. What has happened to call these once-unchallenged beliefs into question?

By 1985 an international recession, the persistence of widespread poverty, and the failure of growth policies in numerous countries precipitated a reassessment of economic development models and policies. Key to this reassessment was the recognition that the interconnected dilemmas of debt, trade, and the environment have not only global dimensions, but also particular consequences for women. While the world was visibly shaken by these and other global crises at the macro level, women (and their children) were also being buffeted by a less evident but equally consequential, and not unrelated, micro-level crisis within the family itself. Due to the death of older husbands, the migration of working spouses and companions, and high rates of desertion and divorce worldwide, many women today are maintaining families virtually on their own (Bruce et al., 1995). In some parts of the developing world, one out of every three households is headed by a woman. Elsewhere in the developing world, this figure is as high as one in two.

What impact have these global and local forces had on the lives and work of women? The evidence is somewhat contradictory. In the developing world, women have made considerable progress over the last two decades: life expectancy, literacy rates, educational attainment, and political participation of women have all increased. But the absolute number of women living in poverty has also grown. Moreover, certain human development indicators reveal that poverty is increasingly a female problem, a phenomenon that has been called in both the developing and developed worlds the "feminization" of poverty.[1]

Indeed, evidence from around the globe establishes two fundamental, interrelated facts about women and poverty: women bear a disproportionate share of poverty worldwide, and women shoulder an unequal burden in coping with poverty at the household level.

The Feminization of Poverty: Women's Unequal Share

A large majority — 62 per cent — of the world's women live in countries with gross domestic production (GDP) of less than US$1,000 per year. A still larger proportion — 75 per cent — live in countries where the annual per capita GDP is declining, staying the same or increasing at a rate of less than US$10 per year (UN, 1994: 96). Of course, looking at macro-

23

economic indicators, the same can be said of a large majority of the world's men; however, macro-level indicators that are not gender-disaggregated obscure the fact that, within poor countries, women are more impoverished than men. However, before turning to the gender gap in development, let us first consider where low-income women predominate, and examine selected differences between women from the developing world and their counterparts in industrialized countries.

The Development Gap The following table shows the percentage of women in industrialized countries, developing countries, and least-developed countries (LDCs) achieving a variety of key human development goals (UNDP, 1994; UNICEF, 1995).

Achievement of Key Human Development Goals
(Women from Different Groups of Countries)

	Developed	Developing	LDCs
Adult Female Literacy (%)	nearly universal	57	32
Mean Years of Schooling (female as % of male)	95	55	42
Labour Force Participation (female as % of male)	73	58	n/a
Contraceptive Prevalence (%)	72	54	16
Births Attended by Trained Health Personnel (%)	98	55	27

But perhaps the statistic most starkly indicative of the development gap between women in developing countries and women in developed countries is the rate of maternal mortality. Almost all countries in the developed regions of the world have reduced maternal deaths to extremely low levels, and many developing countries have also made dramatic reductions (UN, 1991: 57). Rates of fewer than five maternal deaths per 100,000 live births are found in parts of the developed world, whereas rates of more than 1,000 maternal deaths per 100,000 live births have been estimated in some developing areas. On average, maternal mortality rates in Africa and South Asia are over 30 times those in developed regions (UN, 1991: 58).

The Gender Gap Although women's average life expectancy now exceeds that of men in most parts of the world, women lag behind in almost every other key area of human development. The following table shows the number of women in the developing world who achieve a variety of development goals for every hundred men who do (UNDP, 1994: 147).

Achievement of Development Goals in Developing Countries
(Number of Women for Every 100 Men)

	Women	Men
Adult Literacy	71	100
Secondary School Enrolment	72	100
Labour Force Participation	58	100

In the developing world as a whole, women occupy just 11 per cent of parliamentary seats. In much of Africa and Asia, three-quarters of all women aged 25 and over are still illiterate, and girls' secondary-school enrolment still lags behind boys' (UN, 1991). Although illiteracy rates are falling for young women, they are still much higher for young women than for young men, and the illiteracy rates of young women in rural areas remain much higher than those of their urban counterparts.

Between 1970 and 1990, women's share in the labour force increased in almost every region. However, the gap between women's and men's recorded economic activity remains wide. In developing regions, economically active women are concentrated in low-productivity agricultural or service activities. Throughout most of the world — including developed countries — women continue to earn, on average, two-thirds of what men earn.

The statistic most grimly illustrative of the gender gap between men and women in the developing world is the sex ratio of the population. Although women's life expectancy is increasing everywhere and women live longer than men in almost every region (UN, 1991), tens of millions of women — now being referred to as the *missing women* — die prematurely or are never born due to manifestations of sexual discrimination: female foetuses aborted after ultrasound tests reveal their sex; newborn girls killed at birth; girl children given less food or health care than their brothers; unattended women prematurely dead of pregnancy or birth-related complications; and widows slain by in-laws covetous of their property or loath to support them.

Amartya Sen was the first to call attention to the plight of missing women. His investigation started with a basic fact: although five to six per cent more boys than girls are born, under normal circumstances males die at higher rates at every age thereafter. Therefore, under normal circumstances, the number of men and women evens out by the time a population cohort reaches its 20s or 30s and then shifts among the elderly as women come to be disproportionately represented (Kristof, 1991). Overall, then, in relatively developed regions, 105 females can be found for every 100 males in the population. In many developing regions, on the other hand, there are fewer than 95 females for each 100 males; this trend is most notable in the world's most populous countries (India has fewer than 93 females per 100 males, China fewer than 94 females). How can this difference be explained?

The key consideration is this: what sex ratio would exist if males and females were treated equally? Given that more boys than girls are born and that the number of males and females does not balance out until a population cohort is well into adulthood, a population with a relatively low average age should have a higher proportion of males than one with a relatively high average age. Because the populations of developing countries are younger than those of industrialized nations, developing countries could be expected to have fewer females than the 105 females per 100 males typical of developed countries.

Yet would they have as few as 95? The answer is no. In sub-Saharan Africa, there are 102 females for every 100 males and in the southern Indian state of Kerala, there are 104 females for every 100 males. In both of these developing regions, society generally values women. One may assume, then, that in a gender-equitable developing country there would be approximately 103 women for every 100 men. A comparison using this figure of 103 women per 100 men indicates that more than 100 million females are missing around the world (Kristof, 1991).

Women and Poor Households The relationship between household poverty and female poverty is not straightforward or unidimensional. In analyzing the linkages between female poverty and household poverty, growing evidence from developing regions suggests the following:

- Women who are earning members, dependent members, or heads of poor households are poorer than men of the same categories. Women who are non-earning dependents are worse off than women who are earning members or heads of poor households.
- Women allocate more of their cash incomes to household subsistence and nutrition than men do, and are more oriented toward meeting the basic needs of the household (Burke and Huq, 1981: 175). The higher a woman's income, the less likely are her children to suffer from hunger and malnutrition. Furthermore, women spend more time than men producing free goods and services for households. Fairly consistently, women in all parts of the world put in more work hours, paid and unpaid, than do men of the same age.
- Household poverty leads to higher rates of male mortality, as well as spurring more men to migrate in search of jobs; these phenomena, in turn, increase the likelihood of female headship. When men leave home to seek employment or higher wages, responsibility for the well-being of the family falls entirely to women.
- Households headed by women alone have a higher risk of poverty than households headed by men and women together because they have fewer resident working members, more dependents, smaller landholdings, and inferior access to extension services, information, credit, and labour markets.[2]

The Feminization of Poverty: Unequal Burden

Women not only suffer an unequal share of poverty, but also carry an unequal burden in dealing with its injurious effects. The reason is that women typically manage the day-to-day cash flow and family subsistence requirements in low-income households, both those that are female-headed and those in which men are the primary breadwinners.

Female-headed Households Recent evidence suggests that many women live outside marriage for significant portions of their adult lives. The reasons are many: husbands migrate in search of work; men desert, divorce, or die before their wives; and women themselves sometimes leave home to seek employment or become separated from their families during natural disasters, wars, and other crises. For these reasons, more and more women find themselves as heads of households or as the primary source of economic support for families over long periods of time.

In Africa, Latin America, and the Caribbean, 9 per cent of women aged 15–59 are heads of households, as are 6 per cent of women in Asia. Of course, the percentage of households headed by women is far higher than the percentage of women who are heads of households; according to *The World's Women* (UN, 1991), up to 30 per cent of households are now headed by women.

Male-headed Households In low-income households headed by men, the economic contributions of women are known to be most important *during times of economic contraction and in areas of economic marginalization*. During periods of economic contraction, women manage the meagre resources available to poor households day to day and continue to work for low wages while men seek higher-income opportunities. In areas of economic marginalization, such as dry or hilly farming areas where only marginal seasonal agriculture is possible, women become the de facto farmers when men leave home in search of jobs.

Factors Contributing to the Feminization of Poverty

The factors that contribute to the feminization of poverty can be grouped under several headings.

Individual Skills and Knowledge In the developing world there are only 71 literate adult women for every 100 literate adult men. Women have inferior access to extension services and training, as well as to information about the wider economic and political environment. In traditional artisan communities, women are sometimes barred from learning certain skills. Therefore, many women enter the labour force or engage in productive activities on an unequal footing due to their lack of basic literacy, numeracy, and entrepreneurial and technical skills.

Traditional Family Structures Aspects of most traditional family systems continue to perpetuate gender inequality and women's poverty; among them are discriminatory customs and norms regarding marriage and family, a lack of inheritance and property rights for women, and the gender division of labour. Most marriage and kinship systems dictate, for instance, where and with whom women can live; where and with whom women can work; whether and under what conditions women can own property; and whether and with whom they can remarry in the event of divorce, desertion, or widowhood. In return for the rules and responsibilities societies impose upon them, women are entitled to maintenance by their fathers (or their fathers' lineages) before marriage and by their husbands (or their husbands' lineages) after marriage — at least in principle.

A corollary to the early feminist belief that increased participation in gainful employment would improve women's status within the household was the expectation that modern capitalist development would loosen patriarchal or male control in family and kinship systems. However, growing evidence shows that while recent economic development has served to undermine traditional kinship-based systems of reciprocity and mutual obligation, it has not loosened patriarchal control over women's labour and mobility or lessened the degree to which women's access to markets (land, labour, and credit) is mediated by men. Many scholars have concluded that the loosening of the informal system of social security in the absence of a state-based system of social security, coupled with the unleashing of market forces without state regulation to correct market distortions, has generally served to disadvantage women (Chen, 1995a). In short, women are losing the few protections offered by traditional systems without gaining significant privileges and freedoms in the modern, capitalist structures that are supplanting them.

27

At particular risk during this socioeconomic transformation are women living or managing on their own. Two myths about family structures and women on their own prevail. The first is that families, particularly sons, care for women who live alone, particularly elderly women. The second is that families and family values are disintegrating. Familial bonds are thus seen either as still protecting women no matter what their marital status or as no longer protecting single, widowed, divorced, or deserted women. In both scenarios, the younger woman on her own is seen to be at special risk.

A third dimension of how family ties "bind" women — the ways in which marriage and kinship rules curtail and constrict the options available to them — is seldom addressed. As noted above, across most regions and social groups in the developing world, marriage and kinship rules impose restrictions upon women in the following domains: postmarital residence, inheritance rights, divorce and remarriage, employment and economic opportunities, and social interactions and relationships (Chen, 1995b). How a woman fares, particularly one who must or chooses to manage alone, depends in large measure upon the precise marriage and kinship rules that govern her social group.

Structures of the Market-Place Traditional family structures affect women's interactions with markets in three main ways. First, the gender division of work is reflected in segmented and discriminatory labour markets in which women are concentrated in the lowest-productivity activities and the lowest-earning jobs. Second, women's limited property rights restrict their access to capital and credit markets, and their lack of economic independence obstructs their access to labour and product markets. Third, given the dearth of resources and information to which they have access and their unremitting day-to-day task of ensuring the food security of their families, women are less able than men to respond to price, wage, or other market incentives.

Economic liberalization and privatization call for the removal of distortionary policies to promote dynamic, open, and competitive free markets. But women's ability or inability to compete in markets depends upon not only distortionary policies, but also powerful and discriminatory customary rules and structures. As long as women cannot own land and other productive assets, as long as women's economic mobility is constrained by social rules, as long as women are burdened with primary responsibility for daily food security, and as long as women's access to education, training, and information is circumscribed, women cannot compete freely in markets. And markets in which half of humanity cannot fully and equally participate cannot truly be thought of as dynamic, open, competitive, or free.

Development Policies In addition to discrimination within the private and the market spheres, women face discrimination in the public realm; this public-sphere discrimination girds gender inequality and perpetuates women's poverty. Differential access to public-sector services and discriminatory policies and regulations are two such examples. In many countries in the developing world, social services (health and education), development services (credit, extension, technology), and the institutional structures that support development (local government, cooperatives, trade unions) are universally open to men but either closed or inaccessible to women. Furthermore, many economic policies have differential impacts on women and men; chief among them are policies that affect income and prices (as women are less able to shift occupations or to respond to price incentives), public expenditures (as women are more likely to absorb the effects of decreased subsidies), and labour conditions (as women workers are often the first to lose worker benefits and protection).

Models of Development The realities women face are not generally reflected in economic models of development. Standard economic models of household behaviour, both neoclassical and Marxist, suffer from two types of blindness: they can see neither *what women do* nor *how households behave*.

In terms of what women do, standard economic models of households overlook or undervalue women's role in the reproduction and maintenance of human resources (i.e., caring for children, gathering fuel and water, processing food, managing the household, etc.). In addition, standard economic definitions of work, income, and employment disregard or minimize the importance of women's work in the informal sector and in production geared toward household use and subsistence.

Regarding how households behave, standard economic models recognize neither that different family members have distinct and sometimes competing needs, rights, and responsibilities nor that both cooperation and conflict exist within households. Standard economic models of behavior do not take into account the preference of many households firstly to diversify their economic activities rather than specialize in and expand specific economic activities, and secondly to minimize the risks inherent in their working environment rather than take risks to maximize return.

Development Crises Global and national-level economic and political currents and crises also have specific impacts on women's lives and work. Chief among them are political tides of militarism, fundamentalism, and ethnonationalism and the economic crises of debt, trade, economic restructuring, and environment. Of particular concern are the impacts of economic recession and economic reforms on women's work (Chen, 1995a).

- Economic recession. In much of the world, women continue to be the last to benefit from job expansion and the first to suffer from job contraction. This imbalance frequently forces women to create their own jobs and enterprises, usually with few resources and little support (UN, 1991). *Across most countries, the lower the per capita income, the lower the proportion of women in formal-sector employment.*

- Informalization of labour relations. Many of the so-called jobs created by recent industrial expansion represent a shift to decentralized and flexible labour relations in which labour-intensive, lower-paid, informal activities are subcontracted to women workers (Standing, 1989: 1080). *In South-East Asia, women factory workers are often dismissed when they marry and have children and become engaged in industrial subcontracting within their own homes* (Pongpaichit, 1988).

- Pursuit of lower wages. The pursuit of lower wages by businesses and industries often leads to the substitution of women for men since men are less likely to work for subminimum wages. *This phenomenon is most notable in the export-oriented manufacturing sector* (Standing, 1989).

- Labour market deregulation. The deregulation of labour markets, associated with privatization and liberalization, is likely to affect women in various ways, including undermining whatever protective effect regulations might have had on the wages, benefits, job security, and working hours of women labourers. *Women workers in the export-oriented, labour-intensive "free trade zones" tend to enjoy fewer rights and benefits than women workers in the private formal sector outside the zones* (Standing, 1989; Elson, 1991).

Key Differences Among Women

The precise ways in which class, race, social norms, and other cultural forces interact to constrain women differ across regions and social groups. Although societies shape women's roles and responsibilities everywhere in the world, the ways in which they do it differ; for example, land-scarce, labour-surplus communities are more likely to confine women to tasks within the homestead. Similarly, the specific norms of good and bad behaviour for women differ from community to community: again, women's mobility outside the home tends to be condoned more in labour-scarce communities than in labour-surplus communities. Although most women everywhere are conditioned to be economically dependent, the precise nature of that dependence differs; in more traditional societies, women's economic dependence on men is structured by social norms and customary law, whereas in more modern societies women's economic dependence on men is structured by market forces, public policies, and modern law. Moreover, the functions (and failures) of government and market institutions differ across countries and regions; these differences pose different constraints and opportunities for low-income women.

Despite these significant differences, however, across the diverse countries of Latin America, Africa, Asia, and the Caribbean, marked similarities in the experiences of women (especially rural women) are found. The first is that women's lives are conditioned and constrained by traditional family systems and by gender relations at the household level. The second is that most low-income women work. The third is that low-income women cater to the basic needs of their families and, in order to do so, take on the triple burden of domestic work, income-saving work, and paid work. The fourth is that low-income women everywhere want work (not charity), want income, want opportunities, want self-esteem, want respect, and want self-reliance.

WOMEN AND POVERTY ALLEVIATION: PRIORITIES FOR THE 21ST CENTURY

There is a general consensus that economic growth is a necessary, but not sufficient, condition for poverty to be addressed. What has been generally recommended is a macro-economic strategy that will promote growth and a set of pro-poor policies that will affect the distribution of growth. Among those concerned with poverty alleviation, however, there is growing demand for equitable and job-led (rather than jobless) growth; for redistribution as well as, and preferably prior to, growth; and for more appropriate and better targeted pro-poor policies. The most recent demands (at the 1995 World Summit for Social Development and in the draft document for the 1995 Fourth World Conference on Women) are for participatory development and social integration.

In the debates on these alternative development strategies, women tend to get omitted in discussions on growth and redistribution. Furthermore, they get relegated as a "vulnerable" group along with the poor, children, the elderly, and the disabled, to deliberations on the pro-poor set of strategies. If the specific poverty of women is adequately to be addressed, then low-income women should be integrated into all development and poverty alleviation strategies.

Women and Growth

There are several dimensions to the link between women and economic growth, most notably how women contribute to growth, how different patterns of growth affect women, and how women should be integrated into growth strategies.

Women's Contribution to Growth The growth or efficiency potential of women is still largely overlooked and undervalued. This potential can be understood in six key ways:

- Women are now widely recognized as reproducers and maintainers of human resources; therefore, "investing in women" can be seen as investing in children and human resource development more broadly.
- Women are increasingly recognized as producers of free goods and services for households.
- Women's role in subsidizing marketed output through their unpaid or underpaid domestic labour still goes largely unrecognized.
- Women's role in subsidizing men's search for higher-return activities still goes largely unnoticed. Women commonly continue to work for low wages or low returns to meet daily consumption needs while men search for better-paying work.
- Women's informal sector activities often subsidize formal-sector activities. For example, women in Bombay provide cooked food to industrial workers at low prices, which in turn "allows" industries to continue to pay low wages to their workers (who would likely protest if their wages did not cover their food bill).
- Women are still widely overlooked or undervalued as productive workers in different sectors of the economy and are, therefore, often left out of sector-specific economic policies and plans.

Impact of Growth on Women Different patterns of economic growth, as well as growth that is uneven, can have quite diverse impacts on women, some of which can be negative. Clearly, jobless (capital-intensive) growth rather than job-led (labour-intensive) growth can have negative consequences for women, as women are often the last hired and the first fired. Because women are more likely than men to be shifted or "casualized" to part-time or contract work, the deregulation of working conditions that often accompanies liberalization and privatization can also have negative consequences for women. And the cut-backs in social services that accompany structural adjustment lead either to those services being performed by unpaid (rather than paid) workers or to those services being dropped all together. In either case, women suffer because they are expected to provide the services. Their existing unpaid work remains undercounted and undervalued because — to use a term from economics — it is considered "elastic," and as a consequence, their well-being and that of their children deteriorates.

Integrating Women into Growth Strategies Mainstream economic programmes and policies are typically developed along sectoral lines; that is, critical sectors of the economy are assigned significant budget appropriations, and their support and development are managed by specialized ministries or departments. Unfortunately, women are typically left out of sectoral economic planning because government policy makers do not view women as productive workers. A sectoral approach in support of women workers can help close the gap between the often "invisible" work of women and mainstream macro-economic planning by increasing the visibility of women within specific sectors of the economy, as well as by identifying appropriate interventions to address the constraints faced by women in those sectors.

Women and Redistribution

In general, redistribution is politically difficult, as it involves taking from one group or individual and giving to another group or individual. Few are those who willingly give up what

31

they have. The resources that might be redistributed include land, other productive assets, public investments, and incomes (through tax and price policies, subsidies, and interest rates). Typically, redistribution policies are conceived of and designed along class lines between the rich and the poor. Some attention has been given to redistribution of public investments between men and women through mechanisms like greater investments in primary health and education services. In general, however, the redistribution of private resources between men and women is seen as a "private" matter, not to be addressed by public policy. Even when statutory modern laws dictate equality between men and women, many governments are loath to "interfere" with local inheritance systems and other customary practices that discriminate against women.

Thus, in many developing countries women have limited, if any, rights to private land. Because of this general taboo on women owning land, women also have limited access to community-owned or government-owned land. Moreover, in many countries women have limited ownership or access in their own right to other productive assets, such as animals, ploughs, water resources, and artisan equipment.

Women and Basic Needs

Although women have not been integrated into the growth and redistribution strategies of many countries, they have received increasing attention as people with special basic needs arising from their sex and their reproductive role and have subsequently been specifically targeted by service-providing entities. In addition to the standard package of basic human needs — food, shelter, safe drinking water, sanitation, primary health care, and primary education — women have additional basic needs. These basic needs of women include reproductive health care to address the particular health issues related to their sex and their reproductive role; child care, a traditional responsibility of women; housing in the event of divorce, desertion, or widowhood, as women typically face difficulties in finding adequate shelter when marriages end; economic safety nets in the event of divorce, desertion, or widowhood; and old-age pensions from the government, as women workers are concentrated in the informal sector, which provides no benefits or pensions.

There are two important caveats to this increased attention to women as special targets of a distinct basic-needs package. First, under many basic needs policies, women are categorized as a "vulnerable" group along with children, the elderly, the sick, and the disabled. This categorization of women as vulnerable has two drawbacks: it fails to distinguish among groups of women, some of whom are not vulnerable, and it fails to distinguish between men and women in vulnerable groups (young, old, sick, disabled).

Second, providing basic needs to women is seen, by some, as a *means* to other ends and not as *an end in and of itself.* For instance, investing in women's education is seen to have the following benefits: reduced infant mortality, healthier children, reduced fertility rates, and reduced maternal mortality (Summers, 1994). While these and other happy by-products of educating women may well arise, they should not be seen as the *justification* for meeting women's basic needs for education; having their basic needs met is the right of all people, women as well as men.

Women and Economic Opportunities

Recent debates on growth and economic development have highlighted the differences between jobless (capital-intensive) and job-led (labour-intensive) growth; between creating jobs (in the formal sector) and creating economic opportunities (in the informal sector); and between promoting productivity (of given activities) and promoting sustainable livelihoods (based on a portfolio of activities). In these debates, however, the specific impact of different patterns of growth on women, the concentration of women in the informal sector, and women's roles in sustaining livelihoods have not been sufficiently highlighted. As a result, the need to integrate women into sector-specific growth strategies, the need to protect women from the negative impacts of uneven or jobless growth, the need to create opportunities for women in the formal sector, the need to protect women within the informal sector, and the need to support women's roles in sustaining livelihoods have not been adequately addressed.

To promote economic opportunities for women, several new strategies are called for. In the formal sector, attention should be paid to creating jobs for women and protecting women from low wages and informalization of working conditions. In the informal sector, where women are concentrated, efforts should be made to provide financial services to low-income women; to provide productive assets to women; to help women resist exploitation and overcome barriers in their working environments; to link women to existing infrastructures and services; to develop infrastructure and provide services as needed; and to shift women to new tasks and new markets (Chen, 1995c).

Addressing Common Constraints

Removing the Biases in the System The low returns on and productivity of women's enterprises are often due to policy biases, to market distortions, or to other structural constraints, such as:

- Policy biases that overlook women's work while promoting a dynamic subsector in which women are concentrated (for example, in organizing dairy cooperatives in India, the government initially overlooked women, who in fact do the bulk of the work in rearing dairy animals);
- Policy biases that neglect a potentially dynamic subsector in which women are concentrated (for example, the poultry subsector in Bangladesh was long neglected but now has been revitalized into a dynamic and growing subsector, thanks to a working partnership between a non-governmental organization (BRAC) and the government of Bangladesh);
- Policy biases that disadvantage women in gaining access to institutional sources of credit;
- Policy biases that overlook sectors in which women are concentrated when regulating markets (for example, overlooking home-based workers when legislating worker's benefits) or in licensing investments (for example, overlooking traditional, manual rice millers when licensing mechanized rice mills);
- Policy biases that subsidize larger firms that compete with women's enterprises, such as those that provide subsidized prices to large firms buying raw materials or selling finished goods in bulk;
- Policy and cultural biases that deny women access to labour markets or that relegate women to lower-return niches in labour markets;
- Legal and customary barriers that deny women equal rights to land and other property; and
- Policy biases that provide more social security and other benefits to the formal sector of labour (where male workers are concentrated) than to the informal sector of self-employed workers (where women are concentrated).

Household-level Constraints Women workers in most parts of the developing world

33

face a common set of constraints at the household level. Some of these constraints are also faced by male workers in the same settings. Among these are the need to adjust to seasonal fluctuations; the need to balance and synchronize multiple economic activities; the need to balance short-term cash flow requirements against longer-term investment requirements; and the need to negotiate both formal market institutions and informal economic networks. Some of the constraints women workers face are not faced by male workers in the same setting, however, particularly those posed by socially defined gender roles and relationships that determine who *does* what within the household and within the wider economic arena, who *gets* what, and who *owns* what.

Micro-economic Constraints Women workers also face constraints specific to the economic subsector or trade in which they operate. Some of these constraints result from the *relationships of production and distribution* within the specific subsector or trade. For example, because they lack access to institutional credit, women vegetable vendors are often forced to buy vegetables at high rates of interest from vegetable wholesalers.

Other constraints are the result of barriers imposed by (or biases inherent in) *local institutions, infrastructures, or services.* For example, women street vendors are often forced to pay bribes to the local police or municipality in order to secure a space from which to sell.

Macro-economic Constraints Women workers also face constraints resulting from the macro-economic policies of governments, including policies related to taxation and investment, trade and tariff structures, credit and financial markets, and labour and product markets. Macro *financing and licensing policies* can affect the choice of technology which, in turn, can affect the demand for women's labour. In Bangladesh, for example, the introduction of mechanized rice mills displaced large numbers of self-employed women (who earned their livelihoods from manual husking of paddy), but offered wage employment to other women (as wage labourers in pre- and post-husking operations at the rice mills). A more commonly cited example is of policies relating to *credit and financial markets*, which typically limit the access of women workers to formal sources of credit and broader financial services. Third, in some countries, the macro-economic policies associated with *structural adjustment* have meant loss of jobs in the formal sector and increased competition in the informal sector.

Alternative Approaches to Promoting Women's Enterprises
The standard approach to promoting women's enterprises is to adopt and specialize in a particular intervention or a mix of interventions. These interventions include:

- delivering services to women workers;
- mobilizing demand for goods and services produced by women workers;
- lobbying for appropriate policies in support of women workers;
- addressing structural constraints faced by women workers; and
- organizing women workers into trade associations, cooperatives, or solidarity groups.

Each of these main services is characterized by specific assumptions and strategies. The most common type of intervention is the delivery of services designed to raise the productivity of women's enterprises. Of these services, the most common is *credit delivery*, which is generally guided by the assumption that women workers need credit either because they are too poor to save or because they have been denied access to institutional sources of credit. The strategy is generally to provide credit along with a savings component. *Training and technical assistance* is informed by the assumption that women workers lack skills, management capacity, entrepreneurship, and social consciousness; the strategy is the provision of training programmes and technical consultants. *Technology transfer* starts with the assumption that women's enterprises have low productivity, which is addressed with appropriate technology development and transfer.

Transforming Structures that Perpetuate Gender Inequality

Even an optimal mix of growth, redistribution, basic needs, and economic strategies for women will fail to reduce women's poverty if the basic structures that perpetuate gender inequality are not transformed. These include social, economic, and political structures at the local, national, and global levels. At the global level, international trade and financial institutions need to be reformed and economic restructuring must be re-evaluated. At the national level, the target should be macro-economic and sector policies, as well as regulations and laws. At the local level, marriage and kinship rules and other social structures still hold women back.

Empowering and Organizing Women

Unless women are empowered to demand services, to demand their rights, and to fight discrimination and exploitation, the basic structures that govern their lives will not be transformed. Paradoxically, until the structures that perpetuate gender inequality are transformed, women acting alone cannot bring about real change. Therefore, unless and until women organize, they cannot be fully empowered.

CONCLUSION

The interdependent crises of worldwide poverty, social disintegration, and the dearth of productive employment cannot be addressed in isolation, nor can there be any hope of surmounting them without the active involvement of women at all levels. To address these crises in a meaningful way, the end that development practitioners seek and the manner in which development is practiced must change.

Development policies must be informed by an understanding of the unequal burden women bear in coping with the effects of poverty. The factors furthering the feminization of poverty — lack of skills, repressive family and social structures, gender-blind development policies and models, and over-reliance on market mechanisms — must be tackled. Structures that perpetuate gender inequality and obstruct the advancement of women at the global, national, local, and household levels must be transformed. Women's invisible contributions to growth — performing unpaid household and community labour, subsidizing the higher-return activities of men, meeting the daily consumption needs of their families, and undergirding the economy by caring for the workers of today and tomorrow — must be recognized. For poverty to be meaningfully addressed, women must have services like education and health care; they must have resources like training, credit, technical assistance, and technology; they must have legal rights and protections; and they themselves must organize, mobilize, and demand change.

Martha Alter Chen is a research associate at the Harvard Institute for International Development (HIID), a lecturer at Harvard's Kennedy School of Government, and founder-director of a new Programme on Non-governmental Organizations at HIID. She has lived in India and Bangladesh and has written extensively on poverty and gender issues in both countries.

Parts of this article draw upon the author's introduction to A. Leonard (ed.), *SEEDS 2: Supporting Women's Work Around the World.* New York: The Feminist Press, 1995.

Notes

1. The term *feminization of poverty* was coined by Diana Pierce to describe the worsening economic position of female-headed households in the United States.

2. Studies on the income and expenditure levels of female-headed households suggest that it is important to adjust income and expenditure levels to include such variables as: economies of scale; consumption of non-purchased goods; consumption of durables; opportunity for long-term consumption.

References

Boserup, Ester. 1970. *Women's Role in Economic Development.* New York: St. Martin's Press.

Bruce, J., A. Leonard, and C. Lloyd (eds.), 1995. *Families in Focus: New Perspectives on Mothers, Fathers, and Children.* New York: The Population Council.

Burke, Shahid Javid, and M. U. Haq. 1981. "Meeting Basic Needs: An Overview," *World Development* 9 (2).

Chen, Martha A. 1995a. Introduction, in Ann Leonard (ed.), *SEEDS: Supporting Women's Work Around the World.* New York: The Feminist Press.

Chen, Martha A. 1995b. *The Lives of Widows in India* (forthcoming).

Chen, Martha A. (ed.). 1995c. *Beyond Credit: A Subsector Approach to Promoting Women's Enterprises* (forthcoming). Ottawa, Canada: The Aga Khan Foundation Canada.

Downing, Jeanne. 1990. "Gender and the Growth and Dynamics of Microenterprises". Gemini Working Paper No. 5. Washington, D.C.: Development Alternatives, Inc.

Elson, Diane. 1991. "Structural Adjustment: Its Effect on Women," in T. Wallace and C. March (eds.), *Changing Perceptions: Writings on Gender and Development.* New York: Oxfam.

Elson, Diane. 1992. "From Survival Strategies to Transformation Strategies: Women's Needs and Structural Adjustment," in Lourdes Beneria and Shelley Feldman (eds.), *Unequal Burden: Economic Crises, Persistent Poverty, and Women's Work.* Boulder, CO: Westview Press, pp. 26–48.

Feldman, Shelly. 1992. "Crises, Poverty, and Gender Inequity: Current Themes and Issues" in Lourdes Beneria and Shelley Feldman (eds.), *Unequal Burden: Economic Crises, Persistent Poverty, and Women's Work.* Boulder: Westview Press.

Folbre, Nancy. 1988. "The Black Four of Hearts: Toward a New Paradigm of Household Economics," in D. Dwyer and J. Bruce (eds.), *A Home Divided: Women and Income in the Third World.* Stanford, California: Stanford University Press.

Grown, Caren, and J. Sebstad. 1989. Introduction, *World Development* 17 (7), pp. 937–52.

Kristof, Nicholas D. 1991. "Stark Data on Women: 100 Million Are Missing," *New York Times*, 5 November.

Moser, Caroline. 1989. "Gender Planning in the Third World: Meeting Practical and Strategic Gender Needs," *World Development* 17 (11), pp. 1799–1825.·

Sen, Amartya. 1990. "More than 100 Million Women Are Missing," *New York Review*, 20 December, pp. 60–66.

Sen, Amartya. 1990. "Gender and Cooperative Conflicts," in I. Tinker (ed.), *Persistent Inequalities.* New York: Oxford University Press.

Sen, Gita, and Caren Grown. 1987. *Development, Crises and Alternative Visions: Third World Women's Perspectives.* New York: Monthly Review Press.

Standing, Guy. 1989. "Global Feminization Through Flexible Labor," in C. Grown and J. Sebstad (eds.), *Beyond Survival: Expanding Income-Earning Opportunities for Women in Developing Countries. World Development* 17 (7) (Special Issue), pp. 1077–95.

Summers, Lawrence H. 1994. "Investing in All the People: Educating Women in Developing Countries." EDI Seminar Paper no. 45. Washington, DC: World Bank.

United Nations Children's Fund (UNICEF). 1995. *The State of the World's Children.* New York: Oxford University Press.

United Nations Development Programme (UNDP). 1991. *Human Development Report 1991.* New York: Oxford University Press.

United Nations Development Programme (UNDP). 1994. *Human Development Report 1994.* New York: Oxford University Press.

United Nations (UN). 1991. *The World's Women: Trends and Statistics 1970–1990.* New York: United Nations.

World Bank. 1990. *World Development Report 1990.* New York: Oxford University Press.

THE ECONOMICS OF MOTHERHOOD

JUDITH BRUCE

Across cultures and throughout history, women have been defined primarily as mothers. Indeed, most women do become sexually active, marry, and bear children whether they welcome or fear the demands of motherhood.

Several decades of research and advocacy at local, national, and international levels have fostered public appreciation of women's roles apart from motherhood, including their contributions to society through wage-earning labour, political participation, creative and intellectual endeavours, and community service. Now a similar re-education is needed with respect to how motherhood itself is conceptualized and valued.

Contrary to myth, motherhood is not limited to bearing children and caring for family members, activities at once celebrated and vastly undervalued. Motherhood has always involved a number of functions as well — notably providing economic support to the dependent family members, especially children.

PREVALENCE OF MOTHER-SUPPORTED FAMILIES

Conventional economic policy in developed and less developed countries alike assumes that most families are headed by a fair-minded, male decision maker whose income is the central, if not only, income resource for the family. In this schema, women's income contributions to families are supplementary to the earnings of men, and women's unpaid labour is of limited economic value to families.

These assumptions are belied by the everyday experience of people everywhere. They are also challenged by an abundance of evidence that there is a high, and probably growing, proportion of mother-supported families in the world. This evidence includes 1) data illustrating the trend toward increasing proportions of female-headed and single-parent households; 2) analyses of women's economic contributions to households that count both cash income and the market value of all saleable goods and services not remunerated in cash; 3) data showing that mothers' workload increases more than fathers' when families grow and that women put more hours into income-generating work than men in many places; 4) studies showing that women's cash income is vital to meeting basic family needs and that women often contribute relatively (and sometimes absolutely) more of their income to meeting these needs; and 5) data on determinants of single motherhood.

Statistics on female-headed and single-parent households suggest the prevalence of mother-supported families but do not provide an exact measure of their numbers for the following reasons:

- Household headship is determined subjectively by survey respondents, who, when asked to name the head of their household, usually name the oldest male affiliated with the household, even if he is not economically active or in regular residence (Rosenhouse, 1989). Thus, household-headship data say less about the real economic support structure of households than they say about status hierarchies in households. Households are usually identified as female-headed only when there is no resident adult male, but almost all "male-headed households" include adult women and many are, in fact, economically supported by women. For this reason, statistics on female-headed households underrepresent the actual number of households that are economically supported by women, many of whom are mothers.

• Households and families are not synonymous. A large and growing number of families extend beyond the boundaries of household. Data on household headship tell us little, if anything, about the economic organization of these families.

• Most female-headed and single-parent households are supported by mothers, but some are not. Some female-headed households do not have children; some that do have children are headed by grandmothers, aunts, or women unrelated to the children; a small but growing number of single-parent households are headed by fathers; and some single mothers and women identified as household heads are not the sole, or even primary, supporters of their household — for example, women receiving substantial remittances from husbands or brothers.

Because of these caveats we cannot assume a one-to-one correspondence between female-headed and single-parent households on the one hand and mother-supported families on the other. No data are currently collected that allow us to determine the exact proportion of mother-supported families in the world; nevertheless, we can assert that this proportion is large and probably growing.

WAGE-EARNING AND DOMESTIC WORK: MOTHERS' DUAL PRODUCTIVE DUTIES

In determining who supports families, it is imperative to measure the value of non-cash work (to which women contribute disproportionately), to identify all income sources, and to document how income is allocated within families. Such an analysis reveals that mothers make — indeed, have always made — major economic contributions to their families.

Mothers perform many tasks that are vital forms of economic production, though often not recognized as such because they are not remunerated in cash. An increasing number of mothers are also making cash contributions to their families as more women join the formal labour force — out of necessity as well as in response to new economic opportunities. When both wage-earning and non–wage-earning forms of economic activity are accounted for, it becomes evident that mothers provide substantial, primary, or sole economic support to a large proportion of families in the world.

Formal measurements of women's economic activity — which includes all work for pay as well as production and processing of agricultural products, whether for the market or home consumption — indicate that rates among women 15 years or older are highest in eastern Asia and the former USSR, where roughly 60 per cent of women in this age group are economically active. Rates in South-East Asia, sub-Saharan Africa, and developed regions (Australia, Europe, Japan, New Zealand, and North America) range from 45 to 50 per cent. Rates are 32 per cent in the Caribbean and Latin America; 24 per cent in southern Asia; 21 per cent in western Asia; and 16 per cent in northern Africa (UN, 1991).

In documenting mothers' economic contributions to families, we are forced, once again, to rely on data related to households rather than to families. We must also infer mothers' and fathers' relative economic contributions to households from data on *women's* and *men's* relative contributions, assuming that a large share of these women and men are mothers and fathers.

Community studies in Nepal find that women contribute an average of 27 per cent of household monetary income; however, when economic value is attached to all the goods and services they produce — e.g., gathering wood for fuel, collecting and toting water, preparing food — women's average economic contribution to the household rises to 50 per cent (Acharya and Bennett, 1982). Women in farming households in Thailand contribute an average of half of their households' economic resources when these are calculated to include domestic consumption derived from home production (Richter, Kerry, and Havanon, 1993). An extensive study of how women and men use time in the Philippines indicates that women's share of market income is a third of men's on average; when the economic value of women's home production is added to the equation, women's economic contribution to the household exceeds men's by about 10 per cent (King and Evenson, 1983, p. 51). Another study estimated that Indian women contribute 30 per cent of India's net domestic product — excluding their services as housewives (Mukerjee, 1985, pp. 259-274). Analyses of data from Ghana indicate that in terms of market hours of work, 33 per cent of households with children were maintained primarily by women in 1988 (Lloyd and Gage-Brandon, 1993, pp. 115-131).

Until recently it was assumed (largely without empirical evidence) that a mother's participation in the labour force comprises the well-being of her children. In reality, choosing between working for wages and caring for children is possible only for mothers in developed countries (though fewer and fewer of them) and for a handful of women in the formal labour force of less developed countries who have access to paid domestic help. For the vast majority of the world's women, meeting children's needs requires mothers to engage in both domestic and wage-earning work. As a result, motherhood increases women's overall work load enormously.

Mothers' earning strategies and pattern of time use change in response to the shape and intensity of their motherhood role. Data from the Philippines show that each young child increases the average length of a mother's work week by 8.4 hours and that each new infant increases it by 6.5 hours (Popkin, 1983, p. 166). In general, a mother's participation in the labour force does not excuse her from household responsibilities; as a result, many mothers who work outside the home must sacrifice rest and leisure time to meet all their work responsibilities. In the Philippines working outside the home reduces a mother's rest and leisure time by 28 hours per week, a study reports (Popkin, 1983, p. 166).

Parallel changes in father's work and rest/leisure schedules are not observed. Studies in the Philippines comparing mothers' and fathers' total work time when children are added to the family show that a father's time spent in child care, food preparation, marketing, and other domestic chores averages 1–2 hours daily, regardless of whether he is the father of one child or seven. By contrast, maintaining five children increases a mother's work load by 22 hours per week (King and Evenson, 1983).

Some evidence suggests that when men and women live together in a household, men add to, rather than share, women's workload. Men's superior bargaining power may allow them to transfer domestic responsibilities to female family members, reducing men's expected workload. In an observational study of child feeding practices in Nicaragua, mothers of 12- to 18-months-olds were observed to spend more minutes in the household production (e.g., cleaning and food preparation) when the father was living with the family than when he was absent (Engle, La Montagne, and Zeitlin, 1992). Data from Ghana show that women who do the least work (domestic and market) live *without* men; men who do the least work live *with* women. Women who live with men work an average of 13 hours more per week than men who live with women.

Comparative studies of women's time use in diverse countries show that women, whether mothers or not, work much longer hours than men in general. This disparity is apparent in both developed and less developed countries. One early study of time-use data from 12 countries — including the United States, the former Soviet Union, and countries in eastern and western Europe — reports that employed women work roughly 20 per cent longer than employed men, on average (Szalai, 1975). A survey of 17 time-use studies in less developed countries finds that women's work hours exceed men's by 30 per cent (Leslie, Lycette, and Buvinic, 1988, pp. 307-348); a similar survey estimates the differential to be 40 per cent (McGuire and Popkin, 1990). Kenya's 1991 census reported that women of reproductive age work 50.9 hours per week, while men of a similar age work 33.2 hours per week, on average (Hill, 1992). In rural Java women work an average of 11 hours per day, while men average 8.5 hours per day (Nag, White, and Peet, 1978, pp. 293-306).

MOTHER'S CASH INCOME: A FAMILY NECESSITY

As subsistence economies modernize, survival and investment in the next generation increasingly require access to cash. Parents' ability to marshal cash for school fees can determine whether their children have any hope of entering the modern economy — yet even nominal school fees of US$25 per year are prohibitive for many families in less developed countries. An African woman described the disintegration of the rural subsistence economy and the changing demands upon families this way: "We farm our land for food and this is good. But we cannot farm for fuel, or soap, or school. For these we need money" (Hammerslough, 1991).

Mothers are the primary or sole source of income in most single-parent households and in many two-parent households as well. Fathers in two-parent homes may earn little or nothing because they cannot find steady (or any) employment or because they are physically disabled or otherwise impaired. In both developed and less developed countries the excessive use of drugs and alcohol by males has been cited among the causes of de facto female-headed households (Blumberg and Lesser, 1994; Richter and Havanon, 1993). A woman from Montserrat describes how this phenomenon affects women in her society:

> A lot of West Indian men like to drink. Those that do work to support their families usually do not make enough to support their drinking habits and their families. So women have to go to work too…. Women are used to supporting themselves, so they do it when the men are here and when the men are gone as well. They tell their daughters not to depend on men, but on themselves. They should tell the sons to have responsibilities, but they don't. It is the women who become responsible. (Moses, 1977)

Male un- and underemployment and the national debt-reduction programmes ("structural adjustment") have increased the pressure on women (and sometimes children) to earn in both developed and less developed countries. The same economic pressures that force mothers to earn income to support their families also break up families — by promoting labour migration or creating conflicts over limited income (Bianchi, n.d.) — leaving mothers with even greater economic responsibility for their children.

In countries ravaged by the AIDS epidemic, which primarily afflicts people of

41

reproductive age, the disease has increased some women's need to earn by creating single-parent households and requiring women to support extended-family members. Caring for the rapidly growing number of AIDS orphans has been largely left to women, whose family support networks may be dramatically depleted by the disease. This situation is illustrated by the case of a woman living with her daughter and teenaged son in Lusaka, Zambia:

> Her husband died of AIDS several years ago, followed by an older daughter. Her married son then assumed responsibility for the family, but he too recently succumbed to the disease, leaving a family behind. Now the woman is caring for her younger daughter who also has AIDS, while trying to keep her son in school. (Leonard, 1994)

In households with two wage-earning parents, fathers' income usually exceeds mothers' (as is true of men and women in general), yet mothers usually contribute a larger proportion of their income (and sometimes a larger absolute sum) to their household, according to studies in a number of countries. Recent research on intra-household resource allocation reveals a striking difference between men and women in proportion to their daily earnings devoted to meeting basic family needs (Haddad, Hoddinot, and Alderman). Even in cases in which the father earns substantially more than the mother, the mother's modest income may constitute the primary source of meeting family needs.

Father's relative cash contribution to their household may be small for a number of reasons. Some fathers contribute a portion of their income to one or more other households in which they are supporting children and/or past or current sexual partners (Bledsoe, 1993). In some societies husbands' and wives' relative economic contribution to their families is dictated by cultural norms prescribing that certain expenditures must be made by males and others by females, as a result of which mothers may be expected to provide a disproportionate share of overall and daily family resources (Fapohunda, 1988). For example, in much of Africa wives are expected to supply staple foods, while husbands are expected to pay intermittent, visible expenses, such as state-mandated school fees. In other instances, husbands are responsible for providing the family house, but the recurring cost of its upkeep, water, and fuel fall to wives. In parts of West Africa monetary exchanges are encouraged between blood kin — e.g., between brothers and sisters — rather than between husbands and wives; thus, a man pays more toward the support of his sister's children than his own.

Fathers sometimes divert a large portion of their income to personal uses; such expenditure patterns unnecessarily intensify mothers' share of economic responsibility for children (Engle and Zeitlin). Usually the barest minimum of a woman's income is withheld for what might be called personal expenditures. This is especially true among the poorest of women. A study of 14 typical villages in South India, consisting primarily of poor, landless families, reveals a striking pattern of systematic differences in the proportion of income women and men devote to household uses. While women appear to retain virtually no personal income, men retain up to 26 per cent of their earnings for personal use. Though the ratio of husbands' to wives' earnings is typically more than 3:2, the proportion of income withheld for personal use by husbands is five to six times the proportion withheld by wives (Mencher, 1988).

Mothers' cash earnings are often critical to children's health and access to health care and education. Evidence from micro-economic household studies and macro-level analyses confirm the "child orientation" of mothers' income (Thomas, 1990, pp. 635-664). Researchers in Kenya and Malawi recently found that among sugarcane farmers, "the level of income controlled by women has a positive impact on household caloric intake, over and above the effect of [overall household] income" (Kennedy and Peters, 1992, pp. 1077-1085). They also found that "while most female-headed households [in Malawi] allocated a larger share of their budgets to food, they spend 25-50 per cent less on alcoholic beverages than do male-headed households." (Peters, Herrera, and Randolph, 1989, pp. 1080).

Projections based on data on 300 children from urban Guatemala suggest that the attainment of an additional half of a standard deviation in children's average height-for-age through improved nutrition would require US$11.40 per month if earned by the mother but US$166 a month if earned by the father (Engle, 1993, pp. 1303-1312). Another analysis of these data suggests — as many previous studies have indicated — that the per cent of family income earned by the mother positively correlates with children's nutrition status indicators (Engle, 1991, pp. 954-965). Thus, even poor working mothers can attain respectable health, nutritional, and educational outcomes with a limited income (Bruce and Lloyd).

Given the fact that a mother's wage earning work is as vital to family survival as her equally demanding domestic work, it seems logical that families would facilitate the integration of mothers' dual roles. Yet paradoxically, the very families that rely upon mothers' earnings often encumber them with restrictive notions of appropriate work. Though we commonly attribute women's economic disadvantages to labour markets and wage discrimination, severe limits are also often imposed by the family system.

In some societies, women must carry on productive work within community or household compounds; in many others, propriety dictates that women should pursue only a limited range of jobs and economic activities. Both forms of confinement restrict women's access to remunerative work. Such constraints, upheld by men's authority within the home, can impair mothers' ability to meet either basic family needs or their own.

Mothers' ability to provide for their families is further eroded by a lack of effective control over their own income. In many societies, it is common for men to control earnings derived from the economic participation of women in family farming and business (Greenhalgh, 1991), or even from women's work outside the home. Husbands and elders exacerbate women's poverty when they control women's labour but do not give them fair compensation for their work. In an agricultural development scheme in Cameroon, for example, employers turned over families' wages, including the wives' share, exclusively to husbands. The husbands confiscated 50 per cent of their wives' wages for their own use (Jones, 1984). Many agricultural modernization schemes result in a double economic assault on women and, by extension, on their children. Women's labour is diverted to work on crops from which only male family members obtain income, while women are left with inferior land and less time to raise and process the crops needed for family consumption.

PATHWAYS TO SINGLE MOTHERHOOD

Nowhere is mothers' income more vital than in single-parent families. There are a variety of mechanisms by which mothers become single parents: separation, divorce, or abandonment; widowhood; polygamy; non-marital child-bearing; and economic, environmental, public health, and political crises that separate family members.

Separation and Divorce

Divorce rates are increasing in developed countries — and probably less developed countries as well — and a growing proportion of divorces involve couples with young children. In North America and northern Europe, 30 to 55 per cent of marriages end in divorce. In less developed countries, an average of about 25 per cent of first marriages have dissolved, many as a result of divorce or separation, by the time women are 40-49 years old. The rupture or attenuation of a parenting partnership generally worsens the economic condition of mother and child. Separation or divorce may stigmatize a mother, reducing her social status and shrinking her support network in cases where community members or her ex-partner's kin reject her.

Widowhood

Given that women usually have a higher life expectancy than men and that women are usually younger — sometimes considerably younger — than the men they marry, it is a demographic certainty that a far greater proportion of women than men will be left without a spouse. The number of widows is not insignificant: In India alone in 1991 there were 30 million widows (Chen and Drèze, 1992). In less developed countries in which spousal age differences are traditionally large (7-10 years) and marital fertility continues late in life (e.g., Bangladesh, Ghana, Morocco, Nigeria, and Sudan), widows are often left with dependent children to support.

In some parts of the world, wars have left large numbers of widows with dependent children. This phenomenon has been observed in Afghanistan and regions of the Middle East in the last decade (Forbes-Martin, 1991). Similarly, a study in rural Cambodia shows that fully 20 per cent of households are headed by widows (Forbes-Martin, 1991). A recent analysis of data from Vietnam revealed that 21 per cent of women aged 50 to 54 (who were in their twenties and thirties during the Vietnam war) are widows (Desai, 1994).

Widowhood can have serious financial consequences for women, who may lose property as well as spousal income when their husbands die. In much of sub-Saharan Africa widows often do not inherit from their husbands, regardless of the age and number of their common children or the closeness of the marriage (Potash, 1986). After a husband's death, it is not uncommon for his kin to take away key possessions. In some parts of India a widow is seen as being the "cause" of her husband's death and is treated as a "stranger" by her deceased husband's family. Though she may remain in the family compound, she must sleep and eat in a segregated space and provide for herself and her children. In upper-caste communities she is prohibited from working for wages, making the pursuit of a livelihood difficult, if not impossible.

Restrictions on residence, ownership, and employment place widows in a situation of acute dependence on economic support from others, yet such support may not be forthcoming. A study of widows in seven states in India reports that less than half live with adult sons, the most dependable source of economic support for widows (Chen, 1995). Less than 10 per cent live with and are supported by in-laws, parents, or brothers. This leaves nearly half of widows, many of whom must also support dependent children, to live and manage on their own.

The economic deprivation and vulnerability of widows is reflected in their high morbidity and mortality rates compared with married women in corresponding age groups. In India mortality rates are 86 per cent higher among widows than among married women, a recent study reports (Bhat, 1994). In Bangladesh there is a measurable increase in the mortality of women after their husbands die if they do not have a number of sons to provide for them and to protect their rights (Cain, 1978, pp. 421-438).

The dismal economics of widowhood argue for a full review of the legal and cultural practices contributing to widows' poverty, particularly where they are likely to have dependent children.

Polygamy and Multiple Unions

Polygamy is a legal institution in some countries and an informal practice in others. Legally sanctioned polygamy is still extensively practiced in a variety of traditional cultures in sub-Saharan Africa and is allowed under Islam. Polygamous men in positions of influence and relative wealth often contract second and third marriages with women who are much younger than they are.

Social norms and legal systems that encourage, or do not censure, men's multiple sexual partnerships are likely to leave many of the women who become mothers through such unions economically vulnerable. Few men have sufficient wealth to adequately support multiple families and invest equally in each mate and her offspring (Bledsoe, 1993), yet in some countries many men continue to father children with multiple partners, often late into their lives. Demographic and health surveys report much higher rates of male than female fertility in several African countries, primarily as a result of polygamy. In Ghana women aged 45-49 report having an average of 5.7 surviving children; men aged 50 and over report 8.5 surviving children. In Mali married women aged 40-49 report having an average of slightly more than four surviving children; men aged 50-55 report having about twice that many surviving children on average (Lloyd, 1994). Much of these men's excess fertility occurs after they are 45 years old; thus many of these fathers are likely to die while the children in their second or third families are still young.

Multiple sexual relationships and families are accepted in many societies (Elias and Heise, 1993). In Jamaica, for example, it is very common for men to have multiple parenting partners: 34-40 per cent of men participating in one study had two or three parenting partners; 14 per cent had four or more (Brown, Anderson, and Chevannes, 1993). Research conducted to help contain the spread of AIDS has played an important role in demonstrating the frequency of multiple sexual (and sometimes parenting) partnerships.

Non-marital Adolescent Child-bearing

Within the universe of mother-supported families, those that spring from early and unplanned child-bearing are arguably the most socially marginalized. Unprotected early sexual activity often robs a girl of her childhood, impoverishes her in adulthood, and compromises the future of her children. Because unmarried adolescent mothers are likely to have less education, low (if any) income, and an uncertain claim on the father's earnings (if he has any), their prospects — short- and long-term — are often grim.

In the past, most adolescent childbearing either took place within, or led to, marriage or a sanctioned union. Indeed, in many less developed countries a girl could be rejected by her spouse, his family, or her family if she failed to conceive soon after sexual relations were established. As the cultural desirability of early marriage has receded, the consequences of adolescent child-bearing have become increasingly favourable. Current evidence from a variety of settings reveals that women who conceive children at a young age and out of the socially accepted sequence — i.e., marriage, followed by sexual initiation, followed by pregnancy — have poor economic prospects (Engle, 1992).

Bonds between unmarried, pregnant, adolescent women and the fathers of their children-to-be are typically weak (Morris, 1993). Even when an unplanned pregnancy leads to marriage, the union is often unstable. A study in Barbados found that only 23 per cent of children of such unions still reside with their fathers by age eight; in Chile, about 40 per cent of such children are abandoned and unacknowledged by their fathers by age six (Russell-Brown, Engle, and Townsend, 1992; Buvinic, Valenzuela, Molina, and González, 1992).

Sexually active, unmarried adolescents account for a large portion of the unmet need for contraception and safe abortion services in many countries, yet adolescent girls lack effective access to, or power to use, contraception. In Latin America typically no more than one-fifth of sexually active adolescent girls report using contraception at first intercourse, and only 20 to 70 per cent of unmarried adolescents report using a contraceptive method during their most recent sexual encounter (UN, 1989; Singh and Wolf, 1990).

Non-consensual sex plays a significant role in adolescent pregnancy in developed and less developed countries alike (Youri, 1994; Rosas, 1992). In a study of a representative sample of adolescent mothers in Seattle, Washington, more than two-thirds reported that they had been sexually abused, and 44 per cent had been victims of forced intercourse at some point in their lives (Boyer and Fine, 1992, pp. 4-12). Nearly half of sexually active schoolgirls in Kenya report that their first intercourse was forced or that they were "tricked" into it (Youri, 1994). The unwilling adolescent mother is plausibly the most vulnerable of all parents.

Migration: Voluntary and Forced

Labour migration may lead to *de facto* single parenthood for a mother whose migrant husband is absent for extended periods of time. In regions where migration flows are increasing, this condition of single motherhood may be common, at least for a portion of women's lives. While some of the best-supported single mothers are those with migrant husbands or male kin who send back remittances on a steady basis, for many mothers and children left behind the benefits of male migration are illusory.

Men (and women) may initially leave home to earn wages for the family's benefit, but their commitment to sending money home, or the practical possibility of doing so, sometimes fades. Data from southern Africa suggest that although remittances to women and children may be substantial during the first year of a migrant male's absence, they appear to dwindle over longer periods of time (Palmer, 1985, pp. 24, 29). Even repeated day- or week-long absences can weaken mothers' and children's claims to fathers' earnings (Hoodfar, 1988).

One observer writes compellingly that fathers live away from the cries of their children (Whitehead, 1981). The implication is that a mother left alone with children bears day-to-day witness to the children's needs and is compelled to meet them, unlike the absent father. In some cases, the migrant men start new families elsewhere, creating a new set of obligations that undercut economic support to the first family. It is understandable, but problematic, that fathers who must reside far from their family for longer periods of time might lose their sense of connection to the family.

Forced migration also leaves many mothers with the sole responsibility for their children. As noted in the previous chapter, the number of refugees in the world has increased dramatically in the last decade. Refugee streams from all sources are dominated by women and children, who represent 80 per cent of the 18 million refugees awaiting resettlement (10 per cent more than the average proportion of women and children in the population of a less developed country) (UNHCR, 1993). This figure may even be low, given the disturbing fact that younger women are proportionately underrepresented in refugee populations, suggesting that the substantial members are being abducted or detained (UN, 1993). Young widows with children are heavily represented among refugee populations from Cambodia and Vietnam (Forbes-Martin, 1991).

Many of those deemed most destitute within the refugee populations live in female-headed households. In the Near East it is estimated that roughly 50 per cent of the poorest refugee households are headed by women (Forbes-Martin, 1991). Because refugee movements uproot whole communities, family and neighbourhood support networks that would usually provide critical assistance to single mothers and widows with young children often disintegrate, leaving refugee mothers to provide full share of economic and emotional support for their children.

WOMEN'S UNEXPECTED ECONOMIC LIFE CYCLES

The data on women's actual experiences in family life present a very different picture from one most women have been raised to expect. In sharp contrast to cultural mythology, the marriage of a girl or woman is not the beginning of a long cycle of economic protection or security. Many women will spend a significant proportion of their reproductive years (15-49) unmarried or living without a partner in residence. After age 49 there is an even higher probability of a woman living apart from a spouse as a result of the increased incidence of widowhood in later life; marital dissolution through divorce, separation, or abandonment may also be common in women's later years. When the number of years in which women are unmarried, living apart from a spouse, divorced, or widowed are combined, they comprise a sizable proportion of women's lives. This fact underscores the need to preserve and expand women's earning opportunities and legally recognize women's economic rights as individuals rather than as adjuncts to their fathers, brothers, and sons.

The increasing proportion of single-parent households — documented in developed countries and thought by many to be occurring in less developed countries as well — coincides with a trend called the "feminization of poverty," in which the poorest quartiles of society are increasingly made up of women and children. A review of data gathered in the mid-1980s from five Latin American cities — Bogotá Caracas, Lima, Panama City, and San José — indicates that female-headed households are overrepresented in the lower-income groups in the last four of these cities; only in Bogotá was there a greater proportion of female-headed households in the total population than in lower-income groups (UN, 1984, p. 246) The feminization of poverty is also a rural phenomenon. A review of global literature undertaken by the International Fund for Agricultural Development found that in the two decades preceding 1988, the number of rural women living below the poverty line increased by 47 per cent, while the number of impoverished rural men increased by only 30 per cent (International Fund for Agricultural Development, 1992, p. 273).

MARRIAGE AND MOTHERHOOD AS FREE CHOICES

By all indications, women want and need satisfying sexual relationships. Most women probably also want to have a close partnership with a man and want to have children (whether because of innate desire or socialization). The issue for most women is not the value of these experiences but rather the conditions under which they experience them. Women's weak bargaining power in the arenas of sexual relationships, child-bearing, and child-rearing is the difficulty.

Sexual relationships often brings risks of disease, unwanted pregnancy, and unforeseen lifelong responsibilities. Women's lack of control over their own sexuality and fertility remains one of the most threatening aspects of their lives. Men and women, including husbands and wives, often hold very different views about the need for protection against sexually transmitted diseases and unwanted pregnancy. Even in stable marital unions, discord over the number of desired children and the lack of communication concerning sexual matters are common (Lloyd, 1994; Bongaarts and Bruce, 1994). Women cite a fear of their partner's disapproval or violence and fear of abandonment as reasons why they cannot use contraceptives. For these reasons, some women must select contraceptive methods that they can use in secret, that have no detectable side effects, and that do not interfere with sexual acts. Women are often unable to gain their partner's compliance for condom use as protection against sexually transmitted diseases, even when their partner is a likely carrier of HIV (Elias and Heise, 1993). Many women carry responsibility for the most intimate aspects of their relationship alone and unprotected.

What explains the ease with which husbands and families control and direct women — particularly when they become mothers — to act in others' interest before their own? Gender role ideologies are partly to blame: Women are socialized from the time they are little girls to find social affirmation in caring for and submitting to others (Papanek, 1979). From their earliest years, young girls wait on adults and often on male siblings as well. There may be harsh social penalties for girls and women who defy gender expectations, particularly with respect to family roles. Gender ideologies that curtail women's rights within families, combined with market-place discrimination against women, impede women's exit from disagreeable, unjust, or even violent family circumstances (Sen, 1990). In sum, women's behaviour in families is powerfully shaped by economic and social incentives to uphold traditional male-female divisions of labour and social hierarchy.

Not only do women have fewer social alternatives than men — having to join or create families almost perforce in order to survive — but once married into the families, many women appear not to be much more secure than they would be outside of marriage. While gathering of statistics on violence against women proceeds unevenly, one global study finds that where such data are recorded, 40 to 80 per cent of all physical abuse suffered by women takes place at the hands of a close family member (usually a husband) (Bunch, 1991, p. 7). The authors conclude that in terms of both morbidity and mortality, "the home is often the most dangerous place for women and frequently the site of cruelty and torture." An insightful study into the causes of violence against women in Peru notes the significant features of the family system that reinforce women's dependence. These include the "domestic isolation of women where male figures are the final authority, early marriages before women have developed a sense of autonomy, poor communication in family conflicts, the identification of the family as the sole institution that shapes women's identity, and the tendency to treat domestic conflict between men and women as a private matter" (Vasquez and Tamayo, 1989, p. 34).

What is the fate of a woman who seeks to leave a marriage? What is the value placed on an infertile woman? What future awaits a mother with too few sons? What befalls a woman who chooses to be sexually inactive and/or not to become a mother? In most societies social rejection and economic insecurity attend such choices. Despite the advances of the international women's movement, and much supportive rhetoric from national governments, most women are far from having a true choice regarding their sexuality, marital status, or motherhood.

CONCLUSION

Family policies that support women as mothers and individuals must confront a paradox. The same families that rely upon women to assume ever-growing responsibility for family support and to function as good wives and mothers undermine women in their efforts to fulfil these roles. Abuses of family-based power — in particular, destructive abuses of husbands' superior strength and access to resources — demote women from partners in marriages to juniors in marriage, from effective advocates for their dependents to dependents themselves.

These undermining family forces are frequently reinforced in the wider social arena. Women are treated under some systems of family law more as a property than as free adults. Women's economic claims are regularly ignored by policy, leaving them doubly discriminated against on the basis of their gender and their normatively ascribed family roles.

Not only are women — especially mothers — often not economically protected by spouses and society, they often become more economically vulnerable after marriage. This vulnerability increases when wives become mothers. While mothers may cease being wives, they rarely resign from being mothers and, thus, rarely escape the long-term economic and emotional responsibilities of motherhood.

Nothing in the data we have reviewed suggests that women in the future will be under any less pressure to generate cash income to support their families. The volatility of marital and sexual relationships is also not likely to abate. With pervasive, cross-cultural evidence of shifting family arrangements, diminishing co-residence of spouses, and women's intensifying economic responsibility for children, there can be no plausible justification for policies that limit women's access to economic resources on the basis of their marital or fertility status. Needing a husband's or father's or son's consent for a woman to have access to credit, market activity, or ownership of assets is not only offensive, it is unproductive. The removal of gender bias from economic policy must include removal of explicit or implicit constraints on women based on their sexual, reproductive, or family roles. Tests of women's unencumbered access might include: Can a celibate, childless woman support herself? Can a pregnant, unmarried woman hold a job? Can a poor, working mother procure affordable child care?

Removing gender biases from economic policy may increase women's access to labour markets and reduce the male-female wage gap, but it is not enough to reduce women's disproportionate share of poverty. In the future, being a mother will be the most important factor disposing women to poverty unless women's family roles are more fully valued and responsibility for children is more equitably balanced between men and women. Safe and secure motherhood requires a fundamental recognition that women have the right to pursue livelihoods on their own behalf, to enjoy freedom of choice in marriage and child-bearing, to find equality in the workplace, and above all, to share the economic and social responsibilities for children with willing partners.

Judith Bruce *is Programme Director, Gender, Family, and Development and a Senior Associate in the Programmes Division of the Population Council.*

This article draws upon the author's "The Economics of Motherhood," in J. Bruce, C.B. Lloyd and A. Leonard (eds.), *Families in Focus: New Perspectives on Mothers, Fathers, and Children*. New York: The Population Council, 1995.

References

Acharya, Meena, and Lynn Bennett. 1982. "Women and the Subsistence Sector: Economic Participation in Household Decision-making in Nepal." Working Paper no. 526. Washington, DC: The World Bank.

Bhat, P. N. Mari. 1994. "Widows and Widowhood Mortality in India." Paper presented at the Conference on Widows in India, Bangalore, March.

Bianchi, Suzanne M. n.d. "Marital Separation and the Economic Well-being of Children and Their Absent Fathers." Washington, DC: US Bureau of the Census, HHES Division.

Bledsoe, Caroline. 1993. "The Politics of Polygyny in Mende Education and Child Fosterage Transactions," in Barbara Diane Miller (ed.), *Sex and Gender Hierarchies*. Cambridge: Cambridge University Press.

Blumberg, Rae Lesser. 1994. "Women's Work, Income and Family Survival Strategy: The Impact of Guatemala's ALCOSA Agribusiness Project," in Esther Ngan-ling Chow and Catherine White Berheide (eds.), *Women, the Family and Policy: A Global Perspective*. Albany: SUNY Press.

Bongaarts, John, and Judith Bruce. 1994. "The Causes of Unmet Need for Contraception and the Social Content of Services." Research Division Working Paper no. 69. New York: The Population Council.

Boyer, Debra, and David Fine. 1992. "Sexual Abuse As a Factor in Adolescent Pregnancy and Child Maltreatment." *Family Planning Perspectives* 24 (1), pp. 4-12.

Brown, Janet, Patricia Anderson, and Barry Chevannes. 1993. *Report on the Contribution of Caribbean Men to the Family: A Jamaican Pilot Study*. Kingston, Jamaica: Caribbean Child Development Centre, School of Continuing Studies, University of the West Indies.

Bruce, Judith, and Cynthia B. Lloyd. forthcoming. "Finding the Ties That Bind: Beyond Headship and Household," in Haddad, Lawrence, John Hoddinot, and Harold Alderman (eds.), *Intrahousehold Resource Allocation in Developing Countries: Methods, Models, and Policy*. Baltimore: International Food Policy Research Institute and Johns Hopkins University Press. forthcoming.

Bunch, Charlotte. 1991. "Women's Rights As Human Rights: Toward a Re-vision of Human Rights," in *Gender Violence: A Development and Human Rights Issue*. New Brunswick, NJ: Center for Women's Global Leadership, Douglass College.

Buvinic, M., J. P. Valenzuela, T. Molina, and E. González. 1992. "The Fortunes of Adolescent Mothers and Their Children: The Transmission of Poverty in Santiago, Chile." *Population and Development Review* 18 (2), pp. 211-242.

Cain, Mead T. 1978. "The Household Life Cycle and Economic Mobility in Rural Bangladesh." *Population and Development Review* 4 (3), pp. 421-438.

Chen, M. 1995. *The Lives of Widows in India*. forthcoming.

Chen, M., and J. Drèze. 1992. "Widows and Well-being in Rural North India." Development Economics Research Programme Paper no. 40. London: London School of Economics.

Desai, Sonalde. 1994. Personal communication.

Elias, Christopher J., and Lori Heise. 1993. "The Development of Microbicides: A New Method of HIV Prevention for Women." Programmes Division Working Paper no. 6. New York: The Population Council.

Engle, Patrice L. 1991. "Maternal Work and Child Care Strategies in Peri-urban Guatemala: Nutritional effects." *Child Development* 62, pp. 954-965.

Engle, Patrice L. 1992. "Consequences of Women's Family Status for Mothers and Daughters in Guatemala." Final report. New York: The Population Council.

Engle, Patricia L. 1993. "Influences of Mother's and Father's Income on Children's Nutritional Status in Guatemala." *Social Science and Medicine* 37 (11), pp. 1303-1312.

Engle, Patrice L., J. La Montagne, and M. Zeitlin. 1992. "Caring Behaviors and Nutritional Status of Weaning-Age Children in Managua, Nicaragua." Report to UNICEF, New York.

Engle, Patrice L., and M. Zeitlin. forthcoming. "Father's Money, Mother's Money and Parental Commitment: Nicaragua and Guatemala," in R. Blumberg (ed.), *Engendering Wealth and Well-being*. Boulder, CO: Westview Press.

Fapohunda, Eleanor R. 1988. "The Nonpooling Household: A Challenge to Theory," in Daisy Dwyer and Judith Bruce (eds.), *A Home Divided: Women and Income in the Third World*. Stanford: Stanford University Press.

Forbes-Martin, S. 1991. *Refugee Women*. New Jersey: Zed Books.

Greenhalgh, Susan. 1991. "Women in the Informal Enterprise: Empowerment or exploitation?" Research Division Working Paper no. 33. New York: The Population Council.

Haddad, Lawrence, John Hoddinot, and Harold Alderman (eds.). forthcoming. *Intrahousehold Resource Allocation in Developing Countries: Methods, Models, and Policy*. Baltimore: International Food Policy Research Institute and Johns Hopkins University Press.

Hammerslough, C. 1991. "Demographic Approaches to Studying the Effects of Maternal Mortality on Children," in *The Effects of Maternal Mortality on Children in Africa: An Exploratory Report on Kenya, Namibia, Tanzania, Zambia, and Zimbabwe*. New York: Defense for Children International USA.

Hill, C. 1992. "Gender Planning and Kenya's Development Planning Processes: A Critical Evaluation." Master's thesis, York University, Ontario, Canada.

Hoodfar, Homa. 1988. "Household Budgeting and Financial Management in a Lower-Income Cairo Neighborhood," in Daisy Dwyer and Judith Bruce (eds.), *A Home Divided: Women and Income in the Third World*. Stanford: Stanford University Press.

International Fund for Agricultural Development, 1992. *The State of World Rural Poverty: An Inquiry into Its Causes and Consequences*. New York: New York University Press.

Jones, C. 1984. "Intrahousehold Contractual Arrangements and Farming Systems Research." Paper prepared for the joint Rockefeller Foundation/Ford Foundation conference on Intrahousehold Processes and Farming Systems Research, Bellagio, Italy.

Kennedy, Eileen, and Pauline Peters. 1992. "Household Food Security and Child Nutrition: The Interaction of Income and Gender of Household." *World Development* 20 (8), pp. 1077-1085.

King, Elizabeth, and Robert E. Evenson. 1983. "Time Allocation and Home Production in Philippine Rural Households," in M. Buvinic, M. Lycette, and W. McGreevey (eds.), *Women and Poverty in the Third World*. Baltimore: Johns Hopkins University Press.

Leonard, Ann (ed.). 1994. *Community-Based AIDS Prevention and Care in Africa: Building on Local Initiatives — Case Studies from Five African Countries*. New York: The Population Council.

Leslie, J., M. Lycette, and M. Buvinic. 1988. "Weathering Economic Crises: The Critical Role of Women in Health," in D. E. Bell and M. R. Reich (eds.), *Health, Nutrition, and Economic Crises: Approaches to Policy in the Third World*. United Kingdom: Suburn House.

Lloyd, Cynthia B. 1994. "Family and Gender Issues for Populations Policy," in *Proceedings of the UN Expert Group Meeting on Population and Women*. New York: United Nations. Shorter version in Laurie Ann Mazur (ed.). 1994. *Beyond the Numbers: A Reader on Population, Consumption, and the Environment*. Washington, DC: Island Press.

Lloyd, Cynthia B., and Anastasia J. Gage-Brandon. 1993. "Women's Role in Maintaining Households: Family Welfare and Sexual Inequality in Ghana." *Population Studies* 47 (1), pp. 115-131.

McGuire, J., and B. M. Popkin. 1990. "Helping Women Improve Nutrition in the Developing World: Beating the Zero Sum Game." World Bank Technical Paper no. 114. Washington, DC: The World Bank.

Mencher, Joan P. 1988. "Women's Work and Poverty: Women's Contribution to Household Maintenance in South India," in Daisy Dwyer and Judith Bruce (eds.), *A Home Divided: Women and Income in the Third World*. Stanford: Stanford University Press.

Morris, Leo. 1993. "Determining Male Fertility Through Surveys: Young Adult Reproductive Health Surveys in Latin America." Paper presented at side-meeting of International Union for the Scientific Study of Population, Committee on Anthropology and Demography, IUSSP General Conference, Montreal, Canada.

Moses, Yolanda T. 1977. "Female Status, the Family, and Male Dominance in a West Indian Community," in Ximena Bunster B. et al. (eds.), *Women and National Development: The Complexities of Change*. Chicago: University of Chicago Press.

Mukerjee, M. 1985. "Contributions to and Use of Social Product by Women," in Devaki Jain and Nirmala Banerjee (eds.), *Tyranny of the Household: Investigative Essays on Women's Work*. New Delhi: Shakti Books.

Nag, M., N. White, and R. Peet. 1978 "An Anthropological Approach to the Study of the Economic Value of Children in Java and Nepal." *Current Anthropology* 19, pp. 293-306.

Palmer, I. 1985. *The Impact of Male Out-Migration on Women in Farming*. West Hartford, CT: Kumarian Press.

Papenek, H. 1979. "Family Status Production: The 'Work' and 'Non-work' of Women." *Signs* 4.

Peters, P., and G. Herrera, with T. Randolph. 1989. "Cash Cropping, Food Security and Nutrition: The Effects of Agricultural Commercialization Among Smallholders in Malawi." Final Report to AID, NIPD. Cambridge: United States Agency for International Development.

Popkin, Barry. 1983. "Rural Women, Work and Child Welfare in the Philippines," in M. Buvinic, M. Lycette, and W. McGreevey (eds.), *Women and Poverty in the Third World*. Baltimore: Johns Hopkins University Press.

Potash, Betty (ed.). 1986. *Widows in African Societies: Choices and Constraints*. Stanford: Stanford University Press.

Richter, Kerry, and Napaporn Havannon. 1993. "Women's Economic Contribution to Households in Thailand: Implications for National Development and Social Welfare." Report submitted to the United Nations Development Programme.

Rosas, M. Isabel. 1992. "Violencia Sexual y Política Criminal." CLADEM Informativo no. 6. Comité Latino Americano para la Defensa de los Derechos de la Mujer, Lima, Peru.

Rosenhouse, Sandra 1989. "Identifying the Poor: Is Headship a Useful Concept?" The Living Standards Measurement Study Working Paper no. 58. Washington, DC: The World Bank.

Russell-Brown, P., P. L. Engle, and J. Townsend. 1992. "The Effects of Early Child-bearing on Women's Status in Barbados." Paper prepared for the joint Population Council/International Center for Research on Women project on Family Structure, Female Headship and Maintenance of Families and Poverty.

Sen, Amartya. 1990. "Gender and Cooperative Conflicts," in Irene Tinker (ed.), *Persistent Inequalities: Women and World Development*. New York: Oxford University Press.

Singh, S., and D. Wolf. 1990. *Today's Adolescents, Tomorrow's Parents: A Portrait of the Americas*. New York: Alan Guttmacher Institute.

Szalai, A. 1975. "The Situation of Women in the Light of Contemporary Time-Budget Research." Paper prepared for UN World Conference on Women, Mexico City.

Thomas, Duncan. 1990. "Intrahousehold Resource Allocation: An Inferential Approach." *The Journal of Human Resources* 25 (4), pp. 635-664.

UN (United Nations). 1989. *Adolescent Reproductive Behavior: Evidence from Developing Countries*. vol. 2. New York: United Nations.

UN (United Nations). 1991. *The World's Women: Trends and Statistics 1970-1990*. New York: United Nations. Table 6.6.

UN (United Nations). 1984. *La Mujer en el Sector Popular Urbano: Amárica Latina y el Caribe*. Santiago, Chile: United Nations.

UNHCR (United Nations High Commissioner for Refugees). 1993. *The State of the World's Refugees: The Challenge of Protection*. New York: Penguin Books.

Vasquez, R., and G. Tamayo. 1989. *Violencia y Legalidad*. Lima: Concytec. Cited in R. Carrillo. 1991. "Violence Against Women: An Obstacle to Development," in *Gender Violence: A Development and Human Rights Issue*. New Brunswick, NJ: Center for Women's Global Leadership, Douglass College.

Whitehead, A. 1981. "'I'm Hungry, Mum': The Politics of Domestic Budgeting," in K. Young, C. Wolkowitz, and R. McCullagh (eds.), *Of Marriage and the Market: Women's Subordination in International Perspective*. London: Routledge, Chapman, and Hall.

Youri, Pat (ed.). 1994. *Female Adolescent Health and Sexuality in Kenyan Secondary Schools: A Survey Report*. Nairobi: African Medical and Research Foundation and The Population Council.

WOMEN IN INTERNATIONAL MIGRATION

GEERTJE LYCKLAMA À NIJEHOLT

"Females are more migratory than males," observed Ravenstein more than a hundred years ago in his pioneering work on the laws of migration (Ravenstein, 1885). In the century that followed, this observation remained unexplored in migration research. In fact, until the 1970s women were invisible in migration research (Morokvasic, 1983). It was taken for granted that they were part of the family of the male migrant; when travelling alone they were seen as joining a husband who had gone ahead. As a consequence, they have not been the subject of policy-making.

This situation changed during the second half of the 1970s, when several studies were done focusing on migrant women as migrants in their own right, and which made policy recommendations to deal with their particular situation (Abadan-Unat, 1979; Youssef, Buvinic, and Kudat, 1979; Chaney, 1980). Two reasons explain the emergence of migration literature on women in the 1970s. One is the wider questioning of women's role in society. The other is the increasing recognition of the economic importance of migrant women (Morokvasic, 1983: 19).

Today millions of women worldwide are on the move, migrating across borders. Their reasons for doing so are many. Next to a category of women moving as family migrants or for reasons of family reunion, the most important categories of international migrants are women refugees and women migrating for economic reasons. The focus in this paper is on the latter category — on women migrating in their own right as workers. The paper draws on available literature, in particular the extensive study on international migration of domestic workers in the Asian region (Heyzer, Lycklama à Nijeholt, and Weerakoon, 1994). It seeks to identify some key issues and challenges for activists, policy makers, and programme planners.

THEORETICAL DEVELOPMENTS

In the 1980s one of the debates in migration theory emphasized that in order to understand processes of labour migration, it is important to interrelate analyses at different levels (Bach and Schraml, 1982; Wood, 1982; Gibson and Graham, 1986; Penninx, 1986; Selier, 1986). Some researchers point to the household as an important link between the micro and the macro level; others suggest the meso level of the wider networks of family and kinship ties as important in understanding migration processes. However, as acknowledged by some researchers, this is not a simple task: "The perennial problem seems to lie in the difficulty of joining the micro and the macro data. Individual decisions to migrate and the impact on collectivities or areas are still not sufficiently understood, especially since the collection of the two types of information is very difficult to coordinate" (Kubat and Hoffman-Nowotny, 1982: 206).

In reviewing migration theory one basically finds two rather opposing approaches, both of which have a tendency to become reductionist. Wood, in a clear discussion of the major standpoints and drawbacks of these two paradigms, refers to them as the Equilibrium Model of Migration and the Historical-Structural Perspective (Wood, 1982).

Within the Equilibrium Model the emphasis is on the individual migrant who moves in the expectation that his or her economic situation will improve. It is a micro-economic approach which emphasizes the rational decision of the individual migrant and implies, for instance, that the migrant has access to the information relevant for making that decision. It is assumed that the migrant moves to wherever the best economic opportunities exist and where returns on his/her labour are highest. In this approach, emphasis is on wage differentials, education and skills, and counting the numbers within the various categories of people who are moving. The perspective represents a rather reductionist economic view on migration. It is a-historic and superficial since little space is given to the underlying structural forces — such as the social, cultural, and political aspects of the labour migration process — which also affect decision-making For example, class background, household structure, and political power structures at national and international levels are often not taken into account. Due to the dominant patriarchal perspective on the division of labour between women and men, little attention is given to women in the migration process. Men are seen as the providers for their wives and children and thus the important actors in this Equilibrium Model of migration. Women are perceived as dependents who stay home and receive (and consume) the remittances. In those cases where women move, it is assumed that they join their husbands (Morokvasic, 1984). These assumptions have proven to be no longer valid in view of the substantial number of studies which show that women migrate on their own, both nationally and internationally, legally and illegally, in all regions of the world.

The second perspective, called the Historical-Structural Perspective, represents quite a variety of standpoints concerning the labour migration process. Overall, however, adherents to this approach hold that "...population movement can only be examined in the context of historical analysis of the broader structural transformations underway in a particular social formation" (Wood, 1982: 302).

According to this perspective, migration is considered in the first place to be a macrosocial process and not an individual decision (Wood, 1982; Selier, 1986). The movement of labour migrants can be explained by their location within the wider class, socioeconomic, and political systems. Due to its focus on the structural conditions which lead to migration, little attention is given to the individual level of decision-making and to people in general. As a consequence of this focus and of the dominant patriarchal assumptions on the gender division of labour, the phenomenon of women migrating — either as wives following their husbands or, in particular, as independent workers — is greatly underexposed.

Interrelating the Two Approaches: The Household Network
Each of these two major perspectives in migration analysis leads to a rather limited understanding of the complex processes that are taking place. This has resulted in attempts to interrelate the two approaches. The argument is made that processes of migration can only be understood when analyses at different levels are interrelated. In particular, ways need to be found to link the individual, micro-level analysis with the structural, macro-level analysis.

Wood (1982), for example, attempts to reconcile the two approaches by proposing the household as the unit of analysis. However, by leaving out family and kinship ties, child-bearing and -rearing, and sociocultural dimensions in general, Wood's concept of household becomes very economistic. The household becomes a set of "unrelated" individuals bound together by a common fund. Bach and Schraml (1982), on the other hand, question whether the two can be fruitfully integrated by shifting to the household as the unit of analysis in migration theory. Instead, they propose to move the historical-structural approach beyond its current theoretical plateau.

In order to understand the labour migration process, it is important, in my view, to stay embedded in the historical-structural approach and consider the structural factors as the forces which bring about migration. Within those parameters, the individual decision to migrate should be perceived as being strongly influenced by collective considerations within the social network of family, household, kin, and community, as well as by the outcome of conflicts of interest within that network. Thus, these levels need to be analyzed in an interrelated way, but it should be understood that the historical-structural forces are the forces which create the conditions on the basis of which a person or a family may or may not decide to migrate. Conditions, however, often leave very little choice.

Within households we find multiple power relations, between husband and wife, mother and daughter, father and daughter, brothers and sisters, and so on. It is well known that within such complex structures of asymmetrical power relations, young girls and young women are among the least powerful. They are usually very dominantly controlled by family rules, its development cycle (Arizpe, 1984), and kinship obligations, e.g., "filial piety" (Salaff, 1981). It is as part of a family, household, and kin network that girls in rural areas are socialized to carry the burden of their part of the gender division of labour. This usually relegates them to household chores and work related to subsistence production. As a foreign housemaid in the household of employment, the young woman is in an even more powerless situation. She may easily become the victim of sexual abuse by male members of the family and, as a consequence, is easily seen as a major competitor in the sexual domain by the wife in that household.

The State as Intermediary Agent

Besides the family, household, and kin network, another dimension that requires attention is the role of the state in migration processes, in particular in processes of international migration. In various regions of the world — for example, in labour migration to South Africa, to the United States, and to Europe — the state plays an important role. Usually it is the labour-importing state which attempts to control and regulate the process. A new phenomenon which has developed in recent years is that the labour-exporting state plays an active role in marketing its workers and controlling the process.

In an attempt to situate Filipino migrant contract construction workers in migration theory, Gibson and Graham advocate a reorientation of the historical-structural migration theory. They do so in view of the increasing role the state plays in migration processes. Their concern is "...to consider historical differences in the way in which migrant labour has articulated with capital *and with the state*" (emphasis added, Gibson and Graham, 1986: 134). It is necessary to examine both the specific economic location of the incorporation of migrant labour and the specific modes of control. In the way the political control of these labour processes is organized, the role of the state has become important. Gibson and Graham (1986: 146–47) see the process as follows:

> Who migrates, and where they migrate to, is then explained by the changing nature of capitalist production and in particular the way in which capitalist competition affects the technical compositions of different industrial sectors; whereas the conditions under which migrants work and live are explained by the covert or overt nature of state involvement in the capital-migrant labour relation.

55

Gibson and Graham's important suggestions for an expansion of migration theory make it possible to analyse the specificities of relatively new forms of labour migration, such as the large-scale migration of contract construction workers to the Middle East, in its articulation with mobile productive capital and with the state. What is lacking, however, in their basically expanded historical-structural approach is the social dimension. As yet, such an approach does not explain why some families send members to the Middle East and others do not. To explain this, it is necessary also to know the social location of the workers, their class position, and the structure of their household. This social dimension is particularly relevant to an analysis of the causes and consequences of large-scale migration of housemaids in South and South-East Asia. These migrant workers articulate with capital in a way which is different from construction workers. For example, in Hong Kong and Singapore, housemaids make it possible for local women to sell their labour power in the market. In the Middle East the situation is different: besides contributing to the maintenance and the renewal of the labour force, housemaids add to the social prestige of a family, and the more servants the higher the status (Sherbiny, 1984: 35). Also, political control as executed by the state shows different dimensions. Pakistan, for example, through the Emigration Ordinance of 1979, set the minimum age for foreign contract employment of women as housemaids at 45 years (Shah, 1983: 415).

The difference in mode of control is most obvious in the work situation. Construction workers may be heavily controlled by the company they are working for in isolated work camps. Housemaids, however, are fully under the control of their employer family. The atomized working conditions, whereby the maids work in separate homes, make it very difficult to build any countervailing power against the forces that control their work and lives. As a consequence, many of these workers are abused, as is indicated by a variety of press reports.

In sum, in order to understand the causes and consequences of the housemaid trade, it is important to develop a theoretical framework which is able to address the distinctive aspects of this particular form of international migrant labour. Recent developments in migration theory give a number of helpful starting points for a further development of such a framework. A first theoretical point is the importance of family, household, and kin networks in interrelating the individual micro dimension of the migration process with the structural macro dimension. This can be realized within a historical-structural approach by moving beyond the current theoretical plateau of this approach, as suggested by Bach and Schraml.

A second theoretical point is provided by Gibson and Graham in their emphasis on the state as a competitive agent in the international labour market, which hires out labour for certain economic sectors, such as construction work or domestic service, and at the same time has substantial political control over these workers. In the case of housemaids, a substantial part of this control is, however, located in the family of employment, which makes the situation of these workers even more vulnerable. It is here that the exploitation and abuse takes place.

Thus, a study of housemaids in the international migration process requires an analysis of the interrelated structural forces (both international and national and, in particular, the role of the state) with the individual situation of the migrant, through the mediating institutions of family, household, and wider kin and community networks.

EVIDENCE FROM LATIN AMERICA, AFRICA, AND EUROPE

Research on the international migration of women for work is scarce — a situation that needs to be addressed in view of the magnitude of the phenomenon. Taking into account only

Asia and the Middle East, it is estimated that currently from 1 million to 1.7 million women have crossed a national border to work as domestic workers (Heyzer and Wee, 1994: 40). There is no doubt that over the past decade a growing market for this type of work has emerged. It has grown into a business which involves large numbers of women, millions of dollars, and dozens of countries importing and exporting this kind of labour.

The phenomenon can be understood only in the context of uneven development. In addition, it exposes inequities in gender relations, family structures, class positions, and both formal and informal economic processes. In regions other than the Asian and Pacific region, international migration of women as workers in their own right is known to exist, but systematic documentation is not available.

In Latin America, women who migrate on their own have as yet received little attention. Their migration is basically seen as being determined by the domestic division of labour (Balan, 1988). Women are the secondary movers; their decision to migrate depends on the decision of a male primary mover. Another article points out that of every three women migrating for employment, whether internal or international, two end up as domestic workers (Weinert, 1991: 20). In a number of Latin American countries, foreign women constitute a much higher proportion of domestic workers than local women. For example, in 1970 in Argentina, about 63 per cent of migrant women from neighbouring countries were employed as domestic workers, as against 5 per cent of the local female population (Weinert, 1991). In Venezuela, due to the country's economic prosperity, national women entered public-sector jobs, leaving space for foreign women to move into the private sector (Weinert, 1991: 21). A significant demand exists for illegal foreign female domestic workers, absorbing the largest proportion of female migrants (Van Roy, 1984, as referred to in Weinert, 1991: 21). As early as 1980, Chaney observed that not only women from South and Central America, but also from the Caribbean, predominate in several migrant streams, such as those to the United States and Canada (Chaney, 1980:15). While the phenomenon of women migrating for work internationally is quite widespread in Latin America and the Caribbean, there is a dearth of precise information.

Africa has a long history of labour migration, of contract workers temporarily employed outside their home countries. Most prominent is the migration of male workers from the surrounding countries to South Africa, which also led to the migration of female migrants to South Africa. However, in the research available, the emphasis is on the impact of male outmigration on the women left behind. A more recent phenomenon is the migration from Africa to Europe and the Middle East. Weyland (1993), in studying the Egyptian peasant migrants heading for the Gulf States, observes that women have not migrated but form the active supporters for the labour migration of their male household members.

Europe has changed from a continent of emigration to a continent of immigration. The early, scarce research available on female migrants focuses mainly on the experiences of Turkish migrant women in Germany (Abadan-Unat, 1977) and female migrants from former Yugoslavia in France and other West European countries (Morokvasic, 1980 and 1984). Little is known about the situation of international women contract workers. In recent labour streams to Europe, however, a growing number of women are found. They migrate as workers in their own right, not under family reunification schemes. According to Böhning, the data show a growth in importance in the category of workers — mainly women — involved in domestic work. It is one of the categories of migrant workers that has expanded considerably in various parts of the world (Böhning, 1991; Weinert, 1991). In Italy a presence of 100,000 Filipina maids is reported. Migration of women from the South started in the 1970s in response to a growing demand for domestic workers. In total, Italy had approximately 220,000 non-national domestic workers in 1989 (Campani, 1993: 192). In Spain, both legal and illegal migrant workers are concentrated in the service sector. More than 90 per cent of Asian immigrants and around 56 per cent of African immigrants work within this sector (Weinert, 1991: 12). In France, sample surveys indicate a high concentration of migrant women in the service sector, particularly in domestic service (Weinert, 1991: 16). The majority of the migrant women find employment through a well-functioning network of personal relationships or through recruitment agencies.

The changes in eastern Europe and the former Soviet Union after the collapse of the socialist system in 1989 have had a great impact on the migratory movements between the eastern and western parts of Europe. In particular, circular migration and commuting across borders constitute new forms of migratory movements in the region. This involves, for example, Poles travelling as tourists to Germany who are then active in the informal sector — in trading, seasonal work in agriculture and construction, and domestic service (Morokvasic and de Tinguy, 1993: 245). Prostitution and trafficking in women is also flourishing. These women often operate in direct competition with women from the South who are migrating or being forced to migrate to Europe to enter the entertainment and prostitution industry. Newspapers report regularly on events related to these types of trafficking (Lycklama à Nijeholt, 1993).

TRADE IN DOMESTIC WORKERS IN ASIA AND THE PACIFIC: FINDINGS

The Asian and Pacific region is characterized by a great diversity not only in history, culture, and ethnicity, but also in resources, economic development, and per capita income. Within this diverse context, the migration of workers within and between countries has been a well-known phenomenon throughout history. It is within this region that the large-scale policy and action research project called "The Trade in Domestic Workers: Causes, Mechanisms and Consequences of the International Migration of Women" was carried out. The project involved nine countries and territories and is thus far the most extensive, systemati,c and coherent study on the international labour migration of women. The findings are very helpful in bringing to the fore the issues and challenges for policy and planning.

One of the features of the booming economies of the high-growth countries in East Asia is a growing middle class which allows its well-educated married women to take up jobs in economies characterized by a high demand for educated and skilled labour. This leaves a niche in the market for foreign workers to take up the burden of housework within the context of the intimate domesticity of the (foreign) home. However, this work is perceived as no-work which fits women "naturally" without the need for training. At the same time, it does not give the worker any kind of status, either as a family member, citizen, permanent resident, or even permanent worker. Since this is treated as informal work not on a par with formal waged employment, policy makers are reluctant to extend legal protection to this kind of work. Yet the magnitude of the phenomenon forces government authorities to pay attention and take measures, in particular with respect to the international political dimensions of the "trade" in domestic workers. An illustration is the resignation of the Filipino Minister of Foreign Affairs as a consequence of the execution of Flor Contemplacion, a Filipina domestic worker in Singapore. The current situation of labour-exporting countries in South and South-East Asia is characterized by low commodity prices, economic adjustments and transitions, high foreign debts and unemployment. For these countries the export of women's labour as domestic workers has become an increasingly important source of foreign exchange, of regular remittances to supplement household incomes, and of labour absorption in a situation of chronic unemployment.

By the mid-1980s the international migration of women as domestic workers began to become visible in the shadow of the large-scale labour migration of single males or males with dependent family members to the Middle East and, to a lesser extent, Hong Kong and Singapore. By the 1990s it became a phenomenon that demanded attention at multiple levels, through research, NGO action, and policy responses from governments. To coordinate efforts at these levels, the Gender and Development Programme of the Asian and Pacific Development Centre (APDC) in Kuala Lumpur initiated in 1987 a regional policy and action research project, "Trade in Domestic Workers: Causes, Mechanisms and Consequences of the International Migration of Women" (Heyzer, 1994).

Aware of the crucial role of the family/household, kinship, and community linkages in the migration process and the dynamic interactions between macro, meso, and micro levels, the researchers, activists, and policy makers involved in the planning of the research decided on a comprehensive analysis of the following:

- the interrelated political, economic, and cultural forces at national and international levels;
- the role of the state;
- the class, gender, and ethnic structures at the macro level;
- the meso-level institutions of family, household, and wider kin and community networks;
- the micro-level interpersonal negotiations of everyday life within and outside the household; and
- the situation of the woman migrant herself, mediated through macro and meso complexities.

Within this framework the research traces the full cycle of international migration, examining both ends of the migration process — from sending country to receiving country and back to the home country.

The major findings of the study can be distinguished for analytical purposes as related to the international, the national, and the local level, thereby recognizing that these levels are interrelated and an integral part of an overall process.

At the international level, the study finds a great unevenness in development with respect to the nine countries and territories involved in the research. The sending countries — Bangladesh, Indonesia, the Philippines, and Sri Lanka — are much poorer than the receiving countries — Hong Kong, Malaysia, Singapore, and the Gulf States. Except for Pakistan, which receives a specific flow of Bangladeshi migrants, the receiving countries are much richer in per capita income than the sending countries. The 1992 overall per capita income for the four receiving countries was on average US$10,376 as against the overall per capita income of US$680 for the sending countries (Heyzer, 1994: xxiii). This leads to an active policy for labour export in countries such as Indonesia, the Philippines, and Sri Lanka.

It is difficult to make an accurate estimate of the magnitude of the "maid trade." Official statistics usually underreport the actual numbers involved, and in addition, many maids use illegal channels to reach their destination. For sending countries, the lowest and highest estimates respectively are 100,000 and 240,000 workers from Indonesia, and 100,000 and 175,000 workers from Sri Lanka. For the Philippines, the estimate is about 275,570 workers.

For the receiving countries involved in the study, the highest estimate is close to a million workers (Heyzer and Wee, 1994: 39–40).

Research on the mechanisms of this type of labour export shows that besides the official government agencies, extensive networks of informal if not illegal agencies are operating internationally. The recruitment network spans sending and receiving countries, permeating down to villages and linking them to towns and cities abroad. It is a multimillion-dollar transnational business which is closely related to other agencies that facilitate the migration process, such as banks, money-lenders, hotels, airlines, illegal money-changers, translation services, medical clinics, and training institutions. All of these profit from the trade in workers. Based on a service fee and a placement fee per worker, recruitment agencies in the Philippines gain an estimated US$121,250,360 to US$319,660,040 from this type of labour export (Heyzer, 1994: 56).

At the national level, governments and government agencies are heavily involved in facilitating the export and import of workers. In an overview of the mechanisms of migration, Dias points out, however, that because of the failure of state agencies to manage labour migration, a proliferation of private recruitment agents, brokers, and middlemen is inevitable. Due to corruption, inefficiency, and lack of resources, the commitment to protect women migrants as reflected in official statements is rarely translated into action (1994: 138–40).

Research in Indonesia shows that while the Manpower Department oversees labour recruitment, it delegates the actual process to licensed recruitment agencies. However, these agencies do not always follow the laws and regulations set for them. Falsification of documents necessary for working abroad in exchange for large sums of money goes unchecked and is accepted as a routine part of the process (Wijaya, 1992: 2–9). These recruitment agencies are supposed to provide training in developing skills and language in preparation for employment in Saudi Arabia. The prospective migrants have to pay a variety of exorbitant fees in order to be eligible for employment overseas. These may range from Rp250,000 to Rp800,000, which is equivalent to about one to three months' work in Saudi Arabia. In practice, however, the services offered, including training programmes, are quite inadequate. In the whole process of recruitment and training, the domestic workers meet with a serious lack of respect. The information given is often incomplete and the women are misled by promises of high earnings and pilgrimages to holy places which may never materialize (Wijaya, 1992: 2–9).

A prospective Sri Lankan migrant domestic worker has some advantages over her counterparts in Indonesia, the Philippines, and Bangladesh in that she can get a passport to go abroad with relative ease and can attend to all the formalities of becoming a housemaid in a foreign country without prior approval from her parents or husband. In addition, the employers can deal directly with prospective workers instead of only with registered recruitment agencies as is the case in other countries. Sri Lankan maids were found to rely on friends and relatives to find a job and reach their destinations (Dias, 1994: 139). The country studies further reveal that the ban on Bangladeshi women to leave their country for domestic work is as ineffective as the refusal of the government of Pakistan to allow Sri Lankan women to enter employment in domestic service. Such measures lead to clandestine and illegal flows of migrant workers (Dias, 1994: 136).

Within the region it is clear that governments face strong competition from other countries as they compete for jobs for their own nationals. This leads them to offer lower wages, while at the same time commitments are made to protect the overseas workers in terms of wages and working conditions. Worker remittances is an issue that plays an important role at the level of the national economy. Initial labour migration policies have focused on this issue (Raj-Hashim, 1994: 120). "Regulation" of remittances is one way for the labour-exporting government to extract money from the migrant workers. Some countries require workers to remit a percentage of their salary; others arrange for foreign-currency deposits, and several countries provide incentives to remit (APDC, 1989: 52). Other ways through which the state benefits from overseas workers include passport issuance fees, revenues from air tickets, sales taxes, import taxes, income taxes, and fees collected from departing workers. The costs are hidden in the sense that no returns are received on the investment in education and skill-training in these individuals, and extra costs need to be made to replace them. Among the maids we find many women with a number of years of education, including college degrees.

At the policy level in sending countries, it was found that compared to the early concern for remittances, concern for migrant workers themselves — their working conditions, welfare, and the fate of returnees — has been slow (Raj-Hashim, 1994: 120). On the other hand, due to unfavourable reports of the experiences of domestic workers in foreign countries, several NGOs have begun to advocate protection of the rights of these workers. It is often due to their pressure that governments have taken action in support of migrant domestic workers.

At the national level in the receiving countries, various policies exist in dealing with migrant domestic workers. As foreigners, the maids fall under the immigration laws of the respective receiving countries. Most of these countries do not welcome these workers as immigrants who can settle permanently. They are seen as a transient workforce. They need work permits and get only a temporary visa tied to the work permit. They face constraints on job mobility and experience an artificial depression of wages due to the fact that they constitute a captive labour pool of foreign workers. In Singapore, domestic work is defined as unskilled work and is thus reduced to a dead-end job. Maids have no possibility to upgrade themselves and regardless of their actual qualifications (even a university degree) cannot apply for long-term employment or permanent residence, options which are open for workers with secondary education in combination with other qualifications such as income and certain skills (Heyzer and Wee, 1994: 57–58). Extremely degrading for foreign maids is the rule that they have to undergo a medical check-up every three months to test for pregnancy and venereal disease. Positive test results lead to instant repatriation (Heyzer and Wee, 1994: 60).

Research further shows that in order to regulate the demand for domestic workers, employers in Singapore are required to pay a foreign maid levy. Starting with an amount of S$120 in the 1980s, the amount to be paid had been raised to S$300 in 1992. If multiplied by the presence of an estimated 65,000 maids, it leads to a monthly revenue of S$19,500,000 and a yearly revenue of S$234,000,000 for the Singaporean government. The levy effectively reduces the income of both employer and employee. In some cases the employer passes the full cost of the levy on to the maid. At the same time, it absolves the government from having to arrange for child care centres for middle-class women who are employed. Malaysia has followed the example of Singapore and has imposed an annual levy of RM360 on the foreign maid herself (Heyzer and Wee, 1994: 60–61).

Research on domestic workers in the Gulf is generally met with a nonexistence of data and statistics (Al-Najjar, 1992: 3). Hiring a domestic worker is, however, relatively simple. To employ a maid, a prospective employer has to arrange for a work permit, for which he has to fulfil certain conditions. In Bahrain, the employer has to give proof that the female head of household is working or sick, and a certificate indicating the employer's salary and that of other family members has to be presented. Once the employer has been granted a work permit, he should choose a candidate and then get an entry visa for her (Heyzer and Wee, 1994: 12–13).

At the local level — the level of the individual worker and her family/household, kinship, and community networks — research shows that economic and family-related motives are the

61

moving forces for women to migrate as domestic workers. The aspiring migrant workers express their hopes and expectations in relation to their families rather than in relation to themselves (Dias and Weerakoon-Goonewardene, 1991). The increase in income is one of the positive consequences for the family of the migrant worker. The income is spent on education for children, housing, buying of land, and also on consumer goods and the settling of debts which may have been caused by the "investments" that need to be made in order to migrate internationally. Indeed, recruitment agents are keen to provide loans on conditions favourable to the prospective migrant.

It has been observed in small communities that domestic servants abroad uphold traditional values and serve as models and symbols of hope for their neighbours. Religion is actively practiced, and it is reported that Indonesian migrant domestic workers abroad facilitate the construction of small mosques (Licuanan, 1994: 104). Because of her income-generating ability, the woman migrant is valued in her family, has a larger say in family affairs (for example, regarding the education of children), and often shows a gain in confidence in herself (Dias and Weerakoon-Goonewardene, 1991: 192).

A negative effect of migration is often its high social cost, which is difficult to measure. Findings at the community level show that migration tends "to increase social stratification and disequilibrium with the families of migrant workers becoming the target of intrigue, envy and gossip by families without overseas workers" (Licuanan, 1994: 107). At the personal and family levels, the migrant woman faces the dilemma, on the one hand, of being able to earn money for the family and, on the other, of having to leave her family and her children behind. According to Dias, the psychological costs are especially heavy on a generation of children who are left without their mothers for several years (1994: 147-8). Literature shows that within family and kinship structures, multiple power relationships operate, and that within these, the young women in the family have little influence. They are controlled by family rules and kinship obligations, often resulting in great pressure to migrate as the earnings are crucial to the survival of the family. Once abroad, many women are very lonely and homesick (Heyzer and Wee, 1994: 48–49). The migration experience often ends in great frustration when upon her return the migrant domestic worker discovers that her remittances have not been spent wisely (Licuanan, 1994: 107).

After their work contracts expire, the majority of domestic workers return home. They do not overstay illegally, marry, or go to a country with relatively easy immigration rules. Compared to Sri Lanka and Indonesia, the Philippines show the highest number of workers with definite or intended plans for repeat migration. Some women have had as many as four serial contracts. Even women who had returned earlier because of bad experiences abroad applied for re-migration (Francisco, 1994: 153). Debts and education of children and siblings are reasons why repeat migration is desired. In the three sending countries just mentioned, programmes for economic reintegration exist for workers returning after their contracts have finished. Those workers who return prematurely and unexpectedly because of major problems, such as physical abuse and sexual molestation, are not taken care of. It is these workers who often need immediate crisis-intervention measures, but none of the sending countries had any social reintegration programmes. It should be further noted that even the available economic reintegration programmes are not known to most women returnees. Overall, the studies show that the returnees did not encounter great difficulties in adjusting again to their families and communities. Few cases are reported of philandering and irresponsible husbands. Marital relationships seem to survive the long periods of separation and anxiety (Francisco, 1994: 155–56). Against the background of the migratory experience, researchers had expected the returnees in Sri Lanka to be "more cosmopolitan and utilitarian, to break with tradition and to be more business-minded." Instead, however, they find that the returned women migrants do not go against the customs and mores of their social groups, but are "content to merge into their familiar surroundings once again with the minimum of disruption to their family and community" (Dias and Weerakoon-Goonewardene, 1991). Other experiences show that after their return, migrant workers have become informal leaders, advising on many matters regarding the community (Licuanan, 1994: 104).

In the receiving countries, maids are subject to a wide variety of experiences. Some of them are very fortunate; others go through humiliating and traumatic experiences. Cases of rape and sexual abuse are regularly reported. The presence of a maid facilitates employment of the wife in the host family. But her presence also creates problems; in several instances, an increase in racial and religious tensions is reported (Licuanan, 1994: 111). The wages of the foreign domestic workers are strongly influenced by their ethnic identity. For example, in Bahrain a Sri Lankan maid earned around BD35 (approximately US$93), an Indian around BD40 (approximately US$106), and a Filipina around BD45 (approximately US$120) (Al-Najjar, 1992: 39). Such differentiation in wages along ethnic lines is common in all receiving countries. The regular payment of wages in itself is also subject to abuse by employers. Another issue that requires attention is that in several countries in the Middle East, a foreign domestic worker has become a status symbol (Dias, 1994: 135). As reported in a communication from Pakistan, in order to enhance one's social status in that country, one needs a Filipina maid and a Bangladeshi cook (Lycklama à Nijeholt, 1994: 10).

Reflecting on the causes, mechanisms, and consequences of international migration of domestic workers, one has to conclude that this is a high-risk undertaking which puts the persons concerned in a very vulnerable position. From beginning to end, the migration process is open to abuse, misinformation, and corruption. A large part of the problem lies in the nature of the work which is perceived as no-work, as private, as women's work. Standards for domestic work are lacking in most countries. Domestic workers are usually not included in protective labour legislation. This makes it difficult, for example, for the UN Convention on Migrant Workers to have an impact, since such conventions depend on national legislation for possible sanctions (Lycklama à Nijeholt, 1994: 23–25). The observations that emerge from this extensive and detailed study on international migration of domestic workers lead to several suggestions for policy and action.

FUTURE CHALLENGES AND POLICY ISSUES

The first issue at the international level is that this type of migration is very much part and parcel of uneven socioeconomic development in various parts of the world. It is unlikely that within the next few decades this problem of uneven development is going to be solved. In fact, policy makers face the historically unprecedented task of creating one billion jobs in the next ten years (Simai, 1995: 13). This leads us to believe that there is little chance for this type of migration to decrease in the immediate future. An example of how new areas of migration are opening up is the situation in eastern Europe, from where women are migrating to try their luck as domestic workers, entertainers, or prostitutes. One of the major challenges facing the world community is to put in place sustainable development focusing on the eradication of poverty and unemployment. Both sending and receiving countries in the migration process need to orient their policies toward socioeconomic restructuring in such a way that sustainable ways of life are possible for all their citizens.

The second issue at the international level relates to the nature of the work. In the industrialized parts of the world we note a shift toward a service economy. Within such an economy there is a growing demand for women as service workers. It is further predicted that well-educated and skilled women will enter the workforce in large numbers, particularly in those developing countries where so far they have hardly been absorbed in the modern sector (Johnston, 1991). This will increase the demand for domestic workers, as developments in Hong Kong and Singapore have already demonstrated. It is vital to the rapidly growing economies that well-educated and skilled women join the labour force, even after they have children. This requires a re-valuation of domestic work, in particular in those countries where governments are not ready to invest substantially in child care centres and related policies which make it attractive for married women to enter the labour market. Domestic work needs to be recognized as work that is vital for the macro-level economy and the micro-level family/household and community and for the woman herself. A manifest supply of workers exists as well as a demand for them. Banning the phenomenon will lead only to more illegality in the process. One of the important policy challenges for the future is that this type of work is appropriately regulated and protected by national legislation, while at the international level it is covered by agreements and contracts, including proper monitoring between receiving and sending countries, leading to mutual benefits for countries and to benefits for the workers themselves.

The third issue at the international level is the urgency for sending and receiving countries to regulate and monitor the activities of the internationally operating recruitment and other related agencies. While governments have an important role to play in such monitoring, the establishment of an International Association of Domestic Workers as proposed at the APDC's Regional Policy Dialogue is a crucial instrument in complementing and critically reviewing the policy measures and actions that are taken by governments. Close linkages should also be made with the NGOs committed to improving the plight of this type of international migrants.

Important issues at the national level include the need for policy measures which make sure that women domestic workers when returning are informed about the existing economic reintegration programmes. In all sending countries included in the research, these programmes do not seem to target the migrant domestic workers. In addition, several social-cost aspects of migration demand urgent attention. Policy measures are needed in both sending and receiving countries which deal with women who are victims of conflict arising from abuse and exploitation of these workers. In particular in receiving countries, mechanisms need to be available which offer the worker possibilities of complaint and appeal, for example, at labour offices at embassies. The receiving countries would also benefit in the long run if they took measures to deal with such complaints. It is only in the receiving country that measures can be taken against employers who have a record of domestic worker abuse. In the sending countries, particularly in those areas where repeat migration is quite common, attention should be given to the sociopsychological consequences which several years of migration of the mother may have for the children. Although support networks of family, kin, and community are most helpful, research suggests that this is not always adequate.

Although governments in the sending countries have been very concerned about remittances at the macro level, at the micro level of the individual worker and her family/household and community, the findings suggest that little is done. It is in particular at this level that governments could make available credit schemes to assist the prospective migrants in dealing with the costs of migration without falling into the hands of unscrupulous agents and money-lenders. Support structures should be set up to advise migrants on how to handle the money that has been earned and transfer remittances safely.

At the local level — the micro level of the individual worker and her family/household,

64

kin, and community — policy measures should ensure that women benefit from their earnings. Their savings ought not only to be channelled to the settling of family debts and family consumption but also put to productive use in benefiting the migrant woman herself. At the community level the issue of increased tension between families of migrant workers, who often demonstrate their newly gained wealth, and families who depend for their livelihood on local earnings only.

At the local level in the receiving country, the issue of racial differentiation in earnings demands the specific attention of policy makers and activists. Although it is embedded in a context of difference in treatment and working conditions, this particular issue touches upon the basic human rights of people and therefore constitutes a key issue for future policy and action. NGOs nationally and internationally already play a major role in exposing the racism involved; their role should be strengthened.

CONCLUDING REMARKS

It is to be expected that the flow of women crossing borders to hire themselves out as workers in their own right will increase. This international phenomenon requires not only the increased attention of policy makers and activists, but also of researchers. In fact, the extensive research on foreign domestic workers in Asia raises more questions than it answers. Information concerning this type of worker is emerging from other parts of the world, but systematic research is lacking. In a world characterized by processes of internationalization and globalization, this phenomenon — due to its size and impact — requires more comparative research in a global context.

Geertje Lycklama à Nijeholt is a sociologist whose research and writing deals with policy issues related to women and development. Within this broad area, she focuses on strategies for change and processes of institutionalization. She recently ended a five-year term as Rector of the Institute of Social Studies in The Hague and has returned to research and teaching in the field of women and development studies.

References

Abadan-Unat, Nermin. 1977. "Implications of Migration on Emancipation & Pseudo-Emancipation of Turkish Women," *International Migration Review* 11 (1), pp. 31–57.

Al-Najjar, Sabika. 1992. "Foreign Domestic Workers in Bahrain" Paper presented by UNDP Bahrain at regional policy dialogue on Foreign Domestic Workers, Colombo, Sri Lanka.

Arizpe, Lourdes. 1984. "Agrarian Change and the Dynamics of Women's Rural Out-migration in Latin America," in *Women on the Move: Contemporary Changes in Family and Society*, Paris: UNESCO.

Asian and Pacific Development Centre. 1989. "The Trade in Domestic Helpers: Causes, Mechanisms and Consequences," in *Selected Papers from the Planning Meeting on International Migration and Women*, Quezon City, Philippines, 30 November-5 December 1987. Kuala Lumpur: APDC.

Bach, Robert L., and Lisa A. Schraml. 1982. "Migration, Crisis and Theoretical Conflict," *International Migration Review* 16 (2), pp. 320–41.

Balan, Jorge. 1988. "International Migration in Latin America: Trends and Consequences," in Reginald Appleyard (ed.), *International Migration Today, Vol. 1: Trends and Prospects*. Paris: UNESCO/University of Western Australia.

Birks, J. S., and C. A. Sinclair. 1980. *International Migration and Development in the Arab Region*. Geneva: ILO.

Böhning, W. R. 1991. Foreword, in Patricia Weinert, "Foreign Female Domestic Workers: Help Wanted!" Geneva: ILO.

Buijs, Gina (ed.). 1993. *Migrant Women: Crossing Boundaries and Changing Identities*. Oxford: Berg Publishers.

Campani, Giovanna. 1993. "Labour Markets and Family Networks: Filipino Women in Italy," in Hedwig Rudolph and Mirjana Morokvasic, *Bridging States and Markets: International Migration in the Early 1990s*. Berlin: Ed. Sigma, Rainer Bohn Verlag.

Chaney, Elsa M. 1980. "Women in International Migration: Issues in Development Planning." Report no. AID/OTR-147-80-46. Washington, DC: Office of Women in Development, Agency for International Development.

Crummet, Maria de los Angeles. 1985. "Class, Household Structure, and Migration: A Case Study from Rural Mexico," Working Paper on Women in International Development no. 92. East Lansing, MI: Michigan State University.

Dias, Malsiri, and Nedra Weerakoon-Goonewardene. 1991. "Female Labour Migration to Singapore and Hong Kong: A Profile of the Sri Lankan Housemaids." Colombo: Center for Women's Research (CENWOR).

Dias, Malsiri. 1994. "Overview of Mechanisms of Migration," in Noeleen Heyzer, Geertje Lycklama à Nijeholt, and Nedra Weerakoon (eds.), *The Trade in Domestic Workers: Causes, Mechanisms and Consequences of International Migration, Vol. 1: Selected Papers from a Regional Policy Dialogue on Foreign Women Domestic Workers,* Colombo, Sri Lanka, 1992. Kuala Lumpur: Asian and Pacific Development Center. London and New Jersey: Zed Books.

Francisco, Josefa. 1994. "Issues of Re-integration," in Noeleen Heyzer, Geertje Lycklama à Nijeholt, and Nedra Weerakoon (eds.), *The Trade in Domestic Workers: Causes, Mechanisms and Consequences of International Migration, Vol. 1: Selected Papers from a Regional Policy Dialogue on Foreign Women Domestic Workers,* Colombo, Sri Lanka, 1992. Kuala Lumpur: Asian and Pacific Development Center. London and New Jersey: Zed Books.

Gibson, Katherine, and Julie Graham. 1986. "Situating Migrants in Theory: The Case of Filipino Migrant Contract Construction Workers," *Capital and Class* 29 (Summer).

Henkes, Barbara. 1995. *Heimat in Holland — Duitse Dienstmeisjes 1920–1950*. Babylon-De Geus.

Heyzer, Noeleen. 1994. "Introduction: Creating Responsive Policies for Migrant Women Domestic Workers," in Noeleen Heyzer, Geertje Lycklama à Nijeholt, and Nedra Weerakoon (eds.), *The Trade in Domestic Workers: Causes, Mechanisms and Consequences of International Migration, Vol. 1: Selected Papers from a Regional Policy Dialogue on Foreign Women Domestic Workers,* Colombo, Sri Lanka, 1992. Kuala Lumpur: Asian and Pacific Development Center. London and New Jersey: Zed Books.

Heyzer, Noeleen, Geertje Lycklama à Nijeholt and Nedra Weerakoon (eds.). 1994. *The Trade in Domestic Workers: Causes, Mechanisms and Consequences of International Migration, Vol. 1: Selected Papers from a Regional Policy Dialogue on Foreign Women Domestic Workers,* Colombo, Sri Lanka, 1992. Kuala Lumpur: Asian and Pacific Development Center. London and New Jersey: Zed Books.

Heyzer, Noeleen, and Vivian Wee. 1994. "Domestic Workers in Transient Overseas Employment: Who Benefits, Who Profits?" in Noeleen Heyzer, Geertje Lycklama à Nijeholt, and Nedra Weerakoon (eds.), *The Trade in Domestic Workers: Causes, Mechanisms and Consequences of International Migration, Vol. 1: Selected Papers from a Regional Policy Dialogue on Foreign Women Domestic Workers,* Colombo, Sri Lanka, 1992. Kuala Lumpur: Asian and Pacific Development Center. London and New Jersey: Zed Books.

"Women in Migration." 1994. *International Migration Review* 18 (Winter) (special issue).

Johnston, William B. 1991. "Global Work Force 2000: The New World Labor Market," *Harvard Business Review* (March-April), pp. 115–27.

Kubat, Daniel, and Hans-Joachim Nowotny. 1982. "International and Internal Migration: Towards a New Paradigm," in Tom Bottomore, Stefan Nowak, and Magdalena Sokolowska (eds.), *Sociology: The State of the Art*. London and Beverly Hills: Sage Publications.

Licuanan, Patricia. 1994. "The Socioeconomic Impact of Domestic Worker Migration: Individual, Family, Community, Country," in Noeleen Heyzer, Geertje Lycklama à Nijeholt, and Nedra Weerakoon (eds.), *The Trade in Domestic Workers: Causes, Mechanisms and Consequences of International Migration, Vol. 1: Selected Papers from a Regional Policy Dialogue on Foreign Women Domestic Workers,* Colombo, Sri Lanka, 1992. Kuala Lumpur: Asian and Pacific Development Center. London and New Jersey: Zed Books.

Lycklama à Nijeholt, Geertje. 1993. "Transformation in the East and Women in the West: Some Preliminary Thoughts on the Effects of a European Revolution." Paper presented at the VIIth General Conference of the European Association of Development Research and Training Institutes, Berlin.

Lycklama à Nijeholt, Geertje. 1994. "The Changing International Division of Labour and Domestic Workers: A Macro Overview," in Noeleen Heyzer, Geertje Lycklama à Nijeholt, and Nedra Weerakoon (eds.), *The Trade in Domestic Workers: Causes, Mechanisms and Consequences of International Migration, Vol. 1: Selected Papers from a Regional Policy Dialogue on Foreign Women Domestic Workers,* Colombo, Sri Lanka, 1992. Kuala Lumpur: Asian and Pacific Development Center. London and New Jersey: Zed Books.

Manila Bulletin, 1 January 1990.

Morokvasic, Mirjana. 1980. "Yugoslav Women in France, Germany and Sweden." Mimeo. Paris: Centre Nationale de la Recherche Scientifique.

Morokvasic, M. 1982. "Why Do Women Migrate? Toward Understanding of the Sex-selectivity in the Migratory Movements of Labour." Paper presented at the Symposium on the Role of Women in Population Redistribution, Cagliari, Italy

Morokvasic, Mirjana. 1983. "Women in Migration: Beyond the Reductionist Outlook," in Annie Phizacklea (ed.), *One Way Ticket: Migration and Female Labour.* London: Routledge & Kegan Paul.

Morokvasic, Mirjana. 1984. "Birds of Passage Are Also Women…" *International Migration Review* 18 (4), pp. 886–908.

Morokvasic, Mirjana. 1984a. "Migrant Women in Europe: A Comparative Perspective" in UNESCO (ed.), *Women on the Move: Contemporary Changes in Family and Society.* Paris: UNESCO.

Morokvasic, Mirjana, and Anne de Tinguy. 1993. "Between East and West: A New Migratory Space," in Hedwig Rudolph and Mirjana Morokvasic (eds.), *Bridging States and Markets: International Migration in the Early 1990s.* Berlin: Ed. Sigma, Rainer Bohn Verlag.

Penninx, Rinus. 1986. "Theories on International Labour Migration: Between Micro and Macro Analysis." Paper presented at the XIth World Congress of Sociology, Research Committee on the Sociology of Migration, New Delhi.

Phizacklea, Annie (ed.). 1983. *One Way Ticket: Migration and Female Labour.* London: Routledge & Kegan Paul.

Raj-Hashim, Rita. 1994. "A Review of Migration and Labour Policies," in Noeleen Heyzer, Geertje Lycklama à Nijeholt, and Nedra Weerakoon (eds.), *The Trade in Domestic Workers: Causes, Mechanisms and Consequences of International Migration, Vol. 1: Selected Papers from a Regional Policy Dialogue on Foreign Women Domestic Workers,* Colombo, Sri Lanka, 1992. Kuala Lumpur: Asian and Pacific Development Center. London and New Jersey: Zed Books.

Ravenstein, E. G. 1885. "The Laws of Migration," *Journal of the Royal Statistical Society* 48:II (June), pp. 241–301.

Rudolph, Hedwig, and Mirjana Morokvasic (eds.). 1993. *Bridging States and Markets: International Migration in the Early 1990s.* Berlin: Ed. Sigma, Rainer Bohn Verlag.

Salaff, Janet W. 1981. *Working Daughters of Hongkong: Filial Piety or Power in the Family?* Cambridge: Cambridge University Press.

Selier, Frits. 1986. "Rural-Urban Migration: Some Theoretical Approaches," in Frits Selier and S. Karim Mehtab, with Mohammad Rafi Qureshi (eds.), *Migration in Pakistan: Theory & Facts.* Lahore: Vanguard Books.

Shah, Nasra M. 1983. "Pakistani Workers in the Middle East: Volume, Trends and Consequences," *International Migration Review* 17 (3), pp. 410–24.

Sherbiny, Naiem A. 1984. "Expatriate Labour in Arab Oil-producing Countries," *Finance & Development* (December), pp. 34–37.

Simai, Mihály. 1995. "The Politics and Economics of Global Employment," in Mihály Simai with Valentine M. Moghadam and Arvo Kuddo (eds.), *Global Employment: An International Investigation into the Future of Work*. Vol. 1. London and New Jersey: Zed Books. Tokyo: United Nations University Press.

Simai, Mihály, with Valentine M. Moghadam and Arvo Kuddo (eds.). 1995. *Global Employment: An International Investigation into the Future of Work*. Vol. 1. London and New Jersey: Zed Books. Tokyo: United Nations University Press.

Stark, Oded. 1991. *The Migration of Labour*. Cambridge: Basil Blackwell.

Trager, Lilian. 1984. "Family Strategies and the Migration of Women: Migrants to Dagupan City, Philippines," *International Migration Review* 18 (4), pp. 1264–78.

UNESCO. 1984a. *Women on the Move: Contemporary Changes in Family and Household*. Paris: UNESCO.

UNESCO. 1984b. *Women in the Villages, Men in the Towns*. Paris: UNESCO.

Van Roy, Ralph. 1984. "Undocumented Migration to Venezuela," *International Migration Review* 18 (Fall), pp. 541–57.

Weinert, Patricia. 1991. "International Migration for Employment: Foreign Female Domestic Workers: Help Wanted!" World Employment Programme working paper. Geneva: International Labour Office.

Weyland, Petra. 1993. "Egyptian Peasant Migrants Heading for the Gulf States: Upon the Relevance of the Households as an Analytical Category for Migration Theory," in Hedwig Rudolph and Mirjana Morokvasic (eds.), *Bridging States and Markets: International Migration in the Early 1990s*. Berlin: Ed. Sigma, Rainer Bohn Verlag.

Wijaya, Hesti. 1992. "Mechanisms of Migration, Including Support Mechanisms: Indonesian Case Study". Paper presented by the Rural Development Foundation Indonesia at Regional Policy Dialogue on Foreign Domestic Workers, Colombo, Sri Lanka.

Wood, Charles H. 1982. "Equilibrium and Historical-Structural Perspectives on Migration," *International Migration Review* 16 (2), pp. 298–319.

Young, Kate. 1982. "The Creation of a Relative Surplus Population: A Case Study from Mexico," in Lourdes Beneria (ed.), *Women and Development: The Sexual Division of Labour in Rural Societies*. New York: Praeger.

Youssef, Nadia, Mayra Buvinic, and Ayse Kudat. 1979. "Women in Migration: A Third World Focus." Washington, D.C.: International Center for Research on Women.

ENGENDERING INTERNATIONAL TRADE: CONCEPTS, POLICY, AND ACTION

LOURDES BENERÍA AND AMY LIND

During the 1980s and early 1990s, the neoliberal view of "free trade" as a way to foster economic growth by internationalizing domestic economies has been largely undisputed and widely promoted. In the past year we have witnessed the conclusion of long and complex Uruguayan Round negotiations for trade liberalization under the General Agreements on Tariffs and Trade (GATT), as well as the agreement to create the successor to GATT, the World Trade Organization (WTO). We have also observed the creation of numerous multilateral trade organizations, such as Mercosur and the Association of Caribbean States (ACS) in Latin America and the Caribbean; the North American Free Trade Agreement (NAFTA); and other trade arrangements in Africa and Asia. In addition, we have seen the final stages of formation of the European Community (EC), the most established common market. All of this represents a dramatic new emphasis on the economic integration of large areas. To illustrate, the Mercosur countries in South America[1] have agreed to set up a customs union and, in time, free movement of labour and capital; this agreement, among countries which represent about half of the GDP of Latin America (*The Economist,* 1994) is viewed as a step toward free trade in the American continent. However, some of the more recent trade agreements, such as NAFTA, have not been approved without strong opposition from various sectors of the population. In particular, researchers, policy makers, and activists have increasingly begun to question the effects of trade policy on women.

The benefits of trade may be both positive and negative, since its impact on economic activity produces both winners and losers. Therefore, any discussion of trade liberalization is not a simple matter of taking a "pro-trade" or an "anti-trade" position; rather, a substantive discussion requires an understanding of the nature of the process generated by trade liberalization and its likely consequences, so that appropriate policies may be developed and appropriate actions taken, particularly to compensate those negatively affected. Given the predominance of labour-market segmentation and segregation in production by gender, it makes sense to assume that trade will have a differential impact by gender. Yet most trade policy analysis, even when dealing with social redistribution, has failed to address these impacts. Therefore, if we want trade negotiators and policy makers to understand the gender-differentiated implications of trade and avoid gender biases, it is urgent that we develop a feminist perspective on trade policy that will include gender as a variable in its analysis. More empirical research is necessary to achieve this, to provide a stronger basis from which to address policy.

This paper is an attempt to address both the engendering of the trade debate and the gender implications of trade policies and actions. It conceptualizes some of the relevant issues for future policy research on gender and trade. An initial question is the extent to which gender is a relevant notion in trade discussions. The paper will explore the various areas in which connections between the two can be traced; these areas range from the effects of trade on employment (more specifically, women's employment) to issues of gender and technology, the feminization of the labour force, free trade zones (FTZs), and the gender and trade aspects of structural adjustment. The need for such an agenda should be obvious. Efforts to promote women's micro-enterprises may be fruitless, for example, if such enterprises cannot survive the competitive pressures arising from trade liberalization. It is important to discuss the gendered implications of trade policy with issues such as this in mind. Empirical studies which incorporate a gender awareness will serve to enrich both theoretical discussion and policy-making.

The paper begins by discussing trade liberalization schemes as they have developed in NAFTA and the European Community. These well-documented cases serve as examples on which to base a broader discussion of trade liberalization schemes. It then surveys the gender dimensions of trade, including its impact and policy implications, in order to lay the groundwork for examining potential strategies that actors in the trade arena may adopt in order to adjust and respond to processes of trade liberalization at local, regional, and international levels. This is followed by a discussion of future areas of inquiry concerning trade and gender, including areas which traditionally have not been addressed in trade policy research.

GLOBALIZATION, FREE TRADE, AND THE FORMATION OF REGIONAL TRADE BLOCS

Overview of Current Global Economic Processes

Since the early 1980s we have witnessed tremendous changes in the global economy and in the political climate that contextualizes it. The current hegemony of the neoliberal model has resulted in a rush of policies aimed at eliminating all obstacles to the "free" exercise of economic activity, including trade liberalization; the deregulation of production, the labour market, and the market of goods and services; and the implementation of regional and international trade agreements. The latter emerged in the context of a perceived need for further expansion of domestic markets to accommodate the forces of globalization. In the Third World, these trends unfolded through shifts from import-substitution to export-promotion development models, or as part of structural adjustment packages implemented to address foreign debt, as is the case in many countries in Latin America and Africa.

Underlying all of these factors is the process of economic globalization, facilitated in part by the technological revolution in transportation and communications of the last 25 years. The transnationalization of production and finance, together with other economic policies imposed as a result of the hegemony of neoliberalism, have brought about profound changes in the world economy; in particular, the increase in power of the private sector (and of large transnational corporations) relative to that of the public sector has undermined the nation-state's ability to control and effectively manage domestic economic policy — changing dramatically the role of the nation-state in the international economy. Critics of "free trade" have addressed the "antidemocratic and inequitable" nature of trade liberalization and have shown how trade agreements potentially "transfer significant powers to non-elected and unaccountable bodies and institutions, and give the highest guarantees of expression to the rights and freedoms of transnational capital" (Grinspun and Kreklewich, 1994). Likewise, these authors have also pointed out that free trade is being used as a "conditioning framework" for the dramatic changes associated with economic and social restructuring that have taken place under the umbrella of a global neoliberal regime.

In this context the new WTO, which has replaced GATT as of January 1995, will have a profound influence on how international trade will be conducted in the future. This is due, in part, to the widespread membership of industrialized and developing countries in the organization, as well as to its role in monitoring and regulating the global trading system. Tariffs are expected to be reduced by about 40 per cent in the first ten years for developing countries and in the first six years for developed countries; rules and regulations are being standardized in an unprecedented fashion; and plans are under way to integrate previously "non-GATT" sectors such as textiles and clothing, agriculture, services, and intellectual property rights on the basis of strengthened GATT rules and regulations. The WTO framework seeks to ensure a "single undertaking approach"; members of the organization must agree to accept the results of the Uruguay Round "without exception" (GATT Secretariat, 1994). This means, essentially, that member countries must reduce current protectionist policies, and in some cases introduce dramatic domestic change, in order to conform to global trade liberalization.

Many countries have already begun this process, including those in Africa and Latin America that have undergone structural adjustment programmes (SAPs) in which trade liberalization is a major component. Mexico, for example, did not become a member of GATT until 1986. It did so as part of eligibility requirements for debt assistance from the World Bank and the International Monetary Fund (IMF). Given that trade liberalization "is no longer confined to reducing barriers to imports and exports at the border" (Joekes and Weston, 1994) and is being conceptualized in much broader terms, it has affected other areas of domestic policy as well. Trade liberalization schemes, for example, raise important questions about trade and production standards and their differences among countries; they also raise questions about which social groups will be affected and in what ways. The same can be said for their effects on foreign investment, the enforcement of technology patents, and intellectual property rights (Weston and Joekes, 1994).

Given that the WTO framework will discourage protectionism and force even the "weaker" economies to liberalize trade in order to compete in the world market, it will be important to monitor the impact of this process on certain countries and local economies. It will be important, for example, to watch the extent to which the notion of "managed trade" will be accepted as a way to create or cultivate comparative advantages, or to compensate the possible negative effects of trade liberalization. This would imply the use of "interventionist" policies that are not in harmony with the prevalent trade discourse. Yet events such as the late

> *"Economic activities, through which individuals express their initiative and creativity which enhance the wealth of communities, are a fundamental basis for social progress. But social progress will not be realized simply through the free interaction of market forces. Public policies are necessary to correct market failures, to complement market mechanisms, to maintain social stability and to create a national and international economic environment that promotes sustainable growth on a global scale. Such growth should promote equity and social justice, tolerance, responsibility and involvement."*
>
> — *World Summit for Social Development Declaration and Programme of Action, Chapter I, para. 6.*

1994–early 1995 Mexican financial crisis and its international repercussions, particularly in Latin America, have raised doubts about the extent to which, without some form of protection, these countries can adjust to free trade and regional integration.

In some cases, the less developed countries and less competitive sectors and industries are likely to be at a disadvantage. For example, it is feared that as restrictions on patent laws are lifted, multinational corporations (MNCs) will increasingly be allowed to patent the medicinal qualities of plants that historically have been the preserve of indigenous or local knowledge. This is already taking place in countries, such as India, that have signed the new GATT agreement (Krishnakumar, 1994a). Given their relative lack of weight in the global economy, there is a danger that local communities might be overlooked and essentially lose their rights to any traditional knowledge about the medicinal quality, production, and processing techniques of local plants. This situation also has important implications for women, as will be shown below.

Regional trade liberalization can take place under a number of schemes. It is important, for example, to differentiate between common markets and free trade areas, because the institutional framework associated with each has implications for the way the processes are handled. As exemplified by the EC, a common market aims at integrating the economies of member countries by eliminating economic borders between them and allowing the free circulation of people within the community. A common external tariff is established through the gradual harmonization of individual country tariffs. Other provisions include the harmonization of social and monetary policy among member states, the provision of compensatory mechanisms to deal with the negative effects of economic integration, and the adoption of policies to deal with regional differences within and among countries. Thus, obstacles to trade are eliminated by gradually reducing export and import duties and other intercountry practices limiting exchange. This process establishes the conditions that gradually lead toward wage equalization, standardization of labour market conditions, and, more recently, environmental regulation. In addition, this is done through the gradual creation of supranational political and economic institutions that can monitor the trade liberalization process and gradually encourage economic and political integration.

On the other hand, a free trade area emphasizes trade liberalization without harmonization of external tariffs, equalization of social policy, provision of compensatory mechanisms for national and regional differences, or harmonization of employment conditions. (Some harmonization of policies may take place either as a result of practical needs or a specific effort on the part of the member countries, as in the case of the labour and environmental agreements negotiated before NAFTA was adopted.) In this scheme, the free circulation of people among member countries is not envisioned. As well, there are no provisions for setting supranational economic and political institutions to facilitate and monitor the process of integration. The emphasis is on economic liberalization, not on the creation of an "enlarged community" with economic, social, and political dimensions. Again, the Mexican economic crisis in many ways reinforced the fear that under NAFTA, the least economically-developed country in the area — Mexico — will not have sufficient guarantees of protection as it opens its borders to competition from the US and Canada. Mexico's case has been compared to that of Spain within the EC. Despite its booming economy during the initial years after joining the EC, Spain's rapid integration with the more advanced EC countries has resulted, since 1992, in chronic balance-of-payment difficulties, a depressed economy, and very high levels of unemployment (Conroy & Glasmeier, 1992). Provisions in the EC agreement to protect its weakest members have not been sufficient in this case. The Mexico crisis illustrates that a trade deficit of the size accumulated by Mexico results in a decrease in reserves, a very significant loss in the value of the domestic currency, and, ultimately, an enormous financial crisis resulting from the ensuing flight of capital.

72

THE GENDER DIMENSIONS OF TRADE

Very little has been written about the implications of all these processes from a gender perspective, and it is difficult to generalize about the gender dimensions of trade agreements. Since there may be both positive and negative effects, analysis requires a detailed breakdown that includes different trends and takes into account the complexity of issues involved. For example, in the case of intellectual property rights, it is often women who play a major role in passing on local knowledge from generation to generation, both in industrialized and developing countries. In many cases, women's roles in this process are overlooked, despite the fact that they perform multiple tasks in the production and preparation of plant foods, forestry, and breeding and caring for animals, as in women's participation in the indigenous dairy industry in rural India (Mies and Shiva, 1993). Assumed "gender neutral" analyses that reinforce the invisibility of women therefore need to be challenged.

One way of approaching these questions is to analyse the impacts of trade expansion according to industry, sector, and geographic/regional location. Another way is to look at the macro-economic effects on employment, price, consumption, and income. It is also important not to overlook non-economic implications. Trade liberalization intensifies the processes of commodification that accompany a market economy and often opens up new areas to the "law of the market"; existing types of production previously not subject to pressures of global markets are thereby eliminated, as are the cultures and ways of life associated with them. Sectors of women, as underprivileged groups in societies and industries, and most represented in the informal sector, are affected by trade and accompanying changes in important ways. In the following section, we will emphasize the gender dimensions associated with the above effects, with the purpose of drawing conclusions for action and policy.

Employment, Price, Consumption, and Income Effects

Employment Effects Employment effects result from the impact of trade liberalization on economic activity; they depend specifically on where women are located in the process of production. If located in industries or sectors with a comparative advantage in international trade, the effects for women are likely to be positive, as opposed to employment in industries losing ground to foreign competition. Employment effects will also depend on the extent to which trade liberalization has an impact on relocation of production. One recent illustration is provided by the relocation of Smith Corona, a producer of typewriters. In the summer of 1993, Smith Corona began to move its plant from Cortland, New York, to Tijuana, Mexico. Fifty-eight percent of about 1,000 employees in the Cortland plant were women; in Tijuana, women currently comprise 75 per cent of the new Smith Corona workforce (Benería and Hualde, work in progress). The displaced workers in Cortland are having difficulty obtaining new employment in the depressed local economy, and in many cases are facing downward mobility as a result, with lower wages and precarious job security (Benería, work in progress). At the same time, the shift of the Smith Corona production site has led to an increase in the proportion of women employed in Tijuana, even though total employment in the plant has decreased. That is, relocation has been accompanied with downsizing and has led to a feminization of the plant's workforce. To be sure, wages in Tijuana are much lower than in Cortland, which means that the Mexican workers do not receive what the North American workers have lost; to the extent that productivity levels are similar in both locations, the difference represents extra profits for Smith Corona. This illustrates how employment effects also have a redistributive impact and how they are gendered.

73

Price and Consumption Effects Conventional international trade theory suggests that "freer" trade will lead to lower prices in domestic markets, since goods that are produced more cheaply in the exporting country are imported at lower prices than goods locally produced. To the extent that prices do decrease, it can benefit consumers who are likely to find a larger selection of goods available in the domestic market and whose incomes are "stretched" through the availability of similar or better quality products at lower prices. Women will benefit from these price effects, as individual consumers, and as household members primarily responsible for the family budget. So will consumers in general.

Another effect of price competition is its impact on retail trade. For example, initial reports about the effect of NAFTA on the retail sector indicate that US discount chain stores are proliferating at a rapid pace in Mexico, resulting in strong competitive pressures on local businesses. This is the case with K-Mart and Wal-Mart stores that have opened up in Mexico City and Monterrey (*The Economist*, 1994). As Mexicans are opting to purchase the imported products over the locally produced goods, this is likely to generate a process of long-term changes in consumer patterns that is likely to be intensified under NAFTA.

Changes in price structure, then, will also lead to consumption effects over and above price effects as a result of shifts in consumer preference and in cultural norms and values associated with the new goods. As individual consumers and as those in charge of household consumption, women will be affected by these changes. In the case of countries with traditional crafts, it will be important to watch closely the effects of these processes on domestic production, including local and indigenous crafts produced by women. The importance of closely monitoring these processes with research that is closely connected to policy and action should not be underestimated. Women who work in local craft production, domestic policy makers, and other trade actors all have important roles to play in shaping the future outcomes of trade initiatives as well as the impact of these initiatives on small-scale production and marketing. Once the effects of trade on these sectors are identified, craft producers are more likely to stand a chance of surviving globalization and trade liberalization processes.

Income Effects These effects of trade liberalization derive from shifts in production associated with increasing trade. As with respect to employment impact, the tendency for sectors, industries, and regions with comparative advantage in the production of exports will be to register an increase in income. This will benefit those who work in these areas, although a "trickling down" process cannot be considered automatic and will depend, for example, on trends in unemployment, wages, and other benefits and on the relative power of the workers involved. Given that women tend to be concentrated in low-wage industries with a relatively low degree of unionization, their relative power also tends to be low. It is therefore important that they be empowered so as to be able to benefit from increasing trade.

In industries that are hurt by the competitive pressures created by freer trade, income will decrease. The negative employment effects referred to above will tend to create a downward pressure on wages and employment conditions. In such cases, workers are likely to need help finding new jobs and readjusting to the changing conditions of the labour market. Women workers in particular may need help with the upgrading and acquisition of skills, particularly if trade fosters the introduction of new technologies and the reorganization of production processes. There are indications, for example, that women tend not to benefit as much as men from the training programmes associated with new technologies (Roldan, 1991). This is obviously likely to have long-term income effects for them. It is important to monitor these processes in order to design appropriate policies, such as the establishment of "women friendly" training programmes that include incentives and structures to facilitate their participation.

The indirect effects of trade liberalization are often realized through complex linkages and interactions. For example, the market-oriented World Bank and IMF–inspired structural adjustment policies (SAPs) adopted by debtor countries since the early 1980s have placed a great deal of emphasis on trade liberalization. Despite the fact that "freer" trade has broadened markets, increased the availability of products, and brought down consumer prices, many of those who have suffered the negative consequences of SAPs have not benefited from the potential advantages of trade liberalization. The polarization of income associated with these processes (Benería, 1992; Cortes and Rubalcava, 1993) creates a bias with respect to the benefits associated with freer trade. While middle- and upper-income households may potentially benefit from the new markets for imported goods, poor households are less likely to be in a position to take advantage of these changes.

To give another example, in China it is not trade liberalization per se but rather the sweeping economic reforms undertaken in conformity with China's greater reliance on the market that have severely affected women workers. In the past 15 years, 20 million workers have been laid off as part of the reforms — 70 per cent of them women. Because government legislation requires employers to provide day care and up to five days of paid leave, female workers have been viewed as "too costly in this new era of profitability" and, as a result, have been laid off, forced to take extended maternity leave for as long as three years, or forced into early retirement (Kerr, 1994). To the extent that trade policy promotes the opening of economies in the world market, other countries undergoing economic reform must also be aware of these potentially negative effects for women. Expansion of the market needs to be monitored, therefore, in order to design appropriate policies that take into consideration both women's employment and social and family responsibilities.

Sectors, Industries, and Regions

The few studies that have, in fact, analysed the gender impact of trade liberalization have for the most part used a sectoral, industrial or regional approach (Cohen, 1987 and 1994; Zabin, 1992; Anderson and Dimon, 1994). In this sense, empirical studies showing the degree of gender segregation and labour-market segmentation are useful to measure the anticipated gender effects of freer trade. A pioneer empirical study is Marjorie Cohen's work on the 1989 Canada-US Free Trade Agreement (CUFTA). Her analysis followed an industry approach, focusing on the textile and clothing, electrical and electronic, footwear, and food processing industries, which have a predominantly female workforce and where women would be disproportionately affected by the trade liberalization resulting from CUFTA. Although the study has some problems, which in our opinion derive from a too-rigid anti-trade position, it nevertheless must be recognized as an important pioneer effort to approach empirically the difficult questions of gender and trade. In a more recent article (1994), Cohen argues that the type of economic restructuring in Canada that has paralleled freer trade is "a gendered issue." In particular, she argues that the feminization of the work force often associated with increased globalization and competition has not occurred in Canada, the general implication being that it is difficult to generalize about what exactly the gender dimension of trade liberalization will be. This implies that country- and region-specific studies and policies should be promoted, both in industrialized and lower-income countries.

Anderson and Dimon's study (1994) compares the cities of Tijuana and Torreon on the US-Mexico border. It shows that increased export processing and tourism, the expected effect of NAFTA in Mexico, is likely to reduce the wage gap between men and women, but only to the extent that exports and tourism generate an increased demand for labour. The study also shows that (a) labour force participation rates are likely to increase for both men and women; (b) although the wage gap between men and women may be reduced in the export processing and tourism sectors, this is not likely to be the case for the labour force as a whole; and (c) even in the face of high demand for female labour in export processing, occupational segregation appears to remain strong.

Finally, Zabin's study (1992) of the fresh fruit and vegetable sector in California (US) and Baja California (Mexico) provides an interesting case that sheds light on the possible effects of trade liberalization between the two countries. This sector employs both men and women; the gender ratio, however, is different in each area. The study's main question is whether wages between the two countries will tend to converge and, if so, whether this convergence will be upward or downward. The main conclusion is that, in some cases, economic integration between the two countries can entrench the differences in opportunities for men and women. This is because "a clear hierarchy has developed in the bi-national farm labour market which is highly correlated with differing proportions of men and women." This hierarchy has to do with gendered migration patterns and cultural constructions of gender, as a result of which women stay in the lower-wage Baja California area while men migrate to the higher-wage California labour market.

In the following sections, we have selected some areas/sectors where women are concentrated and which are likely to undergo important economic transformations as trade expands worldwide.

Trade, Agriculture, and Rural Women   In many Third World countries, women play crucial roles in agricultural production. The dismantling of protective trade measures will stimulate production in cash crops that are competitive in the international market; to the extent that they rely on female labour, there is likely to be an increase in employment for this category of women (ACWW/IAC, 1994). However, an increase in agricultural production and in women's employment will not always raise their wages if, for example, surplus labour is available. The scenario may be different, however, if agricultural workers are organized and are able to use collective bargaining power to demand higher wages. On the other hand, women who work in export-oriented cash crop production are likely to benefit from the dismantling of protective trade measures if they are direct recipients of increased prices in the crops they export; this, however, depends on other factors as well, such as the gender division of labour in the household and farming community, women's access to land and technologies, and women's unpaid work in social reproduction (Elson, 1991). The question then becomes one of determining how and under what circumstances women can be direct recipients of trade benefits and to what extent this would benefit them, given both economic and non-economic factors. Again, this necessitates country- and region-specific monitoring and policies.

Despite women's participation in the production of cash crops, a more common scenario is their involvement in subsistence production, typically farming on their own account to sustain their households or to sell in local markets. To the extent that this type of production is not for export, it is likely to be displaced when trade liberalization leads to increased imports of cheaper foreign products. For example, several studies of the likely impact of NAFTA on corn imports in Mexico indicate that small farmers in the corn sector, who constitute 29 per cent of total rural employment, or 1.7 million workers, will find it difficult to compete with imports of corn from the United States (Hinojosa, 1992). This situation could lead to an increase in Mexican imports of corn from the United States and is likely to have a strong negative effect on Mexican corn production, especially if no measures are taken to ameliorate the regressive distributional impact of removing protection from low-income corn farmers. The result could be a dramatic change in the Mexican countryside, as the rural population might be forced to migrate to urban areas in Mexico (or to the United States) in search of employment. Trade liberalization in agricultural sectors therefore may profoundly change demographic patterns and result in a variety of gender dimensions that merit attention by researchers and policy makers.

In the same way, small farmers, both in developing and industrialized countries, increasingly cannot compete with large-scale production and are driven out of the world commodity markets. Although the extent of women's participation varies so that it is not possible to generalize, we do know that in Africa, for example, women have been the main food producers while men have traditionally had a higher degree of participation in export crops (Boserup, 1970). Given this gender division of labour, male farmers may have easier access to the best land, reserved for export crop production, and to new technologies (Elson, 1991); they thereby reap the benefits of trade to a greater extent than women farmers.

The Informal Sector   During the past two decades, a large body of literature has documented women's participation in the informal sector. It is characterized by a variety of factors — small-scale production, marginality, poor working conditions, low earnings, and often illegal and underground activities (Scott, 1979; Tinker, 1985; Benería and Roldan, 1987; Portes, Castells, and Benton, 1989; Mitter, 1994). Some of these studies have situated women's informal-sector work within the context of economic globalization. Others have dealt with the reasons for women's concentration in the sector — exploring, for example, their need to balance both productive and reproductive roles in their daily life activities.

To our knowledge, the implications of increased trade for this sector have not been investigated. It is important to point out that it is a sector with a great deal of variation — generally and in terms of its significance for trade. While some productive units are geared directly to the international market and may even be leading producers (as with the case of micro-enterprises in Italy's Emiglia Romana region), others are characterized by low productivity and can only survive under trade liberalization if they do not compete with imports. Examples of the first are garment shops and craft production units that are organized for the international market; they are globally subcontracted out at very low wages and typically employ predominantly women (Mies, 1982; Truelove, 1990; Kabeer, 1991; Petras, 1994). The highly competitive character of this form of production has also made it quite volatile, even in terms of location, and sensitive to marginal shifts in costs and trade regulation. Such is the case of segments of the US garment industry, which in recent years have returned to the United States after a period of relocation in low-wage countries (Petras, 1994). For the workers engaged in this type of production, such volatility contributes to instability of employment and precarious working conditions — in both low- and high-income countries.

Trade liberalization, therefore, can have contradictory effects on small producers in the informal sector. They can be either expansionary (by stimulating production and employment) or contractionary (by driving non-competitive firms out of the market). To the extent that subcontracting reaches the informal sector, an expansionary effect from trade among large firms with comparative advantage would reach the smaller firms (and even industrial homework) via subcontracting; thus, the search for lower production costs (a result of competitive pressure) could result in further expansion of the informal sector. The opposite would happen in the case of contraction of production — trade competition would have a negative effect on employment in the affected firms, which would have a multiplier effect throughout the subcontracting chains. The effects on sectors of the informal economy where women tend to be concentrated are likely to vary according to specific industrial and regional circumstances; regardless of the outcome, these processes need to be monitored in order to make adjustments that take into consideration the gendered impact of trade on women's and men's informal employment.

One of the difficulties in analysing the gender dimensions of trade in the informal sector is the lack of statistics and information. Despite important attempts on the part of the United Nations and other institutions to design ways to gather information about the sector (UN, 1993), there continues to be a lack of documentation, which implies that new research will still have to rely on survey and case-study work until better baseline data can be compiled.

Free Trade Zones Research on women's participation in free trade zones (FTZs) is well established, although there is very little work on the likely effects of trade liberalization on the reorganization of production and women's employment in FTZs. Currently there is much concern in countries that rely heavily on FTZs that "freer" trade might wipe out existing trade privileges granted them under this rubric; that is, there is fear that FTZs might become obsolete as free trade becomes the norm. In the Dominican Republic, where 160,000 workers — two-thirds of them women — are employed in 26 FTZs, the fear is that increased US-Mexico trade under NAFTA may displace Dominican imports by the United States, its largest market, and make its FTZs obsolete (*The Economist*, 1994). This would have a devastating effect on the (mainly female) employees and further deteriorate their bargaining position. The same issues have been raised concerning the maquiladora industries at the Mexico-US border, where it is feared that the predominantly female labour force will be greatly affected by changes in policy towards the maquila sector (Hualde, 1993).

A pivotal concern in this process is the question of labour rights and practices in FTZs. The AFL-CIO in the United States, for example, has charged the government of the Dominican Republic with unfair labour practices, claiming that the abuse of workers in FTZs in developing countries means unfair competition for US workers. This issue was raised by labour representatives during the NAFTA negotiations as well, and efforts have been made, in US law as well as by labour groups such as the AFL-CIO, to institutionalize a set of internationally recognized labour standards (*The Economist*, 1994; Lee, 1993). The US Department of Labour, for example, found that very few developing countries have special labour laws for their FTZs, and that those that do usually adopt them to restrict unions, prohibit strikes, or limit the scope of collective bargaining (US Department of Labour, 1989/90). Since women constitute the majority of workers in FTZs, research addressing the gender implications of FTZ labour laws and practices deriving from national and regional trade liberalization schemes is important and timely.

Emerging Issues in Gender and Trade

Researchers and policy makers are increasingly taking an interest in many new areas of research that have implications for gender and trade, such as environment, biotechnology, intellectual property rights, and technology transfer. Initial efforts have been made to build analytical frameworks to address these issues (Shiva, 1994; Mitter, 1994; Mies and Shiva, 1993; Agarwal, 1991), but their connections with trade are not always direct or self-evident. It is nevertheless important that these connections be traced, in order to provide substantive information for policy makers and for action-oriented organizations.

Gender, Environment, and Trade Previous research on gender and the environment has established the gender-specific relationship of men and women to the environment; the differential impact of environmental degradation; and the active roles women have played in movements of environmental protection and regeneration (Agarwal, 1991; Shiva, 1994). To the extent that trade promotes growth and industrialization, the connection between it and environmental issues is quite obvious. As new technologies are introduced in agricultural production, and as protective measures continue to be dismantled, allowing foreign investors more accessibility to market natural resources, we are likely to witness further environmental degradation (Harcourt, 1994). In the primary sector, this degradation may include deforestation, increased contamination from the introduction of pesticides and the use of other chemicals in agriculture, and the erosion of local forms of sustainable development.

All of this has repercussions for rural women, who play key roles in gathering wood, fetching water, and sustaining the family. As the pioneering work of Ester Boserup showed and as further research has confirmed (Boserup, 1970; Sen, 1982; Tadesse, 1982; Agarwal, 1991), there already exists a gender imbalance in men's and women's access to productive and subsistence resources. With the introduction of export-oriented agricultural production, these resources will become even less accessible to women in cases where men tend to concentrate in export-oriented crop production and women concentrate in subsistence-based production (Elson, 1991; Mies and Shiva, 1993; Harcourt, 1994).

Gender, Trade, and Biotechnology Research that has been conducted on women, biotechnology, and agriculture to date has focused primarily on plant technologies, making links between biotechnological advances in plant production, on the one hand, and the environmental and cultural degradation of indigenous knowledge systems on the other. Local communities have had little input in the decisions of large multinationals to commercialize plant production for biotechnical purposes (Shiva, 1994). And when communities have, in fact, been included in the discussions and given part of the patenting and intellectual property rights, typically men are the members of the community who manage the financial and legal transactions (Agarwal, 1991). Unless women, who play crucial roles both as producers and consumers of biotechnology, participate in discussions on this from the start, they will continue to lose out in the negotiations. Further, existing development strategies have made little attempt to tap or enhance indigenous knowledge and skill, especially women's knowledge. This is in addition to the fact that women have been absent from the institutions through which modern scientific knowledge is created and transmitted (Agarwal, 1991). Thus, empowering women implies an effort to open their access to scientific studies, to combine their indigenous knowledge with it, and to empower them, individually and collectively, as participants in political and economic processes.

With the new WTO taking effect, traditional farmers will face many changes deriving from the liberalization of patent laws, intellectual property rights, and farmers' rights. In many Third World countries, this implies that traditional indigenous knowledge systems of plant breeding, for example, may now become patented by foreign companies (Keayla, 1994). For example, as multinational pharmaceutical companies increasingly are able to patent medicines and drugs from indigenous sources in India, local companies will no longer be able to produce their products, and local consumers will become more dependent on medicine and drug imports (Keayla, 1994). Global efforts have been made to protect intellectual property rights and farmers' rights, such as through the FAO Commission on Plant Genetic Resources and the Keystone Dialogue (Shiva, 1994), but with limited success. The new WTO framework provides for protection of plant varieties either by patent laws or by an effective *sui generis* system (by which each country evolves its own system of protecting farmers' and breeders' rights), but critics argue that, especially recently, as plant breeding research has become

79

increasingly privatized, this works more in favour of large corporations than it does for small farmers (Krishnakumar, 1994b; Keayla, 1994). The gender impact of this process lies in the extent to which women participate in preserving indigenous knowledge systems and their roles in the production and consumption of biotechnologies. As the scope of patentability is extended to cover not only industrial and agricultural technology sectors, but also the biotechnology sector, research must focus more attention on the gender dimensions of patent laws and on women's roles in these processes so that appropriate actions and policies can be undertaken to ensure their inclusion in and advantage from them.

Aside from research focusing on biotechnology and agriculture, there has been some initial work done on biotechnology and human reproduction with respect to implications for gender and trade. Feminist research on biotechnologies of gender has focused on how women's reproductive functions are becoming a site of technological development and appropriation (Haraway, 1992; Shiva, 1994). The rise in parts of Latin America in the past decade of black markets for surrogate mothers is one example of how biotechnology may directly affect women's bodies (Stalone and Steinberg, 1987; Mies and Shiva, 1993). It seems clear that biotechnologies of bodies as well as plants or crops have widespread implications for women, both in advanced industrialized countries and in developing countries. We are quite unprepared to deal with the economic aspects of these issues and perhaps even less with the ethical issues. Given the potential of trade liberalization schemes to intensify advances in biotechnological research and development at the international level, it will become increasingly important to understand these issues, especially as they affect poor women in developing countries, and to connect these seemingly disparate areas of inquiry.

Trade, Technology Transfer, and Gender   Trade can intensify as well as inhibit the transfer of technology. It intensifies technology transfer when, for example, producers who use less efficient technologies are compelled to introduce more advanced methods in order to compete in the international market. However, to the extent that trade eliminates a nation's ability to compete, and to the extent that this reinforces the concentration of production in the more technologically-advanced countries, it is likely to inhibit technology transfer. In today's world we can observe both tendencies. While the first leads to convergence between rich and poor countries, the second leads to divergence, at least in the sectors/industries affected. Thus, while the East and South-East Asian countries have seen rapid economic growth, increased trade, and technological convergence with the high-income countries, this has not been the case for many African and Latin American countries or for eastern Europe, although there are variations among sectors and industries.

The gender dimensions of trade and technology transfer depend largely on the effects of new technological systems in particular regions or industries. Research needs to be carried out to determine the regional or sectoral variations in impact, and the subsequent implications for different categories and sectors of women. For example, the technological revolution in computing, telecommunications, and transport has affected offshore production in that it has facilitated the geographic dispersion of some industries. The resulting effects on women's employment in information technology (IT) need to be examined. Changes in the global economic landscape, such as the transfer of production to low-wage countries seen in recent decades, have led to the feminization of wage labour at a global level, particularly but not exclusively in labour-intensive industries. Policies of export promotion have tended to create, for a variety of reasons, a preference for women workers on the part of MNCs (Mies, 1982; Heyzer, 1985; Ong, 1987; Feldman, 1992), resulting in the feminization of the labour force at a global level. This has meant a reversal of the employment trends that predominated under previous import-substitution models of industrialization, which saw a predominantly male workforce, and has been viewed as part of the informalization and deregulation of the labour market since the 1970s (Standing, 1989).

Thus, trade and technology have contributed to changes in the gender composition of the workplace; in addition to FTZs, labour-intensive industries — transnational as well as domestic — in low-wage countries have hired high percentages of women (Beneria and Roldan, 1987). As existing literature on the subject has shown, the effects on women are complex, not always easy to evaluate, and clearly not generalizable from country to country. A general feature, however, has been their production for the world market at relatively low wages and in poor working conditions.[2] While many women have benefited from the increasing autonomy provided by greater access to jobs and income, others have continued to be subject to discrimination and exploitative conditions at the workplace and as wage earners (Elson and Pearson, 1981; Ong, 1987).

In a gendered workplace, it is important to see these changes as taking place in a contested terrain where the outcomes depend on a variety of economic, social, cultural, and political factors. There is some evidence, for example, of the possibility of reversal of the feminization of wage labour, leading toward the defeminization of some industries. Although it is too early to generalize, three examples illustrate this tendency. First, there are indicators to show that the introduction of Japanese just-in-time technologies has led to a shrinking of the proportion of women workers in specific industries (Roldan, 1991). This is because the flexibility and multilayered skills demanded by this type of production organization requires the retraining and reorganization of the workforce, a process that often bypasses women. As Roldan has shown in the case of an Argentinean metal industry, this results from a combination of factors, ranging from management and workers' views that men constitute the primary workforce to the opposition of male workers to the retraining of women. This example illustrates an essentially political contest, rooted in the competitive pressures created by the opening of the Argentinean economy to international competition as a result of SAPs.

Another example concerns the decrease, since the mid-1980s, of the proportion of women in the maquiladora industry located along the US-Mexico border — from an earlier high of 69 per cent to 54 per cent in 1993 (De la O, 1993). This decline in the predominance of women in these industries has reversed previously held notions and practices of gender segregation along the border. Although no systematic study concerning the reasons for this change has been carried out, preliminary research indicates that there are several, ranging from the adoption of new technologies to the reorganization of the work process to the availability of young men ready to take jobs previously held by women (Benería and Hualde, research in progress). Behind these factors there are competitive pressures generated by the global market and particularly by the implementation of NAFTA.

A third example relates to the textile and garment industry in Catalonia, Spain, which has undergone a process of intensive restructuring since the 1970s. Traditionally a predominantly female industry, its proportion of women workers decreased from 67 per cent in 1978 to 55 per cent in 1988 (Benería, work in progress). Here, too, there would seem to be several reasons for the decrease — the introduction of highly automated machinery, which eliminates many of the jobs previously held by women; the introduction of night and weekend shifts; and experimentation with new work schedules, such as ten hours per day and four days per week. At the root of these changes is the profound restructuring of the industry resulting from Spain's membership in the EC.

The implications of these changes for women's relative access to employment indicate a need to monitor processes of industrial restructuring, design policies that are less discriminatory toward women, and incorporate training programmes that address women's specific gender needs.

CONCLUSION

Analysis of the gender dimensions of trade requires a new approach both in theory and practice. This paper argues that trade liberalization is not necessarily neutral with respect to gender. Until now, the debate on trade has remained seemingly "gender neutral"; little discussion has taken place concerning the gender dimensions and possible outcomes of free trade models for women in specific sectors. As we have discussed, the implications of the new trade policies for women depend upon women's position in the process of production and social reproduction. Only empirical research will show us what the gender effects and policy implications of specific trade liberalization schemes are, and how they will affect women in particular industries, sectors, or regions. It is important to emphasize that as the world's economic integration accelerates through trade liberalization schemes, women and men need to understand that trade is an issue affecting their daily lives. In particular, it makes sense to argue that trade liberalization schemes should be implemented only if trade-related research and policy demonstrate that the negative effects can be counterbalanced or if winners compensate losers.

The current emphasis on neoliberal trade reform will only continue to accelerate integration of local and national economies into the international market. The implications of this process are manifold and complex; not only are there positive and negative effects, but the introduction of new technologies and the search for lower production costs are likely to affect social, cultural, and political structures throughout the world. It is therefore crucial to introduce gendered conceptual frameworks in those sectors concerned with the impacts of trade liberalization on people's daily lives and its contributions to social, cultural, and environmental change. Policy makers, research institutions, schools, activists, politicians, women's organizations, church groups, labour organizations, human rights groups, and international organizations, among others, can play larger roles in understanding these issues and can contribute to trade negotiations from the start. Various channels of participation in trade processes have opened up; however, much work has yet to be done to include these voices in the trade decision-making process.

Alternatives to the dominant approach to trade liberalization must also be proposed. As Grinspun and Kreklewich point out, a progressive response does not need to be based on "myopic nationalism." Instead, it must be based on a clear understanding of the major forces involved and of their consequences for specific social groups. In particular, they argue, the rhetoric of globalization must be unmasked to show that the transfer of power to unelected and unaccountable bodies and institutions enhances "the rights and freedoms of transnational capital" and then "is invoked to deny similar countervailing rights and freedoms to community-based organizations, associations and unions" (1994: 54). This implies the need not only to expose these facts but to find ways to increase the power of communities and local governments in exercising power over decisions that affect them. This will not succeed, however, unless local governments and organizations make collaborative efforts to work at regional or international levels.

Among the UN organizations, UNIFEM has taken the initiative to foster discussion and research on trade and gender, and has recently published a study, *Women and the New Trade Agenda*, by Joekes and Weston (1994). Other organizations, women's groups, and individuals have attempted to "get women and social issues on the trade agenda" (Marsden, 1992 &

1993). These efforts, however, cannot by themselves affect the rules of global trade; we also need more women professionals with an understanding of the often complex issues of trade and international exchange who can participate in the formulation of trade policy and theory. There is a need to publicize the importance of trade negotiations among women's organizations at all levels, for inclusion in their agendas for action; governmental agencies, international organizations, NGOs, regional networks, and grass-roots organizations can all play significant roles in making information on trade issues accessible and in constructing strategies that respond to the political, economic, and cultural implications of trade liberalization and globalization. It is crucial that organizations work across national borders in order to contend with the transnational nature of trade. This can be done at different levels, depending on the level at which action-oriented organizations operate — regional agreements, bilateral negotiations, local policies, and multilateral negotiations. We need, as well, to add a human dimension to the trade debate by discussing solutions to the negative effects of trade liberalization, such as compensatory measures and long-term measures. Compensatory measures may include job retraining and help in finding new sources of employment for workers displaced by the new trade policies. Long-term measures include reassessing domestic and industrial policies from a gender perspective and promoting more equitable and non-discriminatory employment, health, and social conditions for women workers. Measures of this kind, coupled with more critical examination of the gender dimensions of trade frameworks and processes, are crucial if we are to transform the arenas in which these issues affect women and men most directly, in their work environments, in their cultural practices, and in their daily lives.

Lourdes Benería is Professor of City and Regional Planning and Women's Studies at Cornell University. Her work on gender and development has dealt with issues related to women and work, labour markets, the underestimation of women's economic activities and structural adjustment.

Amy Lind is currently conducting research on the politics of neoliberalism and women's movements in Ecuador. She is the author of "Power, Gender and Development: Popular Women's Organizations and the Politics of Need in Ecuador," in Arturo Escobar and Sonia Alvarez, The Making of Social Movements in Latin America, Boulder: Westview Press, 1992.

This article was originally prepared for the Gender, Science and Development (GSD) Programme of the International Federation of Institutes for Advanced Study (IFIAS) and UNIFEM's collaborative project on International Trade and Gender, January 1995. The authors thank them for their comments and editing suggestions. It has been slightly revised and shortened for this publication.

Notes

1. Argentina, Brazil, Paraguay, and Uruguay.

2. There has been debate about the effects of transnational employment on women workers. While the early literature emphasized negative effects linked to low wages and exploitative working conditions facing women, the debate intensified when Linda Lim argued that multinational employment was in fact beneficial for women because it provided them with employment at competitive or higher wages than other forms of local employment, and in some cases gave them a sense of freedom and more autonomy (1990).

References

Abramovitz, Janet N. 1994. "Biodiversity and Gender Issues: Recognizing Common Ground," in Wendy Harcourt (ed.), *Feminist Perspectives on Sustainable Development*. London: Zed Books.

Agarwal, Bina. 1991. "Engendering the Environment Debate: Lessons from the Indian Subcontinent." CASID Monograph No. 8, Michigan State University.

Anderson, Jean, and Denise Dimon. 1994. "Economic Integration and the Mexican Male/Female Wage Differential." Paper presented at the XVIII International Congress of the Latin American Studies Association, Atlanta, Georgia, March.

ACWW/IAC (Associated Country Women of the World/International Agrarisch Centrum). 1994. Proposal for a conference on Women and Agricultural Trade Agreements (WATA) for Rural Women Leaders.

Benería, Lourdes. "Economic Restructuring and the Plight of Communities." Research in progress.

Benería, Lourdes, and Alfredo Hualde. "Capital Mobility, Economic Restructuring and the Plight of Communities: A Case Study of Smith Corona's Relocation." Research in progress.

Benería, Lourdes. 1992. "The Mexican Debt Crisis: Restructuring the Economy and the Household," in Lourdes and Feldman (eds.), *Unequal Burden*, pp. 83-104.

Benería, Lourdes, and Shelley Feldman (eds.). 1992. *Unequal Burden*. Boulder, CO: Westview Press.

Benería, Lourdes, and Martha Roldán. 1987. *The Crossroads of Class and Gender*. University of Chicago Press.

Boserup, Ester. 1970. *Woman's Role in Economic Development*. New York: St. Martin's Press.

Cohen, Marjorie Griffin. 1987. *Free Trade and the Future of Women's Work*. Toronto: Garamond Press and the Canadian Centre for Policy Alternatives.

Cohen, Marjorie Griffin. 1994. "The Implications of Economic Restructuring for Women: The Canadian Situation," in Isabella Bakker (ed.), *The Strategic Silence: Gender and Economic Policy*, London: Zed Books/North-South Institute.

Conroy, Michael and Amy Glasmeier. 1992. "Unprecedented Disparities, Unparalleled Adjustment Needs: Winners and Losers on the NAFTA 'Fast Track', *Journal of Interamerican Studies and World Affairs*, 34 (4) (Winter), pp. 1-37.

Cortes, Fernando, and Rosa Maria Rubalcava. 1993. "Cambio estructural y concentracion: un analisis de la distribucion del ingreso familiar en Mexico: 1984–89." Manuscript, El Colegio de Mexico.

De la O, Maria Eugenia. 1993. "Cambio tecnológico y empleo en la industria de maquila." Research report, El Colegio de la Frontera Norte.

De la O, Maria Eugenia. 1994. "Mexican Retailing: The Fiesta." *The Economist* 18 June, pp. 72–75.

The Economist. 1994. "Labour and Trade Freedom." 30 April, pp. 50–51.

Elson, Diane. 1991. "Male Bias in Macro-Economics: The Case of Structural Adjustment," in Diane Elson (ed.), *Male Bias in the Development Process*. Manchester: Manchester University Press.

Elson, Diane. 1992. "From Survival Strategies to Transformation Strategies: Women's Needs and Structural Adjustment," in Lourdes Beneria and Shelley Feldman (eds.), *Unequal Burden*. Boulder, CO: Westview Press.

Elson, Diane, and Ruth Pearson. 1981. "The Subordination of Women and the Internationalization of Factory Production," in Kate Young et al. (eds.), *Of Marriage and the Market*. London: CSE Books.

Feldman, Shelley. 1992. "Crisis, Islam and Gender in Bangladesh: The Social Construction of a Female Labour Force," in Lourdes Beneria and Shelley Feldman (eds.), *Unequal Burden*. Boulder, CO: Westview Press.

GATT Secretariat. 1994. "The Final Act of the Uruguay Round: A Summary." *International Trade Forum* 1, pp. 4–21.

Grinspun, Ricardo and Robert Kreklewich. 1994. "Consolidating Neoliberal Reforms: 'Free Trade' as a Conditioning Framework," *Studies in Political Economy*, 43 (Spring), pp. 33-61.

Harcourt, Wendy (ed.). 1994. *Feminist Perspectives on Sustainable Development*. London: Zed Books.

Haraway, Donna. 1992. *Simians, Cyborgs and Women: The Reinvention of Nature*. London: Routledge.

Heyzer, Noeleen. 1985. "From Rural Subsistence to an Industrial Peripheral Workforce: An Examination of Female Malaysian Migrants and Capital Accumulation in Singapore," in L. Beneria (ed.), *Women and Development: Sexual Division of Labour in Rural Societies*. New York: Praeger.

Joekes, Susan and Ann Weston. 1994. *Women and the New Trade Agenda*. New York: UNIFEM.

Kabeer, Naila. 1991. "Cultural Dopes or Rational Fools?: Women and Labour Supply in the Bangladesh Garment Industry." *The European Journal of Development Research* 3 (1) (June), pp. 133–61.

Keayla, B. K. 1994. "Final Dunkel Act: New Patent Regime: Myth and Reality." *Frontline* 6 May, pp. 14–16.

Kerr, Joanna. 1994a. "Chinese Women Taking the Great Leap…Backward?" *Progressions* 1 (1) (April) (North-South Institute, Ottawa), p. 2.

Kerr, Joanna. 1994b. "A Workable Alternative: How to Implement Plant Breeders' Rights." *Frontline* 11 March, pp. 102–103.

Krishnakumar, Asha. 1994a. "Harnessing a Heritage: The Rights of Local Communities," *Frontline*, 11 March, pp. 100-101.

Krishnakumar, Asha. 1994b. "A Workable Alternative: How to Implement Plant Breeders' Rights," *Frontline*, 11 March, pp. 102-103.

Krugman, Paul. 1984. "Import Protection as Export Promotion," in Henryk Kierkowski (ed.), *Monopolistic Competition and International Trade*. Oxford: Blackwell.

Lee, Thea. 1993. "Happily Never NAFTA." *Dollars and Sense* 183 (Jan-Feb), pp. 12–15.

Lim, Linda. 1990. "Women's Work in Export Factories: The Politics of A Cause," in Irene Tinker (ed.), *Persistent Inequalities*. Oxford: Oxford University Press.

Marsden, Lorna. 1992. "Timing and Presence: Getting Women's Issues on the Agenda." Working Paper GSD-3, Gender, Science and Development Programme, IFIAS, Toronto, July.

Marsden, Lorna. 1993. "Getting Women and Trade Issues On the Agenda." Paper presented at Structural Change and Gender Relations in the Era of Globalisation, North-South Institute Workshop, Toronto, October.

Mies, Maria. 1982. "The Dynamics of the Sexual Division of Labour and Integration of Rural Women into the World Market," in Lourdes Beneria (ed.), *Women and Development: The Sexual Division of Labour in Rural Societies*. New York: Praeger.

Mies, Maria, and Vandana Shiva. 1993. *Ecofeminism*. London: Zed Books.

Mitter, Swasti. 1994. "What Women Demand of Technology." *New Left Review* 205 (May-June), pp. 100–110.

Mitter, Swasti. 1994. "On Organising Women in Casualised Work: A Global Review," in Sheila Rowbotham and Swasti Mitter (eds.), *Dignity and Daily Bread: New Forms of Economic Organising Among Poor Women in the Third World and the First*. London: Routledge.

Nash, June (ed.). 1993. *Crafts in the World Market*. Albany: SUNY Press.

Ong, Aihwa. 1987. *Spirits of Resistance and Capitalist Discipline*. Albany: SUNY Press.

Pastor, Robert A. 1992. "NAFTA As the Center of an Integration Process: The Nontrade Issues," in Nora Lustig et. al. (eds.), *North American Free Trade*. Washington, DC: The Brookings Institution.

Petras, Elizabeth. 1994. "The Global Garment Industry." Paper presented at the International Studies in Planning Seminar, Cornell University, Spring.

Portes, Alejandro, Manuel Castells, and Lauren E. Benton (eds.). 1989. *The Informal Economy: Studies in Advanced and Less Developed Countries*. Baltimore: Johns Hopkins University Press.

85

Portes, Alejandro, and Richard Schauffler. 1993. "From Surplus Labour to Dynamic Enterprise: Competing Perspectives on the Latin American Informal Sector." *Population and Development Review* 19 (1) (March), pp. 33–60.

Roldan, Martha. 1991. "JIT (Just In Time) Techological Innovations, Industrial Restructuring and Gender Relations." Paper presented at the conference on Women Organizing in the Process of Industrialization, Institute of Social Studies, The Hague, April.

Scott, Allison MacEwen. 1979. "Who Are the Self-Employed?" in Ray Bromley and Chris Gerry (eds.), *Casual Work and Poverty*. London: John Wiley and Sons.

Shiva, Vandana. 1994. "The Seed and the Earth: Biotechnology and the Colonisation of Regeneration," in Vandana Shiva (ed.), *Closer to Home: Women Reconnect Ecology, Health and Development Worldwide*. Philadelphia and Gabriola Island, BC: New Society Publishers.

Shrybman, Steven. 1993. "Trading Away the Environment," in Ricardo Grinspun and Maxwell Cameron (eds.), *The Political Economy of North American Free Trade*. New York: St. Martin's Press.

Stalone, Patricia and Deborah Steinberg. 1987. *Made to Order: The Myth of Reproductive and Genetic Progress*. New York: Pergamon Press.

Standing, Guy. 1989. "Global Feminization Through Flexible Labour." *World Development* 17 (7), pp. 1077–95.

Tadesse, Zenerbeworke. 1982. "The Impact of Land Reform on Women in Ethiopia," in Lourdes Beneria (ed.), *Women and Development: The Sexual Division of Labour in Rural Societies*. New York: Praeger.

Tinker, Irene. 1985. "Street Foods as Income and Food for the Poor." Paper presented at the Society for International Development conference, Washington, DC, May.

Truelove, Cynthia. 1990. "Disguised Industrial Proletarians in Rural Latin America: Women's Informal Sector Factory Work and the Social Reproduction of Coffee Farm Labour in Colombia," in Kathryn Ward (ed.), *Women Workers and Global Restructuring*. Ithaca: Cornell University Press.

United Nations Statistical Office/ECA/INSTRAW. 1991. *Handbook on Compilation of Statistics on Women in the Informal Sector in Industry, Trade and Services in Africa*. Santo Domingo and New York: United Nations.

United States Department of Labour. 1989/1990. *Worker Rights in Export Processing Zones*. Bureau of International Labour Affairs Foreign Labour Trends Series, vol. 1.

University of Arizona. 1992. "Free Trade: Arizona at the Crossroads." Background report prepared for the Sixty-First Arizona Town Hall, October.

Wacker, Corinne. 1994. "Sustainable Development Through Women's Groups: A Cultural Approach to Sustainable Development," in Wendy Harcourt (ed.), *Feminist Perspectives on Sustainable Development*. London: Zed Books.

Zabin, Carol. 1992. "Binational Labour Markets and Segmentation by Gender: Agriculture and the North American Free Trade Agreement." Paper presented at the XVII International Congress of the Latin American Studies Association, Los Angeles, September.

GLOBAL MARKETS: THREATS TO SUSTAINABLE HUMAN DEVELOPMENT

MANFRED BIENEFELD

For women, as for men, the hope for a better future rests on the world's ability to achieve sustainable human development. But this is no small challenge. Sustainability requires that today's growth must not compromise or diminish the natural and human-made endowments available to future generations (Brundlandt, 1987). Human development demands that people's lives become more secure, more fulfilling, and more prosperous, and that is only possible if the societies to which they belong become more mutually supportive, more coherent, more tolerant, and more productive. Unfortunately, the world is not doing well on these fronts, and there is little prospect of significant change until a new international regime can restore the capacity of individual societies to set ethical, social, and environmental limits to the competitive global market.

The past 20 years have severely damaged the prospect of sustainable human development. Stress on the global ecosystem has increased; societies have become less coherent and more intolerant; social safety nets and other mutual support systems have been eroded or stretched to breaking point; and even the growth of output and productivity has languished. And these trends will continue so long as the world is dominated by neoliberal policy prescriptions that consistently fail to take account of every society's limited capacity to adjust to the demands of a volatile, amoral, and fiercely competitive global market.

Once the competitive process slips the leash of socially and politically rooted national regulation, the complaints of the disadvantaged and the voices of those who would sacrifice some growth for increased equity or for greater social stability are rapidly marginalized. Now, not even the threat of social unrest or civil war will yield significant policy compromises unless a major power sees some strategic interest under threat. The demand for sound economic policies becomes virtually unconditional, impervious even to catastrophic social and economic reversals. The real short-term pain that is to be endured for a hypothetical long-term gain turns out to be effectively unlimited in duration and intensity as policy comes to be made by people and institutions that are more and more remote from the suffering. Indeed, in those distant air-conditioned offices, the willingness to take tough decisions, even when these trigger political opposition becomes a sign of courage and a source of pride (Williamson, 1994). The fact that those who make the tough decisions rarely share the pain is not irrelevant.

As markets become more unregulated, short-term and private interests gradually come to dominate long-term and public ones. Competitiveness becomes the arbiter of all things good and bad; and debt service becomes a first charge on society, even if the loans were made by speculative investors who used their leverage and their alleged expertise to persuade beleaguered governments that it was safe and sensible for them to borrow.[1] Squeezed by competition and burdened by unbearable debt-service obligations, many societies have been forced to neglect issues that are critical for future social stability, economic efficiency, and sustainable human development. Public institutions have been stripped of resources and authority while persistent and open-ended demands for austerity, cost reduction, downsizing, and expenditure cuts have mortgaged the future by reducing investment and maintenance, curtailing learning and skill acquisition on the job, and bankrupting a large section of the local business community. Ironically, this has left many societies more vulnerable and divided and less capable of responding constructively to the challenge of the global market.

Such perverse outcomes are widely documented[2] (Rodrik, 1990; Taylor, 1988; Taylor, 1993; Sachs, 1987), and the multilateral financial institutions have always acknowledged that the possibility (IMF, 1987; Yagci et al., 1985),[3] but they have tended to treat the danger as more hypothetical than real. Moreover, whenever such costs do arise, they have argued that they must be endured while being combated by yet further economic liberalization. Unfortunately, the underlying belief that market liberalization will always eventually yield welfare gains turns out to be largely a matter of faith.

Many who do not share this faith in largely unregulated markets believe that only a relatively regulated social market can support sustainable human development or yield social efficiency. But this group is divided between those who believe that the regulation of markets must now occur primarily at the global level, and those who argue that it must be primarily a national matter because the regulation of markets is a political task that cannot be divorced from the political process that gives it content. This is the argument presented in this paper. According to it, sustainable human development will not be achievable unless we can reconstruct an international system that can restore the sovereign power of societies to manage their internal economies in accordance with democratically determined priorities and values. Although global governance is recognized as an important objective, it is not a substitute for national sovereignty. Good global governance will depend on the existence of stable, internally coherent states.

Women have a particular interest in such matters since they generally play a more central role in the social construction of society due to their primary responsibility for reproduction and child-rearing. That is why they have suffered disproportionately as the deregulation of markets has undermined the ability of societies to protect the social conditions of reproduction from the full force of the global market's demand for cost minimization. And that, in turn, is why women have a particularly direct stake in the establishment of a world order that would allow societies to make choices regarding their social structures and the equitable distribution of parental responsibilities. To be sure, this is no simple matter. Although the sovereign power of societies to make such choices may be important to both women and men, the question of how that power will be used in any particular case will remain open. And this will always entail the possibility that in certain societies, women might prefer the mixed blessings of the global market to the outcomes that would result if their own society had more power to shape its social reality. However, those who would choose the global market under such conditions should be clearly aware of the costs that that choice will exact from many of them in due course.

SUSTAINABLE HUMAN DEVELOPMENT: A GLASS HALF FULL OR HALF EMPTY?

The past 20 years have been deeply disappointing from a human development point of view, especially when the outcomes are compared to the high hopes of the 1960s and 1970s. While such global generalizations will always remain controversial, the current spread of social and political instability around the world is forcing even those who are prepared to declare the global economic glass "half full" to voice concerns about the social and political disintegration that afflicts so much of the world (Griffin, 1995). There are good reasons for that concern. There is no doubt that, outside of Asia, the past 20 years have eroded the quality of life of people around the world. That decline is reflected in well-known statistics on incomes, inequality, war and civil conflict, refugees, and important aspects of the environment. But the biggest losses may have come in a form that is more difficult to measure, namely the rising tide of political, social and economic insecurity that has been imposed on working people around the world in the name of flexibility and efficiency.

There is no denying the remarkable progress made by sizeable parts of Asia, and the significance of that experience is certainly enhanced by the fact that the truly dynamic part of this continent contains roughly a third of the world's population. A majority of these people have enjoyed significant improvements in their quality of life, and since they were initially very poor, their per capita income gains may have reduced global income inequality. However, these gains merely highlight the losses experienced by people in other parts of the world, and those losses have been so dramatic that it is impossible to speak of an overall improvement in the human condition over that period. Nor can the Asian experience lead us to an optimistic prognosis for the future, because the Asian growth model's sustainability is increasingly in doubt and because the policies that were used so successfully by the most dynamic East Asian economies (South Korea, Taiwan, and China) are no longer tolerated under the new global trading rules.

The region's growth model is threatened by economic, social, and environmental development. The most significant threat may be that posed by the progressive liberalization of its financial markets under severe pressure from the United States and the multilateral financial institutions. Although this has been useful in the short run by making some additional capital available to the region, it is leading to increased instability and uncertainty in many cases. Such problems are well known from other experiences (Rodrik, 1990; Collier and Mayer, 1989). In Asia they manifest themselves in rising debt levels, in the frequency of bank failures, in the development of speculative bubbles in both property and asset markets, and in the increasing difficulty of raising tax revenue to finance the infrastructure of the future. Ironically, it is Japan, the region's strongest economy, that is most deeply troubled in this regard as it struggles to contain the damage done by the speculative frenzy that followed the full liberalization of its financial markets in the early 1980s. However, in Indonesia, Thailand, and South Korea there are indications that these risks are rising.

Other threats include the volatility of the world's currency markets, which has recently imposed heavy costs on those who earn their foreign exchange in dollars but pay loans or shareholders in yen; the increasingly intrusive nature of world trade law, which is forcing countries to abandon agricultural subsidies and industrial policies that have served to build domestic economic linkages and stable political coalitions; and the environmental degradation that has accompanied the frenetic growth of the past decades, especially in places like Thailand, South Korea, Indonesia, and China's Special Economic Zones. In addition, income inequality is becoming a more insistent problem, even in economies such as those of China, South Korea, and Taiwan, whose earlier phase of rapid growth was characterized by a relatively egalitarian pattern of income distribution. Together with the region's gradual social and political liberalization, this is threatening to undermine the social cohesion and the political stability that were such striking and important ingredients of their success. Finally, the slow growth of the world economy is imposing significant constraints on the region's dynamic export expansion and this, in turn, may restrict their capacity to maintain rapid domestic

89

growth. While these problems have not reached chronic levels, they are serious and they are growing. And they should caution against any simplistic extrapolation of the region's past experience into the future.

The other reason why this region's experience cannot be a source of optimism for the world economy is that the relatively interventionist policies that were so extensively used by the region's economic engines of growth — Japan, South Korea, Taiwan, and China (Wade, 1990; Amsden, 1989; World Bank, 1993; Lall, 1994) — are no longer tolerated in today's more global economy. Thus the World Bank concludes its recent study of the East Asian miracles with a reluctant acknowledgment that their interventionist trade and industrial policies did appear to be associated with positive outcomes. However, it denies that this might hold any lessons for other developing countries, if only because, in the 1990s, "developing economies that seek access to the emerging regional trading blocs may find that it comes tied to increased obligations that could inhibit the adoption of [such] interventionist policies" (World Bank, 1993, p. 365).

In this context it is worth remembering that the experience of these East Asian economies is unique not only because they have achieved rapid growth, but because these formerly very poor economies have become major and growing markets because they have achieved sustained and rapid real wage increases over a period of thirty years; because they have created nationally based industrial firms that have become major competitors in global markets for technologically sophisticated and design intensive products, including cars, home electronics, and Random Access Memory chips; and because they have become such major sources of outward investment that they were the main driving force behind the more recent rapid growth of the South-East Asian region.

The success of this region cannot, therefore, be ascribed to the neoliberal policy regimes that have today become a condition of access to the global market-place. The most successful East Asian economies pursued coherent, national development strategies that emphasized the need to build strong national industrial and technological foundations; that intervened heavily in financial markets to channel long-term investment toward strategic industrial sectors, firms, and projects; that managed trade extensively in support of their industrial policy objectives;[4] that explicitly fostered domestic economic linkages, especially between industry and agriculture, for both economic and political reasons; and that took steps to contain income inequality in order to protect the economic and political foundations of their strategy.

Of course, the strategies pursued by the East Asian economies were neither new nor unique. Indeed, these countries consciously set out to emulate the Japanese strategy, just as Japan had once emulated what they called "the German strategy." The significance of this observation is enhanced by the fact that no national economy larger than a city-state has achieved remotely comparable success in this century, even though many have deregulated their markets far more extensively. Indeed, many of the latter now face an increasingly serious set of social, political, and economic problems.

The other regions of the world have all failed to make significant progress in laying the foundations for sustainable human development over the past twenty years. This is most obviously so in Africa, which has suffered enormous human, social, and economic losses since the mid-1970s, with a growing number of states facing the complete collapse of their social and political order. According to UNCTAD's *1994 Trade and Development Report*, the "growth performance in Africa remains highly unsatisfactory. With output continuing to lag behind population growth, per capita incomes are heading downward, as they have done for a decade and a half...Structural Adjustment Programmes have failed to bring the turnaround they promised [and]...in several African countries, the main factor behind poor economic performance has been political unrest or armed conflict" (UNCTAD, 1994, p. i).

In Central and Latin America the brief euphoria of the early 1990s has given way to a more sober reassessment. Most countries have yet to make good the losses incurred during the "lost decade" of the 1980s, and wages and working conditions continue to be squeezed, especially in the informal sectors that have now grown explosively for more than a decade. In many cases, social and political tensions remain high, and even in the few economic success stories such as Chile or Colombia, there is little to suggest the emergence of the sort of national industrial or technological base that has allowed the East Asian economies to support rapidly rising real wages over an extended period. In sharp contrast, the much-touted Mexican miracle witnessed a sharp decline in real wages through most of the 1980s, and after a brief respite in the early 1990s, that decline has now resumed with a vengeance as the austerity measures imposed in the wake of the recent peso crisis wreak havoc with the domestic economy.

For the moment, the flow of international finance to the region has declined abruptly, revealing just how tenuous and shallow the so-called boom of the nineties had really been. For the region as a whole, "growth continues to be much better than during the debt crisis, though weak when viewed in an historical perspective. The rise in output since the 'lost decade' has stemmed more from the increased capacity utilization made possible by higher imports than from additional investment and improved productivity. With few exceptions, investment rates are modest, in some cases even lower than during the debt crisis"(UNCTAD, 1994, p. ii).

In social and political terms, the situation is more serious than this economistic summary would suggest. Political tensions are pervasive, and social structures are under severe strain as work is casualized and as the informal sector becomes the norm. In some cases, the authority of central governments is being challenged by beleaguered provincial or local authorities; in others, health services and sanitation have deteriorated to the point where cholera has once again become endemic; in yet others, crime and lawlessness have reached chronic proportions. In short, sustainable human development is not being achieved in this part of the world, and it is not likely to be achieved under the current policy regimes.

This leaves only the industrial world, where the dismantling of the welfare gains that were achieved by working people during the early postwar period continues apace; where rates of growth of output and productivity have been low for 20 years; where real interest rates and debt burdens remain historically high; where the number of unemployed has remained stubbornly above 30 million, even during the so-called recovery of the early 1990s; where the casualization of work is undermining job security and creating a generation of workers with few accumulated pension rights, no career path, no job security, and less and less protection on the job; where income inequalities are growing rapidly;[5] where short term financial flows have risen to previously unimaginable levels, destabilizing currencies and interest rates and blackmailing public authorities with their callous and self-interested demands for social-service cuts; and where political processes are becoming more volatile and unstable, as an increasingly disenfranchised electorate is suspended between anger and apathy, both encouraged to cherish its democratic rights and to despite the parties and the politicians for which it votes. This is not the road to sustainable human development.

THE NEOLIBERAL AND "GLOBAL REGULATION" SOLUTIONS

The neoliberals' solution is to deplore the irrationality of politics and politicians; to urge the more comprehensive deregulation of all markets, including those for labour, intellectual property, and pollution rights; and to paint a more upbeat picture of the world on the grounds that despite the current problems, most countries have laid the foundations for sustainable human development by adopting sound (in other words, neoliberal) economic policies. The fact that outcomes remain so disappointing merely confirms their contention that short-term pain is the price of long-term gain, and that there are still market imperfections to be removed. Because the duration of the short-term pain is not specified, this argument cannot be falsified by any empirical evidence. It is effectively a matter of faith. The truth is that empirical evidence plays only a minor role in the justification of neoliberal policy prescriptions, which are largely derived by deduction from certain axiomatic assumptions about human behaviour. Time and again, policies have been implemented in the absence of any significant empirical support.

Those who understand that unregulated markets will yield neither optimum efficiency nor a socially acceptable outcome, must address the question of *how* markets *are* to be regulated. Many answer this question by calling for global regulation on the grounds that the nation-state has been overtaken by history and that, in a global world, markets can only be regulated globally. This belief rests on the mistaken assumption that regulation is a technical task when, in fact, it is an inherently political one. The operation of competitive markets can be reconciled with a society's values and priorities only on the basis of a meaningful political process that can legitimize the choices that have to be made. But such a political process does not, and probably cannot, exist at the global level, so that global institutions — the IMF, the WTO, the World Bank, the United Nations — simply cannot play this role. To ask them to do so is both impossible and undesirable. Impossible for reasons of scale and distance; undesirable because different societies ought to be able to make different choices according to culture, history, and circumstances.

Because global institutions tend not to be politically accountable, because their diversity makes it difficult for them to make clear political choices, and because they have recently been dominated by a small number of relatively neoliberal states, they have tended to play the opposite role of that which is needed. Instead of imposing socially and politically derived limits on the operation of competitive markets, they have tended to impose limits on the efforts of societies to regulate the market. In effect, they have been in the business of enforcing the logic of the global market, for the sake of "levelling the playing field." Indeed, they have become the central driving force behind the process of globalization that is currently undermining the internal coherence of so many societies. They impose neoliberal conditionalities on struggling debtor nations; they demand the deregulation of markets and the downsizing of public sectors; and they play a leading role in reducing the range of policies that a developing country can employ without being subjected to retaliation of some kind. In short, the proposal that the regulation of markets should occur at the global level is, at best, misguided. And the continued pursuit of this non-solution will ultimately end in failure or disaster.

We must hope that it is failure and not disaster. Failure would mean that the current neoliberal project was abandoned in favour of a more realistic and hopeful one that sought to rebuild an international system that supports and encourages the development of sovereign political entities that have the power to reconcile the market's relentless drive for cost reduction and efficiency, with other needs and priorities.

The alternative to such failure would be a disaster that would take the form of a descent into an anarchic Dark Age of violent confrontation and social disintegration. As more societies are overwhelmed by the unbearable demands of a volatile and ultimately irrational global market, the social bonds will either rupture or they will tend to be replaced by stronger chains that are forged in the furnace of fanaticism or in the preparations for war. History is replete with examples. Once this road is travelled but a short distance, the disaster becomes a self-fulfilling prophecy because the resulting chaos makes demands for a more coherent and constructive political response seem increasingly unrealistic and naive. The banner under which the world is currently marching to this appointment with destiny is "Adjust at any cost."

A self-regulating global market is an impossible dream. To be successful, markets must be embedded in societies capable of moderating their dangerous centrifugal tendencies and forcing them to work within politically defined limits. That is why the emergence of the nation-state was historically so closely linked to the successful emergence of capitalism and why capitalism's perpetual tendency to transcend the nation-state has historically been so closely linked to capitalist crises, which arise whenever the congruence of economic and political spheres is diluted to the point where competitive markets can no longer be reconciled with political and social stability.

LEARNING FROM HISTORY

The regulation of markets is so important because excessively unregulated markets are socially and politically destructive and, therefore, ultimately even inefficient. Moreover, since such regulation must be based on political processes that can command the consent of the governed, it must remain primarily a national task so long as such political processes remain largely national in scope. Until that changes, the current crisis can be resolved only if the declining fortunes of the nation-state can somehow be reversed. Although that will prove extremely difficult, the challenge must be met because there is simply no alternative if sustainable human development is to remain a possibility.

Governments around the world are losing their capacity to respond to the needs and wishes of their citizens. Economic deregulation robs them of the power to do so in a world of heavy accumulated debts, high real interest rates, volatile exchange rates, and massive short-term capital flows. In such a world, governments are forced to shape their policies in accordance with the whims and prejudices of foreign bond and currency traders who care little about the long-term effects of their demands for social-service cuts. In this process, governments gradually turn into executive agencies responsible for persuading their citizens that there is no alternative to those policies; for servicing the country's international debt; and for protecting the rights of private property, irrespective of its nationality.

Within these tight constraints, an increasingly disenfranchised populace is abandoning the apparently discredited nation-state in favour of more narrowly defined "identities" that are often ethnically or culturally rooted. While this is an understandable reaction to the impotent hostility that flourishes in societies facing endless austerity in the midst of plenty, together with mounting personal and economic insecurity, it is not likely to solve any problems. Indeed, it is likely to make matters worse by further fragmenting political power, increasing uncertainty and insecurity, and deepening the latent social and political divisions that lie below the surface of every society. Ultimately, those who would burden the nation-state and the concept of citizenship with ethnic or cultural qualifications will only rediscover the dangerous futility of such an enterprise. But the real responsibility for these disastrous developments must lie with those who are allowing globalization to destroy the secular, territorial states in which social solidarity could be primarily based on the fact that citizens had a personal and a financial investment in the future of "their" society. That must be the only qualification for citizenship if the dream of building fair, tolerant and non-racist societies is to remain alive.

The belief that, to be successful, the market economy must be embedded in strong, stable, coherent and activist nation-states is based on an inductive (as opposed to the mainstream's deductive) theory, in which theoretical propositions are derived from the historical record

93

itself. In this case, there are five broad historical observations that lead to this proposed link between coherent nation states and capitalism. First, the early rise of capitalism was inextricable linked to the emergence of the modern nation-state (Senghaas, 1985; Bienefeld, 1982, 1995). Second, the excessive economic deregulation of the 1920s was so disruptive that it triggered both an economic depression and strong, often violent, political reactions that eventually led to war (Polanyi, 1944; Bienefeld, 1989). Third, the world economy's remarkable and historically unparalleled success between 1948 and 1973 was achieved under an international regime in which the capitalist nation-states had enough economic sovereignty to pursue full employment as a first policy priority, and to require both capital and labour to operate on the basis of nationally negotiated compromises that could reconcile the social, political and economic objectives of society (Marris, 1984; Milward, 1984; Bienefeld, 1982). Fourth, the transformation of the successful East Asian economies was led by states that were encouraged and allowed, largely for geopolitical reasons, to implement coherent national development strategies that set out to create viable national economies by emphasizing the development of strong domestic linkages between sectors and regions; the creation of nationally owned and controlled strategic industries that played leading roles in the acquisition of technology and skills and in the development of export capabilities; and the maintenance of a relatively egalitarian income distribution (Wade, 1990; Amsden, 1989; World Bank, 1993; Bienefeld, 1988). And fifth, almost 20 years of neoliberal deregulation have today produced results highly reminiscent of those in the late 1920s, when fierce competition among unbalanced, debt-ridden economies was also generating increasing levels of social polarization and political conflict (Bienefeld, 1988).

Had the effective national regulation of markets not been destroyed over the past 20 years, there is no reason why the stable prosperity of the industrial world could not have spread gradually to the developing world, especially since that stability would have allowed the industrial countries to pursue more far-sighted and benign policies *vis-à-vis* the developing world. Had they provided capital and technology at a much lower cost, the developing countries could have developed industries focused more heavily on their own expanding domestic markets. Such a growth model might have progressed a little more slowly in the beginning, but it would have provided a foundation for political integration and social solidarity that would contrast sharply with the present model, in which domestic markets are permanently constrained by the voracious appetite of foreign bond holders and investors feeding off the debts of the past. In these countries, such industry as does survive tends to be foreign controlled and primarily oriented toward export markets. Even when it is controlled by nationals, this means that its main interest in the domestic economy is not as a market for its products, but as a source of cheap labour, cheap infrastructure, and subsidized capital. It is easy to see why that is not conducive to the emergence of the social and political integration that is the prerequisite for the emergence of a social market, the only viable and desirable form of capitalism.

Everyone accepts that some state regulation is needed for the market to work efficiently. Even the minimalist state espoused by the neoliberals must "create the conditions for efficient contract enforcement." According to them, such a lean state would have few responsibilities, apart from the clear definition of property rights and the establishment of a legal and correctional system to enforce contracts. Minimal as this may sound, the creation of the conditions for efficient contract enforcement may turn out to be a more complex task than these partisans would like to believe.

The theoretical discussion of this question only reminds us that in theory, anything is possible. Yes, one could imagine a world in which contract enforcement was easily accomplished. In this make-believe world, producers would have no power to influence market prices or the government; consumers would have perfect information and exogenously given, stable preferences; people would readily accept the existing distribution of property rights and the rules that govern the market; and those rules would be constructed so that each individual's rational calculation of the costs and benefits of rule observance would lead them to obey those rules most of the time. In this world, the task of government would be a a minor one. But then, too, there would be no economic problem, since money would grow on trees and the streams would flow with milk and honey.

In the real world, producers are constantly seeking to extend their power over markets. Information is highly imperfect and is systematically hoarded, manipulated, and distorted because it is a source of power in the market and elsewhere. Consumers' tastes are constantly shaped and manipulated by producers. People do not necessarily accept the given distribution of property rights as fair and legitimate. And efficient law enforcement is impossible if everyone merely calculates the individual costs and benefits of compliance. In this real world, the neoliberal minimalist state will create an unstable, conflict-ridden, and ultimately inefficient economy that will be burdened by the ballooning cost of litigation, law enforcement, personal protection, labour supervision, and fraud. In fact, the achievement of a society in which contracts can be easily and efficiently enforced requires the state to understand that no law can be efficiently or effectively enforced unless people believe it to be legitimate and fair. And that requires a public authority that is considered legitimate and fair, which in turn requires both a meaningful political process and a public authority that is able to respond to the wishes of its citizens. But that requires a degree of sovereignty that allows the state to mediate domestic conflicts, to moderate income inequalities, to insure its citizens against catastrophic uncertainty, to exploit social externalities, to protect the "commons" (i.e., the environment) and to build a sense of social solidarity. In short, it requires a social market.

Over the past 20 years, neoliberalism has so undermined that sense of social solidarity in many societies that concerns are being voiced even by more thoughtful conservatives. Thus, a British Conservative backbencher wrote recently that "conservatives have become wary of relying as heavily on the free market as we appeared to do in the 1980s" because they have come to understand that the "neo-Liberals . . . simply think in terms of the individual economic agent without any understanding of the institutions, values and ties which are not just good in themselves but are anyway essential for the free market to thrive." These views are echoed in the pamphlet's Preface, which suggests that the "counter-revolution against a rationalist, abstract and universalist free market triumphalism continues to gather pace"; as well as by a *Financial Times* columnist who ends his discussion of the pamphlet by warning that people now "fear an unravelling of our polity, a disconcerting process whose end is not in sight" (Rogaly, 1994, p. 16).

In the US, this process has gone much, much further. Federal employees are now unable to perform their duties for fear of harassment in many states of the Union. Membership in that country's unofficial militia movement, which vows to protect US citizens from an oppressive federal government, has risen sharply after a "militia" member was charged with the bloody terrorist bombing of a federal building in Oklahoma. Meanwhile, the voters of California's wealthiest county have chosen to default on Orange County's debt rather than accept a marginal increase in taxes. This is surely the road to ungovernability, not that to efficient or sustainable human development.

Meanwhile, austerity measures are slashing social services around the world in the name of deficit reduction and efficiency, but there is a growing realization that this may neither reduce the debt nor improve efficiency. We know from the 1930s that public spending cuts can increase deficits by reducing the level of economic activity and can reduce efficiency because performance losses can outweigh the immediate savings. Even in the corporate sector there is talk of "bulimic corporations" that took downsizing so far that they eroded their long-term viability. At the national level that lesson may take longer to sink in, but by the time it does, the damage that will have been done will be infinitely greater. The efficiency of a society is rooted in the existence of a stable, well-trained labour force that cumulatively develops its skills in regular jobs, requiring only limited supervision to perform well; an efficient infrastructure that provides reliable and low-cost access to transport and communication; a financial system that has the incentive to invest in that society's long-term future; and legal and health systems that enhance the quality of people's lives and protect them from arbitrary or catastrophic risks at a low cost. Current austerity measures do not enhance efficiency when it is defined in this way. Indeed, they pose a significant threat to its achievement.

Efficiency cannot be created, measured, or understood at the level of the firm. It is a social phenomenon, a joint product of past investment in social and economic infrastructure, in the creation of a cohesive and law abiding society, and in specific firms and projects. And the returns generated by economic activities belong to all those who invested in that entire process. That is why taxes are not some appropriation of someone's private income by government but represent both a return on past public investment and a source of future investment. Because this social investment is organized and financed at the national level, the regulation of markets must occur at that level. After all, most of it is about the collection and allocation of the social surplus; the coordination of public and private investment; and the rules determining who has the right to create credit, what risks they can run, and who should bear the costs when things go wrong. Citizenship denotes one's partnership in this joint national enterprise and it confers both the right and the responsibility to determine the ways in which that enterprise should be regulated.

Even from a purely economic point of view, regulation must ensure that the citizens who have invested in a society's future should reap the benefits, or bear the costs, of those investments. This is the material base on which one can construct the sense of social solidarity on which society's cohesion and stability ultimately rest. Without such a base, social and political instability will ultimately destroy efficiency and undermine sustainable human development.

A successful market economy thus depends on the development of a citizenry that is prepared to pay taxes and to obey the law, not primarily out of fear but because it understands the value of social investment and the vital importance of fairness and trust. But that foundation for social efficiency cannot be laid if public authorities cannot respond to the wishes and priorities of their citizens, cannot restrict the competitive process for ethical or political reasons because foreign competitors refuse to do so, cannot punish free riders who wish to take advantage of the social infrastructure but evade their "fair" tax assessment, or cannot resist the demand for policy changes from foreign investors who have no concern or responsibility for the long-term impact of their policy proposals. That is why national sovereignty is a prerequisite for long-run efficiency as well as for sustainable human development.

Those who endlessly celebrate the efficiency gains that are said to result from the freeing of trade and finance must be forced to acknowledge that deeper international entanglements will also impose significant costs if they undermine the social solidarity on which true efficiency ultimately rests. And if they do, those costs could easily outweigh the gains. It is time, in other words, to consider the impact of market liberalization more seriously and more comprehensively. The stakes are too high to leave matters in the hands of the economists.

CONCLUSIONS

The world's current difficulties are not primarily due to the fact that national economic regulations interfere with global allocative efficiency, and the further deregulation of the world's markets will not solve those problems. In fact, that deregulation is now the problem because it has allowed too many economic actors to free themselves of any social, ethical, or political constraints. Moreover, until the competitive process can once again be embedded within such a set of constraints, it will continue to threaten sustainable human development by eroding the social solidarity on which even efficiency ultimately depends.

Human beings are social animals, and sustainable human development requires sustainable social development. But that becomes impossible if societies cannot manage the centrifugal forces that always threaten their solidarity. If humanity is to make progress, it must finally learn to sustain that solidarity by means other than external threats, aggression, or religious fanaticism. History has shown that this is not impossible, though it has also shown that it is difficult. The emergence of territorial, tolerant, and secular welfare states demonstrated that it is possible to unite people as citizens in a collective struggle to create a fair and peaceful society that marginalizes poverty and insecurity while leaving people the freedom to focus their lives on family, community, and friends. Unfortunately, the last 20 years have shown that such outcomes are constantly threatened by the Scylla of excessive conformism and the Charybdis of excessive individualism.

The former threat stems from those who are so anxious to defend that precious social solidarity that they threaten to smother it with a humourless and sterile conformism. The latter threat emanates from the potential free riders who, in a capitalist world, will try to transform their private property rights into more or less absolute rights which can then be used to expand the individual's power and wealth unconstrained by any ethical or social concerns. Globalization gives such people the freedom to jettison their social responsibilities, their moral principles, and even their responsibility for social debts incurred in their name, as citizens. They declare themselves citizens of the world and quite literally take their money and run.

The pendulum will continue to swing between Scylla and Charybdis, if only because each generation lives in a new world and fashions its priorities in accordance with its own experience. At best, we might hope to moderate the amplitude of the pendulum's swings, but even that modest hope seems far-fetched today as the market radicals rush headlong toward anarchy, armed only with their abiding faith in the magic of the market.

Like true ideologues, they respond to apparent policy failures with the fervent demand that their remedies must be applied even more radically. If the freeing of trade and the deregulation of finance have not brought the expected benefits, then it must be time to deregulate the world's labour markets. And after that? Maybe privatization of security services? Or of military power? After all, why should states have exclusive control of such power when we "know" that they are the source of most of our problems? Why should such power not be wielded by the corporations, who are forced to act in the public interest by the iron laws of a competitive market? It is frightening that such thoughts are no longer confined to the lunatic fringe, but it is important to remember that their progress has little or nothing to do with their plausibility or with the support that they receive from the empirical evidence. It has everything to do with power and the production of knowledge in its service.

The current swing of the pendulum is driven by the relentless assertion of the power of private property over the power wielded by public authorities or by ideologically rooted institutions like the church. Globalization is a process that undermines the power of politically constituted public authorities, and it challenges the power of localized ideologies or cultures.

97

In so doing, it frees the power that is rooted in private property rights, and it is those who hold the bulk of those rights who are driving this process forward. Globalization is not some technologically determined, inevitable "fact of life." It is a politically driven process that furthers the interest of countless corporations and individuals seeking to free themselves from the burdens of history and social responsibility. Having acquired their property and their skills as members of particular societies, they would now declare themselves citizens of the world. If "their" society has become too deeply indebted, they wish to be free to move their money into other, less vulnerable currencies; having refused to support the social past investment needed to secure their society's future prosperity, they wish to be free to take advantage of the social investment in other jurisdictions; and, having grown up with the help of extensive state support, they would now lay claim to all of the resulting profits while denying potential competitors the state support that they would need to overcome any barriers to entry.

Of course, this process of social asset-stripping will not endure. It is not efficient, it is not just, and it is not sustainable. In time the world will once again come to understand that sustainable human development is a social enterprise that cannot succeed unless those who take decisions on behalf of society and those who take advantage of the resulting social investment, must bear full responsibility for their actions, both as individuals and as citizens. So long as that is not the case, sustainable human development will remain a fading dream for the vast majority of people. We know that the pendulum will reverse its swing, but we must struggle to ensure that it does so before too much more damage is done.

Manfred Bienefeld is a Professor in the School of Public Administration at Carlton University in Ottawa. He has worked extensively in the development field, especially in East Africa, the Pacific and the Caribbean. Currently his main research interests are in the structural adjustment, financial deregulation and the economic function of nation states. He has worked for numerous international agencies and national governments and published widely on development questions.

Notes

1. It is noteworthy that after almost ten years of enforcing debt repayment through structural adjustment programmes, the 1989 *World Development Report* saw fit to remind its astonished readers that the lending and borrowing that led to the debt crisis of the 1980s should be seen as evidence that "even competitive financial markets can make mistakes" (World Bank, 1989, p. 4). But if that is so, then the costs of those mistakes should surely have been distributed rather differently. As it was, structural adjustment was premised on the idea that the debt had to be repaid and it was the responsibility of the debtor countries to deflate and restructure their economies to do so, whatever the cost. And, in many cases, the cost was very high.

2. Taylor concludes one of his careful empirical surveys as follows: "Thinking about alternatives to the WC (Washington Consensus) package is important, because it has been applied widely with modest results and high social costs. The WC's major intellectual drawback is that its underlying assumptions and empirical generalizations do not fit the facts" (1993, p. 39). And Sachs suggests, "The basic ideas in most stabilization programs supported by the IMF and the World Bank are quite straightforward.. The sobering point is programs of this sort have been adopted repeatedly, and have failed repeatedly over the past thirty years" (1989, p. 29). Interestingly enough, Sachs remains a strong supporter of the neoliberal policy prescriptions because he has persuaded himself that "there is no alternative."

3. The IMF's 1987 study of the *Theoretical Foundations* concludes by noting that under certain circumstances, its policies could trigger a destructive and costly destabilization of an economy (IMF, 1987, p. 55). What it did not acknowledge was that the "special conditions" that were said to create this danger applied to most of the countries that came to the IMF for help.

4. Despite the rhetoric about the neutral nature of these trade regimes, the truth is that in South Korea, the

export drive was undertaken without any significant reduction in import tariffs. Moreover, these tariffs were highly discretionary, varying sharply from sector to sector and even from product to product. And those variations were designed to complement the country's industrial policy objectives. The claim that this amounts to a "neutral trade regime" because a similarly discretionary set of export subsidies happened to be of roughly equal value in aggregate, misrepresents the point at issue. The fact is that these countries made extensive use of trade barriers to support their industrial policies and to shape patterns of investment within the economy. This is extensively documented in the previously cited literature, but it is also evident from the data presented by the World Bank in its 1985 *World Development Report* (ch. 5).

5. *The Economist* recently reported that rising income inequality was an increasingly serious problem in the industrial countries. According to this authoritative voice of conservatism, "It is no coincidence that the biggest increases in income inequalities have occurred in economies such as those of America, Britain, and New Zealand, where free-market economic policies have been pursued most zealously" (*The Economist*, 1994, p. 19).

References

Amsden, A. 1989. *Asia's Next Giant: South Korea's Late Industrialisation.* New York: Oxford University Press.

Beaucheshe, E. 1994. "Social Programs Give Canadian Firms Edge, Study Says," *The Ottawa Citizen,* 26 April, p. D2.

Brundtland, G. H. 1987. *Our Common Future.* World Commission on Environment and Development. New York: Oxford University Press.

Bienefeld, M. A. 1982. "The International Context for National Development Strategies: Constraints and Opportunities in a Changing World," in M. A. Bienefeld and M. Godfrey (eds.), *The Struggle for Development.* Chichester: John Wiley & Sons.

Bienefeld, M. A. 1983. "Efficiency, Expertise, NICs and the Accelerated Development Report." *Institute of Development Studies Bulletin, IDS Sussex (UK),* 14 (1) (January).

Bienefeld, M. A. 1988. "The Significance of the Newly Industrialising Countries for the Development Debate." *Studies in Political Economy* 25 (Spring), pp. 7-40.

Bienefeld, M. A. 1989. "The Lessons of History and the Developing World." *Monthly Review* 41 (3) (July-August), pp. 9-41.

Bienefeld, M. A. 1993. "Structural Adjustment: Debt Collection Device or Development Policy?" Advanced Development Management Program Series No. 5. Institute of Comparative Culture, Sophia University: Tokyo.

Bienefeld, M. A. 1995. "A Comment on Keith Griffin's 1994 CASID Address on 'Global Prospects for Development and Human Society.'" *Canadian Journal of Development Studies* (forthcoming).

Collier, P., and C. Mayer. 1989. "The Assessment: Financial Liberalization, Financial Systems, and Economic Growth." *Oxford Review of Economic Policy* 5 (4).

Economist, The. 1994. "For Richer, for Poorer." 5 November, p. 19.

Freeman, Richard, 1992. "Labour Market Institutions and Policies: Help or Hindrance to Economic Development?" *Proceedings of the World Bank Annual Conference on Development Economics.* Washington, DC: World Bank, pp. 117-156.

Griffin, K. 1995. "Global Prospects for Development and Human Society." *Canadian Journal of Development Studies* (forthcoming).

Hahn, F. 1982. "Reflections on the Invisible Hand" *Lloyd's Bank Review* (April).

Heller, P. S., et al. 1988. "The Implications of Fund-Supported Adjustment Programs for Poverty." IMF Occasional Paper No. 58. Washington, DC: IMF.

IMF. 1987. "Theoretical Aspects of the Design of Fund-Supported Adjustment Programs." IMF Occasional Paper No. 55. Washington, DC: IMF.

Khan, M. S., and Knight. 1985. "Fund-Supported Adjustment Programs and Economic Growth." IMF Occasional Paper No. 41. Washington, DC: IMF.

Lall, S. 1994. "The East Asian Miracle: Does the Bell Toll for Industrial Strategy?" *World Development* 22 (4) (April).

Marris, S. 1984. "Managing the World Economy: Will We Ever Learn?" Princeton Essays in International Finance No. 155.

Mayer, C. 1987. "The Assessment: Financial Systems and Corporate Investment." *Oxford Review of Economic Policy* 5 (3) (Autumn).

Milward, A. S. 1984. *The Reconstruction of Europe 1945-51*. London: Methuen.

Polanyi, K. 1944. *The Great Transformation*. Boston: Beacon Press (1957 edition).

Rodrik, D. 1990. "How Should Structural Adjustment Programs Be Designed?" *World Development* 18 (7), pp. 933-947.

Rogaly, J. 1994. "Think of It As Protection." *Financial Times* (London) 11/12 (February 1995), Sec. 2, p. I.

Sachs, J. 1987. "Trade and Exchange Rate Policies in Growth-Oriented Adjustment Programs," in V. Corbo et al. (eds.), *Growth Oriented Adjustment Programs*. Washington, DC: IMF/IBRD.

Seers, D. 1983. *The Political Economy of Nationalism*. New York: Oxford University Press.

Senghaas, D. 1985. *The European Experience*. Dover, NH: Berg.

Taylor, L. 1988. *Varieties of Stabilization Experience*. New York: Oxford University Press.

Taylor, L. 1993. "Stabilization, Adjustment and Reform," in L. Taylor (ed.), *The Rocky Road to Reform*. Cambridge, MA: MIT Press.

UNCTAD. 1994. *Trade and Development Report, 1994*. Geneva: UNCTAD.

Wade, R. 1990. *Governing the Market: Economic Theory and the Role of Government in East Asian Industrialization*. Princeton, NJ: Princeton University Press.

Williamson, J. 1994. "In Search of a Manual for Technopols," in J. Williamson (ed.), *The Political Economy of Reform*. Washington, DC: Institute of International Economics.

World Bank. 1981. *Accelerated Development in sub-Saharan Africa: An Agenda for Action* (The "Berg Report"). Washington, DC: World Bank.

World Bank. 1985. *World Development Report*. Washington, DC: World Bank.

World Bank. 1992. *World Bank Support for Industrialization in Korea, India and Indonesia*. Washington, DC: World Bank Operation Evaluations Department, World Bank.

World Bank. 1993. *The East Asian Miracle: Economic Growth and Public Policy*. Washington, DC: World Bank.

Yagci, F., et al. 1983. "Structural Adjustment Lending: An Evaluation of Program Design." World Bank Staff Working Paper No. 735. Washington, DC: World Bank.

PART 2

RE-THINKING GOVERNANCE: THE POLITICAL EMPOWERMENT OF WOMEN

"We urge the World Conference (on Human Rights) to declare that women's access to decision-making power in all fields should be a worldwide priority and recommend (that)...national governments set goals and timetables to secure equal representation of women at all levels of decision-making, including in...politics, development and the economy, and to establish measures for the effective implementation of them."

— Position Paper of the Working Group on Women's Rights at the NGO Forum at the World Conference on Human Rights, 1993

AGENCY AND WELL-BEING: THE DEVELOPMENT AGENDA

AMARTYA SEN

Over the last couple of decades, an important evolution has begun to alter the basic nature of the women's movements in developing countries. Not long ago, the tasks faced by these movements were primarily aimed at working toward achieving better treatment for women — a more square deal. The concentration was mainly on women's well-being — and it was a much-needed corrective. The objectives have, however, gradually evolved and broadened from this "welfarist" focus to incorporate — and emphasize — the active role of women's agency. No longer the passive recipient of welfare-enhancing help, women are increasingly seen — by men as well as women — as active agents of change: the dynamic promoters of social transformations that can alter the lives of both women and men.

The nature of this shift in concentration and emphasis is sometimes missed because of the *overlap* between the two approaches. The active agency of women cannot, in any serious way, ignore the urgency of rectifying many inequalities that blight the well-being of women and subject them to unequal treatment; thus, the agency role must be much concerned with women's well-being also. Similarly, coming from the other end, any practical attempt at enhancing the well-being of women cannot but draw on the agency of women themselves in bringing about such a change. So the *well-being aspect* and the *agency aspect* of women's movements inevitably have a substantial intersection. And yet they cannot but be different at a foundational level, since the role of a person as an "agent" is fundamentally different from the role of the same person as a "patient." The fact that the agent may have to see herself as a patient as well does not alter the additional modalities and responsibilities that are inescapably associated with the agency of a person.[1]

This paper addresses the "agency" aspect of the task and its relation with the "well-being" aspect, in the specific context of women's agency in the developing countries in the contemporary world. This distinction and the shift in focus in the women's movement are seen here from a little distance. That distance is perhaps to some extent inescapable in any investigation undertaken by a male analyst (no matter how supportive of the cause he might be), but there may actually also be some merit in having a slightly distant picture — if only to enrich the different perspectives in which a social change can be observed and analysed.

The broadening of the tasks of women's movements as it has evolved is well reflected by the wide-ranging manifesto *Towards a Women's Development Agenda for the 21st Century*, presented by UNIFEM in early 1995 and identifying a number of "key challenges" that women's development agenda must address at this time.[2] The list ends with the exacting "challenge of promoting ethical principles of good governance that recognize women's leadership and decision-making roles." Women's agency is, obviously, central to this particular challenge.

In the deliberations that will occur at the Fourth World Conference on Women in Beijing, the agency issue must be extensively discussed. It is important in this context to make the agency role of women adequately concrete, with precise illustrations of the extensive reach and power of women's agency. It is particularly appropriate in this context to see the relevance of women's agency in advancing those variables which are widely recognized as being crucial to the process of development itself. In this short essay, I shall try to discuss briefly this general approach and also seek illustrations to make the "development connection" more concrete.

WELL-BEING AND AGENCY: ASPECTS OF PERSONHOOD

I begin with some conceptual issues. The medieval distinction between an "agent" and a "patient," to which I made reference earlier, is critical to the broadening of "women's agenda." A *patient* is a person whose well-being should interest others and who needs the help of people in general. An *agent*, on the other hand, has an active role in pursuing whatever goals she has reasons to support and promote. These goals can be as broad as the agent can reasonably value, though they would typically include, inter alia, her own well-being. In terms of objectives, the agency role can, thus, be much *broader* than the promotion of self-welfare.

To see individuals as entities that experience and have well-being is an important recognition, but to stop there would amount to a very restricted view of the personhood of these people. Focusing on the agency role is, thus, central to recognizing people as responsible persons: not only are we well or ill, but also we act or refuse to act, and can choose to act one way rather than another. And thus, we — women *and* men — must take responsibility for doing things or not doing them. It makes a difference, and we have to take note of that difference. This elementary acknowledgment — though simple enough in principle — can be exacting in its implications, both to social analysis and to practical reason and action.[3]

The changing focus of women's movements is, thus, a crucial *addition* to previous concerns; it is not a rejection of those concerns. The old concentration on the well-being of women, or to be more exact, on the "ill-being" of women, was not, of course, pointless. The relative deprivations in the well-being of women were — and are — certainly present in the world in which we live, and are clearly important for social justice, including justice for women. For example, there is plenty of evidence that identifies the biologically "contrary" — socially generated — "excess mortality" of women in Asia and North Africa (with gigantic numbers of "missing women" — "missing" in the sense of being dead as a result of gender bias in the distribution of health care and other necessities).[4] That problem is unquestionably important for the well-being — indeed even the survival — of women, and cannot but figure prominently in exposing the treatment of women as "less than equal." There are also pervasive indications of culturally neglected needs of women across the world. There are excellent reasons for bringing these deprivations to light and keeping the removal of these iniquities very firmly on the agenda: women are certainly the victims of various social iniquities.

But it is also the case that the limited role of women's active agency seriously afflicts the lives of *all* people — men as well as women, children as well as adults. While there is every reason not to slacken the concern about women's well-being and ill-being, and to continue to pay attention to the sufferings and deprivations of women, there is also an urgent and basic necessity, particularly at this time, to take an agent-oriented approach to the women's agenda.

The agenda, thus, must transcend the view of women as patient solicitors of social equity, and see women as potentially active agents of major social change. There is not only the question of what is *done to* women, but also the issue of *how* this is done — in particular, through whose decisions and operations. And this issue, in turn, relates to the question of what is done to less privileged men, and to children of either sex, and how that comes about. Once this broader set of agency questions is put firmly on the agenda, the focus of the agenda has to include what women can do — for themselves and also for others. What began as an inquiry into women's passive misfortunes can thereby get transformed into an analysis of women's active capability to make the world a more livable place.

WOMEN'S AGENCY AND OWN WELL-BEING

Perhaps the most immediate argument for focusing on women's *agency* may be precisely the role that such an agency can play in removing the iniquities that depress the *well-being* of women. Empirical work in recent years has brought out very clearly how the relative respect and regard for women's well-being is strongly influenced by such variables as women's ability to earn an independent income, to find employment outside the home, to have ownership rights, and to have literacy and be educated participants in decisions within and outside the family. Indeed, even the survival disadvantage of women compared with men in developing countries seems to go down sharply — and may even get eliminated — as progress is made in these agency aspects.[5]

Different characteristics such as women's earning power, economic role outside the family, literacy and education, property rights, and so on may at first sight appear to be rather diverse and disparate. But what they all have in common is their positive contribution in adding force to women's agency through independence and empowerment. For example, working outside the home and earning an independent income tend to have a clear impact on enhancing the social standing of a woman in the household and the society. Her contribution to the prosperity of the family is then more visible, and she also has more voice, because of being less dependent on others. Further, outside employment often has useful "educational" effects, in terms of exposure to the world outside the household, making her agency more effective. Similarly, women's education strengthens women's agency and also tends to make it more informed and skilled. The ownership of property can also make women more powerful in family decisions.

> *"It is necessary to change the prevailing social paradigm of gender to usher in a new generation of women and men working together to create a more humane world order."*
>
> — *World Summit for Social Development Declaration and Programme of Action, Chapter I, para. 7.*

The diverse variables identified in the literature, thus, have a unified empowering role. This role has to be related to the acknowledgement that women's power — economic independence as well as social emancipation — can have far-reaching impacts on the forces and organizing principles that govern divisions *within* the family, and can, in particular, influence what are implicitly accepted as women's "entitlements."[6]

To understand the process, we can start by noting the fact that women and men have both *congruent* and *conflicting* interests affecting family living. Decision-making in the family, thus, tends to take the form of the pursuit of cooperation, with some agreed solution — usually implicit — of the conflicting aspects. Such "cooperative conflict" is a general feature of many group relations, and an analysis of cooperative conflicts can provide a useful way of understanding the influences that operate on the "deal" that women get in family divisions. There are gains to be made by both parties through following implicitly agreed-upon patterns of behaviour. But there are many alternative possible agreements — some more favourable to one party than others. The choice of one such cooperative arrangement from the set of alternative possibilities leads to a particular distribution of joint benefits.[7]

Conflicts between the partially disparate interests within family living are typically resolved through implicitly agreed-upon patterns of behaviour that may or may not be particularly egalitarian. The very nature of family living — sharing a home and leading joint lives — requires that the elements of conflict must not be explicitly emphasized (dwelling on conflicts will be seen as a sign of a "failed" union), and sometimes the deprived woman would not even have a clear assessment of the extent of her relative deprivation. Similarly, the perception of who is doing how much "productive" work, or who is "contributing" how much to the family's prosperity, can be very influential, even though the underlying "theory" regarding how "contributions" or "productivity" are to be assessed may rarely be discussed explicitly.

The perception of individual contributions and appropriate entitlements of women and men plays a major role in the division of a family's joint benefits between men and women.[8] As a result, the circumstances that influence these perceptions of contributions and appropriate entitlements (such as a woman's ability to earn an independent income, to work outside the home, to be educated, to own property) can have a crucial bearing on these divisions. The impact of greater empowerment and independent agency of women, thus, includes the correction of the iniquities that blight the lives and well-being of women *vis-à-vis* men. The lives that women save through more powerful agency may be their own.

That, however, is not the whole story. There are other lives — men's and children's — also involved. In the next two sections, I discuss some evidence of the reach of women's agency in the regional contrasts within India.[9] The illustrations will concentrate on the role of women's agency in (1) reducing child mortality and (2) restraining fertility. Both deal with concerns that are central to the process of development, and while they clearly do influence the well-being of women as well, their relevance is undoubtedly substantially wider.

CHILD SURVIVAL AND THE AGENCY OF WOMEN

These positive links between women's empowerment and agency, on the one hand, and the status and well-being of women, on the other, are also relevant to the survival of children (girls, of course, but also boys). The influence works through many channels, but perhaps most immediately, it works through the importance that mothers typically attach to the welfare of the children, and the opportunity they have, when their agency is respected and empowered, to influence family decisions in that direction.

Countries with basic gender inequality — including India, Pakistan, Bangladesh, China, Iran, Egypt, and so on — often tend to have higher female mortality of infants and children, in contrast with the situation in Europe or America or sub-Saharan Africa, where female children typically have a substantial survival advantage. In India itself, male and female death rates in the 0–4 age group are now quite close to each other in terms of the average for the country as a whole, but a strong female disadvantage persists in regions where gender inequality is particularly pronounced, including most states of north India.[10]

In an important statistical contribution, Drèze, Guio, and Murthi have presented an analysis of variations in under-five mortality rates between different districts of India in 1981 (the latest year for which adequately detailed data are available).[11] One aspect of this analysis is an examination of the relationship between an index of female disadvantage in child survival (reflecting the *ratio* of female to male mortality in the 0–4 age group at the district level) and a number of other district-level variables such as the female literacy rate, the female labour force participation, the incidence of poverty, the level of urbanization, the availability of medical facilities, and the proportion of socially underprivileged groups (scheduled castes and scheduled tribes) in the population.[12]

What should we expect to be the impact of the different agency variables — in this case women's participation in the labour force and women's literacy and education — on child survival? It is natural to expect this connection to be entirely positive as far as women's literacy and education are concerned. But in the case of women's labour force participation, researchers have tended to identify factors working in different directions. First, involvement in gainful employment has many positive effects on a woman's agency roles, which often include greater emphasis being placed on child care and greater ability to attach more priority to child care in joint family decisions. Second, since men typically show great reluctance to share the domestic chores, this greater desire for more priority being given to child care may not be easy to execute on the part of the women when they are saddled with the "double burden" of household work and outside employment. The net effect could, thus, go in either direction. In the Drèze, Guio, and Murthi study, the analysis of Indian district-level data does not yield any statistically significant, definite relation.[13]

Female literacy, on the other hand, is found to have an unambiguously negative and statistically significant reducing impact on under-five mortality, even after controlling for male literacy. This is consistent with growing evidence of a close relationship between female literacy and child survival in many countries, including India.[14] In this case, the greater empowerment and agency role of women are not reduced in effectiveness by the problems arising from inflexible male participation in child care and household work.

There is also the further issue of *gender bias* in child survival (as opposed to *total* child survival). For this variable, it turns out that female labour force participation rate and female literacy rate *both* have very strong ameliorating effects on the extent of female disadvantage in child survival, with higher levels of female literacy and labour force participation being strongly associated with lower levels of relative female disadvantage in child survival. By contrast, variables that relate to the *general* level of development and modernization *either* turn out to have no statistically significant effect *or* suggest that modernization (when not accompanied by empowerment of women) can even *strengthen*, rather than weaken, the gender bias in child survival. This applies *inter alia* to urbanization, male literacy, the availability of medical facilities, and the level of poverty (with higher levels of poverty being associated with *higher* female-male ratios). In so far as a positive connection does exist in India between the level of development and reduced gender bias in survival, it seems to work mainly *through* variables that are directly related to women's agency, such as female literacy and female labour force participation.

It is worth making a further comment on the impact of enhanced women's agency through greater female education. Drèze, Guio, and Murthi's statistical analysis indicates that, in quantitative terms, the effect of female literacy on child mortality is extraordinarily large. It is more powerful an influence in reducing child mortality than the other variables which also work in that general direction. For instance, keeping other variables constant, an increase in the crude female literacy rate from, say, 22 per cent (the actual 1981 figure for India) to 75 per cent reduces the predicted value of under-five mortality for males and females combined from 156 per thousand (again, the actual 1981 figure) to 110 per thousand.

The powerful effect of female literacy contrasts with the comparatively ineffective roles of, say, male literacy or general poverty reduction as instruments of child mortality reduction. The increase in male literacy over the same range (from 22 to 75 per cent) only reduces under-five mortality from 169 per thousand to 141 per thousand. And a 50 per cent reduction in the incidence of poverty (from the actual 1981 level) only reduces the predicted value of under-five mortality from 156 per thousand to 153 per thousand.

Here again, the message seems to be that some variables relating to women's agency (in this case, female literacy) often play a much more important role in promoting social well-being (in particular, child survival) than variables relating to the general level of opulence in the society. These findings have important practical implications, since both types of variables can be influenced through public action, but respectively require rather different forms of intervention.[15]

AGENCY, EMANCIPATION AND FERTILITY REDUCTION

The agency role of women is also particularly important for the reduction of fertility rates. The adverse effects of high birth rates powerfully include the denial of substantial freedoms — through persistent child-bearing and -rearing — routinely imposed on many Asian and African women. There is, as a result, a close connection between women's *well-being* and women's *agency* in bringing about a change in the fertility pattern. It is, thus, not surprising that reductions in birth rates have often followed the enhancement of women's status and power.

These connections are indeed reflected in interdistrict variations of the total fertility rate in India. In fact, among all the variables included in the analysis presented by Drèze, Guio, and Murthi, the *only* ones that have a statistically significant effect on fertility are female literacy and female labour-force participation. Once again, the importance of women's agency emerges forcefully from this analysis, especially in comparison with the weaker effects of variables relating to general economic progress.

The link between female literacy and fertility is particularly clear. This connection has been widely observed in other countries, and it is not surprising that it should emerge in India too.[16] The unwillingness of educated women to be shackled to continuous child-rearing clearly plays a role in bringing about this change. Education also makes the horizon of vision wider and, at a more mundane level, helps to disseminate the knowledge of family planning. And of course educated women tend to have greater freedom to exercise their agency in family decisions, including in matters of fertility and childbirth.

The particular case of the most socially advanced state in India, that is, Kerala, is also worth noting here because of its particular success in fertility reduction based on women's agency. While the total fertility rate for India as a whole is still as high as 3.7, that rate in Kerala has now fallen below the "replacement level" to 1.8. (even lower than China's fertility rate of 2.0). Kerala's high level of female education has been particularly influential in bringing about this decline in birth rate, falling from 44 per thousand in 1951–61 to 18 by 1991. Since female agency and literacy are important also in the reduction of mortality rates, that is another — more indirect — route through which women's agency (including female literacy) may have helped to reduce birth rates, since there is some evidence that a reduction of death rates, especially of children, tends to contribute to the reduction of fertility rates. Kerala has also had other favourable features for women's empowerment and agency, including a greater recognition of women's property rights for a substantial and influential part of the community.[17]

Recently there has been a good deal of discussion of the imperative need to reduce birth rates in the world, and those in India in particular. China's achievement in cutting down birth rates over a short period through rather draconian measures has suggested to many the need for countries such as India to emulate China in this respect. These coercive methods do involve many social costs, including the direct one of the loss of the effective freedom of people — in particular, women — to decide themselves on matters that are clearly rather personal. It is perhaps worth noting in this context that compulsion has not produced a lower birth rate in China compared with what Kerala has already achieved entirely through voluntary channels, relying on the educated agency of women.

In fact, it is not quite clear exactly how much *extra* reduction in birth rate China has been able to achieve by resorting to coercive methods. China has brought about many social and economic changes that have enhanced the power of women (for example, through raising female literacy rates and expanding female participation rates in the labour force) and made conditions more favourable to fertility reduction through these voluntary channels. These factors would themselves have reduced the birth rates (well below that of the Indian average, for example). While China seems to get some unscrutinized credit for its coercive measures, it gets far too little credit for other — supportive — policies that have helped to cut down the birth rate in China.

Kerala's low birth rate — lower than China's — also suggests that these supportive influences may be effective enough to render compulsion largely redundant, even if it were acceptable otherwise. As has been noted before, Kerala not only has a much higher level of female literacy (87 per cent) than India as a whole (39 per cent), it is also well ahead of China's female literacy rate (68 per cent).[18] The fact that the ranking of female literacy is exactly the same as that of birth rates is in line with *other* evidence for the close connection between the two. It might also be mentioned here, in passing, that the increasing popularity of sex-selective abortion of female foetuses in China, as well as in parts of India, contrasts sharply with the absence of such a practice in Kerala. While the solution of this problem has been sought in India through banning sex-selective abortion — a ban that may well be evaded easily enough — the real resolution of the problem must lie ultimately in a shift in family preference away from the rejection of female children. Here again, the agency role of women would be quite crucial as would be the influences that enhance that agency of women, including female education and the opportunity to work outside the home.[19]

A FINAL REMARK

The UNIFEM manifesto is right to claim that "the women's development agenda is not just for women," and to identify the role of "a vision by women for the transformation of the global development agenda." The focus on the agency role of women has a direct bearing on women's well-being, but its reach goes well beyond that.

In this essay, I have tried to present some conceptual clarifications in the distinction between — and interrelations of — agency and well-being, and then have gone on to illustrate the reach and power of women's agency in promoting child survival and helping to reduce fertility rates. Both these matters have general developmental interest that go well beyond the pursuit specifically of female well-being, though — as we have seen — female well-being is also directly involved and has a crucial intermediating role in enhancing these general achievements.

These illustrations can be supplemented by considering the functioning of women in other fields, including in political and social leadership.[20] The development agenda has to pay attention to these issues as well. Understanding the role and extensive reach of women's agency is one of the momentous challenges the contemporary world faces at this time. The integration of the agency role of women in the general development agenda must receive the attention it deserves. A lot would depend on it.

Amartya Sen is a Lamont University Professor and Professor of Economics and Philosophy at Harvard University. He has written on welfare economics, social choice theory, development economics, economic methodology, and also in ethics and political philosophy. He is Past President of the Econometrics Society, the International Economics Association and the American Economics Association.

This article draws upon the following publications by the author: "Population: Delusion and Reality," *New York Review of Books*, 22 September 1994; and the forthcoming book, jointly written with Jean Drèze, *India: Economic Development and Social Opportunity*, Oxford: Oxford University Press, 1995.

Notes

1. My paper "Well-being, Agency and Freedom: The Dewey Lectures 1984," *The Journal of Philosophy* 82 (April 1985) investigates the philosophical distinction between the "agency aspect" and the "well-being aspect" of a person, and attempts to identify the far-reaching practical implications of this distinction, applied to many fields (not only to gender inequality — important as it is).

2. Noeleen Heyzer, "Toward a Women's Development Agenda for the 21st Century," New York: UNIFEM, 10 February 1995.

3. The relevance of this distinction to ethics, political philosophy, and social thought is explored in my "Well-being, Agency and Freedom," cited in note 1.

4. Alternative statistical estimates of the extent of "extra mortality" of women in many countries in Asia and north Africa are discussed in my "Missing Women," *British Medical Journal*, March 1992, and Stephan Klasen, "'Missing Women' Reconsidered," *World Development*, 1994.

5. There is a vast literature on this; my own attempts at analysing and using the available evidence can be found in "Gender and Cooperative Conflicts," in Irene Tinker (ed.), *Persistent Inequalities*, New York: Oxford University Press, 1990, and "More than a Hundred Million Women are Missing," *New York Review of Books*, 20 December 1990.

6. These issues have been discussed in my *Resources, Values and Development*, Oxford: Blackwell, and Cambridge, MA: Harvard University Press, 1984; and in "Gender and Cooperative Conflict" and "More Than a Hundred Million Women Are Missing," both cited in note 5. A pioneering study of this general field was presented in Ester Boserup's classic work *Women's Role in Economic Development*, London: Allen & Unwin, 1971. The recent literature on gender inequality in developing countries includes a number of interesting and important studies of different types of determining variables. Examples of the main arguments can be found in Martha Loutfi (ed.), *Rural Work: Unequal Partners in Development*, Geneva: ILO, 1980; Mark R. Rosenzweig and T. Paul Schultz, "Market Opportunities, Genetic Endowment, and Intrafamily Resource Distribution," *American Economic Review* 72 (1982); Myra Buvinic, M. Lycette and W.P. McGreevy (eds.), *Women and Poverty in the Third World*, Baltimore, MD: Johns Hopkins University Press, 1983; Pranab Bardhan, *Land, Labor and Rural Poverty*, New York: Columbia University Press, 1984; Devaki Jain and Nirmala Banerjee (eds.), *Tyranny of the Household: Investigative Essays in Women's Work*, New Delhi: Vikas, 1985; Gita Sen and C. Sen, "Women's Domestic Work and Economic Activity," *Economic and Political Weekly* 20 (1985); Martha Alter Chen, *A Quiet Revolution: Women in Transition in Rural Bangladesh*, Dhaka: BRAC, 1986; Jere Behrman and B.L.Wolfe, "How Does Mother's Schooling Affect Family Health, Nutrition, Medical Care Usage, and Household Sanitation?" *Journal of Econometrics* 36 (1987); Monica Das Gupta, "Selective Discrimination against Female Children in India," *Population and Development Review* 13 (1987); Gita Sen and Caren Grown, *Development, Crises, and Alternative Visions: Third World Women's Perspectives*, New York: Monthly Review Press, 1987; Alaka Basu, *Culture, the Status of Women and Demographic Behaviour*, Oxford: Clarendon Press, 1992; Nancy Folbre, Barbara Bergmann, Bina Agarwal and Maria Flore (eds.), *Women's Work in the World Economy*, London: Macmillan, 1992; United Nations ESCAP, *Integration of Women's Concerns into Development Planning in Asia and the Pacific*, New York: United Nations, 1992; Bina Agarwal, *A Field of One's Own*, Cambridge: Cambridge University Press, 1995; among many other contributions. Bina Agarwal's work particularly stresses the important effects of land ownership by women.

7. Gender divisions within the family are sometimes studied as "bargaining problems"; the literature includes, among many other contributions, Marilyn Manser and Murray Brown, "Marriage and Household Decision Making: A Bargaining Analysis," *International Economic Review* 21 (1980); M. B. McElroy and M. J. Horney, "Nash Bargained Household Decisions: Toward a Generalization of Theory of Demand," *International Economic Review* 22 (1981); Shelly Lundberg and Robert Pollak, "Noncooperative Bargaining Models of Marriage," *American Economic Review* 84 (1994). For approaches different from that of "bargaining models," see Nancy Folbre, "Hearts and Spades: Paradigms of Household Economics," *World Development* 14 (1986); J. Brannen and G. Wilson (eds.), *Give and Take in Families*, London: Allen & Unwin; and Marianne A. Ferber and Julie A. Nelson (eds.), *Beyond Economic Man*, Chicago: Chicago University Press, 1993; among other contributions.

8. On this, see my "Gender and Cooperative Conflict," cited in note 5. See also the papers of Julie Nelson, Shelley Lundberg, Robert Pollak, Diana Strassman, Myra Strober, Viviana Zelizer in the "1994 Papers and Proceedings," *American Economic Review* 84 (1994).

9. These two sections draw heavily on chapter 7 of my forthcoming joint book with Jean Drèze, *India: Economic Development and Social Opportunity*, Oxford: Oxford University Press, 1995. The book, incidentally, views women's empowerment as a central requirement of economic and social development of India — not just for "gender justice."

10. In 1991, the death rate per thousand in the 0–4 age group was 25.6 for males and 27.5 for females at the all-India level. The female mortality rate in that age group was lower than the male mortality rate in Andhra Pradesh, Assam, Himachal Pradesh, Kerala, and Tamil Nadu, but higher in all the other major Indian states. The female disadvantage was most pronounced in Bihar, Haryana, Madhya Pradesh, Punjab, Rajasthan, and Uttar Pradesh.

11. Jean Drèze, Anne-Catherine Guio, and Mamta Murthi, "Demographic Outcomes, Economic Development and Women's Agency." Discussion paper, Centre for Development Economics, Delhi School of Economics.

12. There were apparently not enough data with adequate interdistrict variations to examine the impact of different forms of property rights, which are relatively more uniform across India. On an isolated basis, there is, of course, the strong and much-discussed example of the Nairs in Kerala, who have had matrilineal inheritance for a long time (an association that confirms, rather than contradicts, insofar as it goes, the positive impact of female property rights on child survival in general and the survival of female children in particular).

13. There is, it appears, a positive association between female labour-force participation and under-five mortality in these fits, but this association is not statistically significant.

14. See, among other important contributions, J. C. Caldwell, "Routes to Low Mortality in Poor Countries," *Population and Development Review* 12 (1986); and J. R. Behrman, and B. L. Wolfe, "How Does Mother's Schooling Affect Family Health, Nutrition, Medical Care Usage, and Household Sanitation?" *Journal of Econometrics* 36 (1987).

15. On this, see Drèze and Sen, *India*, cited in note 9.

16. See, for example, the studies cited in footnote 14. See also Robert J. Barro, and Jong-Wha Lee, "International Comparisons of Educational Attainment," Washington, DC: World Bank, 1993 (paper presented at a conference on How Do National Policies Affect Long-Run Growth?; and Robert Cassen et al., *Population and Development: Old Debates, New Conclusions*, Washington, DC: Transaction Books for Overseas Development Council, 1994.

17. On these and related general issues, see my "Population: Delusion and Reality," *New York Review of Books*, 22 September 1994.

18. Life expectancy at birth in Kerala is 73 years for women and 69 years for men. The average figure (71 years) is only marginally higher than China's average (69 years), but the gap is larger for women, in favour of Kerala. The gap is largest in infant mortality rates: 17 for boys and 16 for girls in Kerala, and 28 for boys and 33 for girls in China.

19. Kerala is not alone in India in having achieved a rapid reduction of the birth rate without compulsion. A somewhat similar success has also occurred in Tamil Nadu, where the total fertility rate (2.2 in 1991) is now very close to the replacement level (down from 3.5 in 1979). In this achievement, women's reasoned agency

and informed participation seem to have played significant parts, along with well-organized voluntary programmes at the state level. What is also quite striking is that the states where fertility decline remains extremely slow (including Uttar Pradesh, Bihar, Rajasthan, and Madhya Pradesh) are precisely the ones with low female literacy and other handicaps that restrain women's agency role. Interestingly enough, these states have also used some forms of coercion in the cause of birth control — evidently with rather little success.

20. UNDP's *Human Development Report 1995*, New York: United Nations, 1995, presents an intercountry investigation of gender differences in social, political, and business leadership, in addition to reporting on gender inequality in terms of more conventional indicators.

DEVELOPMENT AS A MORAL CONCEPT: WOMEN'S PRACTICES AS DEVELOPMENT PRACTICES

ELIZABETH REID

Two decades after the exuberance of the first International Women's Year Conference in Mexico City and well into the last decade of a century of struggle, we are still contending with the hard "How?" questions. How can the values of care and respect be integrated into daily life? How can the well-being of those who are subjugated and daily humiliated, assaulted, or neglected be improved? How can relationships become sanctuaries, ways of being with another person that do not cause misery or hardship? How can power and wealth be differently accessed and differently used? How can women contribute their insights, skills, and knowledge to the quest for different and better ways of living and interrelating? How do we bring about different ways of living in this world?

The uneven distribution of time, income, property, legal and social entitlements, and public representation has been well documented, at least between women and men. The basis for outrage is now incontrovertible. Courage, competence, and articulateness have marked the protagonists. But change has been limited. Development, it is now argued, should have a human face, but that face is still rarely female. Most women are not among the people at the centre of development, are not the people spinning development.

Why is it that there has been more success in charting the inequalities and developing the analyses than in changing the practices of development? Part of the reason, I would contend, is that insufficient attention has been paid to the link between analysis and practice, between how a situation is conceptualized and the strategies designed to address it. The way a problem is conceived shapes and determines practice: development practice, social policy, research hypotheses, and social activism.

In the past decade, there has been a significant amount of emphasis on institutionalizing gender analysis as a primary analytical tool for addressing women's concerns. This has contributed significantly to the mapping out of inequalities in access and opportunities between men and women but has been less successful in transforming the quality of women's lives. A series of problems emerge from the use of gender analysis, in itself and as a basis for praxis, that is, practice or action.

Gender analysis was born with the women's liberation movement, one of the few social movements of our time which embraced the challenge to link theory and praxis. In its origins, the concept of gender was used to describe social relationships as they manifested themselves in the interactions between women and men. At its best, gender analysis supports the development of a strategic theory for exploring how the dynamics of these social relations can

113

be transformed. It named the processes of social construction of gender within interpersonal relations, both public and private, and led to a practice of transformation of these processes and interactions through social activism and social change.

However, this original endeavour has ossified into analyses which create a static topology of roles or fixed dichotomous categories.[1] Although the tendency to use these categories as undifferentiated entities is almost ubiquitous, I give as an example a statement by Susan Brownmiller: "Rape is a conscious process of intimidation by which all men keep all women in a state of fear."[2] Even though the use here may be both literal and metaphorical, the analysis of rape as a non-consensual and destructive form of relating between certain human beings has been replaced by a set of universal predications: all men rape, all women are in fear of it.

So too, following suit, have our language and thinking ossified. When asked who among us has a well-developed sense of smell, who can tell by smelling when a cake is cooked or the stove left on, the answer is "Women" rather than "Whoever spends a lot of time in the kitchen cooking." We have slipped into seeing and understanding the world in this divided way. But this is to substitute an effect for a cause, and it may now be strategic to resist this tendency. It is not because one is a woman that one has this sense of smell. It is learned from experience. Anyone could have it; most women do. But this is an accidental quality derived from the tasks socially allocated to us.

This tendency to universalism is particularly evident in gender analysis as it is used in development theory. In this discipline, gender becomes an analytical tool for dividing the world into two categories — men and women — and mapping out the distribution of assets or the patterns of access or the allocation of tasks between them. It provides a descriptive topology which is essentially static and time-bound. Both men and women are theorized as internally undifferentiated categories. Gender analysis sets up the gender categories as a simplistic line of demarcation in social and economic life, adding complexity by mapping out differences over time or across cultures. It is a tool for mapping.

Thus, a gender analysis of labour would sketch out the division of labour by gender. Examples can be drawn from simple situations: in this community, men clear the fields and women do all other agricultural tasks. Or: women perform 80 per cent of all agricultural tasks. Or: women trade on the footpaths, men in the market. Or: men use their disposable income to buy consumer goods, women to feed their families. Seductive and even accurate as such statements may seem, they reduce complexity to undifferentiated universals.

Such a gender template is not strategic. It substitutes a static and incomplete description for a dynamic analysis of power and of difference. This is not to say that such a descriptive topology may not have value in increasing understanding of patterns of distribution. It may create a sense of outrage and certainly provides a basis for complaint. But it creates binary opposites — men and women — without concerning itself with the construction of these categories or with the social relations that give one a dominant position in sexual politics and that underpin distinctions in people's social interest.

Static gender analysis disempowers rather than empowers. It does not generate or even identify the fault lines of change nor unearth the practices required for social transformation. It cannot contain within its analysis the basis for social activism and social change: choice, capabilities, freedom, moral commitment, doubt, failure, and transformation.

The practice which developed out of this analytic approach was a politics of access, the demand that women (or sometimes men, e.g., access to secondary schooling in Jamaica) have access to what the other has in greater abundance. For example, demands are made for more women in political life, in law, in private sector management, greater access for women to education and skills training. These demands have had significant results: there are now more women in these positions — especially, for example, in Asia and Latin America, where there have been dramatic increases in women's access to education, health, and the workplace.

However, a politics of access assumes that women need what men already have and that equality with men is the overarching goal for women. It would make women's lives more like, or just like, men's, which may not be where most women would like to be. It does not create opportunities for the reconstruction of masculinity. Nor does it question the social arrangements that helped create disparities in access. It gives women access to a workforce, for example, which remains structured around the assumption that the worker has a home-based service industry that provides for him all the domestic services needed to allow him to function efficiently in the workplace. Without a restructuring of the domestic workplace, women do not and cannot enter the formal workplace as equals. They are thus bound to fail to conform to workplace expectations as they juggle conflicting responsibilities or they choose not to have a "career," to refuse promotions, to take positions not commensurate with their abilities and training, or to leave. The politics of access do not address the restructuring needed to allow for the interweaving of personal life with changing social and economic structures and social practice.

Furthermore, even where women's access to health, education, employment, and political life has improved, there has been little or no improvement in the rate of maternal mortality or disability, of illegal and illicit abortions, of female infanticide or physical or emotional deprivation, of violent and abusive behaviour toward women — that is, of any variables which allow glimpses of how women are treated and valued in a society. Being better educated or earning an income remains compatible with a culture of indifference, neglect, or contempt. Yet it is these qualities in the lives of girls or women which often cause the most harm or pain.

Nor does a politics of access reach anywhere near the social and psychological condition that marks the lives of women more profoundly that those of men: shame. The feeling of shame is a pervasive sense of personal inadequacy, the distressed apprehension of the self as inadequate or diminished.[3] Listen to Marge Piercy's voice:

> A strong woman is a woman in whose head
> a voice is repeating, I told you so,
> ugly, bad girl, bitch, nag, shrill, witch,
> ballbuster, nobody will ever love you back,
> why aren't you feminine, why aren't
> you soft, why aren't you quiet, why
> aren't you dead?[4]

The feeling of shame does not arise just from women being so thoroughly objectified, so continually on display. It is the internalization into a disabling condition of the surrounding cultures of violence and violation, neglect, indifference, reproach, scorn, of the silencing of their voices, the contempt for their strengths. This disempowering attunement of women to their social environment cannot be captured in a gender analysis. Yet it is a constant and crippling quality in their lives which works against the emergence of a sense of solidarity. Access to education, health, and employment do not necessarily, or even often, reduce this feeling of shame.

In creating two undifferentiated blocks, gender analysis also creates the conditions for confrontation between men and women. Gender analysis is often heard as an accusation that

115

men have benefited from the exercise of extractive power, of having extracted social, economic, and political benefits from or at the expense of women. Its mapping out of a pattern of pervasive exploitation creates a backlash of outrage, self-justification, repudiation, even verbal or physical violence. Thus it can prejudice processes of dialogue and partnership between men and women.

By theorizing human complexity into two internally undifferentiated categories, gender analysis also leads to exceptionalism. If all men are whatever, then one has to deal with those who are not, or not so, whatever. Thus, one begins mapping out exceptions: Men dominate conversations, speaking over or ignoring women, although I must say that my male colleagues always listen without interrupting. It is interesting that even extensive exceptionalism often does not put in question the tendency to undifferentiated universalism.

Sexuality has also been theoretically and metaphorically positioned within gender analysis as the plane of interface between these two universal categories. It derives its point of view from its unrelenting focus on the relations between men and women. This set of relations is understood and postulated to structure the social and sexual relations of all humans. This has rendered gender analysis heterophallic and heterosexist. In consequence, all other ways of sexually relating find themselves marginalized, colonized, devalued, excluded, or considered as derivative or as instances of otherness.

By placing heterophallic intercourse at the centre of sexuality, gender analysis also makes penetrative intercourse the instantiation of male-female sexual relations. But as women have experienced, sexuality or the exercise of sexual power is not only about intercourse. It permeates all aspects of public and private life.[5]

But is this true of men and male sexuality? Reflection on this question leads to the realization that the historical basis of gender analysis has been an exploration of *women's* experiences and problems. Women have established the problematic, and gender analysis has been used to try to elucidate it. A gender analysis is essentially women-centred.

To use a women-centred gender analysis as a framework for structuring our understanding of male sexual relations is to presuppose that all the elements required to understand male sexuality can be drawn from the context of male-female relations. However, the framework provided by a women-centred analysis may not help us understand why men enter sexual spaces or provide insights into men and the nature of their relations with women.

The framework determines the questions, but will these questions provide the insights? Should the focus of the analysis be changed? Should men be the focus? Should the tools of the analysis be changed? It may be that men's heterosexual behaviour and gender relations are derivative, being in some way a reflection of or a consequence of the relations men have with other men: between fathers and sons, of men to themselves, and between and among men. To understand the way male sexuality is expressed in their relations with women may require an understanding of the nature of their relations with other men. A gendered analysis may not be relevant.

That is, a gender analysis is from a woman's perspective and would have its analogues in the perspectives of any subjugated group. The analysis is and must be centred in the reality of their lives, its textures, silences, and topologies, but the strategies must be constituted in relation to the other, the subjugator. With men, the analysis must also be centred on their own lives, and undertaken by themselves, but the central strategies will be addressed to themselves. A gender exercise, mapping out imbalances of access and inheritance, would give them more insight into women's lives than their own. The techniques they will require to understand the pain and purposes of their own lives must be self-reflexive, able to create their own spaces for introspection, reflection, and shared exploration. How can men be motivated to undertake this quest for the reconstruction of self and society? This becomes one of the most critical "How?" questions for women, for it is only after this has happened that there can be a coming-together.

In critiquing the practice of gender analysis in the context of development, I do not wish to argue that our language, history, social forms, and organizational cultures are not shaped by gender. They are, and this textures the lives of both women and men. But gender manifests itself in the context of lives shaped by a multitude of other influences as well, a clustering of differences, communalities, and inequalities. What I am searching for is an analysis or analytical tools or structuring concepts that will provide a more adequate or complex basis for strategic development.

It may be that to move away from or complement the confrontational impact of gender analysis, we need to search for a different type of analytical concept — for example, one akin to the musical concept of timbre. Timbre is defined as that characteristic quality of a sound, independent of pitch and loudness, from which its source or manner of production can be informed. It is the characteristic quality of sound produced by a particular instrument or voice: tone colour. Timbre depends on the relative strengths of the components of different frequencies, which are determined by resonance. Thus, the saxophone and the clarinet have different timbres, but so too can one saxophone have a different timbre from another.

If a conceptual tool could be found which enabled us to differentiate among women as well as between women and men, such a tool might not have the same difficulties as the concept of gender. Perhaps it would help to identify some elucidatory quality which all people shared, such that our differences, both as women, as men, and as people, would lie in the relative strengths of the components of this quality. Sensitivity to the needs of others might be such a concept.

Similarly, rather than ascribing power to men as an undifferentiated whole, a topology that describes in whom it in fact resides and how it is exercised would facilitate a more complex understanding. But to do this, one would have to be able to identify those with power, and this, in less than obvious situations, has proven to be a slippery endeavour. The places from which power is exercised are often hidden places.

To some extent, those with power may be able to be named only by negation: they are not the dissenting voices, they are those absent from the imagery of solidarity, absent from the barricades. They are absent because there is no imperative for them to call into question the values and norms of everyday life. It is they who benefit materially from them. The complication here, however, is that the exercise of power generates relationships of dependency, numbs the capacity to resist, and saps the sense of agency. As such, those absent from the barricades could be either the oppressors or the oppressed.

More important than this mapping-out of the exercise of power could be a rejection of the definition of power as consisting only in the exercise of authority and control. Power as control and arrogance is incompatible with the experience of vulnerability, of incertitude and doubt, conditions inherent in being a woman. If power is redefined as the ability to create or change, the exercise of this form of power is an ability shared by men and women alike. Herein lie our creative powers, our powers of self-transformation, of imagination, of empowerment. Power as creativity is not finite. The exercise of power by newcomers does not necessarily mean its loss by others.

This form of power is somehow linked to doubt, to vulnerability, to tentativeness. Listen to the voice of Josephine Miles:[6]

Preliminary to Classroom Lecture

My quiet kin, must I affront you
With a telling tongue?
Will not a mission or request content you
To move as you belong
The fields of doubt among?

The voice to burden down a tale upon you
Were indolent with din.
Would better ask and have the answer from you.
And would you then begin
Querying too, querying, my quiet kin?

In this sense, doubt is a willingness to relinquish the arrogance and invulnerability of power. It is an acceptance that there may be no absolutes, an ability to be wrong, a querying, the initiation of a quest. Doubt makes possible curiosity, openness, and mystery. It creates the possibility of a diversity of paths. Self-doubt as a component of shame is a disempowering condition inherent in the lives of women. But when doubt turns outward, it can be a constructive force for restoring a sense of capacity and of agency and so, paradoxically, of power. Doubt becomes transformative.

The transformative practice of development could have to do with feelings, with querying, with turning outward, with interaction. It could be grounded in a lived and conscious practice of interaction which was non-dominating. Resistance to domination has to be learned, and a collective will has to be created that will lead people to act, to create, to change. For this to occur, there must be the spaces and the occasions to come together, to pause, to reflect, to reconsider, to heal, and so to create the possibility of transformation. How can this be brought about?

Any answer to this question will need to capture the dynamics of inclusion and exclusion, of domination and subordination, of thesis and antithesis, of self- and other-centredness, and the ways these dynamics are played out in multiple and shifting settings, influenced by desire, thwarted or strengthened by self-esteem. It will also need to point toward the fault lines and pressure points through which change could more easily occur and contain within itself means to trigger these changes.

We do not need to start from scratch to shape an answer to the question of how development can be a transformative practice. We need only to turn to women's own past. And present. For there are many practices from our own history which could provide insights into and point the way to good development practices.

One of the sources of feminism's transformative impetus was the women's liberation movement of the late 1960s and 1970s, and of course, of the early decades of this century, which had a highly developed theoretical framework strategically linked to change. It promoted some powerful practices for social transformation which, through a process of trivialization and defamation, have long been discredited. Perhaps it is time to reclaim and reconsider them.

The first such conceptual and strategic practice was that of sisterhood. This strategy mirrored the practice common among African American women of referring to each other as "sister."[7] The concept of sisterhood was to apply to all women: all women were part of the sisterhood.[8] Women writing to women, including strangers, signed their letters, "In sisterhood." Women referred to each other as "sister." The concept of sisterhood responded directly to the lack of trust and the suspicion generated among women when they gain their identity and derive their value only from the men in their lives. In such societies, women become created as competitors and strangers, without links to each other except through the patriarchy.

The relationship of women to the patriarchs provides a powerful metaphor for development. Underlying, or explicit to, development theory has been a concept of development as vertical supplication, the international analogue of client-patron politics, of sinner-confessor relationships, of the colonized to the colonizers, of the have-nots to the haves, and of other vertical relations of entreaty. Vertical relations act against the creation of social trust and cooperation among supplicants, and between them and the patron, and against the development of collective solutions.[9] Cultures of domination undermine agency and the practices of interaction.

As a strategic tactic, the use of the concept of sisterhood did not directly challenge the patriarchy. But it provided women with an alternative sense of identity and membership in a new and different world. Its use led to the recognition of diversity and the acceptance of difference among women. It promoted a sense of oneness in diversity and so of trust and respect. It wove women together as the warp and weft of this unity of sisterhood. It did not destroy their vertical patriarchal, bureaucratic, or political linkages but created new horizontal ones, directly, woman to woman. Women began to think of women as "we." It made possible the emergence of a sense of solidarity, a precondition for collective action and social change.

The second tactical approach developed by the women's liberation movement was the valuing of active participation of all interested women in the movement. The voices of all women were to be listened to, and the realities these voices were expressing were to be appreciated, reflected on, and incorporated into the whole. It was acknowledged that some women are articulate, others not. It became important that awareness be created, or rules introduced, that there be no domination by the articulate and no hegemony of their experiences and insights in the analysis.[10]

The theoretical basis for this technique was perhaps more intuitive, less articulated. But for women, the experience of being silenced was so commonplace that there was a shared sensitivity to becoming themselves silencers. It was believed that the understanding of women's condition was dependent on all women being able to contribute, that there were significant differences as well as commonalities and that these too needed to be explored. The understanding of the whole required the perspectives and realities of all, not just the more articulate few.

This valuing of the voices of all was not held to be incompatible with the existence of leaders. There were the theorists and the strategists, the poets and the orators. In fact, in my own country, Australia, it was the demise of the intellectual leadership that contributed significantly to the transformation of the women's liberation movement into a movement of women. The period of political foment and activism of the 1970s showed women that it was possible, individually and collectively, to change their lives. No longer were they prisoners of hopelessness. They had changed themselves and their worlds and, whether or not there was a women's liberation movement or national political commitment, they were determined not only to hold on to these changes but to continue moving forward.[11]

In the valuing of all voices and in their third strategy, the creation of consciousness-raising groups, the women's liberation movement was exploring a different approach to research methodology and theory construction. Women's stories, insights, and life histories were being used to question classical canons of objectivity and subjectivity, to dismantle accepted notions of the public and the private, and to develop new analytical concepts to assist in understanding and elaborating issues around the quality and purpose of women's lives.

The approach was one of theorizing through autobiography or through storytelling (since, for many women, the use of the personal pronoun "I" was difficult). For the women speaking, the confessional moment(s) of sharing were transformative, a stepping out of a self constructed by others, a revelation of other aspects of self, a start of a journey toward becoming who they are, allowing themselves to grow. Identity came to be perceived as capable of (re)construction, invention, and change. The idea that people are inherently or essentially anything was challenged. For the listeners, the symphony of voices was a way of understanding complexity and differences, for constructing a holistic understanding. It helped to put individual stories into context and thus made the construction of theory from voices a more systematic, less idiosyncratic undertaking.[12]

The third critical instrument of the women's liberation movement was the establishment of consciousness-raising groups: the collective sharing of the unarticulated, the festering, the pain, the desire, the dreaming. Consciousness-raising groups were symbolic shelters and sanctuaries, spaces and sites where women could come together, talk, and give each other support. They were the created analogues of wells and water-taps, of river banks where clothes are washed, of sweat shops and factories, of hairdressing salons, of kitchens and school canteens.

Consciousness-raising groups embodied in their very structures the way women themselves relate to the world, not as individual and solitary selves but as being and growing in connectedness with others. These groups rejected the accepted canons of objectivity to embrace the subjective and the empathetic. They were based on the premise that women could come to understand societies and their structures *because of* the lives that each woman had led, not *despite* them. They brought the whole person into the process rather than insisting that a person could and should in some sense stand outside of their situation and critically assess it. Together women strove to give voice to and comprehend the reality of women's lives from within the process of living them.

The creation of purposeful spaces, of sites of reflection and retreat, may be one of the most powerful of development practices. For these spaces can be sites of healing and recovery, sites of resistance, sites of connecting across difference, sites of consensus-building and collective problem-solving, sites of creativity and exuberance. The greater the diversity of the group members, the more complex the analysis and the more extensive and inclusive the networks and the communities created.

The shared naming of women's experiences of gender, sexuality, violence, indignity, power, and subordination in these groups created a radically new way of understanding and rethinking women's relations to reality. They transformed women's consciousness, changing their ways of feeling about themselves. They began to name the truth in groups to one another and to see themselves collectively, not individually, trapped in the meshes of patriarchal power. Sharing what was previously private and painful led to determination and the courage to work toward a different world.

Consciousness-raising groups were not sites for the creation of new forms of conformism, of the imposition of the politically correct. For they were not themselves sites of theory construction that occurred over time, cumulatively and with reflection. Rather they were sites of exploration. But the exploration of oppression, silencing, and belittling did not mean that one did not place one's head on the pillow at night next to that of an oppressor.[13] Again, a woman contemplating, for example, something as vexing as shaving her body hair or the use of cosmetics or cosmetic surgery could explore the basis of that desire in the gratification of male fantasies but at the same time explore it in relation to her own canons of self-esteem and public comfort. Talking about such things was a way of thinking aloud, of finding one's own individual path to balancing objectification and personal freedom. Not all women took the same path.

Consciousness-raising made possible the emergence of a sense of empowerment. It became an expression of a collective will to change and itself a means of creating some of the required changes: self-confidence, laughter, audacity, bravery. It created a space for tactical and strategic planning and provided a safe haven for forays into the world outside.

These practices transformed the context of women's lives by transforming those lives directly, by making women themselves the agents of change. The forces of change flowed from within women to encompass all others who came within the orbit of their lives. These practices also created the trust, the respect and the network of alliances which are the constitutive elements of social capital. They built communities of women and created the possibility of social amelioration, the improvement of the lives of all through the improvement of their lives.

Where social capital exists or can be created, mutual aid societies spring into existence, and credit and training schemes, social investment funds, and other such development initiatives are more effective. Where women trust each other and share a concern for the well-being of all, there one finds successful rotating credit schemes, communal mills, community banks, labour exchange, cooperative production, shared child-minding, and the flows of information and advice which draw women into the world of political and economic participation. These are less effective or fail where there is a lack of trust and weak community norms of collective, rather than individual or familial, advancement.

Social capital makes possible participatory development and good governance.[14] It ensures that human resource development, investment in human capital, will be for the common good and not just for individual advancement, that investment in physical capital will be maintained, usable, and used, that institutional development will address human issues of nepotism, corruption, inefficiency, and ineffectiveness. When people turn outward, encompassing others and those who are different from themselves, they become interested and active in improving the well-being of all. We saw this in the women's liberation movement. This too could be an intrinsic part of development — and must be if development is to reflect people's own dreams and aspirations and not be imposed on and irrelevant to their lives.

Analyses which begin from the realities of women's daily lives create a textured and intricate understanding of what needs to be changed. However, strategic development — the attempts to answer the question of "How?" — which encompasses *only* women will often just create safe havens or intermissions in a continuing context of disempowerment, discrimination, and humiliation. For the quality of women's lives is determined not only by their own actions but by the attitudes and behaviour of husbands, children, mothers-in-law, employers, public servants, and also by the economic, cultural, and political values of their countries.

To understand this better, let us join Helen, Stephan, Miriam, and other friends who are sitting around in the evening, chatting over a glass or two of beer. Helen, not long returned from her fields, is presiding behind the counter. The setting is rural Uganda.

Stephan, smartly dressed, an electrical technician, exclaims that he wants to marry. But, he laments, none of the possible brides is going for less than five cows and his father says that times are hard and he cannot afford more than two and so his son must wait.

Bitterly, Stephan points to the Health Ministry anti-AIDS poster above the refrigerator: Love

121

Carefully! Stick To One Partner! Why, he demands, is there no poster telling parents how to behave. Miriam points out that since coming to power, President Museveni has repeatedly begged parents to bring down the bride price but without success, at least, Miriam adds, around Bushenyi.

Well, ventures someone from outside, the notion of buying a wife is barbarous and must change if women are to be equal.

You don't understand, bursts out Helen, you think a woman feels bad if she's exchanged for cows or money. But if there's no exchange she feels worth nothing. I cost my husband ten cows. I had a good education from Irish nuns at Mbarara, I speak English and can run a business. My father spent money on me, why give me away for nothing? You want a healthy, educated bride, you pay for it.

Stephan raises his voice: I only want my own woman. I'm not crazy, I know all about AIDS. With a wife I wouldn't live risky. Why must men pay to make women feel better? A wife costs money, you have to keep her. Her family would have to keep her if she didn't marry. Why must I pay to get her so she costs her family no more?

That's bad thinking, retorts Helen. Women must feel valued or we can't look for equality. If my husband got me free, I couldn't start a revolution. A free bride's a slave — no worth, no status, no respect. Everyone knows my bride price was ten cows. When I talk revolution they listen, with respect.

So you see, Jill smiles softly at the outsider, for us, women's liberation has to start from where we're at, not where you're at![15]

And so the evening ends but the problem remains unresolved. Stephan and other men in Bushenyi remain bitter and scared. Helen and the other women continue to demand that women be valued. And similar conversations are occurring in communities around the world.

In this situation, there might be some women who individually can negotiate or demand protection from HIV infection. They may be able to refuse to have intercourse with their husbands if they do not trust them or to leave with their children. However, such a strategy would not slow down the spread of the virus among men. And such women are few and far between. Most women are economically, socially, and emotionally dependent on their husbands in such a way as to make them unable to negotiate safety.

Helen has given a great deal of thought to this problem, as have many women. She sees it as a question of survival. The evening before she had argued that women have to say no to risky husbands but they can't, on their own. They are scared but they reject divorce. So, she said, we get together. A husband living risky comes home and sees not only his scared wife, waiting to obey. He sees a *group* of women, all with the same problem, all saying the same thing! This is revolution. It is bigger than our political revolution. It is men being compelled to hear women.

However, strategies of women individually or collectively attempting to protect themselves and their children — even if effective — can only be short-term stratagems. A decision to forego sexual expression or relationships which have a sexual dimension may not be sustainable over the longer term, or the personal price of sustaining it may not be acceptable. It also means that these women must forego the creation, nurturing, and raising of children. This is a form of emotional deprivation that few women would wish to endure for a lifetime. Women-centred strategies show that women can empower themselves in certain ways but there are limits to what they alone can achieve.

Thus, in both the shorter term and more particularly the longer term, any strategy will have to encompass the Stephans of the world as well. The men and women of the community will have to start discussing women's value and men's behaviour and come to some decision about how the impasse might be broken. Consensus will have to be built throughout the community, and decision-making will need to be collective. It is not just a question of *how* to build communities and sanctuaries, it is also a question of *where* and *with whom* to build them.

Women-focused strategies need to be complemented by strategies that bring together and transform the lives of all those who yearn for and dream of a better way of living *now*. Certain changes can be brought about by women together. Other changes will require that men work together to develop a language that names some of the tragedies and distortions of their own growing up in a sexist society, a society where they are both oppressed and oppressing. Others will require not only broader-based alliances but also inclusive collectives of men and women, rich and poor, young and old, healthy and unwell, the articulate and the inarticulate.

The same practices that women have used to create social capital could be used wherever people are united in a desire for a different world, a different set of values, a different way of living. This site of shared desire — be it a concern about rising food prices, about women's right to make decisions about their bodies, about better education for their children, about the degradation of the environment, or about keeping women and children from becoming infected with HIV — could be the meeting place. Whenever people are drawn together by a commonality of feeling, they have created a space, a site for building community.[16] The building of community requires that trust, understanding, respect, and concern for others exist or be created among those coming together.

This sense of connectedness and the collective will to change are in fact the preconditions for development to be based on people's own dreams of the world they would wish to live in. For social change, if is to be sustainable, must come from within, and all, men and women, need to participate. Thus, the fundamental challenge to development practice is to facilitate and stimulate such preconditions, and this in turn brings with it a changed role for the outsider, the development practitioner. The outsider becomes the facilitator and the consensus builder. Empowerment, along with the confidence and hope that it creates, becomes the catalysing concept.

These women's practices point the way to the sort of practices which development must incorporate if social capital is to be created and strengthened, that is, if trust is to be instilled and norms of individualism changed to include concern for others, if empathy and compassion are to be respected and volunteerism valued. These practices will include ways to bring diverse people together to seek and reach collective solutions: networks, meetings, social occasions. Development assistance should be funding soccer clubs and choral societies,[17] guilds, chambers, and poetry circles, mutual aid societies and trade unions, cafés and clubs. The more diverse the groups, the more extensive will be the associative links and alliances so formed.

All of these processes lead to rethinking development as not only establishing conditions for economic growth and institutions for good governance but also as a moral activity. At its centre will be the improvement of people's well-being through, *inter alia,* improving the quality of, ways of, and structures for human interaction. The vocabulary of social capital formation is an ethical vocabulary: trust, respect, concern, solidarity, dignity. Its practices will lead to a strengthening of moral practices: consensus-building and collective decision-making rather than the disempowerment of authoritarian dictums. The moral communities that form the core of development evolve only in the context of such meaningful human relations and interactions.

This is a part of women's dreaming, but we must dream together with our oppressors if our dreaming is to change our lives more radically. For if the dreaming is to help shape the development agenda, radical changes will be required. It can happen only if new social processes emerge, in which:

123

- value is placed on people being able to come together, face to face, to interact in a myriad of ways;
- decisions are made as a result of consensus-building between competing forces, not by force or authority;
- free expression and discussion, doubt, imagination, reason, and feeling are all able to shape the outcome;
- words, metaphors, and images are not handmaidens of state power, of religious or corporate institutions, or of gender, class, patriarchal, or ethnic privilege, but rather are expressions of desire and dreaming and instigators of change;
- networks are extensive and inclusive and alliances and acquaintances stretch across differences; and
- emphasis is placed on the nature and quality of human interactions, rather than on individual advancement, so as to create and strengthen relationships of thoughtfulness, generosity, and caring, the bases for trust.

These new processes will need to be supported by the development of cooperative and non-exploitative productive capacities and socio-economic structures based on the organizational principles of networks as a balance to more centralized controlling institutions.[18]

Within women's own past, there are practices which can contribute significantly to a better understanding of those difficult "How?" questions and of the practice of development. Gender analysis provides a basis for advocacy and a needed reminder that gendered lives are socially constructed. The practices of the women's liberation movement provide tactical models not only for women but also for others united in a desire for social change.

Development has yet much to learn from the practices that women and their organizations and movements have developed. These practices create processes of change which are essentially endogenous, arising from within collectivities yet able to be supported from without. They lead to a shared consciousness which grounds social movements in the daily realities of deprivation and human creativity and creates consensus and mutual respect within and among the groups and organizations which make up civil society and nations. In undertaking these practices, communities and nations may come to value women and their ways of thinking and acting. Only then will women and their dreaming truly become a part of them.

Elizabeth Reid is the Director of the HIV and Development Programme, United Nations Development Programme (UNDP), New York. She has extensive experience in the design and delivery of development assistance in Asia, the Pacific, the Middle East and Africa, and a lifetime's lived experience of women and social change.

124

This article draws upon the author's "Women's Dreaming: Women, Sexuality, and Development," a paper presented at the Women's Studies Conference on Women, Sexuality, and Development, Sydney University, November 1994.

Footnotes

1 For an early critique of gender analysis, see R. W. Connell, *Gender and Power,* Sydney: Allen & Unwin, 1987, and for an insightful and thoughtful defence of its retention within the feminist armoire, see Susan

Bordo, "Feminism, Postmodernism and Gender-Scepticism," in Linda J. Nicholson (ed.), *Feminism/Postmodernism,* New York: Routledge, 1990.

2 Susan Brownmiller, *Against Our Will: Men, Women and Rape,* New York: Simon and Schuster, 1975.

3 For a sensitive analysis of this condition, see Sandra Lee Bartsky, *Femininity and Domination: Studies in the Phenomenology of Oppression,* New York: Routledge, 1990.

4 "For strong women," in Marge Piercy, *The Moon is Always Female,* New York: Knopf, 1994.

5 See, for example, the work of Ann Game and Rosemary Pringle, especially *Gender at Work,* Sydney: George Allen & Unwin, 1983.

6 In Richard Ellman and Robert O'Clair (eds.), *Norton Anthology of Modern Poetry,* New York: Norton, 1973, p. 826.

7 Other social movements have adopted a similar strategy, for example, the use of the terms "Brother" and "Comrade."

8 I still find within myself a deep reluctance to write this phrase. "The Sisterhood" quickly became a sneering and derogatory way of referring to women activists, a phrase used particularly, in my experience, by journalists, politicians, and staffers. It was often reinforced by phrases like "The Boilers," with their offensive sexual innuendos. A boiler is a hen that has stopped laying. It is not even valued for the table. The phrase "in sisterhood" could not be debased in the same way, since only women used it.

9 This is why the demand of the developing countries in the mid-1970s for a new international economic order was in itself, irrespective of its outcome, so important. It forged bonds among the previously isolated and suppliant countries and transformed them into an empowered collective. See Elizabeth Reid, "Women and the New International Eonomic Order: A Critique," in Khadija Haq (ed.), *Equality of Opportunity Within and Among Nations,* New York: Praeger, 1977.

10 To ensure that this was achieved, some groups handed out tokens at the beginning of meetings. Each time that a person spoke, she handed one back. Women who had used all their tokens could reenter the conversation when all tokens were in the middle or when all those with remaining tokens had finished whatever they wanted to say. This strategy has its analogues in modern management training and facilitation techniques. See, for example the Appreciation technique developed by Organizing for Development: An International Institute (ODII), Washington.

11 For an elaboration of this, see Elizabeth Reid, "The Child of Our Movement: A Movement of Women," in Jocelynne A. Scutt (ed.), *Different Lives: Reflections on the Women's Movement and Visions of Its Future,* Melbourne: Penguin, 1987.

12 This radical innovation in approaches to theory construction is still not widely accepted by the gatekeepers of acceptable research methodologies. For an excellent example of its use in the exploration of issues of male sexuality and class, see Gary W. Dowsett, "Working-Class Homosexuality, Gay Community and the Masculine Sexual (Dis)Order," *Revue Sexologique* 2(2): 1994, pp. 75–105.

13 An image of Robin Morgan's in her poem "Monster," from her volume of poems of the same name, New York: Norton, 1972.

14 For an important account of why some governments fail and some succeed, of how people's participation can be constructive or suppliant, see Robert Putnam, *Making Democracy Work: Civic Traditions in Modern Italy,* Princeton: Princeton University Press, 1993.

15 The story is taken from Dervla Murphy, *The Ukimwi Road: From Kenya to Zimbabwe,* London: Flamingo/HarperCollins, 1994, pp. 123, 127–28.

16 See bell hooks, "Moving Into and Beyond Feminism", *Outlaw Culture: Resisting Representations,* New York: Routledge, 1994.

17 For an elaboration, see Robert Putnam, cited in note 14.

18 For an interesting discussion, see Virginia Held, *Feminist Morality: Transforming Culture, Society and Politics,* Chicago: University of Chicago Press, 1993.

THE EVAPORATION OF POLICIES FOR WOMEN'S ADVANCEMENT

SARA HLUPEKILE LONGWE

Ten years ago, in the UN *Nairobi Forward-Looking Strategies for the Advancement of Women to the Year 2000 (FLS)*, governments of the world set out formidable goals for themselves, agreeing to a host of recommendations for achieving women's equality and empowerment. The plain fact is that these goals have not been achieved, and little or no progress has been made. In many developing countries, the position of women has worsened over the past ten years, and there has been a worldwide pattern of increased feminization of poverty.[1]

This is despite the fact that after the 1985 World Conference on Women, all major development agencies altered their policies to ensure a better focus on various aspects of women's equality and empowerment. We are left, therefore, with the large question of why such a large collective development policy has produced so few results.

The usual assumption is that the development agencies are trying hard enough, but are facing resistance from the patriarchal governments and traditional societies of the Third World. This author's experience would suggest that the situation is not so simple. This paper argues that in the area of women's advancement, lack of progress on policy implementation has to be seen in terms of the common interests of both the development agency and the Third World government. In other words, lack of progress is better understood in terms of a patriarchal alliance between the two sides.

This paper looks at the various ways in which policies on women's advancement evaporate, even when these are fairly explicit in the guidelines and regulations of a typical development agency. The argument here is that the patriarchal culture of most development agencies impedes the organization's ability to implement policies concerned with women's equality and advancement. The principles and values of feminism would not only contradict the agency's internal norms and traditions, but stand in the way of cozy and comfortable alliances with the patriarchal governments of the Third World.

To examine this process of policy evaporation, this paper introduces the notion of a development agency as a "patriarchal pot." A development agency is here seen as a complex cooking pot, on which the lid normally remains closed. The pot is filled with male bias, implicit in the agency's values, ideology, development theory, organizational systems, and procedures. This is the pot into which policies for women's advancement are thrown. It is a strange patriarchal pot of much input but no output. Officially the policy exists, and the pot does not. But this paper says that the policy has evaporated, and what remains is the pot.

WELCOME TO SNOWDIDA

For a concrete example of a patriarchal cooking pot it would be most useful to look at the real-life world of a particular development agency and its programmes in a particular country. To provide this example, I will take the reader to the country of Snowdia, a very isolated nation in the North which no foreigner (except myself) has ever visited. Snowdia has its own government development agency called SNOWDIDA, which is an administrative extension of the Ministry of Foreign Affairs in the Republic of Snowdia.

We shall look at SNOWDIDA's development activities in the People's Republic of Sundia, one of the least developed countries in Southern Africa.[2]

THE SNOWDIDA POLICY ON WOMEN'S EMPOWERMENT

Nine years ago SNOWDIDA adopted a radical new policy called Women's Empowerment for Development. The policy followed the recommendations contained in the *FLS* adopted in Nairobi in 1985. The policy was approved by the Parliamentary Committee on Development, after consultation with PODA, a network of NGOs in Snowdia concerned with women's advancement. Through PODA, the women's movement in Snowdia managed to strengthen the policy to incorporate definite commitments to work for women's advancement in developing countries.

Previously SNOWDIDA policy was concerned with improving the welfare of women, taking the existing social system and traditions as given. The old policy focused on supporting separate "women's projects" concerned with improving women's income and access to resources. By contrast, the new policy is concerned with enabling women's advancement by increasing opportunities for mobilization and empowerment to overcome discriminatory practices and to give women an equal place in society. The new policy involves *mainstreaming*, or addressing issues of gender equality in all projects supported by SNOWDIDA. By comparison with the earlier welfare approach, the new policy represents a radical shift.

This change in SNOWDIDA policy does not contradict the policy of the government of Sundia. On the contrary, Sundia has assented to the 1985 *FLS* and in 1983 ratified the UN Convention on the Elimination of All Forms of Discrimination Against Women (CEDAW). Furthermore, the government of Sundia has published its own fairly radical policy statements on women's advancement. The Sixth National Development Plan has a chapter entitled "Women and Development," which states that women must be "equally the participants and beneficiaries" in the development process. In addition, women's participation in decision-making is an explicit objective of the government's new policy on decentralization, which gives more political power and autonomy to district government. At the administrative level, the government has established a Women in Development (WID) Department in the Ministry of Finance and Planning.

POLICY EVAPORATION

Despite these pronouncements, all of these bilateral policy commitments have evaporated in Sundia. Before we begin to look for the underlying reasons, we should first examine some of the main external signs of this evaporation.

Imagine a gender consultant who has been called in to look at the attention to gender issues in a SNOWDIDA programme in Sundia. The consultant is instructed to look at the SNOWDIDA Programme of Support to the Health Sector. The initial gender assessment is undertaken by considering the provisions of this plan against the requirements of the SNOWDIDA 1985 policy of Women's Empowerment for Development. The table on the next two pages summarizes the consultant's findings, and provides an example of the process of gender policy evaporation.

Looking at the "gender critique" of the SNOWDIDA health programme shown in the table, the reader may get the uneasy feeling of already having visited Sundia, or at least other places very much the same. Gender policy evaporation is a common phenomenon. Sometimes the policy evaporates bit by bit, between policy and implementation. Sometimes you only have to turn over a page of a development plan, and all the gender issues previously mentioned have suddenly disappeared. Evaporation can be a very rapid process!

When we review the original policy of Women's Empowerment for Development, we can see that the main aspects of the 1985 policy reform — gender equality, empowerment and mainstreaming — have effectively been discarded. The gender critique shows that the SNOWDIDA office in Sundia has not adopted the 1985 policy and, at best, is operating under the pre-1985 policy of confining women's development to an interest in welfare and increased access to resources.

We might have spent more time, and had more fun, identifying the further evidence of policy evaporation in Sundia. But this is not our main purpose here. The surface evidence is presented merely for the purpose of provoking an interest in its underlying causes. Who is doing what, and why?

POLICY EVAPORATION IN SUNDIA: THE LARGER PATTERN

Policy evaporation is not peculiar to SNOWDIDA. It is common across most development agencies operating in Sundia. Gender policy evaporation is the norm in all bilateral and UN agencies there. The only development agencies which are making a serious effort are some international NGOs whose programmes are concerned with linking up with Sundian NGOs, particularly those which form part of the growing Sundian women's movement.

Policy evaporation among the major development agencies is closely mirrored by policy evaporation within the Sundian government. This process of evaporation follows the same pattern as in the development agencies; there is some enthusiasm for the gender-oriented development policy at the political level of government, but there is rapid evaporation when these policies reach the government bureaucracy. Although the government has established a WID Department, this department has made little progress in persuading the sectoral ministries to produce gender-oriented policies and plans.

FEMINIST ANALYSES OF BUREAUCRACY

Our interpretation begins with the general notion that SNOWDIDA is a patriarchal organization which automatically repudiates any feminist ideas and policies. In this, SNOWDIDA is merely following the pattern of all other institutions within the Snowdian government bureaucracy.

There is a growing feminist theory of organizations which interprets bureaucracy as being inherently patriarchal.[3] The general theoretical framework for this literature is Weberian: the starting point for analysis is that the Weberian ideal for bureaucratic organization is male-gendered, and women are incorporated only on male terms. In other words, women are accommodated either in subordinate female gender roles or otherwise as honorary males.

128

PROGRAMME CYCLE AND GENDER POLICY EVAPORATION IN HEALTH REFORM

Situation Analysis: There is an overview of the main health problems in Sundia and the deteriorating health status of the rural population. There is a separate section on gender issues, which states that there is a general problem of discrimination against women in Sundia, but a lack of gender-disaggregated data and a lack of information on how customary and discriminatory practices affect the health status of women.

Critique of Situation Analysis: It is noteworthy that gender issues have been mentioned. However, the separate section on gender issues indicates that the policy of mainstreaming gender issues is being ignored from the outset. The separate section on gender issues does not identify the particular gender issues affecting the health sector. The claim that gender-disaggregated data is not available is untrue.

Policy Environment: The Health Sector Support Programme is justified as a means of softening the effects of structural adjustment and as supporting government policy on decentralizing control over the health sector. SNOWDIDA's policies of focusing benefits on the most vulnerable and increasing women's access to resources for improved health are mentioned.

Critique of Policy Environment: There is no mention of the gender issues and inequalities arising from policies of structural adjustment (despite the significant amount of literature on this subject). The SNOWDIDA policy on women's participation and empowerment is not mentioned or interpreted for the health sector. Instead, the SNOWDIDA policy is reduced to an interest in "access to resources."

Overall Programme Strategy: The strategy is to provide improved health services and packages to the most needy, to enable increased home care and increased capacity in rural health clinics, and to promote community participation in the planning and implementation of health reforms.

Critique of Strategy: Now all sign of gender issues, or even women's concerns, has disappeared. This is despite the need for a strategy to pursue the previously mentioned policy interest in increasing women's access to resources. It is also despite the need to ensure women's participation as a component in community participation.

129

PROGRAMME CYCLE AND GENDER POLICY EVAPORATION IN HEALTH REFORM

Programme Goals: These are mainly concerned with outlining purpose in terms of delivery of health packages, supporting the Ministry of Health Planning Unit, and supporting the formation of district health management boards. There is one goal concerned with improving women's access to health resources.

Critique of Goals: The goal concerned with a gender issue has been separated from other goals. All of the urgent and glaring gender issues in the health sector have been overlooked. The remaining goal is low-level in term of SNOWDIDA's and Sundia's policies on gender.

Programme Objectives: The Programme is divided into twelve projects, each with detailed objectives. No objective explicity mentions women or gender, and no objective can be construed as being concerned with addressing a gender issue.

Critique of Objectives: The minimal interest in gender issues which remained in the Goals has not been translated into any objectives aimed at improving women's access to health resources. Obviously the process of gender policy evaporation is now complete.

Programme Management and Organization: Here there is some detail on the distribution of responsibility among SNOWDIDA, the ministry, and the district. There is a short section on community participation which does not mention women's participation.

Critique of Programme Management: Women's participation in project planning and management is a necessary part of community participation. This would enable women's control over the reform process, ensure that there is a fair gender distribution of labour in home care, and ensure that the health care needs of women and children are met.

Programme Implementation: The SNOWDIDA health adviser claims that gender issues have been omitted from project documents to avoid unnecessary argument at the planning stage. But the health adviser says staff have been trained to be "gender sensitive" and issues of women's participation and gender equality are addressed at the implementation stage.

Critique of Programme Implementation: Visits to several project sites reveal that the claims that projects are addressing gender issues are completely untrue. The claim may have been made in good faith by a person with no understanding of gender issues. The programme has no gender adviser. One project manager flatly states, "This is a health project, not a women's liberation project."

130

From this perspective, the very structure and rationality of bureaucracy is interpreted as intrinsically patriarchal. The hierarchical chain of bureaucratic authority is contradictory and antagonistic to women's more participatory way of making and implementing decisions. Similarly, Weber's model of a legal-rational system of bureaucratic thinking is interpreted as contradictory to the more open, pragmatic and consensual modes of thought which characterize female ways of thinking.[4]

Investigations into the patriarchal nature of bureaucracy have primarily been confined to an analysis of its internal gender relations. In other words, there has been a concern with how domestic relationships of male gender dominance are reflected in the pattern of gender relations in the office and factory.[5] Bureaucracy is seen as a "male club" where women, if admitted, are domesticated and subordinated.

However, in this paper our interest is very different from the approach of the existing literature, in two important ways. First, we are not here concerned with how women employees are placed and treated within the bureaucracy, nor the positions that women hold (subordinated though they may be). Instead, we are looking at how a bureaucracy maintains and reproduces patriarchal culture in the wider society. More specifically, we are interested in how SNOWDIDA contributes to the continued subordination of women in Sundia, despite having been given the opposite mandate.

Second, I would argue that the Weberian interpretation of bureaucracy does *not* explain the evaporation of policies on women's advancement. On the contrary, the Weberian model of bureaucratic principles and rules should ensure that such policies are taken seriously.

Instead of looking for patriarchy inherent within bureaucracy, we should instead be looking for the non-bureaucratic aspects of SNOWDIDA's organization which are responsible for this diversion from the formal obligation to implement the policy on women's advancement. Therefore, we should consider SNOWDIDA as a combination of two different and antagonistic organizations: overt bureaucracy but covert patriarchy. This line of analysis is pursued further in the remainder of this paper.

SNOWDIDA AS A BUREAUCRACY

Let us first look at how SNOWDIDA functions in its overt form, as a Weberian-style bureaucracy. From a Weberian theoretical perspective of bureaucracy, policy evaporation is incomprehensible at three levels: policy, planning, and organization. Let us look at each of these three levels in turn.

Policy
SNOWDIDA does not make policy. Policy is made at the political level of government, and the job of SNOWDIDA is to implement policy. To some extent it may have to interpret policy and to balance policy priorities, but such policy activities are then subject to scrutiny at the political level of government, especially in the form of the Snowdian Parliamentary Committee on Development.

According to the Weberian theory of bureaucracy, implementation of policies is the central purpose of the chain of command (from the government). Bureaucratic rules and procedures are primarily concerned with ensuring that policy guidelines from the top generate appropriate action throughout the organization.

It follows that wilful policy evaporation within SNOWDIDA cannot be justified within Weberian theory. When a SNOWDIDA official "waters down" or ignores the policy on women's advancement, the official is actually remaking policy. Negation of a policy automatically becomes policy intervention, entailing assumption of powers which are not given in the chain of command and which therefore contradict a basic principle of bureaucracy.

Whereas in other policy areas an official's repudiation of policy would merit dismissal, in the area of women's advancement the official may instead be praised for being honest and pragmatic. There must a different value system operating in this policy area. Something else is going on.

Planning

Similarly, policy evaporation during the planning process is incomprehensible, according to Weberian principles. The bureaucratic planning process works according to given rules and procedures. Development plans are formulated to address the problems which have been identified in the process of setting the development policy against the facts of the actual situation in Sundia.

This identification of problems should lead into the formulation of goals, since goals should be concerned with overcoming the problems. Goals give way to objectives which will address the problems. This is part of a logical planning sequence which is an essential aspect of the due process of a Weberian bureaucracy.

Therefore, the gradual evaporation of policy during the planning process is bureaucratically irrational. It entails slippage from the rationality of due process, and this slippage contradicts a basic ideal of Weberian bureaucracy. It can only be understood as a mistake, which must be corrected if procedures are being followed properly. However, if there is a *pattern* of evaporation throughout the area of policy on women's advancement, then this cannot be a mistake. There must be other norms operating, quite outside bureaucratic norms.

Organization

A third aspect of Weberian-style bureaucracy is that it adapts to new policy and new demands by developing specialized departments, staffed by professionals with training in the area of the new policy interest. But when one asks the SNOWDIDA office in Sundia why the health sector programme has overlooked gender issues, the answer is likely to come back like a shot: "We have nobody with the training to understand these things."

According to the policy, each SNOWDIDA programme is supposed to have a gender adviser. But when one looks at the plan for the Health Sector Support Programme you find that there are detailed terms of reference for three or four specialized advisers, but no mention of a gender adviser. Such a situation, ten years after the publication of a new policy, reveals a clear unwillingness to develop the necessary specialist expertise to interpret and implement the policy. Again this behaviour is incomprehensible within a Weberian theory of bureaucracy. It demands some other form of explanation.

From a Weberian perspective, bureaucrats' official opinions are formed only in terms of given policies, and given rules and procedures. Officially, they do not have their own personal opinions, or if they do, such opinions must not interfere with their work. From Weber's point of view, the whole point of a modern bureaucracy is that it made a break with earlier and medieval systems of administration which were patrimonial, patriarchal, autocratic, arbitrary, inconsistent, irrational and so on.

132

OVERT BUREAUCRACY AND COVERT PATRIARCHY

It is not enough to say that policy evaporation occurs in SNOWDIDA's programmes because SNOWDIDA is a bureaucracy, and bureaucracies are automatically patriarchal. Staffs of bureaucracies are trained to follow rules and procedures, to implement policies. The above analysis reveals that if SNOWDIDA adhered to bureaucratic rules, it would actually be implementing the policy on women's advancement.

Therefore, SNOWDIDA can be seen as encompassing two very different forms of organization: the overt and the covert.

- The overt organization is the government bureaucracy, with its explicit policies and procedures, and legal-rational system of analysis. The Weberian model is the legitimating ideology of bureaucracy.
- The covert patriarchy, or the "patriarchal pot" within the organization, which runs counter to the Weberian model and enables the subversion of all policies and directives which threaten covert patriarchal interests.

The overt organization is a conventional bureaucracy, which is obliged to implement policies handed down by government. The covert organization is what we have called the "patriarchal pot," which ensures that patriarchal interests are preserved. When presented with feminist policies, the overt and the covert organizations have opposing interests, values, rules, and objectives: bureaucratic principles demand implementation; patriarchal principles demand evaporation.

THE CULTURE OF THE PATRIARCHAL POT

If we apply the label "patriarchal pot" to the organization which subverts female gender interests, we need to understand more about the way the patriarchal pot can exist alongside the bureaucracy, given that they would seem to be antagonistic. We need to know more about the structure and behaviour of the pot and how it maintains its existence.

Let us therefore analyze the aspects of the patriarchal pot that lie hidden within SNOWDIDA. We need a better understanding of the interests served by the pot, the ideology which legitimates the pot, and the procedures which maintain the pot. Furthermore, if the pot is actually antagonistic to bureaucracy, we need to know how the contradictory and cancerous pot can continue to survive and thrive in partnership with bureaucracy.

SNOWDIDA's Internal Interests

The patriarchal interests within SNOWDIDA are not hard to find. First, of course, like other bureaucracies North and South, it is male-dominated. Gender inequality in recruitment, conditions of service, and promotion are essential for maintaining the SNOWDIDA tradition of male domination and male culture. SNOWDIDA is run as a wing of the Snowdian Ministry of Foreign Affairs, which has always been a male preserve.

Implementing a development policy for women's advancement therefore threatens the male domination of SNOWDIDA. It immediately suggests the need to recruit more women and — even more threatening — to recruit feminists. Herein lies the internal threat to SNOWDIDA: that feminist recruits would not confine their interests to the advancement of women within Sundia, but would be equally interested in the advancement of women within SNOWDIDA.

133

SNOWDIDA's External Interests

Since we are looking at SNOWDIDA's operations in Sundia, we are here more interested in how SNOWDIDA's external relations serve to sustain the patriarchal pot. We need to look at the North-South patriarchal alliance which forges SNOWDIDA's character and which sets the institutional norms on issues of gender relations in development.[6]

Here we have to understand the commonality of patriarchal interest between SNOWDIDA and its cooperating ministry, the Sundian Ministry of Planning (MOP). Both are government bureaucracies, and therefore both have common experience and procedures when it comes to delaying, subverting, or ignoring government policies which threaten the privileges of class, tribe, religious group, gender, and so on. In fact, when it comes to subverting Weberian ideals of legal-rational behaviour, the Sundian Ministry outdoes SNOWDIDA.

In the area of gender, the Sundian MOP has exactly the same problem as SNOWDIDA. It also has a government which, at the political level, has handed down policies on women's equality and advancement. In fact, MOP officials have a more serious interest in ensuring policy evaporation: the government gender policy threatens not only male domination within MOP, but also threatens the continuance of the patriarchal control of society as a whole. The Sundian government policy on gender equality would challenge the customary laws and traditions which have always maintained male domination of Sundian society.

Therefore, the patriarchal alliance of SNOWDIDA and MOP have a simple basis. The Snowdian Ambassador, who is in charge of the Sundia SNOWDIDA office, always ensures that nothing disturbs such common interests.

The Men's Club Alliance

The easy and cozy relationship between the officials of SNOWDIDA and MOP needs also to be understood in terms of the "men's club" culture to which they both belong. Officials on both sides are part of the Sundian male culture of meetings, cocktail parties, and the golf club. They live in a world of male privilege which, in Sundia, is even more premised on male domination than its equivalent in Snowdia.

The men's club infects both the office and the social world of the high-level bureaucrat in Sundia. At the office, the privileged male work of high-level decision-making is supported by the menial female work of office cleaning, secretarial services, and document production. Similarly, at the domestic level, the husband's full-time professional occupation is enabled by the wife, who looks after the home, children, schooling, and shopping. Leisure hours at cocktail parties and golf clubs are financed by the unpaid or exploited labour of the lower classes, especially female members of the lower classes.

In the Sundian men's club, women are not discussed as equals or even as human beings. Women are sexual objects or commodities, to be hunted as sexual prey or acquired for additional wealth and prestige. SNOWDIDA officials who attempt to introduce policies of gender equality into the development discourse not only upset the workplace, they upset the whole patriarchal culture. In particular, they upset the men's club, which is not only the centre of their social life but also their essential meeting place for informal contacts and influence.

It is this SNOWDIDA membership in the Sundian men's club which, to a large extent, explains the frequent SNOWDIDA claim that "we cannot interfere with the local culture." The culture of male domination is the culture of the men's club; it is a club to which they themselves belong and from which their work profits.

THE STRUCTURE OF THE PATRIARCHAL POT

We have now looked at the common interests and culture of the alliance which sustains the patriarchal pot. But we still need to look at how this pot actually works. How are we to understand the actual process by which a particular policy can evaporate, when other policies do not? We have to look at the structure of the pot in terms of its relationship to the overt bureaucracy and its legitimating theory and ideology.

Diplomacy in Defence of Patriarchy

The Ambassador's simple formula for implementing a SNOWDIDA development support programme in Sundia is, as far as possible, to reduce SNOWDIDA policy in Sundia to the selection of the particular MOP programmes for which SNOWDIDA will provide support. Such a selection process is usually conducted as if there is complete Snowdian-Sundian consensus on development policy.

However, this smooth diplomatic gloss conceals the need for policy-level negotiation in areas where in fact there is lack of policy consensus. All SNOWDIDA development principles have implications for changing the structure of Sundian society. Therefore, all development cooperation between Snowdia and Sundia needs to be based on initial negotiations to ensure that the policy priorities of both sides are being pursued.

In practice, there is currently considerable explicit conditionality for enforcing Sundian conformity to a policy of structural adjustment which has been imposed by the IMF and which has the support of most development agencies in Sundia, including SNOWDIDA. But the imposition of structural adjustment entails no conditionality on gender equality. On the contrary, these structural adjustment policies are actually *detrimental* to policies of gender equality and women's advancement.

In the area of development agency policy on structural adjustment, policy is enforced by conditionality. On structural adjustment, the Ambassador's diplomatic gloss disappears, and he talks tough. But in the area of gender equality, a different rationale comes into play. Suddenly SNOWDIDA behaves as a diplomatic mission, rather than as a development agency. In the area of SNOWDIDA gender policy, the Ambassador suddenly becomes very diplomatic, and states that "we cannot interfere with the internal affairs of Sundia." When the Ambassador talks of structural adjustment, he is in charge of a bureaucracy. When he talks of gender issues, he is in charge of the patriarchal pot.

Theory in Support of Pot Preservation

The most important aspect of preserving the patriarchal pot is that it should remain invisible. One important way of enabling the pot to quietly and invisibly evaporate the policy is to adopt a vocabulary in which a discussion of women's empowerment becomes impossible. This may be achieved by adopting a technical rationale of the development process, which is not theoretically appropriate for the analysis — or even the recognition — of the political and ideological aspects of the development process.

Here the essential technical rationalization is to limit the discourse on women's advancement to the level of *providing for women's basic needs* and *increasing women's access to resources*. Within this vocabulary, it is possible to discuss women's advancement *within the existing social system*, and not in terms of the need to reform the social system.

An equally important theoretical point is concerned with the place of gender issues within the planning process. This is perhaps the most important theoretical principle of the patriarchal pot. Addressing gender issues is a secondary concern in any project and relates only

135

to improved project efficiency. In other words, it is not a primary concern of any project to address a gender issue. The project has its own primary purpose, concerned with purely technical objectives of increasing the water supply, improving institutional capacity, or whatever.

The final important aspect of technical rationalization is that it automatically excludes all awkward normative and political words. This is in contrast to the SNOWDIDA policy document which uses political phrases such as women's participation in decision-making, women's control over resources, and women's empowerment.

But in Sundia, the Snowdian Ambassador has advised all SNOWDIDA staff that, as technical advisers, they should avoid all politically loaded words in planning documents. He has explained that this is particularly important in the area of gender, which is a sensitive area in Sundia. In fact, the Ambassador has advised all SNOWDIDA staff to avoid the phrase "gender inequality," and instead to talk more diplomatically about "gender differences." He has advised that the word "equality" be replaced by "equity" or other non-threatening vocabulary.

The Implicit Ideology of the Patriarchal Pot

Here we see that the purpose of theory is to obscure ideology. The underlying ideological principle is that systems of male domination in Sundia are not to be the subject of development interventions. Any intervention in this area is to be labelled as "interference." Whereas, generally, socio-economic aspects of inequality may be addressed in SNOWDIDA-supported projects, the system of structural gender equality is not to be the subject of development interventions, even in programmes concerned with other aspects of structural adjustment. The principle is that SNOWDIDA will work within the existing patriarchal structure.

This, of course, must remain covert ideology. It must remain covert for the simple reason that the overt principles are the exact opposite. Both SNOWDIDA and Sundia have explicit development policies concerned with promoting gender equality and ending practices of gender discrimination.

This points to the absolute importance of technical rationalization as a system of discourse. Within a technical and non-political vocabulary, the ideological contradiction between policy and practice never comes up for discussion. It remains invisible.

COVERT PROCEDURES OF THE PATRIARCHAL POT

The problem cannot remain invisible simply on the basis of applying vocabulary control. For instance, there may be vocal members of the women's movement in both Snowdia and Sundia who want to know why there seems to be no action on SNOWDIDA's policies of women's advancement.

Within the Snowdian government and parliament, there may be feminists who begin to realize that SNOWDIDA has no intention of putting the policy into practice and is instead actively thwarting the policy. Consultants and evaluators from Snowdia and elsewhere may ask to look at SNOWDIDA-supported programmes, and they are very likely to compare policy with progress. All these situations have to be managed.

So if a gender issue does actually get onto the agenda, how is it to be dealt with? The answer is that it must apparently be dealt with by normal bureaucratic procedure. But this must be done in such a way that the gender issue will slowly evaporate away.

Weberian bureaucracy is, by definition, an efficient method of public administration. By contrast, the procedures of the patriarchal pot ensure that the issue evaporates before it has been addressed. The procedures of the patriarchal pot are concerned with mocking bureaucratic procedure, making sure that what goes in never comes out. The patriarchal pot implements a strange slow-motion parody of bureaucratic procedure. What looks on the surface like bureaucracy is actually the slow, destructive boiling of the patriarchal pot.

Let us take an example from the SNOWDIDA Health Sector Support Programme in Sundia. Let us imagine that the visiting consultant, sent by Snowdia's Parliament Committee on Development, has visited the project and has pointed out that Sundian government family planning clinics are discriminating against women. Specifically, the family planning clinics refuse to provide women with contraceptives unless they bring a letter of permission from their husbands. In effect, this makes contraceptives unavailable to most married women and to all single women. And a major part of the SNOWDIDA Health Sector budget is to provide support for family planning clinics.

Clearly the consultant seems to have revealed the lack of attention to the SNOWDIDA gender policy on ending discriminatory practices. The First Secretary in the SNOWDIDA country office has to respond to this criticism, and may even have to be seen to take action and make changes in the office.

There are a variety of ways in which the First Secretary may respond and react to such criticism. These are the standard procedures of the patriarchal pot which may be used to ensure that this gender issue soon evaporates.[7]

We may divide his responses into three actions: verbal defence, diversionary action and organizational change. Let us look at each of these categories in turn. If possible, the First Secretary will want to confine his reaction to *verbal defence*, which involves demonstrating that the consultant's criticisms of the programme are mistaken.

Procedures for Verbal Defence
Denial. "The consultant, who was only here for a week, has misunderstood the problem. It is Sundian policy that contraceptives are made available only to couples. Therefore, the clinic is only following government policy, to which SNOWDIDA also must also conform." (The flat denial is a dangerous procedure, because it usually involves obvious lies. In this case, the claim about Sundian government policy is completely untrue.)

Inversion. "There is a problem here, but it originates in the home and not in the clinic. It is husbands who insist that wives can only be given contraceptives with their permission, and Sundian wives accept this situation. This is therefore a domestic problem, in which the Sundian government cannot interfere, let alone SNOWDIDA." (This should be recognized as yet another version of the old strategy of blaming the victim.)

Policy Dilution. "SNOWDIDA policy is concerned with increasing access to resources, which we have done by providing more clinics and stocking them with a variety of contraceptives. We have done our part from a development point of view. The rules of who is eligible to receive contraceptives must remain in the hands of the government, and this is a very sensitive cultural issue in which we could not possibly interfere." (It is not true that SNOWDIDA policy is limited to providing resources to government. The policy also involves enabling women's empowerment and overcoming the obstacles of discriminatory practices.)

Since verbal defence must entail misrepresentation, the First Secretary may choose alternative procedures, admitting the problem and proposing action to address it. This is the basis of *diversionary action*.

137

Procedures for Diversionary Action

Lip Service. "The consultant has pointed to a problem which has been worrying us for some time. We are most grateful for her clear analysis of the problem, and her recommendations for action. We intend to establish a Consultative Committee to look at these recommendations, which have implications for improving our attention to gender issues in all SNOWDIDA programmes." (This is often a procedure for sounding good at the time, but with absolutely no intention of taking any action.)

Research Study. "The consultant has pointed to just one aspect of a larger problem, which is very sensitive and touches on matters of Sundian custom and tradition. We have decided to appoint a team from the Sundian Research Institute to look at gender issues in all sectors, in the context of structural adjustment, and to make recommendations on the implications for SNOWDIDA." (By the time the report comes out, at the end of next year, the original problem should have been forgotten. In any case, the report will be written like a Ph.D. thesis, and most readers will not be able to understand it.)

Shelving. "The research report 'Gender Issues in the Context of Structural Adjustment in Sundia' has recently been completed. It has been sent to headquarters in Snowdia for their consideration, since it is one of several reports on this issue which were commissioned in different parts of the world." (The report has been shelved. It will never be seen again.)

Even more diversionary is *organizational change*. This will require significantly more time, which is viewed as a positive aspect on the road to doing nothing. Moreover, if the organizational change is inappropriate for addressing gender issues, there never will be any appropriate outcomes.

Procedures for Ineffectual Organizational Change

Compartmentalization. "We are now establishing the new post of WID Counsellor to head the new WID Section in the SNOWDIDA office in Sundia. The WID Counsellor will advise on gender issues in all projects, will supervise the planning of support for women's projects, and will be in charge of gender training for SNOWDIDA staff and counterparts." (The SNOWDIDA country office is divided into Sections by conventional sector: health, education, and so on. Therefore the creation of a separate WID Section effectively treats gender as a separate sector, when it is actually supposed to be an intersectoral concern. This compartmentalization contradicts the SNOWDIDA policy of mainstreaming gender issues in all sectors of development assistance. The WID Counsellor will soon understand that this is a very junior post and that promotion prospects depend very much on confining her interest to the separate women's projects, and otherwise keeping quiet about gender issues.)

Subversion. "I have appointed our Second Secretary, Mrs. Patrison, to take on the additional responsibility of WID Counsellor in our office here in Sundia. I know she is very young and has no previous experience in gender issues. But I am sure she will soon pick it up." (This appointment is an act of pure cynicism. Patrison is a junior official well known for incompetence and administrative confusion, and famous for immediately losing any document given to her. As a junior official, she will not be in a position to influence the planning of sectoral programmes, which are overseen by more senior officials. In this way, the SNOWDIDA policy of having a WID Counsellor in each country office is followed in principle but subverted in practice.)

Tokenism. "I am pleased to announce that the wife of the Vice-President, Mrs. Charity Wander-Wander, has agreed to sit on our Sundia-SNOWDIDA Health Programme Committee. Until now the Sundian members of this Committee have all been men, but now we shall hear women's voices on some of these difficult issues concerning tradition and custom." (Mrs. Wander-Wander is a well-known traditionalist. In fact, she is known for telling women to obey their husbands. There are many women prominent in the Sundian women's movement who could have been invited to sit on this Committee. Furthermore, half the members of this Committee should be women if the SNOWDIDA policy on women's participation is to be followed. Mrs. Wander-Wander has been invited as a token woman. In any meeting she will be allowed to speak for five token minutes to ensure that "the woman's point of view has been heard" before the men take their decision.)

CONCLUSION

Let us return from the mythical People's Republic of Sundia, and ask ourselves how mythical it really is. Is SNOWDIDA not like an agency which we know very well? Is Sundia not a country which seems familiar?

If any of this description of the patriarchal pot rings true in our own experience, then we need to think again about how the women's movement, North and South, can contribute to the process of women's advancement.

We may have previously, unthinkingly, regarded government and UN development agencies as a means toward women's advancement. And perhaps they could be. But the above analysis suggests that patriarchal agencies are very much part of the problem and an obstacle to progress.

For the global women's movement, the unearthing of the patriarchal pot has endless implications. For instance, it shows that it is not enough to ensure the establishment of gender-oriented development policies on the assumption that these policies will then be pursued. Instead, it shows that the women's movement, North and South, must also mobilize to monitor the activities and progress of these development agencies, on the assumption that this gender-oriented policy will not be pursued unless there is independent monitoring.

The women's movement makes a mistake if it does not take an interest in the workings of government bureaucracy. If we want to change the world, we cannot dismiss bureaucracy as part of the "male world," as if patriarchy can be defeated elsewhere — in the NGO movement, in issue politics, and in alternative forms of organization and government. Bureaucracy is the means by which patriarchy is perpetuated.

Feminist politics will have limited impact if they are confined to the conventional political arena. Feminists must also reform the government bureaucracy, which otherwise has an endless capacity to evaporate policies for women's advancement.

This paper — written merely to analyse a problem, not to explore the implications of the analysis — has peered briefly into a government bureaucracy and revealed some of the ways in which it can work to maintain and reproduce patriarchy in the wider society. It is not merely the internal patriarchal culture of bureaucracy which needs be reformed. Related, and more important, is the need to reform bureaucracy so that it will implement, rather than evaporate, policies on women's equality handed down from the political level of government. Bureaucracy must be converted to femocracy — a task that may be necessary for all government bureaucracies in the North, not merely development agencies.

Sara Longwe is a gender consultant, based in Lusaka, Zambia. She is known for her original work in the analysis of gender issues in development. Her "Women's Empowerment Framework" provides the basis for the UNICEF Gender Training Package. She is an activist for women's human rights and a founding member and current Vice-Chairperson of FEMNET (the African Women's Development and Communication Network).

This article is a slightly edited version of the author's presentation at the "Women's Rights and Development: Vision and Strategy for the 21st Century" seminar organized by One World Action and held at Wolfson College, Oxford, May 1995.

Notes

1. In the draft UN Platform for Action for the Fourth World Conference on Women (Beijing, 1995), it is flatly stated that, "the goals set forth in the Forward-Looking Strategies have not been achieved" (para. 35), and summarizes the pattern of women's increased impoverishment (para. 39).

2. Some readers may already be familiar with some aspects of Sundia from my discussion of an earlier visit in "Towards Better North-South Communication on Women's Development: Avoiding the Roadblocks of Patriarchal Resistance," presented at a Women in Development Europe workshop on gender planning, February 1992, Dublin. I am grateful to my partner, Roy Clarke, for the endless discussions which led to the invention of Snowdia and Sundia. My analysis of patriarchal resistance within development agencies was carried further in a subsequent paper, "Breaking the Patriarchal Alliance: Governments, Bilaterals and NGOs," *Focus on Gender* 2 (3) (1995).

3. For a recent overview of the literature in this area and some of the latest contributions, see Mike Savage and Anne Witz (eds.), *Gender and Bureaucracy*, Oxford: Blackwell, 1992.

4. Carol Gilligan. *In a Different Voice*. Cambridge, MA: Harvard University Press, 1982.

5. See, for instance, Rosemary Pringle. *Secretary's Talk: Sexuality, Power and Work*. London: Verso, 1989.

6. My earlier paper, "Towards Better North-South Communication," cited in note 2, represents my previous attempt to analyse this alliance.

7. I first wrote about these "procedures" in "From Welfare to Empowerment: The Situation of Women in Development in Africa." Women in International Development Working Paper No. 204. East Lansing: University of Michigan.

NATIONAL MACHINERIES FOR WOMEN: A BALANCING ACT

DORIENNE ROWAN-CAMPBELL

At the International Women's Year conference in Mexico City in 1975, representatives of the world's women decided that each government should establish an agency dedicated to promoting equality and gender equity and improving the status and conditions of women. They used — and continue to use — the term "national machineries" (NMs) to refer to these agencies, which have been set up by many national governments worldwide.

Ten years ago, arguing for a bilateral donor's investment in supporting a capacity-building project for the NM in one African country, I wrote: "There has probably never been a time in history when the signs were totally auspicious for promoting women's concerns. It is no different at this point in time. The omens are mixed and to read the auguries requires more oracular powers than a short visit to the country will allow." Today, reflecting on 20 years' experience, it is clear to me that there has never been *a best of times* or *a worst of times* for those working in national machineries. Instead there continues to be a tension between *a season of hope* and *a season of despair:* hope because of the gains made, despair because the pace is so very slow and the resources so minimal when measured against the intensity of women's needs and scope of expectation.

The 1994 UNDP *Human Development Report* reminds us that "all countries treat women worse than men." In the last decade, the restructuring of economies through policies aimed at reducing budget deficits, servicing debts, and increasing foreign-exchange earnings has led to severe cutbacks in social services. The quality of our health care has diminished, with consequent rises in maternal mortality and morbidity, decreases in nutritional levels, and in some countries, a decrease in life expectancy.

Lest we despair, there is also some hope. More women and girls are being educated, there are more of us in decision-making positions, more laws protecting or guaranteeing our equality are being proposed and passed, measures to address violence against us are on most international and national agendas, and it is becoming politically incorrect for politicians and international bureaucrats to neglect to mention women or gender.

How much of the positive changes can be attributed to the work of national machineries is a difficult assessment to make. Most have been responsive to local women's concerns but have not been assertive in agenda-setting. They have remained a pinprick of light in the bureaucratic darkness, a reminder which keeps issues visible and alive. Given few tools and little recognition, NMs have nevertheless succeeded in maintaining an institutional space for women's issues in national and international bureaucracies. Minimal as this achievement may seem, it is significant. We celebrate their commitment, "stick-to-itiveness," and survival skills.

141

We celebrate also a contained but meaningful achievement.

Globally, what other achievements of NMs should we celebrate? To date, gains have been made in institutionalizing a focal point for women's affairs in governments and international agencies, but there has been limited progress toward institutionalizing the issues. It appears that even as more and more people use the language of gender and development and more documents speak of gender equality and equity, less and less direct action is being taken on the issues. One very senior government official confided that "senior policy makers have been educated to use the right words and a measure of forbearance . . ." The state, for the most part, tolerates welfare initiatives, which in no way address fundamental asymmetries in power relations, allocation of resources between men and women, or promotion of more women into decision-making positions. There have been legal changes, but these have served as benchmarks and have not been rigorously applied and monitored.

A common experience of NMs both South and North — which is also shared by the "women's focal points" which often work as their counterparts in bilateral and multilateral organizations — is their need to perform a balancing act. They are pressured by internal demands to respond to the immediate welfare needs of women and by international demands to address policy issues; by the expectations created by governments' declarations and commitments at international conferences but with slight attention and even slighter resources applied to the task at home. Machineries have tried to work within the bounds of what the state allows, fighting for the past 20 years for credibility, validity, and institutional acceptance.

To maintain the momentum of change, NMs must be able achieve more. Pausing on the edge of this new millennium, therefore, we must soberly assess new models through which they can turn rhetoric into reality and protect past gains against potential challenges.

AN ENVIRONMENT OF CHALLENGE

A measure of the challenges likely to confront us in the 21st century is evident in preparations for the Fourth World Conference on Women (WCW) itself — a conference where the language of parity and equity, conveyed in such words as *gender*, is under attack and where there is still no agreement over such fundamental concerns as safe motherhood and reproductive rights. The debates offer a glimpse of a world in which strong religious fundamentalism twists the words of women's movements, with their aspirations of liberation for both women and men, into a litany for social breakdown and family disintegration

Debates over language at world conferences is not the only signal of an adverserial environment. While the United Nations may plead stringency, the WCW Secretariat is more slightly staffed than that of any previous conference and certainly has been allocated fewer resources than the 1992 UN Conference on Environment and Development (UNCED), the 1994 International Conference on Population and Development (ICPD), or the 1995 World Summit on Social Development (WSSD). Despite the positive language adopted by ICPD, the women's focal points in the UN system appear to be finding that they are working with diminishing resources and that vision and achievement are not rewarded. The same is often true at the national level. As rhetoric increases — e.g., *the gender gap, women's rights as human rights* — practical commitments apparently decrease. National machineries in most developing countries find that fewer resources are allocated for women's affairs than in the previous ten years, both from the state and from international sources. In some countries, instruments for empowerment are under attack. In the US, the Republican "Contract with America" is challenging the affirmative action instruments by which that country attempted to address inequality based on sex and race. In many countries, men see themselves as victims of these policies. In the Caribbean and Brazil, in particular, male marginalization is a burning issue, with high drop-out rates of young males from formal education systems, fuelling debate and a backlash which treats gender issues as misguided.

Geopolitical considerations have changed over the 20 years and most countries of the North and South are adopting the same economic pattern: a reliance on market forces, emphasis on export-oriented industries, and greater privatization of services formerly provided by government. As countries seek their competitive advantage, there has been a massive influx of women into low-paying, low-skilled employment in textiles, light manufacturing, and export-processing, the low pay once again being justified by the "pin money" ideology of women as secondary earners. At the same time, fundamentalists are firmly placing the burden of home, hearth, family, and community morals on women.

Does the structure of NMs as developed over the past two decades prepare them to meet these challenges? The tasks allocated to them include issue identification, priority-setting, advocacy, awareness-building, policy development, policy analysis, policy influence, welfare protection, and monitoring — all necessary functions if the wide mandate to transform society is to be realized. In the past 20 years, however, energies have been focused on establishing machinery and continually re-creating institutional room, validity, and credibility as development policies, political trends, or parties change. Emphasis has been placed on the advocacy and awareness-building role of NMs and, aided by the international community, on specific programmes and projects for women. By 1990 many national machineries had progressed beyond the setting-up phase and had managed to convince governments to establish national policies for women. These policies now need to be translated into operational instruments.

The work of NMs has been hindered by isolation. The staff of a women's unit, bureau, or ministry is susceptible to a "women for women by women" syndrome, in which all issues relating to women remain the sole province of that unit and no other segment of government accepts responsibility. Without the authority to compel other departments to take up issues, an NM has only persuasion to fall back on. The resulting organizational vulnerability has received little understanding from NGOs and women's groups, which often attack the machinery's inability to introduce and maintain change. NMs have been working in from the margins, working through erosion rather than through the creation of true alternatives.

NATIONAL MACHINERIES AS AGENTS OF CHANGE

Faced with a wide mandate — of which they are able to deliver only a fraction — innumerable functions, small staffs, little bureaucratic support, and the suspicion of NGOs and women's organizations, national machineries have been assessed as having consistently underperformed. Based on that judgement we can either decide that NMs are no longer relevant or we can change how we do business. Given the enormous unsung struggle in these fragile institutions, changing how we do business would be my option.

How do we do this? Lessons from the past point us in a number of strategic directions: re-examining alliances, providing training for specific skills, rethinking the models for NMs, and exploiting the current policy and development environment.

Alliances

Successes underline the importance of building partnerships and alliances. In countries such as India and the Philippines, changes in the planning processes were not achieved by fiat but through alliances and an active working partnership among academics, experts,

143

sympathetic planners, and the NM. Jamaica adopted a strong national policy statement which was developed in partnership with women's organizations, academics, and bureaucrats and through grass-roots consultations. My own experience in international machinery confirms that a partnership between leading experts and committed academics can move critical issues, such as violence against women and the gender dimensions of structural adjustment, onto the international stage. Alliances with the local academic community can provide the analytic and research skills which few machineries possess and which they sorely require. Indonesia provides an example of a state approach to partnership between an NM and women's studies centres established to strengthen the knowledge base for policy analysis and development.

To be effective, then, the NM needs to consciously develop strategic alliances. The NGO community can push for more radical changes than can an arm of government, and their efforts provide room for negotiating the national machinery's change agenda. As the private sector begins to supply many of the services previously envisaged as being the purview of government, it is clear that alliances need to be built with that sector so as to influence their policies and operations.

The most important new alliance needs to be with men. An environment needs to be created in which men can see change as bringing opportunities rather than confrontation and a positive partnership rather than a female take-over. Men need to understand, as well, that gender is not just another way of saying women but a means of addressing an imbalance in relations between men and women, whether the scales are weighted on the men's side or on the women's.

Are these kinds of alliances possible in a bureaucratic environment? A key role for national machineries is to stimulate changes in attitudes, behaviours, and values of both the civil service and the local population. It is apparent that NM staff do not recognize this primary role as a change agent and have, therefore, done little to equip themselves for the task. Within government, those working on such issues as AIDS and environment face similar challenges. It is not readily apparent that they think of themselves as change agents either. Although innovation is highly touted in the private sector, it is not often rewarded in the public sector and a change agent is usually viewed as a threat to established bureaucratic practice. A starting point in becoming more effective in managing change would be for NMs to develop working relationships with colleagues involved in other social change issues and facing similar challenges. Through informal meetings, workshops, and seminars, they could together examine constraints and potential which might lead to some strategic directions for effectively stimulating and anchoring organizational and community change. These internal alliances are as important as the alliances developed with those outside the bureaucracy.

Training

Considerable interpersonal and strategic negotiation skills, as well as organizational and management capacities, are required to make and maintain alliances. Additionally, monitoring and analysing policies and undertaking policy dialogue requires technical skills in gender analysis. These skills are what most national machineries lack. Their staff tend to be generalists drawn from the social sector. Some have worked with NGOs, some have project management experience, and many are politically appointed "because they are women" and should therefore know what women need. If NMs are going to be a force for change in the new millennium, then training will be needed to build their capacity. Capacity-building has so far concentrated on providing training in gender analysis, project development, and project management, although more recently some training relating to policy has been available. Working toward tomorrow requires a training revolution. NM staff need to understand organizations, public and private, and to be able to assess their tolerance for change. This awareness is crucial to working effectively in bureaucracies and provides a dynamic entry point for working with the private sector. They need, as well, to wield "expert" power (that is, the power of knowledge and skill) in policy analysis, planning, and identification of strategic issues.

Above all, NMs need to critically examine power and power relations, and this is rarely covered in the types of training provided. This understanding is particularly important because machineries have very little legitimate power, as their status in the government hierarchy is generally low. The tendency has been for them to use the "referent power" of their ministers or that of a sympathetic patron, such as the head of state. They thus become dependent on these allies. Some heads or directors of NMs use their personal charismatic power to effect change, failing to understand that when the issues, approaches, and activities are viewed as personal to the head of the agency, it becomes difficult to sustain any gains achieved when that person leaves the position.

Training that embraces this wide curriculum for change needs to be developed, not by NMs but by those who work in gender and development, in women's studies, in international agencies, and in NGOs. There is also a need to exercise creativity in developing materials on management and public administration specifically for NMs.

Structures

Even with training, how much should be expected of an NM? Are the structures so far devised functionally capable of delivering the mandate? For those who have worked in this field for the past 20 years, the term *national machinery* conjures up an image of a small unit, desk, or bureau staffed by a few women and situated at the middle-management level of a social-sector agency or ministry. While some NMs are ministries in their own right, even these suffer from a paucity of funds, staff, space, and authority. While these structures are expected to influence the policy agendas of government, most of their work is directed at welfare activities designed to meet the practical needs of a defined group of women. There are reasons for this. A minister needs a product, and the impact of changing policy directions behind doors in cabinet meetings is not readily apparent to those outside government. A constituency needs visible signals that government is responding to their concerns. NMs are therefore continually trying to be all things at all times to bureaucrats, the minister, and the international agencies that assist them and their constituency, women. Is this the best way of doing business?

Perhaps we should look at the use of the word *machinery* from a different perspective. A machine is a purpose-built tool comprising many mechanical or electronic parts with different functions. The tool works through the interaction of those parts and functions. National machinery has many different functions, and it is through the effective interaction of these functions that the mandates can best be achieved. New models can be visualized if we think of each of the critical functions as a "cog" in the larger machine and reconsider how it is shaped and how it interacts with the other parts.

The international community has long suggested that NMs are best situated in a policy or planning ministry/agency. While this remains valid, an even more efficient working arrangement could be envisaged. The key functions of the machinery — advocacy, policy analysis and influence, issue identification and prioritization, awareness-building, and the modelling of responsive programmes — could be broken down and split up among relevant government agencies. This change is less radical than it sounds. Briefly outlined, the restructuring would be as follows: The welfare and social-sector aspects of the NM's work would remain with the minister currently responsible and thus continue rightly in a welfare or social service area. Women's immediate practical needs could then be met through this agency. This "cog" of the machine would have, as at present, an advocacy role which would extend to strategic issues, such as legal change and the structural nature of violence against women. It would also have a monitoring role, assessing the implications of policy decisions, and a reporting role through the minister. It would remain the lead agency on women's affairs, setting agendas for change through identifying issues and through its close working alliances with women's organizations, NGOs, and the private sector.

The lessons of the past 20 years have clearly demonstrated that a national machinery working alone cannot set and implement policy, even when a specific national policy for women is developed. It is also evident that even the support structures envisaged, such as inter-ministerial committees, have been constituted at too junior a level to have real impact on policy planning and state decisions. The policy-making and -influencing function of the NM should therefore be attached to the key policy and planning body in the country at a decision-making level. This "cog" could be charged with the responsibility for influencing and integrating women-specific and gender concerns into the macro policy-making and planning process and provide technical advice to effect this. Further, this unit should be required to monitor not only its own policy activities and to report on them but to provide a government-wide overview on the development and implementation of policies for women's affairs. This arrangement would relieve the NM of being accountable and responsible for activities that must be undertaken by other ministries and agencies. This restructuring should also legitimate the inter-ministry negotiations and collaborative efforts which NMs have been attempting to set in place for years.

This is not to suggest that the question of accountability will not remain as vexed. The structure simply specifies a mechanism through which direct accountability for policy development and implementation is no longer vested solely in the national machinery but is shared with the policy ministry and, through it, all other ministries. Requirements to report, delicately handled, allow the minister responsible to hold colleagues more directly accountable for contributing to the overall mandate, while the requirement for other ministries to assess and report on their activities places more pressure on each ministry and its minister to accept responsibility for the integration of women and gender equity in their own policies and programmes.

Making Language Live

Sharing mandates and responsibilities should allow the NM more time to explore other mechanisms to advance gender issues and to address the challenges which lie ahead. First, existing tools need to be used more effectively. National machineries seem to have invoked the Convention on the Elimination of All Forms of Discrimination Against Women (CEDAW) very little in their battle to make governments act on their promises, yet it is an obvious negotiating tool. Most NMs appear to refer to CEDAW only when there is a need to report on compliance. In addition, UNCED and ICPD have strong clear language which can be used to bolster arguments, and it is hoped that the WCW Platform for Action emerging from Beijing will be a clear blueprint for policy makers.

A more aggressive and strategic approach needs to be taken to using the international language of development. Slogans can be made real and bring about concrete change. There is also, however, need for caution. For instance, it is very difficult for an agency of government to critique its own government's human rights record. In the transformation of "slogans" into operational policies, the NM is too vulnerable and should not work alone. For example, as preparations moved into high gear for Beijing, it became clear that many countries with dubious human rights records were using the notion of their attention to women's issues to embellish their tarnished images. The NMs in those countries can use these opportunities as an entry point to push for concrete actions. Manipulating the manipulators is part of the work of the NM or of any change agent. Machiavelli would have approved.

This Renaissance political pragmatist might also have had a great deal to say about the emergence of "good governance" as a means to and an objective for development. The elements of good governance, as currently defined, include social justice, political pluralism, administrative accountablity, transparency, and economic liberalism. Without entering the debates as to whether good government can be achieved in all countries and for all people by adopting essentially western models and values or whether loan and aid conditionalities should attach to non-performamce by governments, the elements of the good-governance agenda provide ammunition and negotiating space for NMs. Demands for transparency and accountability can greatly enhance arguments for better monitoring of the impact of policies on women and men and for wider reporting of the outcomes. Some donors are emphasizing women's participation as an important contribution to achieving good governance and wish to see evidence of this.

Ideas discarded in the late 1980s and early 1990s, such as poverty alleviation being linked to social justice and empowerment, are emerging again. Following the WSSD, numerous countries began to develop new poverty alleviation programmes. NMs have opportunities to use the language of the WSSD, ICPD, and good governance to ensure that current interventions differentiate between poverty experienced by women and poverty experienced by men, to target women as the poorest in all societies, and to design equitable interventions.

CONCLUSION

Where will the leadership come from to address required changes? An agenda is needed. The WCW Platform for Action should provide this, but the draft in hand as we approach the Conference presumes business as usual for national machineries. Institutions as frail as most national machineries are not well placed to restructure themselves. They need allies to share the risk-taking and protect hard-won gains. NMs take the burden of responsibility for government action or inaction. They often take the blame for the inaction or inattention of the wider community. It is time to see what we, the people, the intended beneficiaries of NMs, can do to support them, to offer new ideas, and to initiate alternative visions. Formerly, too many people of vision, energy, and commitment shielded themselves from direct involvement with government, preferring to work in the non-government arena. How will NMs build new alliances if we, the vaunted allies, reject this partnership?

Taming the challenges of tomorrow can be achieved only through partnership. Without partnership, we miss an opportunity to forge a moment and a movement of solidarity to defeat the dangers of fundamentalism, economic marginalization, and male fear. Without partnership for change, our heirs will find themselves in the year 2015 still trapped as perfomers in a balancing act with little forward momentum. And the work undertaken by agencies promoting gender equity and equality will still be undertaken in an environment characterized by *the best of times and the worst of times, ever a season of hope, ever a season of despair.*

Dorienne Rowan-Campbell has been involved with institutionalizing change in public broadcasting with the Canadian Broadcasting Corporation, the Women and Development Programme of the Commonwealth Secretariat, and Women and Development Studies at the University of the West Indies. A Jamaican and a Canadian, she now works as an independent consultant. She serves on UNIFEM's Editorial Advisory Committee.

PART 3

SHAPING THE INTERNATIONAL AGENDA: WOMEN'S ACTIONS AT UN CONFERENCES

"The Platform for Action recognizes the importance of the agreements reached at the World Summit for Children, the United Nations Conference on Environment and Development, the World Conference on Human Rights, the International Conference on Population and Development and the World Summit for Social Development which set out specific approaches and commitments to fostering sustainable development and international cooperation..."

— Platform for Action, Fourth World Conference on Women, Chapter II, para. 8.

WOMEN AND THE POLITICS OF SUSTAINABLE DEVELOPMENT

SABINE HÄUSLER

In the 1970s and 1980s, many NGOs and different social movements, both in the South and the North, started to be active on the margins of the dominant Western development model. They sought to formulate and implement alternatives to the mainstream export-led growth model of economic development that has resulted in an exploitation of both natural resources and human beings, women in particular. Over the years they became a force to be reckoned with and wielded considerable influence — both in practice and even more on the level of presenting powerful alternative discourses.

The development establishment in the North and its satellites in the South were engaged in gradually incorporating these valid criticisms. They co-opted ideas from the margins into their discourses and political agendas. A considerable proportion of Northern development funds was shifted from ineffective and slow Southern government bureaucracies to international and national NGOs, in the hope of making development more "people"-oriented — the major point of criticism of mainstream development. Development projects thus became cheaper because NGOs do not require highly paid development experts and equipment. Meanwhile, the pressure of criticism was reduced, and large-scale development projects geared at industrializing the South continued.

In response to the accelerating global crisis of environment and development, in 1989 the United Nations passed a resolution to organize the UN Conference on Environment and Development (UNCED). The goal was to steer the world onto a path of "sustainable development." Within the preparatory process a new mode of partnership and dialogue among an increasing number of actors came into being. For the first time, the United Nations opened the way for a large group of non-governmental actors to participate in the preparatory process for a UN conference.

These new actors on the global scene were different citizens' movements from both North and South, women, indigenous people, environment and development NGOs, as well as business and industry. Even the most radical critics of the development model felt the need to use this opportunity to influence mainstream agendas directly. The different groups, with their very different agendas, were lumped together as the "independent sector" by the architects of the NGO Global Forum that was held parallel to UNCED in 1992. The fact that the term *NGO* was vaguely defined — namely, as any group not a governmental organization — led to the paradoxical situation of transnational corporations fighting for their interests rubbing shoulders with the Amazonian Indians, women's groups, and so on — all in the same forum. The different groups organized in the independent sector engaged in several separate preparatory processes for UNCED and, as a result, reached a new level of cooperation and exchange.

The different groups used a two-fold strategy: on the one hand, they lobbied their governments during the preparatory process for UNCED to incorporate their respective demands into governmental negotiations about global environmental regimes; on the other hand, they prepared for their independent input into the NGO Global Forum.

The citizens' movements drafted treaties reflecting their visions for a sustainable world, alternative and additional to those proposed by the mainstream actors of UNCED. The Business Council for Sustainable Development, representing some of the environmentally most destructive industries and businesses, proposed reformative self-regulation of their own activities. Other NGOs, such as development and environment groups, religious groups, youth organizations, and scientists, and other UN agencies, such as the World Bank, the UN Environment Programme (UNEP), and the Food and Agriculture Organization (FAO), prepared their own proposals for a sustainable future. All of these and more were given a space within the NGO Global Forum.

The net result of UNCED as a whole is still a failure of global proportions. The UNCED *Agenda 21* and the treaties are non-binding. One of the major winners of UNCED is the World Bank, which is now managing the major financial mechanism for sustainable development projects in the South, the Global Environment Facility (GEF). Northern governments got away with continuing business as usual — with minor improvements. One concession from Northern political leaders was commitments to transfer funds into the GEF; Northern aid agencies will reshape their aid policies so as to scale up environmental development projects in the South. Southern political leaders asserted their right to more Western-style development and hence a continued flow of aid funds.

Through their effective advocacy and lobbying of governments, transnational corporations escaped stringent control mechanisms to regulate their activities in the future. Citizens' movements had next to no influence on fundamentally changing the mainstream agenda. They were invited to "cooperate," but in effect, it was only their language that was incorporated into the documents, while the nature of the documents remained largely conservative with respect to the present economic and political order. A large-scale co-option of critical citizens' groups was in full swing during the UNCED process. However, the main success of citizens' movements was an increase in exchange with like-minded groups globally and a new level of communication, particularly by electronic means. What will happen with the citizens' movements' alternative treaties, including the "Women's Action Agenda 21," which were meant to be guidelines for future actions, remains unclear. A great number of groups continue to monitor their governments' implementation of changes proposed in the UNCED *Agenda 21,* the new Commission on Sustainable Development and future international conferences, in the hope of influencing their agendas.

In short, "sustainable development" has become the latest stage in the development discourse, which has shown once again its incredible capacity to survive against all odds. We live in a global economic and political order in which mainstream actors will go on doing business as usual — touched up in "green." A new eco-cratic rationality is forcefully asserting itself.

Looking back at the experience of UNCED, the most important lesson to learn is to understand the new and more sophisticated strategies of power that have developed within the process. Within the partnership-and-dialogue model of consultation with the independent sector, it has become obvious that marginal actors such as women, indigenous people, and other citizens' groups have been unable to change the parameters of the discussion. The lobbying of citizens' groups and NGOs at the UNCED preparatory committee meetings were based on pre-set agendas — which, in effect, critics could only help to improve in formulation — within the set parameters. Hence, elements of alternative development discourse were early on incorporated into the mainstream discourse. The same holds true for gendered language in the documents.

By taking part in the whole process, including the NGO Global Forum, many of the radical critics indirectly legitimized it. Poor media coverage of dissenters from the environmentally destructive mainstream development model, assembled far away from the main venue of UNCED in Rio de Janeiro, effectively silenced their criticism. In the few press reports transmitted from the NGO Forum, the emphasis was on portraying hopeless idealists, exotic Indians, and groups of emotional women. During the UNCED process, many NGOs promoting ideas suited to the interests of powerful funders, and mainstream actors gained access to funding and now increasingly resemble the mainstream in their language and practice.

The great willingness of the different citizens' movements and groups to act as a united force against the mainstream may have been counter-productive in the end. They made it all the more easy for the architects of UNCED, and in particular the NGO Global Forum, effectively to manage and contain their discontent. So successful was this process that UN conferences in the future will operate under the same model of consultation with the "independent sector."

Within the political climate of the 1990s, the results of UNCED seriously put into question the feasibility of changing the dominant institutions from within. One of the main concerns today is whether dialogue between radical critics and mainstream institutions is still possible without the former being co-opted into dominant political and economic frameworks and pre-set agendas. In the final analysis, critics may end up being changed by them, instead of the other way around.

As Donna Haraway (1988) has pointed out, the powers of today no longer work by simple domination and normalization (into the Western mode of development); power today works through networking, communications redesign, and stress management. I think the UNCED process has been a formidable illustration of Haraway's point.

These reflections raise serious questions about the alternatives of today and the futures chosen by those who do not want to be "normalized" and "networked" into the global economic and political order. Can there still be alternatives outside this all-pervasive global economic and political system? Are we not all part of it already? Do the alternatives have to be lived and fought for in spaces within it or within ourselves? Realistically speaking, the visions of citizens' movements, including the "Women's Action Agenda 21," will not become reality in any foreseeable future. We will have to live with this recognition. The challenge is to keep up positions critical of the dominant model of development while continuing to resist becoming co-opted into the very framework of thinking on which it rests. One of the most important tasks is to continue to make visible the ways in which the strategies of power operate and their increasing sophistication, and to analyse how they work in practice. Strategies for change have to start from a realistic assessment of the situation as it is, follow the full complexity and the constantly shifting grounds on which the issues are fought, and still allow room for action on all levels.

The new and ever more sophisticated methods developed by communications specialists who are in the business of managing and engineering consent — the technical term for this is issues management — need to be watched carefully. The new communication strategies aim at shaping public discourse by setting agendas rather than directly reacting to dissent. Some of the techniques used by the engineers of consent are the silencing of critics by depicting them as "confrontational" or "irresponsible," by depoliticizing the issues and casting them in technocratic terminology, by diverting attention through pushing issues of secondary

153

importance, or by fudging critical issues brought up by critical actors (Keysers and Richter, 1993).

The need to involve women on all levels and in all aspects of decision-making and action has been recognized by all mainstream actors in the UNCED process. However, their mention of women, indigenous people, children, and other marginalized groups in the UNCED documents may have been just the promotion of an issue of secondary importance in order to make their documents more acceptable to a gullible public and thus to divert attention from their reluctance to accept fundamental changes within the present economic and political world order. The UNCED formula for the independent sectors' "participation" was so successful that it will be used for upcoming UN conferences.

WOMEN AS ACTORS IN THE UNCED PROCESS

Women as a group gained their official mandate to take part in the UNCED process in the middle of 1991, at a relatively late stage when preparations were already in full swing. Through the activities of a handful of internationally known women, in particular the International Policy Action Committee (IPAC), mobilization of a sizeable number of women to take part in the process was assured. In this mode of mobilizing wider support for women to be heard within the UNCED and Global Forum proceedings and for women's roles in environmental management, their "natural" closeness to nature and hence their special knowledge about environmental processes were stressed. The prevailing image of women as agents fighting the effects of the global ecological crisis cast them as *the* answer to the crisis: women as privileged knowers of natural processes, resourceful and "naturally" suited to provide the "alternative."

A large number of case studies of women active and successful in environmental struggles were compiled for the Women's Tribunal, held in Miami in 1991. "Women's Action Agenda 21," containing a vision for alternative development from women's perspectives globally, was the outcome of the Miami Conference. This document is unique in many ways: for the first time women across the divides of North/South, race, and class and from a variety of professional and social backgrounds agreed on a common position which refuted the Western model of development as such.

A number of women very actively lobbied country delegates at the preparatory committee meetings for the inclusion of women in the UNCED documents. The whole UNCED *Agenda 21* was screened for gendered language; chapter 24, pertaining to women as a major group to be strengthened in bringing about sustainable development, was included. The proceedings at Planeta Femea within the NGO Global Forum in Rio made clear that the prevailing eco-feminist position had been a powerful way to mobilize women forcefully to voice their criticism within UNCED.

Yet during the UNCED process the long-standing statement of opposition between women from the North and the South has been softened, and women across these divides have learned that they can fruitfully work together. It has been my personal experience that women involved in women, environment, and development (WED) issues show a great openness toward working with women from other cultural and political backgrounds.

Analysing the experience of UNCED, we need to ask ourselves: Who participated in the process? Within what political frameworks do the different women participating think? Whom did these women represent? Broad-based coalition-building with other groups and movements, clarification of their political positions, and mobilization of grass-roots women within national settings remain major challenges after UNCED for women active in the struggles for sustainable livelihoods for all people.

A question mark must hover over the many success stories represented in Miami. Do they still continue to be successful or have they already faltered? When everything in society works to marginalize women, how good are the chances for their successful actions to be sustained in the long run?

Another phenomenon should make us suspicious: Virtually all actors within the UNCED process — NGOs, citizens' movements, the World Bank, aid agencies — agreed that women need to be involved in sustainable development. Hence women's aims were also accepted by actors who have a distinct interest in preserving the dominant mode of development. In fact, in many cases, inclusion of women seems to have been one way of making their texts more widely acceptable.

Considering the net results of UNCED, it is likely that women in the South in particular will become further targets of policies for sustainable development. The past experience of such development projects has shown that they put more strain on already overworked rural women without necessarily leading to much-needed wider legal and political changes for these women. Also, a stepping-up of population programmes geared mainly toward women in the South and women of colour in both the North and the South is under way.

The women's visions presented in "Women's Action Agenda 21" and the other NGO treaties drafted at the NGO Forum in Rio are beautiful and powerful, but how realistic is their implementation? The activities of different women and women's groups after UNCED seems to be heading in two directions: either geared toward the integration of women into the mainstream of sustainable development as expressed in the UNCED *Agenda 21,* or toward a criticism of the Western development model as such as expressed in the "Women's Action Agenda 21." Much post-UNCED lobbying of, for example, the Commission on Sustainable Development has been geared at integration of women: equal gender representation within the board, and so on.

Illustrating the problem of differences among women were the struggles within the women's movement on the question of reproductive rights versus feminist population-control programmes that occurred within the preparatory process for the 1994 International Conference on Population and Development (ICPD). Much can be learned and extrapolated from the recent struggles. A deep split is currently running through the women's movement on the not-so-new question of integration vs. autonomy, or to borrow from the Greens, realism ("realos") versus fundamentalism ("fundies"). Further studies of the sophisticated processes of co-option of feminist women into the project of the powerful population control lobby are needed.

Within the present political climate, can we still hope to change the dominant institutions from within without being trapped by having to argue with them within their frameworks — and without being changed by them in the process? How do the alternative visions of development proposed in "Women's Action Agenda 21" and the integrative position proposed in chapter 24 on women in the UNCED *Agenda 21* relate to each other if we agree that the most effective road to sustainable development must be to change the parameters of the framework itself? These are old questions within the women's movement, but we are not much closer to answering them now than we were a decade ago. The answers to these questions and strategies for the future need to take into account the experiences of women organizing within UNCED and the newly emerging methods of co-option and manipulation.

The question arises whether all or most of our efforts should concentrate on the many

UN conferences that will come up in the next few years or whether we should spend a large part of our energies in building up some more lasting organizational structure that can have a long-term impact and survive such mega-events. We need time and space to experiment further with alternative ways of being, thinking, acting, and relating to one another. Also, more analytical clarity on conceptual issues regarding women's alternatives to development is needed.

FUTURE RESEARCH ON ISSUES OF WOMEN AND THE ENVIRONMENT

I do not mean to imply that research can in any way assume a privileged role in the struggle for sustainable livelihood of all people globally. We need a clearer idea of who is doing what in terms of action, research, and policy formulation, and where the crucial gaps are.

What role can research play in the struggles ahead? Starting out from women's lives, the epistemological sensibility of feminist researchers should further help and strengthen grass-roots women North and South to determine their own agendas for change. Recent developments within feminist research methodologies need to be considered. The emphasis should be on situated knowledge. In this sense, research could take a strategic role in the support of alternatives proposed by people at the grass-roots level. Much of the work on the theoretical level needs to be done in order to provide the conceptual basis for alternative visions of development and to help make grass-roots people's experience influential in the theoretical discussions of the architects of "sustainable development." Many of the newly emerging alternative discourses and proposals for change lack women's and feminist perspectives. Further criticism of Western science and technology as the solution to the crisis from feminist position is much needed.

Within the last two decades, research on issues of women and the environment has been mainly about women in the South in the context of development work. The vast majority of earlier studies focused on either proving or disproving women's inherently closer connection to nature and their "nature" interest in safeguarding their environment. Today this question no longer seems relevant; we know that women suffer disproportionately from the many different manifestations of the global ecological crisis. In any event, the question of women's relation to nature/environment must remain open-ended. Women's own perception of their relation to nature and their motives for being involved in ecological action may vary according to cultural, religious, or ideological backgrounds, across the division of North and South. The question is no longer what is the "correct" position on the woman/nature relation, but rather how we situate ourselves as women and agents committed to the fundamental change of the Western development model and how our actions and struggles can be most effective. Within the politics of rainbow coalitions, what are effective strategies to preserve people's, and in particular women's, interests?

There is now widespread recognition that development is not just a problem of the South but a global problem. Frameworks of analysis have to be grounded in the perspective of a global crisis that manifests itself in different forms in the different regions of the world. At issue for sustainability are relationships of power at all levels, the bargaining power of different groups of different people, and their different knowledge bases. Sustainability implies questioning what kind of development we want.

RESEARCH CHALLENGES

One of the major challenges remains providing inroads into dismantling the Western framework of thinking itself. Women researchers in the mainstream natural as well as social sciences have a crucial role in further challenging their disciplines' Western, white, male frameworks of thinking and, accordingly, the solutions and policies they propose for environmental reforms. The implicit values and ideologies behind environmental managerialism need to be further disclosed and challenged. Feminist philosophers, scholars within cultural studies, and in particular non-Western feminists could provide further fundamental criticism of the Western, patriarchal, Enlightenment thinking that is at the very root of the crisis of environment and development. On a theoretical level, the vantage point of women and environment has been a particularly useful perspective from which to criticize the Western development model. Non-Western feminists could make important contributions in challenging the almost all-pervasive Western framework of thinking, not from within its own parameters, but from genuinely non-Western modes of thinking. The development indicators applied at present to assess human well-being may thereby be dismantled as highly reductionist; the validation of local people's experiential knowledge about natural processes also falls into this category.

Western-type environmental education for sustainable development extended to Southern people must be questioned and challenged if the sustainability of existing non-Western modes of living is taken seriously. However, the tendency to romanticize such lifestyles must be avoided.

Further cooperation among Western, Eastern, and Southern researchers will be crucial in the future. Networking of researchers, policy makers, and activists engaged around different environmental regimes — such as biodiversity, forests, climate change, and so on — is necessary to monitor and analyse these highly dynamic fields and their constantly shifting terrains. Ever more complex amounts of information produced within international conferences and negotiations need to be processed, analysed, and made available to action groups. Very often such analysis lacks a feminist perspective and is hence an area in which feminist researchers could well specialize. Together, activists, policy makers, and researchers could think through the effects of international developments in these fields and devise effective strategies for action.

In order to bring women's issues into macro-frameworks of analysis, conceptual work is needed to link women's experiences at the micro-level to macro-level theory. Among these issues are international trade agreements, the neoclassical economic framework, high-tech agriculture, commercially oriented forestry, industrial fishery, and so on. People's, and especially women's, initiatives and self-determined ways of managing natural resources need to be strengthened by our providing conceptual foundations for their validity and long-term sustainability. In this way, the highly environmentally destructive practices in the fields just mentioned can be challenged. Further sex-segregated data collection also is necessary fully to reflect women's contribution to the economy. For example, work on alternative economic frameworks that take into account the real costs of women's work and nature's destruction is needed to provide the basis for development alternatives. The challenge here is to strike a balance between accounting "real" costs while keeping in mind intrinsic and non-accountable values.

Careful analysis and monitoring of the politics of sustainable development and how power relations unfold, shift, and assert themselves are needed. It is necessary to keep an overview of the political process in general as well as women's stake in it. We also have to

157

grapple with the question of women's politics and politics between women. How can women from different backgrounds and from different cultures work together more closely without reproducing the old patriarchal structures of domination? Can we make each other accountable as we work on transformative projects? How can we avoid marginalization of women by women? Certainly, a mere redefinition of power by women which emphasizes women's values and culture may not be sufficient to tackle this issue.

CONCLUSION

These few reflections have made it clear that the UNCED process and the emerging politics of sustainable development present formidable challenges to everyone genuinely interested in sustainable livelihoods for all people. For women active in environmental struggles the real challenges still lie ahead, and the small successes achieved so far need to be fought for continuously. Alliances and bridges built between women and other actors interested in fundamental transformation of development globally need to be nurtured carefully as a long-term project. Looking back to the early 1970s, when the interest in women's role in the management of natural resources first emerged, and reflecting on the last two decades since then, we have come a long way in the WED debate and practice. However, the global mobilization of women around environmental issues which started in the early 1990s within the UNCED preparatory process will have to move into a new phase.

Sabine Häusler is a contributor to and an editor of Women, the Environment and Sustainable Development: Towards a Theoretical Synthesis (Braidotti et al, eds. Zed Books, 1994). Since 1992 she has been working on an interdisciplinary research project at the Institute of Social Studies, The Hague, and the University of Utrecht. She worked in Nepal from 1985 to 1989, advising that country's largest international NGO.

This paper draws upon the author's "Women and the Politics of Sustainable Development," in Wendy Harcourt (ed.), *Feminist Perspectives on Sustainable Development*. London and New Jersey: Zed Books, in association with the Society for International Development, Rome, 1994.

References

ANPED (Alliance of Northern People for Environment and Development). 1992. Agenda Ya Wananchi, Citizens' Action Plan for the 1990s. Global Conference of NGOs, December 1991, Paris.

Braidotti, Rosi, Ewa Charkiewicz-Pluta, Sabine Häusler, and Saskia Wieringa. 1993. *Women, the Environment, and Sustainable Development: Toward a Theoretical Synthesis.* London: Zed Books/INSTRAW.

Haraway, Donna. 1988. "A Manifesto for Cyborgs: Science, Technology, and Socialist Feminism in the 1980s," in Linda Nicholson (ed.), *Feminism/Postmodernism*. New York and London: Routledge.

Keysers, Loes, and Judith Richter. 1993. "Dialogue on Population: Power and Co-option Mechanisms in Women's International Networking Around Reproductive Rights." Paper presented at SID/WUMEN Roundtable on Women, the Environment, and Development Alternatives, Institute of Social Studies, The Hague.

UNCED (United Nations Conference on Environment and Development). 1992. *Agenda 21.*

WEDO (Women's Environment and Development Organization). 1992. Official Report. Women's Congress for a Healthy Planet, Miami, Florida, November 1991.

WOMEN'S HUMAN RIGHTS
AND DEVELOPMENT:
A GLOBAL AGENDA FOR THE
21ST CENTURY

CHARLOTTE BUNCH

The world community has recently begun to recognize women as a new source of energy, ideas, and strategies. Women have contributed greatly to major United Nations global conferences over the past several years: the United Nations Conference on Environment and Development in Rio (UNCED, 1992); the World Conference on Human Rights in Vienna (WCHR, 1993); the International Conference on Population and Development in Cairo (ICPD, 1994); and the World Summit for Social Development in Copenhagen (WSSD, 1995). But women's activism at these fora has not simply been about the events themselves. It reflects our determination to bring gender perspectives into global debates and to become an integral part of policy-making nationally, regionally, and internationally, at these conferences and beyond.

Women are seeking to connect our experiences in local community leadership to global policy-making, where decisions that affect our daily lives are made. Locally, women have been maintaining families and holding communities together, often in the face of adverse economic circumstances and civil strife as well as sexual discrimination and attitudes that diminish our contributions to society. Women's experiences of sustaining life and the perspectives that emerge from these are desperately needed in policy-making, where current systems are failing to provide sustainable human development for the globe.

Active participation of women in making policy means that global issues — peace, environment, development, human rights, democracy — will no longer be viewed without a gender perspective, and that the work done on so-called women's issues — equal pay, the feminization of poverty, violence against women, reproductive rights, and so on — will affect the very framing of social policy questions.

In demonstrating that "women's issues" are interconnected with other global issues, women show that what we know about such questions is also relevant to broader policies. For example, violence against women and children at home can be seen as part of a continuum of violence and domination in the world that includes war and racial conflict as well. Understood thus, it is clear that such societal conflicts will not diminish as long as we continue to tolerate violence in the family — at the core of society — which teaches children to accept and use violence as the way to resolve differences and achieve control over others.

159

Incorporating gender perspectives into the major global policy areas requires both adding new issues to the agenda, such as violence against women, as well as transforming current understanding of familiar concepts. For example, in the area of human rights, it requires moving beyond the divisions between public and private and between socioeconomic and civil-political rights that have allowed vast areas of violation to remain invisible. Such distinctions must be broken down and the divisive "either/or" and "which comes first" debates put aside. Rather, women's lives demonstrate clearly what is also true for most men: all rights must be seen as indivisible. The ability to exercise socioeconomic rights affects one's ability to exercise civil-political rights, just as access to human rights in the private sphere affects one's ability to exercise rights in public.

And just as human rights are indivisible, so too are the major global policy questions interconnected. Human rights, peace, development, environment, population, and many other issues affect one another, and all are critical to an effective women's global agenda for the 21st century.

WOMEN'S HUMAN RIGHTS ARE BASIC TO A GLOBAL DEVELOPMENT AGENDA

Human rights is a system of values and ethical principles that expresses what people determine is fundamental to human dignity and that seeks to cross national, racial, cultural, and gender boundaries. As such, our understanding of what constitutes human rights evolves over time, and as we face the next millennium, it has come to seem that human rights principles must include the indisputable assertion of the universal dignity of all of humankind. Women seek to make this vision more inclusive and to realize such rights for ourselves as well as for others who have been excluded from exercising them.

The development agenda that has been set by the UN world conferences held over the past five years includes a broad range of provisions to support women's potential to participate in and transform development. This development agenda — encompassing environment, employment, poverty alleviation, social integration, and reproductive rights — demands respect for women's human rights to

- speak and participate in the public world, exercising the fundamental rights of citizenship and democracy;
- control their bodies and lives in the private world, without which it is often impossible to exercise public rights; and
- gain shelter, food, education, health, a secure environment, and the right to seek employment in order to secure sustainable livelihoods.

160

These rights are included in the UN Charter and the Universal Declaration of Human Rights. But too much of human rights practice and jurisprudence has been shaped by using men's life experiences as the norm and interpreting, illustrating and enforcing human rights only from that perspective. While some aspects of human rights abuse are the same for men and women, much of it is gendered; that is, the ways in which women are abused and experience torture, imprisonment, slavery, displacement, and other violations are often quite specifically shaped by being female.

Women's lives in all their diversity must be put at the centre of human rights discourse in order to understand what is basic to protecting and promoting the human dignity of the female half of humankind. Women are not waiting for permission to have our human rights recognized but rather are stating that issues like female infanticide and illiteracy, violence against women and female sexual slavery, reproductive health and women's poverty are fundamental to our humanity and must become cornerstones of human rights practice and global development agendas.

Human rights is often treated as quite separate from development. But women's experience of working to meet basic development needs has illustrated that such needs are not met when women lack basic rights. Since 1990 the Human Development Reports of the United Nations Development Programme (UNDP) have defined development as a process of widening the range of people's choices, of empowering them to participate in processes that shape their lives. Yet time after time, efforts throughout the world aimed at empowering women have been hampered by lack of respect for the human rights of women. In particular, violence against women in its many forms has become a fundamental obstacle to our ability to participate in development projects, to exercise our rights to democracy, or to engage in a wide variety of economic, social and political pursuits.

Women today are at the very epicentre of the assault on human rights and human dignity. In the face of national conflict and various chauvinisms, it is imperative that respect for human dignity be a fundamental principle. This moral system is crucial today because it counters the narrow religious fundamentalisms and nationalistic chauvinisms so prevalent in our time. Both exacerbate polarization in much of the world and deny the basic humanity of "the other." Since these reactionary forces demand male control of women and confine women to subordinate positions, the defense of women's human rights is critical to development, democracy and the very notion of human rights itself.

IMPLEMENTING WOMEN'S HUMAN RIGHTS AFTER VIENNA

As a result of the worldwide mobilization of women around the WCHR in 1993, the Vienna Declaration and Programme of Action recognized that women's human rights are universal, inalienable, and indivisible and should not be subordinated to culture or religion. For the first time, the United Nations called for the elimination of "violence against women in public and private life" as a human rights obligation.

Further, women succeeded in gaining widespread recognition of women's rights as human rights and advanced the process of creating specific mechanisms for monitoring and demanding accountability for abuse of women's human rights. Major achievements included the appointment of a Special Rapporteur on Violence Against Women, and efforts toward strengthening the Convention on the Elimination of All Forms of Discrimination Against Women (CEDAW) were reinforced. The Vienna Declaration also called for the integration of women and gender perspectives into all human rights mechanisms and practices, including gender training for those responsible for protecting and promoting human rights.

The organizing that took place around the WCHR also opened up space for other women's rights — such as the right to a secure livelihood and reproductive rights — to be understood as human rights. This resulted in the reaffirmation of the human rights of women to life, liberty, and security of person that was incorporated into the ICPD Programme of Action emerging from the 1994 Cairo conference. This final document also reflects an understanding that an adequate standard of living is critical to sustainable population and development policies.

Women have gained acceptance both as subjects of abuse and as actors for human rights.

They have advanced a more integrated approach to human rights. The challenge before us, at this point, is ensuring meaningful implementation of the declarations that have emerged from all of these conferences. Toward this end, it is vital that

- methods for documenting and redressing gender specific abuses of women's human rights be developed, since these are often complex and have generally been left out of previous approaches to human rights;
- women's human rights not be marginalized as a separate sphere where all women's issues are considered solely by women-specific mechanisms and narrow definitions of women's human rights lead to a limited sphere of action;
- gender becomes an integrated consideration in all human rights mechanisms, rapporteurs, and committees, since most abuses have differential impact on women and men and responses to them must be gender-sensitive;
- human rights mechanisms be used to demand accountability of international financial institutions and private parties such as transnational corporations for violations of women's human rights that occur as a result of their policies, such as structural adjustment; and
- women continue political pressure demanding that resources and energy be committed toward the realization of these promises to promote and protect women's human rights.

In organizing for the WCHR in Vienna, women learned important lessons that are still crucial in mobilizing for the implementation of women's human rights. Since there is still very little integration of gender in mainstream human rights bodies, women's caucuses and special units or projects are still necessary to bring women's voices into the discourse and practice of human rights more forcefully. There is much to be gained by women working at national and regional levels but also collaborating globally by coordinating strategies among women from NGOs, governments, and UN agencies even while working in different spheres. Above all, women must take action on behalf of their human rights and not wait for permission to be included.

WOMEN'S GLOBAL LEADERSHIP FOR THE 21ST CENTURY

Some of the concrete actions to be taken to bring women's visions of human rights as central to development into reality include strengthening and enforcing the Convention on the Elimination of All Forms of Discrimination Against Women (CEDAW); reinterpreting all human rights treaties to incorporate women's experiences and bringing concrete cases and documentation of these to the appropriate national, regional, and international bodies; providing gender training to all UN and government personnel, especially to national military and police forces and international peace-keepers; and placing more women on UN and regional/national bodies such as the Commission for Sustainable Development, human rights committees, and peace negotiation teams. In approaching this work, women must go beyond mobilizing around world conferences to being involved in, monitoring, and pressuring the ongoing mechanisms and bodies of the United Nations and other policy-making agencies at all levels.

Central to achieving this agenda is the work of enhancing and enabling women's leadership in the policy-making process, which involves both strengthening women's activities at the local and national levels and connecting them more effectively to global policy-making.

Only through such a process will women become a strong voice in global discussions around issues critical to human rights and development, such as UN reform, global governance, environmental standards, humanitarian relief, national sovereignty, regulatory processes for the World Trade Organization, and in other important arenas where decisions are shaped.

Funding agencies, UN and development agencies, and others supportive of a women's human rights and development agenda can take many steps to assist this process, such as:

- increasing women's access to international human rights, development, population, and peace-keeping machinery;
- educating women about global economic trends and bringing women's experiences of these into international discussions;
- training women leaders to participate in local, national, and global governance in all its various forms;
- strengthening women's organizations and networks so that they can provide training and act as a base for women's participation in these areas; and
- funding pilot projects that seek innovative solutions to problems such as violence against women, poverty alleviation, and repatriation of women refugees.

The 1995 Fourth World Conference on Women in Beijing and the 50th anniversary of the United Nations provide opportunities for women to continue advancing in this process of global activism, developing leadership, and learning more about global trends and how to affect them. This is particularly important because what happens to women is central to a multitude of the world's concerns today, from religious fundamentalism to the global economy.

At no time has women's leadership been more necessary for determining the direction of our evolution. At no time have women been more ready to move in that direction. But such leadership needs to be mobilized around a global agenda that crosses divisions between issues and understands that development, democracy, human rights, and human security are interrelated and must all be addressed if we are to create a healthy and sustainable planet in the 21st century.

Charlotte Bunch, a feminist writer and organizer for over two decades, was a founder of Washington D.C. Women's Liberation and of Quest: A Feminist Quarterly. She has edited seven anthologies including a collection of her essays, Passionate Politics: Feminist Theory in Action. Bunch is a Professor in the Bloustein School of Planning and Public Policy at Rutgers University and is the founding Director of the Centre for Women's Global Leadership.

This article draws upon the author's presentation at the UNIFEM panel "Visions for a New Women's Development Agenda" that was held during the Preparatory Committee for the World Summit on Social Development, New York, 16 January 1995.

ENSURING WOMEN'S SEXUAL AND REPRODUCTIVE HEALTH AND RIGHTS

ADRIENNE GERMAIN

On 13 September 1994 in Cairo, at the conclusion of the International Conference on Population and Development (ICPD), 184 governments reached an unprecedented consensus on a new 20-year Programme of Action to secure reproductive and sexual health, achieve gender equity and equality, promote women's empowerment, and ensure human rights, including reproductive rights (Germain and Kyte, 1995; UN, 1994). Women's health advocates, who had mobilized worldwide during the previous two years, played a central role in generating this consensus and in making certain that women's experiences, priorities, and perspectives were fully reflected. The Programme of Action specifies two essential and inseparable types of action. The first is action to ensure an adequate *supply* of good quality reproductive and sexual health services to all in need, regardless of age, income, ethnicity, gender, and other such variables. The second, and equally important, action is the creation of enabling social and economic conditions in which women and men can and do effectively *demand* services and enjoy their reproductive rights.

The key challenges facing activists, policy makers and programme managers are to persuade governments, energize donors, and enable women's groups, along with other NGOs, to ensure that the ICPD Programme of Action is implemented in its entirety, not piecemeal. In this way, both the supply and the demand sides should be balanced and interact synergistically. Implementation will not only secure reproductive and sexual health and rights, but also contribute substantially to achieving the broader goals of sustainable development, by addressing power imbalances between women and men, ensuring that people are healthy and productive, strengthening families in all their forms, and encouraging voluntary achievement of population stabilization.

This essay identifies actions specifically for women's sexual and reproductive health and rights, including but not limited to birth control, along with policies and programmes to encourage men to take responsibility for their own fertility, for prevention of sexually transmitted diseases (STDs), and for the health and well-being of their sexual partners and the children they father. All of these actions must, among other requirements, tailor interventions to particular situations (for example, some health infrastructures are not yet strong enough to guarantee safe, nonabusive provision of all methods of contraception). While encouraging men to take responsibility for their own behaviour, policies and programmes must also ensure women's control over their own bodies. It is essential that representatives of the women to be served are included in all levels and aspects of decision-making, design, implementation, and monitoring. Finally, governments — as well as health and other professionals, activists, community leaders, and programme managers — will have to address issues of sexuality and gender-based power imbalances that most would prefer to avoid.

WOMEN'S SEXUAL AND REPRODUCTIVE HEALTH

An estimated 500,000 women die each year due to pregnancy-related causes, most of them in Southern countries. Ten or more times this number suffer acute or chronic illness or injury. Perhaps half of the estimated 250 million new cases of STDs annually occur in girls and women. In many countries, girls and women constitute the fastest growing segment of new HIV/AIDS cases, and in sub-Saharan Africa the female to male ratio is estimated to be six women infected for every four men (WHO, 1995). The rate of transmission of STDs from men to women is higher than from women to men. Women suffer much worse consequences than men from STDs, including increased risk of ectopic pregnancy, pregnancy wastage, and pelvic inflammatory disease (Dixon-Mueller and Wasserheit, 1991; Germain et al., 1992).

The world has so far invested far too little in women's sexual and reproductive health, especially safe pregnancy and delivery, STD prevention and control, and gynaecologic care. Rather, the bulk of resources available for sexual and reproductive health have gone into family planning programmes (Zeitlin, Govindaraj, and Chen, 1994; Brady and Winikoff, 1992). Although these programmes have assisted millions of women to control their own fertility, an estimated 100 million married women of reproductive age still have no access to services, and that number will increase by another 170 million in the 1990s (Merrick, 1994). Uncounted millions more are excluded from services because they are "too young" or unmarried; others are poorly served (Dixon-Mueller and Germain, 1992); most men are not included in family planning services. As many as 38 million induced abortions occur annually in Southern countries, an estimated 20 million of them clandestine and unsafe, a stark testament to the lengths to which women go to prevent an unwanted birth (Germain, 1989). In too many cases, subtle or explicit coercion of one sort or another has been used to "persuade" or force individuals to use contraceptives, to be sterilized, or to have abortions (Boland, Rao, and Zeidenstein, 1994).

The ICPD Programme of Action clearly disallows coercion and incentives in any form in reproductive health services, including family planning programmes. Further, it specifies that truly voluntary fertility control that respects human rights and advances health requires not only improved quality of family planning services, but also expanded service approaches that encompass the multiple dimensions of sexual and reproductive health for both women and men: sexuality and gender education, STD prevention and treatment, safe abortion, pregnancy and delivery services, postpartum and gynaecologic care, and child health. This commitment echoes the "Women's Declaration on Population Policies," which was signed prior to ICPD by over 2,500 individuals and organizations representing hundreds of thousands of women in 110 countries as of September 1994 (Women's Voices '94 Alliance, 1992). Primary objectives of both the ICPD Programme of Action and the Women's Declaration are:

- to ensure that women and men have a healthy, satisfying sexual life, free of disease, violence, disability, fear, unnecessary pain, or death;
- to enable women to manage their own fertility by conceiving when they desire to do so, terminating unwanted pregnancies, and carrying wanted pregnancies to term safely and effectively; and
- to enable women and men to raise healthy children as and when they desire to do so.

To achieve these objectives, changes are needed in the definition of who is to be served; in how services are to be provided, especially the balance between quantity and quality of care; in the mix of services provided; and in measures to monitor and evaluate programmes.

In 1987 the International Women's Health Coalition defined and promoted a reproductive health approach that would encourage and enhance collaboration among disparate vertical programmes for family planning, maternal and child health (MCH), and STD control (Germain and Ordway, 1989). The concept has since been refined by various agencies and recognized by governments in the ICPD Programme of Action.

Many in the population and related health fields have adopted the language of reproductive health, but most programmes still approach women as means to the ends of fertility control and child health. They concentrate on married, fertile women in their reproductive years, leaving many girls and women unserved or seriously underserved. Although family planning has been combined with MCH (see, for example, Coeytaux, 1989; Otsea, 1992, Kay and Kabir, 1988; Kay, Germain, and Bangser, 1991; Si Mujer, 1992), such programmes have had very little interaction with AIDS and STD programmes until quite recently (see, for example, Berer and Ray, 1993; WHO, 1993). Too often, MCH programmes neglect maternal health (Rosenfield and Maine, 1985). Many women have no access to services at all. When they do, debates over integrated versus vertical approaches continue unresolved, leaving most women with no option but to travel to and wait at multiple clinics on multiple days (Aitken and Reichenbach, 1994). Until ICPD, only a few agencies addressed sexuality or sexual health — notably the Ford Foundation, the John D. and Catherine T. MacArthur Foundation, the Swedish International Development Authority, DANIDA, NORAD, International Planned Parenthood Federation, and The Population Council (e.g., Ford Foundation, 1991; IPPF, 1993; Population Council, 1989; Senanayake, 1992; SIDA, 1994). While other international agencies are considering doing so, national governments have taken little action.

Child health programmes have as yet invested little in ending discriminatory and abusive treatment and neglect of girls by families, communities, and health services. Unmarried but sexually active young people who do not have children are generally excluded from services; when served, they may be treated punitively (Hawkins and Meshesha, 1994). At the other end of the age spectrum, preventive health services have generally had no interest in women who are sterile or beyond reproductive age, even though they remain sexually active.

SEXUALITY AND GENDER RELATIONS

Until the advent of HIV and AIDS, and even since then, health and family planning programmes have generally not wanted to come to terms with the fact that reproduction takes place through sexual relations, which are themselves conditioned by broader gender relations (Dixon-Mueller, 1993b). Similarly, health and education policies and programmes in most countries have rarely dealt with sexuality and have understood very little about how gender relations affect achievement of their goals. As a result, we still know very little about these issues or even how to discuss them (Zeidenstein and Moore, 1995). Overall, population and health policies and programmes continue to be rooted in and reinforce existing unequal gender relations and traditional constructions of sexuality, based on double standards for men and women as well as male dominance. Examples include public campaigns on child health that feature only mothers, rarely fathers; family planning education materials or condom packaging that use sexually aggressive images; and STD/HIV campaigns that portray women as the primary vectors of infection.

Socialization into sexuality and gender roles begins early in the family and community and is reinforced by basic social institutions, the mass media, and other factors (Miedzian, 1993; Obura, 1991). Political, economic, legal, and cultural subordination of women generally means they are easily subject to violence by men in the home and outside and are unable to protect themselves from risk beginning at a very young age (Fullilove et al., 1990; Handwerker, 1994; Heise with Pitanguy and Germain, 1994; Worth, 1989). Confusing double standards exist, under which boys are expected to be sexually aggressive and girls to be both chaste and sexually appealing (Ekwempu, 1991; ECOS, 1992; S. Nowrojee, 1993a; Winn, 1992). While women are expected to be submissive, they are also held responsible for sexual interaction. For example, they are the ones expelled from school for pregnancy or publicly shamed for "loose" behaviour, while boys generally go free and may even be rewarded. From Kenya to the United States, boys who rape have been publicly exonerated by parents who say, "Boys will be boys" (Gross, 1993; Perlez, 1991) or school officials who say, "They meant no harm" (V. Nowrojee, 1993).

Women's reproductive and sexual well-being, self-perceptions, and self-esteem are directly and indirectly affected by rape, battery, homicide, incest, psychological abuse, genital mutilation, trafficking of women and children, dowry-related murder, and forced sterilization and forced abortion (Adekunle and Ladipo, 1992; Dawit, 1994; Edemikpong, 1990; Ghadially, 1991; Maggwa and Ngugi, 1992; Pyne, 1992; Toubia, 1993). Such practices are so widespread that it is probable that most women will experience at least one in their lifetimes, almost regardless of where they live. The 1993 World Development Report indicates that "women ages 15 to 44 lose more Discounted Health, Years of Life (DHYLs) to rape and domestic violence than they do to breast cancer, cervical cancer, obstructed labor, heart disease, AIDS, respiratory infections, motor vehicle accidents or war" (World Bank, 1993).

> *"Donors and governments should be held accountable, and their concern for women's health and development should be reflected in their resource allocations and priorities. They should revise their funding categories to promote comprehensive women's health programmes, rather than narrowly defined programmes for family planning. It is essential that women-centred programmes have access to a fair share of the financial resources available for reproductive health."*
>
> *— From the statement produced at "Reproductive Health and Justice: International Women's Health Conference for Cairo '94" held in Rio de Janeiro.*

Other beliefs and practices regarding women's bodies and sexuality also have important health consequences. Beliefs that women should not know about sexuality can result in high risk of STDs, unwanted pregnancy, and inability or reluctance to seek health care. For example, STD symptoms are often believed by women to be normal, not problems to be treated (Bang and Bang, 1992; Dixon-Mueller and Wasserheit, 1991; Pyne, 1992; Ramasubban, 1995). Widespread beliefs that menstrual blood and normal vaginal discharge are dirty, shameful, or distasteful to the sexual partner lead to poor menstrual hygiene or vaginal cleansing, which increase the risk of vaginal infection and reduce women's sexual pleasure (Dixon-Mueller and Wasserheit, 1991; Gupta and Weiss, 1993; Ramasubban, 1990; Sabatier, 1993; Wambua, 1992).

Finally, gender differentials in access to health care put girls and women in unnecessary jeopardy. Women, more than men, have to overcome economic and cultural barriers to seeking and receiving information and care. Social constructions of "proper" female behaviour and

167

sexuality deter women from using STD clinics for fear of being regarded as promiscuous or defiled (Dixon-Mueller and Germain, 1992; Elias and Heise, 1993). Single women and adolescents may not approach family planning services because they fear being seen as sexually active or being refused service. Even medical research has been discriminatory, giving little attention until recently to breast and cervical cancer, using only male subjects for research on heart disease, and excluding female-specific symptoms such as cervical cancer or vaginal candidiasis from the case definition of AIDS (Corea, 1992; Hamblin and Reid, 1991; Reid, 1992).

NEGLECTED ISSUES TO BE ADDRESSED

To meet the sexual and reproductive health needs of girls and women of all ages throughout their life cycles and ensure their sexual and reproductive rights regardless of whether their sexual relations have a reproductive purpose, services need to include the following:

- sexuality and gender education, counselling, information, and services, including special attention for girls and women who have been subjected to violence;
- STD prevention, screening, diagnosis, and treatment;
- services related to childbearing (prenatal and postnatal care, safe delivery, including emergency obstetric care, nutrition, and child health);
- fully voluntary birth control for individuals (a full range of contraceptive methods and safe abortion);
- gynaecologic care (including screening for breast and cervical cancer);
- health counselling and education in all services; and
- strong primary health-care systems and referral mechanisms for other health problems.

How this agenda is accomplished, short- and long-range priorities, and specific investments will of course need to be adjusted for particular settings. What is important is an overall strategic vision against which specific plans can be made, implemented, and monitored. The ICPD Programme of Action provides most of that vision, with the important exceptions of safe abortion services for all women in need and explicit recognition of sexual rights. While basic maternal health and family planning services do not yet have the priority and resources they should have, several other aspects of women's reproductive and sexual health have been particularly contentious and are highlighted here as priority concerns. These are quality of services, safe abortion, STD control, improved technologies, sexual rights, men's responsibility and behaviour, young people's concerns, and older women's needs.

Quality of Services
The ICPD Programme of Action resolved long-standing debates by affirming that while the primary clientele of reproductive health services should continue to be women, persons younger and older than reproductive age, unmarried persons, and persons who are sterile (whether voluntarily or not) should also be included. While increased resources will be needed, a reordering of programme and budgetary priorities would contribute substantially to ensuring that all persons, regardless of gender, age, or fertility status, are reached with a wider range of good-quality services.

Much higher priority than heretofore must be given to improving the quality of services.

168

Bruce (1990) conceptualized the primary elements of quality of care in family planning programmes to include choice among methods, full information on safety and side effects, technical competence, client-provider relations, continuity of use, and constellation of services. More recently, the International Planned Parenthood Federation (Huezo and Briggs, 1992) has codified these "Rights of the Client" and posted them in its clinics (IPPF, 1993). However, systematic implementation of such guidelines has not yet been achieved anywhere.

The terminology of quality of care has gained currency, yet the concepts often have significantly different meanings for women's health advocates and for family planning policy makers (Marcelo and Germain, 1994). Policy makers, international agencies, and clinics are still struggling to define specific standards of care and to establish measures to monitor and evaluate the quality of services. We must bring their understanding closer to women's. Similar standards need to be developed for other aspects of sexual and reproductive health services.

While the actual costs of providing comprehensive, good-quality sexual and reproductive health services have not yet been documented or systematically estimated, achieving good-quality care in existing services need not be expensive (Kay, Germain, and Bangser, 1991; Kay and Kabir, 1988). The motivation of staff and reallocation of human — as well as financial — resources can improve basic programme management and logistics systems and, more important, the technical and interpersonal quality of services (Aitken and Reichenbach, 1994). Above all, treating clients with dignity and compassion is not costly. Good-quality care can begin to be achieved through the following:

- improved supervision of staff;
- new programme statistics and evaluation measures that follow each client to assure proper treatment and positive outcomes;
- training staff to assist clients with emotional or social, not just physical, consequences of seeking health services, including birth control;
- programme managers who are alert to quality control problems; and
- reward systems for staff and programmes based on how well they serve people, not on how many contraceptives they dispense or how many patients they treat (Jain and Bruce, 1994).

Quality can be further enhanced by expanding the range of services offered as resources allow.

Safe Abortion

Contraceptives fail, and people are not always able to use them or may not use them correctly. Thus, safe abortion services will always be needed. Where safe abortion services are not available, women sacrifice their health and their lives to end unwanted pregnancies (Dixon-Mueller, 1993a). It is impractical, as well as unethical, not to provide safe services. The ideal is, of course, both to remove legal restrictions and to assure provision of safe services to all who need them. Even where abortion is severely legally restricted, however, or where political and social factors are serious obstacles, governments and other agencies in a number of countries have found means to provide this critical service for women's health, including modification of regulations (without legal change), staff training, and deciding not to prosecute those who break restrictive laws to provide safe services.

STD Control

In the face of the STD and HIV/AIDS pandemics, it should be mandatory that all

169

programmes that serve sexually active people, such as MCH seervices, family planning services, and youth programmes, offer information and services for the prevention and control of STDs, including HIV/AIDS, to all participants. These programmes should give much higher priority to condom introduction and distribution (Liskin, Wharton, and Blackburn, 1990). Few, if any, family planning programmes and only a few MCH programmes in Southern countries systematically screen and treat clients for STD infection. Yet contraceptive safety is compromised by these diseases; STDs are the major cause of infertility; and the presumed clients of family planning and MCH services, married women of reproductive age, have virtually no access to specialized STD services or AIDS control projects (Dixon-Mueller and Wasserheit, 1991; Elias, 1991; Elias, Leonard, and Thompson, 1993; Germain et al., 1992). Much higher priority needs to be given to using existing diagnostic and treatment technologies.

Improved Technologies

A major reorientation of research priorities and process is needed to pursue three critical technological gaps: woman-controlled methods that protect against infection, with or without protection against pregnancy; emergency contraception and post-ovulatory methods; and male contraceptive methods (Barroso, 1994; Fathalla, 1994; Marcelo and Germain, 1994). Simpler, less expensive diagnostic techniques and treatments for conventional STDs are urgently needed (Wasserheit and Holmes, 1992). Substantial changes are also needed in the research process to determine whether the women to be served are fully represented at all stages, and that introductory trials are conducted in such a way as to ensure that service delivery systems are strong enough to protect and follow up on clients' safety and well-being (García-Moreno and Claro, 1994; Spicehandler and Simmons, 1993; WHO/HRP and IWHC, 1991; "Declaration of the International Symposium," 1994).

Sexual Rights

Prevailing social constructions of sexuality and gender relations are major deterrents to sexual and reproductive health and rights. They are generally considered "politically sensitive," which has prevented necessary policy and programme development in most countries, although an expert group of the World Health Organization developed guidelines as early as 1975 (WHO, 1975). The ICPD Programme of Action recognizes the need to address most of these gender-based problems but falls short of embracing sexual rights per se. It does acknowledge several of the basic elements of sexual rights, namely those that are "already recognized in national laws, international human rights documents and other relevant consensus documents" (UN, 1994), including "the right to the highest standard of sexual and reproductive health," "the right to make decisions concerning reproduction free of discrimination, coercion and violence," and "full respect for the physical integrity of the human body." While health and education systems can be encouraged to develop means to prevent and/or treat the consequences of sexual violence, coercion, and discrimination, the foundation for action would be much more solid were the basic elements of sexual rights understood, recognized, and made explicit. This is a high-priority task, deserving of urgent attention at international and national levels.

Men's Responsibility and Behaviour

Generally, family planning services, national and international agencies, and demographers have focused on women, since it is they who bear children. (An important exception was India, which put very strong emphasis on vasectomy in the national population programme until the early 1970s.) While it is essential for women to have access to services to protect their health and control their fertility, it is equally important for policy and programmes to ensure that men take responsibility for their own fertility, prevention of STDs, and the well-being of their sexual partners and the children they father. The ICPD Programme of Action acknowledges that profound social changes will be needed to increase use of vasectomy and condoms, to ensure men's respect for their partners' contraceptive choices, and to motivate men to take responsibility for their own behaviour (see, for example, Aral, Mosher, and Cates, 1992; Correa and Petchesky, 1994; Savara and Sridhar, 1992).

Although vasectomy is significantly cheaper and safer than female sterilization procedures, tubal ligation is nearly three times as frequent as vasectomy in Southern countries (Fathalla, 1994). The only other male contraceptive method, the condom, has more often than not been offered as a last choice for women who cannot or will not use modern, more "effective" contraceptives. In any case, many men refuse to use condoms consistently, or at all, or with their regular partners (Rosenberg and Gollub, 1992; Stein, 1993). In general, men have not been welcomed or encouraged to participate in family planning services.

It is thus not surprising that contraceptive-use data show that in Southern countries, methods that require men's initiative and cooperation (vasectomy, condom, rhythm, and withdrawal) account for only 26 per cent of contraceptive use. (In Northern countries, these methods account for 57 per cent of use.) Even taking into account the likelihood of underestimation, the great discrepancy between the female and male burdens of responsibility for contraception is stark (Mauldin and Segal, 1988; Ross and Frankenberg, 1993). Refusing to use contraceptives themselves, many men also resist their partners' desire to use a method (Liskin, Wharton, and Blackburn, 1990; Ruminjo et al., 1991). At the same time, in many cases they abdicate responsibility for their children to the woman or women who bore them (Bruce, 1989; Bruce and Lloyd, 1992; Bruce, Lloyd, and Leonard, 1995).

Because their objective has been fertility control, vasectomy services have missed an extremely important opportunity to work with men on other aspects of sexual health (see, for example, Lynam et al., 1993). These programmes could provide information, screening, and treatment for STDs, promote continued condom use beyond the initial period following vasectomy, and provide counselling and educational activities to promote healthy sexuality and equitable gender relations (Liskin, Benoit, and Blackburn, 1992). Groups such as PRO-PATER in Brazil and Profamilia in Colombia have demonstrated how to move from a simple vasectomy clinic to a men's reproductive health programme (Hawkins, 1992; Liskin, Benoit, and Blackburn, 1992; Liskin, Wharton, and Blackburn, 1990; Mtsogolo, 1992; Rogow, 1990). Experimentation is needed to determine suitable approaches in each country. For example, it seems that men may prefer separate service facilities from women and, sometimes, male providers (Rogow, 1990; Mtsogolo, 1992).

Young People's Concerns

Perhaps the most pressing challenge is to reach young people, who are being severely injured, and are dying, as a result of some societies' unwillingness to invest in sexuality and gender education, as well as in information and services for both unmarried and married young people. A narrow message of abstinence and dire warnings about the consequences of poorly managed sexuality are not the answer. Sexuality is a basic dimension of human life, and young people in most societies, especially under contemporary conditions, experiment voluntarily, or under pressure. The message needs to be one of mutual caring and respect, with full information about possible negative consequences and how to prevent them (S. Nowrojee, 1993b).

171

Some innovative efforts have been launched to engage young people in dialogue with each other and with adults on their perceived needs and to provide them with necessary information and services (Francis and O'Neill, 1992; Hawkins and Meshesha, 1994). A number of European countries have adopted transformative approaches to sex education that recognize sexuality as good, lovemaking as something people should know how to do well, and sexual health as central to overall well-being. Many other cultures have, or used to have, social institutions to support young people in their sexual initiation. Although some practices, such as female genital mutilation, are harmful and should be eradicated, much could be accomplished by recovering, re-creating, or building on beneficial traditions.

While experimental programmes are developed to support young people as they explore their sexuality and their gender roles, we must also provide the opportunities for education and work that offer them hope for their futures and that will encourage and enable them to avoid unwanted or otherwise negative sexual and gender relations. We must also work with other major social institutions, especially the mass media, to promote positive images of gender equality and sexuality.

Older Women

The sexual and reproductive health needs of older women, though widely ignored, are serious and widespread. These include the changes that accompany menopause, long-term morbidity and disability associated with poor pregnancy and delivery practices, the long-term consequences of STDs, and reproductive tract cancers, among others. While proper care and prevention at younger ages would help avoid many of these problems and although much is known about how to treat them as well, there is as yet little of the requisite political will to meet the needs of older women.

CONCLUSION

Our proposed approach is to recognize that sexuality and gender relations lie at the centre of reproductive and sexual health and rights. Policies and programmes therefore need to encompass not just services but also specific actions to empower women, to ensure their overall health, and to motivate men to take responsibility for their own behaviour. The outcome should be mutually caring, respectful, and satisfying sexual relationships, and a solid foundation for reproductive and sexual health and rights as well as for human development and rights overall. This is a sweeping agenda that reflects women's perceived needs and experiences. Significant changes are already occurring on a small scale in many countries and even at the level of international diplomatic debate.

The ICPD Programme of Action estimates that approximately US$17 billion will be needed in the year 2000 to provide reproductive health services — including maternal health, STD prevention and control, family planning, and basic research — for all those in need in Southern countries and in countries with economies in transition. While this figure includes a two- to threefold increase in the amount currently expended on family planning in Southern countries and an even more significant increase in funds for reproductive health services, it is a very modest sum in light of the expanded benefits and numbers of people who would be served. At least two-thirds of these expenses would continue to be met by national governments. The remaining US$5 billion to $6 billion of foreign assistance required is extremely modest; this amount is roughly equivalent to the cost of two to three nuclear submarines. The other investments required for human development, such as closing the gender gap in education, improving basic health infrastructure, and protecting the environment may seem costly on their face, but they are the basis for human security, eradication of poverty, empowerment of women, and sexual and reproductive health.

What is urgently needed is the political will to reallocate resources to this agenda for social and human resource development, imaginative strategies to use those resources well in the particular circumstances of each country, and the inclusion of representatives of women, who have the most at stake, in all levels of decision-making, programme implementation, and monitoring.

Adrienne Germain is the Vice-President and Programme Director of the International Women's Health Coalition, a U.S.-based private organization dedicated to improving women's reproductive health and rights in Africa, Asia, and Latin America. She has worked for 25 years on women's roles in development, reproductive health and reproductive rights in Southern countries. Germain served as a Private Sector Advisor on the U.S. Government delegations to the International Conference on Population and Development and the Fourth World Conference on Women.

This article draws upon A. Germain, S. Nowrojee, and H. H. Pyn, "Setting a New Agenda: Sexual and Reproductive Health Rights," in G. Sen, A. Germain, and L. Chen (eds.), *Population Policies Reconsidered: Health, Empowerment, and Rights,* Cambridge: Harvard University Press, 1994. I am grateful for editorial suggestions on this paper by Rachel Kyte, Mia MacDonald, and Susan Wood. Errors remain my own.

References

Adekunle, A. O., and O. A. Ladipo. 1992. "Reproductive Tract Infections in Nigeria: Challenges for a Fragile Health Infrastructure," in A. Germain et al. (eds.), *Reproductive Tract Infections: Global Impact and Priorities for Women's Reproductive Health.* New York: Plenum Press.

Aitken, I., and L. Reichenbach. 1994. "Reproductive and Sexual Health Services: Expanding Access and Enhancing Quality," in G. Sen, A. Germain and L. Chen (eds.), *Population Policies Reconsidered: Health, Empowerment and Rights.* Cambridge: Harvard University Press.

Aral, S. O., W. Mosher, and W. Cates, Jr. 1992. "Vaginal Douching Among Women of Reproductive Age in the United States." *American Journal of Public Health* 82 (2), pp. 210–14.

Bang, R., and A. Bang. 1992. "Why Women Hide Them: Rural Women's Viewpoints on Reproductive Tract Infections." *Manushi: A Journal about Women and Society* 69, pp. 27–30.

Barroso, C. 1994. "Meeting Women's Unmet Needs: The Alliance Between Feminists and Researchers," in P.F.A. Van Look and G. Perez-Palacios, *Contraceptive Research and Development 1984–1994: The Road from Mexico City to Cairo and Beyond.* New Delhi: Oxford University Press.

Berer, M., and S. Ray. 1993. *Women and HIV/AIDS: An International Resource Book.* London: Pandora Press.

Boland, R., S. Rao, and G. Zeidenstein. 1994. "Honoring Human Rights in Population Policies: From Declaration to Action," in G. Sen, A. Germain and L. Chen (eds.), *Population Policies Reconsidered: Health, Empowerment and Rights.* Cambridge: Harvard University Press.

Brady, M., and B. Winikoff. 1992. "Rethinking Postpartum Health Care." Proceedings of a seminar presented under the Population Council's Robert H. Ebert Programme on Critical Issues in Reproductive Heath and Population. New York: Population Council.

Bruce, J. 1989. "Homes Divided." *World Development* 17 (7), pp. 979-91.

Bruce, J. 1990. "Fundamental Elements of the Quality of Care: A Simple Framework." *Studies in Family Planning* 21 (2), pp. 61–91.

Bruce, J., and C. Lloyd. 1992. "Finding the Ties That Bind: Beyond Leadership and Household." Working paper no. 41. New York: The Population Council.

Bruce, J., C. Lloyd, and A. Leonard. 1995. *Families in Focus: New Perspectives on Mothers, Fathers, and Children.* New York: The Population Council.

Coeytaux, F. 1989. "Celebrating Mother and Child on the Fortieth Day: The Sfax, Tunisia Postpartum Programme." *Quality/Calidad/Qualité.* New York: The Population Council.

Corea, G. 1992. *The Invisible Epidemic.* New York: HarperCollins.

Correa, S., and R. Petchesky. 1994. "Reproductive and Sexual Rights: A Feminist Perspective," in G. Sen, A. Germain, and L. Chen (eds.), *Population Policies Reconsidered: Health, Empowerment and Rights.* Cambridge: Harvard University Press.

Dawit, S. 1995 (forthcoming). *The International Human Rights Dimensions of Female Genital Mutilation.* London: Zed Books.

"Declaration of the International Symposium on Contraceptive Research and Development for the Year 2000 and Beyond." 1994. Appendix, in P. F. A. Van Look and G. Perez-Palacios (eds.), *Contraceptive Research and Development 1984–1994: The Road from Mexico City to Cairo and Beyond.* New Delhi: Oxford University Press.

Dixon-Mueller, R. 1993a. "Abortion *Is* a Method of Family Planning, in R. Dixon-Mueller and A. Germain (eds.), *Four Essays on Birth Control Needs and Risks.* New York: International Women's Health Coalition.

Dixon-Mueller, R. 1993b. "The Sexuality Connection in Reproductive Health." *Studies in Family Planning* 24 (5), pp. 269–82.

Dixon-Mueller, R. and A. Germain. 1992. "Stalking the Elusive 'Unmet Need' for Family Planning." *Studies in Family Planning* 23 (5), pp. 330–35.

Dixon-Mueller, R., and J. Wasserheit. 1991. *The Culture of Silence: Reproductive Tract Infections Among Women in the Third World.* New York: International Women's Health Coalition.

ECOS (Estudos e Comunica em Sexualidade e Reprodu o Humana). 1992. "Um Arao (A Hug)." São Paulo.

Edemikpong, N. B. 1990. "Women and AIDS," in E. D. Rothblum and E. Cole (eds.), *Women's Mental Health in Africa.* Binghampton, England: Harrington Park Press.

Ekwempu, F. 1991. "The Influence of Socio-cultural Behavioral Patterns on the Knowledge and Practice of Contraception and Abortion Among the Hauda-Fulani Adolescents of Northern Nigeria." Research supported by the International Women's Health Coalition, New York.

Elias, C. 1991. "Sexually Transmitted Diseases and the Reproductive Health of Women in Developing Countries." Working Paper No. 5. New York: The Population Council.

Elias, C., and L. Heise. 1993. "The Development of Microbicides: A New Method of HIV Prevention for Women." Working Paper No. 6. New York: Population Council.

Elias, C., A. Leonard, and J. Thompson. 1993. "A Puzzle of Will: Responding to Reproductive Tract Infections in the Context of Family Planning Programs." Paper presented at the Africa Operations Research/Technical Assistance End-of-Project Conference, October, Nairobi.

Fathalla, M. 1994. "Fertility Control Technology: A Women-centred Approach to Research," in G. Sen, A. Germain, and L. Chen (eds.), *Population Policies Reconsidered: Health, Empowerment and Rights.* Cambridge: Harvard University Press.

Ford Foundation. 1991. *Reproductive Health: A Strategy for the 1990s.* New York.

Francis, C., and C. O'Neill. 1992. "A Strategy for Supporting the Use of Condoms by Sexually Active Youth: The Eastern Caribbean Experience," in L. Bond (ed.), *A Portfolio of AIDS/STD Behavioral Interventions and Research.* Washington, DC: Pan American Health Organization.

Fullilove, M. T., et al. 1990. "Black Women and AIDS Prevention: A View Towards Understanding the Gender Rules." *Journal of Sex Research* 27 (1), pp. 47-64.

García-Moreno, C., and A. Claro. 1994. "Challenges from the Women's Health Movement: Women's Rights versus Population Control," in G. Sen, A. Germain, and L. Chen (eds.), *Population Policies Reconsidered: Health, Empowerment and Rights*. Cambridge: Harvard University Press.

Germain, A. 1989. "The Christopher Tietze International Symposium: An Overview." *International Journal of Gynecology and Obstetrics*. Special Suppl. Limerick, Ireland: International Federation of Gynecology and Obstetrics.

Germain, A., and J. Ordway. 1989. *Population and Women's Health: Balancing the Scales*. New York: International Women's Health Coalition.

Germain, A. et al. (eds.). 1992. *Reproductive Tract Infections: Global Impact and Priorities for Women's Reproductive Health*. New York: Plenum Press.

Germain, A., and R. Kyte. 1995. *The Cairo Consensus: The Right Agenda for the Right Time*. New York: International Women's Health Coalition.

Ghadially, R. 1991. "All for Izzat." *Manushi: A Journal about Women and Society* (September/October).

Gross, J. 1993. "Boys Will Be Boys and Adults Are Befuddled." *New York Times*, 29 March.

Gupta, G. R., and E. Weiss. 1993. *Women and AIDS: Developing a New Health Strategy*. Washington, DC: International Center for Research on Women.

Hamblin, J., and E. Reid. 1991. "Women, the HIV Epidemic and Human Rights: A Tragic Imperative." Paper presented at the International Workshop on AIDS: A Question of Rights and Humanity, International Court of Justice, The Hague.

Handwerker, W. P. 1995 (forthcoming). "Gender Power Differences Between Parents and High Risk Sexual Behavior by Their Children: AIDS/STD Risk Factors Extend to Prior Generation." *Journal of Women's Health*.

Hawkins, K. 1992. *Male Participation in Family Planning: A Review of Program Approaches in the Africa Region*. London: International Planned Parenthood Federation.

Hawkins, K., and B. Meshesha. 1994. "Reaching Young People: Ingredients of Effective Programs," in G. Sen, A. Germain and L. Chen (eds.), *Population Policies Reconsidered: Health, Empowerment and Rights*. Cambridge: Harvard University Press.

Heise, L., with J. Pitanguy and A. Germain. 1994. "Violence Against Women As a Health Issue." Paper Number 255. Washington, DC: World Bank (Population, Health, and Nutrition Division).

Huezo, C. M., and C. Briggs. 1992. "Rights of the Client." *Medical and Service Guidelines for Family Planning*. London: International Planned Parenthood Federation.

IPPF (International Planned Parenthood Federation). 1993. *Strategic Plan: Vision 2000*. London.

Jain, A., and J. Bruce. 1994. "A Reproductive Health Approach to the Objectives and Assessment of Family Planning Programs," in G. Sen, A. Germain, and L. Chen (eds.), *Population Policies Reconsidered: Health, Empowerment and Rights*. Cambridge: Harvard University Press.

Kay, B. J., and S. M. Kabir. 1988. "A Study of Costs and Behavioral Outcomes of Menstrual Regulation Services in Bangladesh." *Social Science Medicine* 26 (6), pp. 597–604.

Kay, B., A. Germain, and M. Bangser. 1991. "The Bangladesh Women's Health Coalition." *Quality/Calidad/Qualité*. New York: The Population Council.

Liskin, L., E. Benoit, and R. Blackburn. 1992. "Male Sterilization." *Population Reports* Series D (5).

Liskin, L., C. Wharton, and R. Blackburn. 1990. "Condoms: Now More Than Ever." *Population Reports* Series H (8).

Lynam, P. J., et al. 1993. "Vasectomy in Kenya: The First Steps." Working Paper no. 4. New York: Association for Voluntary Surgical Contraception.

Maggwa, A. B. N., and E. N. Ngugi. 1992. "Reproductive Tract Infections in Kenya: Insights for Action from Research," in A. Germain, et al. (eds.), *Reproductive Tract Infections*. New York: Plenum Press.

Marcelo, A. B., and A. Germain. 1994. "Women's Perspectives on Fertility Regulation Methods and Services," in P. F. A. Van Look and G. Perez-Palacios (eds.), *Contraceptive Research and Development 1984–1994: The Road from Mexico City to Cairo and Beyond.* New Delhi: Oxford University Press.

Mauldin, W. P., and S. Segal. 1988. "Prevalence of Contraceptive Use: Trends and Issues." *Studies in Family Planning* 19 (6), pp. 335–53.

Merrick, T. 1994. "Population Dynamics in Developing Countries," in R. Cassen (ed.), *Population and Development: Old Debates, New Conclusions.* Washington, DC: Overseas Development Council.

Miedzian, M. 1993. "How Rape Is Encouraged in American Boys and What We Can Do to Stop It," in E. Buchwood, P. Fletcher, and M. Roth (eds.), *Transforming a Rape Culture.* Minneapolis: Milkweed Edition.

Mtsogolo, B. 1992. "A Male-oriented Child Spacing/Social Responsibility Education and Services Programme: Malawi," in *ODA Annual Progress Report.* London: Marie Stopes International.

Nowrojee, S. 1993a. "Sexuality and Gender: Impact on Women's Health." Paper presented at the Medical Women's International Association, Near East & Africa First Regional Congress: The Health of Women and Safe Motherhood, 29 November–3 December, Nairobi.

Nowrojee, S. 1993b. "Speaking Out for Sexual and Reproductive Health." *DIVA: A Quarterly Journal of South Asian Women* 4 (1), pp. 17–22.

Nowrojee, V. 1993. "Kenya Adopting Rape Culture." *The Nairobi Law Monthly* 50, pp. 29–31.

Obura, A. 1991. *Changing Images.* Nairobi: English Press Limited.

Otsea, K. 1992. "Progress and Prospects: The Safe Motherhood Initiative." World Bank Background Document for the Meeting of Partners for Safe Motherhood, March, Washington, DC.

Perlez, J. 1991. "Kenyans Do Some Soul Searching After the Rape of 71 School Girls." *New York Times,* 29 July.

Population Council. 1989. Annual Report 1988. New York: The Population Council.

Pyne, H. H. 1992. "AIDS and Prostitution in Thailand: Case Study of Burmese Prostitutes in Ranong." Master's thesis, MIT.

Ramasubban, R. 1990. "Sexual Behaviour and Conditions of Health Care: Potential Risks for HIV Transmission in India." Paper presented at the International Union for the Scientific Study of Population Seminar on Anthropological Studies Relevant to HIV Transmission, November, Copenhagen.

Ramasubban, R. 1995 (forthcoming). "Patriarchy and the Risks of HIV Transmission to Women in India," in M. Jasgupta, T. N. Krishnan, and L. Chen, (eds.), *Health and Development in India.* Bombay: Oxford University Press.

Reid, E. 1992. "Women, the HIV Epidemic and Human Rights: A Tragic Imperative." Paper presented at the International Workshop on AIDS: A Question of Rights and Humanity, May, The Hague.

Rogow, D. 1990. "Man/Hombre/Homme: Meeting Male Reproductive Health Care Needs in Latin America." *Quality/Calidad/Qualité.* New York: The Population Council.

Rosenberg, M. J. and E. L. Gollub. 1992. "Commentary: Methods Women Can Use That May Prevent Sexually Transmitted Disease, Including HIV." *American Journal of Public Health* 82 (11), pp. 1473–78.

Rosenfield, A., and D. Maine. 1985. "Maternal Mortality — A Neglected Tragedy: Where is the M in MCH?" *Lancet,* 13 July.

Ross, J., and E. Frankenberg. 1993. "Findings from Two Decades of Family Planning Research." New York: The Population Council.

Ruminjo, J., et al. 1991. "Consumer Preference and Functionality Study of the Reality Female Condom in a Low Risk Population in Kenya." Research Triangle Park, NC: Family Health International.

Sabatier, R. (Southern African AIDS Program, Harare, Zimbabwe). 1993. Personal communication.

Savara, M., and C. R. Sridhar. 1992. "Sexual Behaviour of Urban, Educated Indian Men: Results of a Survey." *Shakti: Journal of Family Welfare,* pp. 30–43.

Senanayake, P. 1992. "Positive Approaches to Education for Sexual Health with Examples from Asia and Africa." *Journal of Adolescent Health* 13 (5), pp. 351–54.

Si Mujer. 1992. *Servicios Integrales para la Mujer.* Cali, Colombia: The Foundation.

Spicehandler, J., and R. Simmons. 1993. *Contraceptive Introduction Reconsidered: A Review and Conceptual Framework.* Prepared on behalf of the Task Force on Research on the Introduction and Transfer of Technologies for Fertility Regulation, and presented at the meeting of the Policy and Coordination Committee, WHO Special Programme of Research, Development and Research Training in Human Reproduction, June, Geneva.

Stein, Z. A. 1993. "HIV Prevention: An Update on the Status of Methods Women Can Use." *American Journal of Public Health* 83, pp. 1379–82.

Swedish International Development Authority/Health Division. 1994. *Sexual and Reproductive Health: Development Cooperation to Promote Sexual and Reproductive Health - An Action Plan of the Health Division at SIDA.* Stockholm.

Toubia, N. 1993. *Female Genital Mutilation: A Call for Global Action.* New York: Women, Ink.

UN (United Nations). 1994. Programme of Action of the International Conference on Population and Development. A/CONF. 171/13, 18 October.

Wambua, L. 1992. RTIs in Cameroon. *Women's Health Journal* 2, pp. 45-50.

Wasserheit, J., and K. Holmes. 1992. "Reproductive Tract Infections: Challenges for International Health Policy, Programs, and Research," in A. Germain et al. (eds.), *Reproductive Tract Infections: Global Impact and Priorities for Women's Reproductive Health.* New York: Plenum Press.

Winn, M. 1992. "Taboo Talk: Reproductive Health Videos by Pacific Island Women." *Quality/Calidad/Qualité.* New York: The Population Council.

Women's Voices '94 Alliance. 1992. "Women's Declaration on Population Policies." New York: International Women's Health Coalition.

World Bank. 1993. *World Development Report.* New York: Oxford University Press.

WHO (World Health Organization). 1975. "Education and Treatment in Human Sexuality: The Training of Health Professionals." Report of WHO meeting. Geneva.

WHO (World Health Organization). 1993. "New Approach to Fighting AIDS." Press release WHO/90. 16 November.

WHO (World Health Organization). 1995. "Calls on Policy Makers to Reduce Women's Growing Vulnerability to HIV/AIDS." Press release WHO/11, 8 February.

WHO/HRP and IWHC (World Health Organization/Special Programme of Research, Development and Research Training in Human Reproduction and International Women's Health Coalition). 1991. "Creating Common Ground: Women's Perspectives on the Selection and Introduction of Fertility Regulation Technologies." Report of a meeting between women's health advocates and scientists, February, Geneva.

Worth, D. 1989. "Sexual Decision-making and AIDS: Why Condom Promotion Among Vulnerable Women Is Likely to Fail." *Studies in Family Planning* 20 (6), pp. 297–397.

Zeidenstein, S. and K. Moore (eds.). 1995 (forthcoming). *Learning About Sexuality: A Practical Beginning.* New York: The Population Council and The International Women's Health Coalition.

Zeitlin, J., R. Govindaraj, and L. Chen. 1994. "Financing Reproductive and Sexual Health Services," in G. Sen, A. Germain and L. Chen (eds.), *Population Policies Reconsidered: Health, Empowerment and Rights.* Cambridge: Harvard University Press.

THE WORLD SUMMIT FOR SOCIAL DEVELOPMENT: ENGENDERING REALPOLITIK

JUAN SOMAVIA

The World Summit for Social Development (WSSD), hosted in March 1995 in Copenhagen, was the largest meeting of heads of state in history — involving 118 world leaders, representatives of more than 2,400 NGOs worldwide, and some 6,000 journalists. Beyond the event itself, the Summit process has made the most political (and, traditionally, parochial) of issues a common concern of countries rich and poor alike; it has taken social development out of the narrow realm of domestic politics and placed it centrally on the global stage.

On the eve of the 21st century — with the effects of war, famine, and natural disasters instantaneously visible to TV viewers worldwide, and the dangers of disease, drugs, terrorism, and financial instability equally rapidly conveyed — no prime minister or president at Copenhagen could afford to ignore the effects of poverty, unemployment, and social tension in her or his own country. The NGOs present would not let them forget, and the journalists reporting on the event would have no doubt seized upon such hypocrisy. Instead, as Prime Minister Gro Harlem Bruntland of Norway so pointedly reminded her colleagues:

> If we implement everything we sign onto here in Copenhagen, we would have done a very good job. If not, we have not....The destitute poor have for too long been kept at arm's length by good wishes and the rest in promissory notes. As Martin Luther King said, the cheque has come back from the bank of justice marked "insufficient funds."

By making the language of civil society — and central to it, the global women's movement — part of the diplomatic lexicon, the Summit served as a critical catalyst in a process aimed at transforming the way people express themselves, relate to one another, build communities together, and herein exercise power. At the heart of the WSSD, integrated within its Declaration and Programme of Action and fundamental to its implementation and follow-up, is the concept of gender equity.[1] A commitment on gender and a corresponding series of policy recommendations figure centrally within both documents; indeed, governments and the peoples they represent are enjoined to work together "to promot[e] full respect for human dignity and to achiev[e] equality and equity between women and men, and to recogniz[e] and enhanc[e] the participation and leadership roles of women in political, civil, economic, social, and cultural life and in development."

As the Summit's central documents acknowledge: "Women bear a disproportionate burden of poverty....Among people living in poverty, gender disparities are marked....Therefore, specific measures are needed to address the juvenilization and feminization of poverty....The eradication of poverty cannot be accomplished through anti-poverty programmes alone, but will require democratic participation and changes in economic structures....People living in poverty must be empowered through organization and participation in all aspects of political, economic, and social life."

The centrality of gender to all the Summit's analyses serves to shift the focus of *Realpolitik* — and with it, traditional UN-speak — from the security of states to the security of people. Leaders in the international women's movement were centrally involved in drafting these documents. And women at the local, national, regional, and global levels will be critical to ensuring the success of the WSSD's implementation.

The Summit process calls upon people everywhere to take a hard look at our present patterns of consumption, time-use, and production — and to acknowledge honestly what they reflect about our priorities and values. How do we spend most of our money, time and effort? Are our economies and societies regenerative or degenerative in nature? How do we reflect the value of families, friendship, and prayer as compared to the worth of goods, services, and status of various kinds?

What could we do to bring our lives, our communities, our nations, and our world back into balance with our shared and abiding human values? Love, compassion, caring, sharing, self-sacrifice, solidarity — these words so often dismissed as "soft" concepts are among the hardest concepts to put into place through practical, concrete strategies for community building. Gender equity is truly operative only in communities in which every woman, man, and child has value and worth and is enabled to develop the capacity to imagine, to invent, and to endeavour to become more than they were before.

In the most general yet profound way, then, the WSSD marks a return to the roots of the United Nations — an echo of the original hopes expressed in the name of "We, the Peoples of the United Nations." The Summit's human vision of social development clashes with current reality. It is an ethical challenge to countries and people, one which proposes a change of course, a collective questioning of the direction in which we are heading. It is as if governments, acting together, found the courage to propose changes which individually many of them are not carrying out.

The Social Summit's emphasis on the feminization of poverty — and the concrete commitment taken by heads of state at Copenhagen to eradicate absolute poverty by a date to be specified by each country — is fundamental to the implementation of the goals set forward in the Declaration and the strategies outlined in the Programme of Action. In effect, the Summit has set up a process of continual review of poverty eradication efforts and progress at the national, regional, and international levels — beginning in 1996, the International Year for the Eradication of Poverty, and again in the year 2000 within the UN General Assembly.

By 1996, national poverty eradication plans should be formulated in each country, aimed at substantially reducing overall poverty and eradicating absolute poverty. These should include country-specific strategies and affordable time-bound goals to create employment, enhance health and education, assign higher political and budgetary priority to basic social services, generate household income, and promote access to productive assets and economic opportunities. National plans should take into consideration the structural causes of poverty — therein reflecting and responding to the differing needs of varied groups at the local, national, and subregional levels. In this connection, the Summit's Programme of Action makes explicit reference to goals put forward at the 1990 World Summit for Children (WSC), the

1992 UN Conference on Environment and Development (UNCED), and the 1994 International Conference on Population and Development (ICPD) — effectively serving as a global "report card" on poverty eradication.

A second major advance of the WSSD is in terms of debt cancellation: for the first time in such a UN forum, the need has been accepted to cancel the external public debt of the poorest countries. The WSSD Declaration and Programme of Action commit governments collectively to case-by-case reduction or cancellation of debt for the least developed countries under the terms of the Paris Club agreements. Yet we are still far from strong language on multilateral debt cancellation under other formulas and far from widespread bilateral debt cancellation.

Indeed, resource questions are central to the challenge of implementing the Summit — and figure centrally within the concept of the "20/20" commitment to funding for human development that was approved at Copenhagen as a helpful benchmark for interested countries. Endorsement of the 20/20 proposal in principle affords us the opportunity to test its strengths, limitations, and feasibility of application; the critical challenge is to enhance our analysis, improve our information-gathering and reporting capacities, and strengthen the ability of governments and grass-roots groups alike to tailor their budgets and programmes around this helpful formula.

Well over and above the resources potentially marshalled through the 20/20 proposal or similar official mechanisms, there is an abundance of money available for social development — in the *private* sector. The real task is that of finding new and innovative ways to mobilize these funds for social development, while in the process working to change the very nature of the economic growth process so as to generate more equitable and sustainable patterns of production and consumption. We are faced with the reality of dwindling resources for official development assistance — which, even if they were to be maintained at current levels, would be dwarfed by the trillions of dollars transacted daily in global financial markets.

Thus, we must make it good business to achieve social development. This means making concrete investments in the future stability and equity of the global marketplace as much as in the local communities in which we live. To do this, we need new vehicles for public/private accountability in decision-making and innovation in investment practice. For example, we need to foster dialogue on socially-sound investing (such as tailored pension and equities portfolios or community venture capital funds) — dialogue which should naturally involve leaders in private finance and pioneers in the field of development finance, such as the Grameen Bank, ACCION International, and Women's World Banking. Through their work, these organizations have all shown that it is profitable to empower women through increased access to credit.

The Summit process has also drawn the attention of the International Monetary Fund and the World Bank to the need to keep the costs of structural adjustment from falling on the weakest and most unprotected. The Declaration and Programme of Action openly acknowledge that it is politically dangerous to balance finances on the basis of unbalancing the lives of people. To see the results of inhumane economics, it is enough to look at Chiapas, Harlem, or Los Angeles (and especially the lives of the women in those communities). The WSSD calls for gender and poverty assessments to be included in the design of any structural adjustment programme. Indeed, these are policy criteria that should affect our spending, lending, hiring, and promotion decisions whether they are taken under conditions of "adjustment" or not.

At the highest political level, then, the Summit has assumed the commitment to achieve equality and equity between women and men and to promote a gender perspective in decision-making processes as inherent to more humane development for all. At Beijing, we must build on the political commitments of the Summit in order to make the Fourth World Conference on Women a resounding success. We cannot acquiesce to the naysayers who would say that people as individuals cannot affect change, that the structures of government and the walls of class and creed and difference that separate us are too thick to penetrate.

Instead, we must renew and remodel these structures to build a shared home in which all have a place. The Social Summit's core documents provide a blueprint for beginning our work. The challenge is not to lose precious time in getting started. Each society must now seek within itself the wisdom, the magnanimity, and the energy to realize its potential in this common task. This will not be easy, because the overemphasis on individualism and competitiveness has led to growing moral indifference worldwide. The documents approved at the WSSD provide for direct participation by organized civil society in designing, applying, and monitoring social policies. The first task is to ensure that these commitments are fulfilled.

The catalyst for action on the Summit's principles is, in fact, the twin task of mobilizing civil society to call for fulfillment of the Summit's commitments and engaging people in proposing policies based on their own experiences so as to ensure that "solutions" are brought close to people. And who better to take the lead than members of the international women's movement? A major world movement of civil society must be organized to link together the sometimes parallel and sectoral work of non-governmental organizations — whether they are concerned with issues of gender, population, ethnicity, environment, social development, human rights, peace, or disabilities. In particular, the challenge remains to link NGOs with an international presence to those that are active only at the national level.

All of this calls for a new vision of how to organize and finance the work of civil society organizations — NGOs, political parties, religious organizations, academic institutions, people's movements. Interesting proposals were made at the Summit by US Vice-President Al Gore and First Lady Hillary Rodham Clinton, who announced, respectively, that 40 per cent of US development assistance will be channelled through NGOs and that grants totalling some $100 million for programmes targeted to meet the needs of adolescent girls in the developing world will be executed by NGOs. Reform of national legislation in the United States and elsewhere will be required in order to support civil society and to encourage greater international cooperation — while still respecting the autonomy of the individuals involved.

Increasingly, the need for a new covenant between governments and organized civil society is apparent — in order to strengthen both parties to meet the challenge of resolving urgent social needs. The women's movement is capable of playing a continued central role in the Summit process — as it did throughout the preparatory process and at Copenhagen, where the women's caucus was far and away the best organized, most effective, and most influential body representing civil society.

In the end, the WSSD was neither confined to the limits of 6-12 March 1995 nor to the documents approved. What happened at the parallel NGO Forum — with 150 activities a day visited by 150,000 people — was and is also part of the Social Summit process. These are merely triggers and first steps toward generating awareness, hope, collective strength, and the ability to bring new insights to bear on the solutions required to humanize this dehumanized world. The value of this Summit will be measurable only over time — its success determined by the degree to which this process enables women and men together to define priorities for human-centred development in the 21st century.

Ambassador Juan Somavia, Permanent Representative of Chile to the United Nations, was Chair of the Preparatory Committee for the World Summit for Social Development. He served as President of the United Nations Economic and Social Council and, as of 1 July 1995, will serve as Chair of the United Nations Research Institute for Social Development. Ambassador Somavia was founder, Executive Director, and President of the Latin American Institute of Transnational Studies; founder and Secretary General of the South American Peace Commission; and President of the International Commission of the Democratic Opposition in Chile.

Notes

1. The Declaration and Programme of Action explicitly highlight the distinct concerns of women at all stages of life, from infancy and childhood through old age, and distinguish among the needs of urban and rural women, women with disabilities, indigenous women, and refugee women, among others.

PART 4

FROM RECOMMENDATIONS TO PRACTICE: SOME REFLECTIONS

"The Success of the Agenda for Equality, adopted in Beijing, rests therefore not in words, but in resources, implementation, enforcement, integration, and accountability. Today women call for: strong institutions and adequate resources for the enforcement of the agreements; firm commitments to the integration of women and gender concerns in all international, regional, and national bodies and policy-making processes; and effective mechanisms of accountability to the world's women in whose name these promises have been made."

—*"A Pledge to Gender Justice" (1995), developed by a working group of NGOs at the third Preparatory Committee meeting for the Fourth World Conference on Women and now endorsed by over 100 organizations worldwide.*

OPPORTUNITIES IN THE GLOBAL CASINO

HAZEL HENDERSON

As the so-called Fourth Development Decade of the United Nations unfolds, the lessons of the previous three decades are becoming clear. Traditional models equating industrialization and per capita–averaged, currency-denominated GNP and GDP growth — which are enshrined in the United Nations System of National Accounts (UNSNA) — have proved failures in most of the countries of the Southern Hemisphere. Even in its 1991 World Development Report, the World Bank addressed some of the sorry realities, a break from its usual upbeat style. In chapter two it noted:

> "Thinking on development has undergone a sea change during the past 40 years . . . Economists have traditionally considered an increase in per capita income to be a good proxy for other attributes of development. But the weakness of income growth as an indicator is that it may mask the real changes in welfare for large parts of the poor population. Improvements in meeting basic needs for food, education, health care, equality of opportunity, civil liberties, and environmental protection are not captured by statistics on income growth."[1]

This historic admission was the result of increasing pressure from grass-roots groups and alternative development practitioners who saw the failures firsthand in the villages, rural areas, and urban slums and, in recent years, from the anti-World Bank campaigns of environmentalists highlighting the environmental destruction caused by the Bank's policies.

In fact, the entire development process not only derailed in the 1980s but, tragically, in most sub-Saharan African countries it went into reverse. This was also the conclusion of a group of experts, convened in Caracas, Venezuela, and co-sponsored by the South Commission, to discuss problems of measuring development. Their report, "Toward a New Way of Measuring Development,"[2] concluded that the traditional development model involved a one-time, historical process — unrepeatable in any case. This is particularly true in today's crowded, polluted world, where natural resources are depleting rapidly and Northern industrial countries are now demanding that Southern countries actually forego this industrial development model as too polluting and instead change their course to pursue only "clean" or "green" technologies and "sustainable development."

After decades of pushing the old prescriptions for GNP-measured economic growth as the path to progress, the World Bank now glosses over past theoretical errors. As of 1991, the Bank's World Development Report has claimed, "Economic development is defined in this Report as a sustainable increase in living standards that encompass material consumption, education, health, and environmental protection." This highly political redefinition avoided addressing the fact that all of the Bank's statistical methods and lending policies require changing, a task still hardly begun even in 1995.

In an interdependent global commons, the key variable is government intervention, i.e., whether, when, where, and how to set up markets and use them, or when, why, who, and how to regulate or devise state or local plans. In other words, the success or failure of development policies seems to boil down to whether any given government intervened expertly or stupidly or has been just plain lucky! Economists from Left to Right are being forced to admit that all economies are "mixed" and that they have, as yet, no theories of mixed economies. It is now

185

clear that "economies" are simply sets of rules, based on the vastly different goals, values, and public priorities of each specific culture. There is more acknowledgement today of this cultural factor by economists, since it is the only way of explaining the "Japanese miracle" (homogeneous cultures; "cronyism"; good conflict resolution; hard-working, well-educated people) and the very different factors that fueled the growth of the "Four Tigers" of Asia: Singapore (a benevolent dictatorship), South Korea (heavy state intervention), Hong Kong (free-market orientation, almost no natural resources), and Taiwan (much state intervention, hard-working people).

These broader analyses show the shallowness of purely economic development formulas regarding "correct" rates of capital accumulation and investment (an insane generality since the key problem is to make *wise* investments), or the old formula of taxing agriculture to invest in industrialization. The influential economic journal *The Economist* now equates good economic growth policies with investments in people, their health, and education — not a free-market idea (in fact, markets tend to fail in such social goals). Yet free-market ideologues in the private sector generally oppose such government investments as unaffordable or as "socialism," and naturally, if the society's scorecard remains the GNP, they will be vindicated, since people are not included in GNP as assets, as are machines and capital investments in technology or plants or equipment.

We can trust the sudden change of heart by economists about the value of people and the environment only if we see them also crusading to correct the GNP. Any citizen knows that when goals change, the scorecard also has to change to reflect the new goal and to measure results in progressing towards it.

RE-VALUING MONEY

GNP, GDP, inflation, interest, and unemployment rates are all loaded with biases and ignore structural issues of power and prior distribution of wealth. They foster an unrealistic view which equates real wealth (natural resources and skills, specific cultural assets, local conditions, and creativity of resourceful human beings) with mere money. A whole treatise would be necessary to elucidate the difference between money and true wealth. It suffices to remind ourselves that money, i.e., currencies, are virtually worthless in themselves. Money acquires value only insofar as human beings use and trust it. Where it is used and trusted, it serves to keep score of human transactions and production. Over half of all the world's production, consumption, exchange, investments, and savings are conducted outside the money economy, even in industrial countries. No wonder, then, that World Bank and other development projects failed, since they overlooked these non-money sectors.

Today we still suffer in the North and South from international systems of finance, debt, and currency manipulation invented in the Northern Hemisphere, which even the respected US-based magazine *Business Week* referred to as "the global casino." This inequitable global casino, unreal as its worldwide electronic funds transfer systems are, has become a structural element blocking the aspirations for real and sustainable development of most of the countries of the South.

Information technology innovations have created a global financial casino where as much as $1 trillion of "virtual securities" (derivatives of underlying real stocks, bonds, commodities, and currencies) are traded each day — bringing new uncertainties such as raids on the dollar, sterling, and other major currencies, and scenarios of financial collapse. Recent examples illustrate the vulnerability of tightly interlinked global financial systems operating without overall rules, such as Germany's Herstatt Bank failure and the US savings and loan crisis.

Worried central bankers and national politicians trying to stave off such scenarios are left with failing textbook economic remedies to support their domestic economies and currencies (such as raising interest rates or buying efforts). These national players, handicapped by eroding national sovereignty, manoeuvre painfully toward the social innovation needed to match the advance of the global casino's computer- and satellite-based technological innovation.[3] The United Nations in its preeminent role as global norm setter, broker, networker, and convenor is well suited to fostering such social innovations in the new electronic commons.

In today's financial markets, bankers, brokers, bond and currency traders themselves — along with growing numbers of finance ministers, parliamentarians, and regulators — see the need for new rules to create a more orderly capital and currency market. Such new market regimes can inspire confidence. Finance ministers acknowledge the loss of domestic controls as well as the diminished tax revenues which came with the financial deregulation of the 1980s. Bond markets more concerned with inflation than unemployment limit "pump priming" projects and jobs while reducing options for social safety nets.

Only global agreements on capital investment, currency exchange stabilization, and restructuring the International Monetary Fund (IMF), World Bank and the World Trade Organization (WTO) can address today's paradoxes. However, prescriptions offered in *The Economist* for closing "the big holes (that) remain in the legal fabric (which) may yet threaten global economic systems"[4] fall far short of addressing the dilemma of national governments squeezed between currency speculators and bond traders on the one hand and the perils of domestic protest of IMF structural adjustments on the other. The prediction, expressed in the same issue of *The Economist*, that "in 1994, the world is closer than ever before to the global cooperative free market arrangements championed 50 years ago by the visionaries who met at Bretton Woods"[5] needs some additional thought. Cooperative agreements do not emerge automatically from free markets and must be designed by human rather than invisible hands.

THE SOCIAL INNOVATION LAG

From the spinning jenny and the steam engine to the automobile and computer, technologies have always outpaced and eventually called forth responding social innovations: double-entry bookkeeping and accounting protocols, national currencies and central banks, standardization of highway signs. The computer industry, now automating service sectors worldwide, underpins today's global casino. Nowhere is the lag in needed social innovation more glaring than in the growing gap between the explosion of computerized global financial trading (over 90 per cent of which is speculation) and the thus far feeble efforts of finance ministers, bankers, and international bodies such as the Bank for International Settlements (BIS) and the IMF to create the needed regulatory regime. The G-7, after the Mexican peso crisis of 1994-95 and the 20 per cent decline of the dollar in 1995, was obliged to address these issues in its Halifax meeting of June 1995. Amid mounting public pressure, the G-7 called for new international safeguards against similar crises by beefing up the IMF's currency stabilization funds. A better idea would be to allow any indebted country whose currency was under speculative attack to seek "bankruptcy" protection similar to the chapter 9-type provisions in US bankruptcy law.

Today's abstracted world trade/global competitiveness model has alienated financial markets from the real economy of "Main Street" (where actual people in real factories produce real shoes or build real houses or grow real food). The global casino is now spinning into cyberspace, divorced from any understanding of the whole picture: human societies with people working, cooperating, and competing while interacting within webs of other species and ecosystems in a fragile, ever-changing biosphere. Thus, the needed paradigm shifts are toward systems and chaos theory and other interdisciplinary, dynamic change models, informed by psychological re-integration to overcome the pervasive fear/scarcity-based strategies of economics. They are now conditions for the shift of our financial system from a pervasive GNP-based, "trickle down" economic growth typified still in Bretton Woods institutions to diversified, decentralized, "trickle up" sustainable development which restores incentives to mutual aid, cooperative informal sectors, and the development of agreements and rules for managing the global commons.

These paradigm shifts begin by rethinking scarcity, abundance, needs, and satisfaction, and lead inevitably to wholesale redefinitions of money, wealth, work, productivity, efficiency, and progress. A prerequisite of this new world view is the understanding that money is not scarce and that its apparent scarcity is itself a major social regulatory mechanism — a social innovation which, when functioning well, provides a beneficial circulatory system for wider human exchange and purchasing power beyond face-to-face barter.

Many of the operating principles derived from industrial paradigms remain unexamined: technological innovation is widely encouraged and subsidized, while social innovation is suspect (as "planning") and occurs only after crises. National societies are assumed to be divided up into a private sector (market competition) and a public sector (government and non-profits) with a "Berlin Wall" inhibiting interaction (buttressed by antitrust laws). Government is enjoined from "competing" with private-sector businesses. Much creativity and inventiveness is dammed up behind rigid definitions and restrictive institutions which operationalize the competitive nation-state–based industrial paradigm now moving toward its logical conclusion: global economic warfare.

BREAKUP OF THE GLOBAL MONEY CARTEL

Today we see the rise of non-money information economies (local, regional, and global networks for barter, counter-trade, reciprocity, and mutual aid) wherever macro-economic management is failing in societies.[6] In G-7 countries, Russia, and Eastern Europe — all challenged by the global casino — people are creating their own local information societies of mutual aid on the Internet and other networks, where users are increasing by 25 per cent per month. In the 1990s information age, democracy is sweeping the planet as people can see for themselves on satellite TV how politics, economics, money, and cultural traditions interact to control human affairs from the global to the local level. A global civil society made up of millions of citizen groups now linking electronically is challenging both governments and corporations as a third "independent sector." Many in governments and at the local level are realizing the implications of the global information age: money and information are now equivalent, and if you have the one, you can get the other. In fact, information is often more valuable. Today money follows information (and sometimes misinformation) and markets are no longer so "efficient."

Thus, the global money monopoly is breaking up, even as its casino becomes more unstable with bouncing currencies, derivatives, and increasing volatility. Socially innovative governments can now go around the money monopoly and conduct sophisticated barter and counter-trade deals directly (as do corporations) using computer-based trading systems. Indeed, one-quarter of all world trade is already done in this way, according to industry estimates. The need to earn foreign exchange, which hung over governments like the sword of Damocles, can now be lifted, and the IMF must face up to this new game which it can never control.

Today's calls for democratizing and restructuring the World Bank, the IMF and the WTO, as well as opening up the still-private BIS, have grown out of new evidence of the irrelevance of structural adjustments and the failure of the economic approach of the UN's Third Development Decade. Protests of grass-roots groups will become more strident as more people see that money is not in short supply and that credits and liquidity often follow politics and could be made available more widely and equitably, not just to governments to shore up alliances and to pander to bond traders and other special interests. Democratic reformers seek wider access to credit for private groups, local enterprises, villages, and many other NGOs and communities for "trickle up" development. Such campaigns will persist until the political assumptions of the Bretton Woods institutions are teased out of their economic models and until their relationships with governments, banks, securities traders, stock exchanges, and bond holders are made much more clear.

WHERE ARE THE WOMEN?

Women all over the world are beginning to realize the extent to which they have been impoverished by the global casino and marginalized by faulty, outdated economic textbooks and their GNP recipe for progress. Women are rightly demanding that unpaid production work in the household, food-growing, and raising the next generation (the most productive activity in any society) must now be recognized by national accounts. Slowly these demands are being heard and framed as legislative reforms and in the 1994 System of National Accounts in many countries, but enormous political pressure must be put on all governments. Governments have become used to the subsidies provided by the unpaid, informal sector of the economy — subsidies which have been provided largely by women — as well as the subsidies from the exploitation of all living systems and the earth's natural riches.

Now that all of the economies of the world are tied together by computerized electronic trading of currencies, bonds, and other securities, women must demand that this global casino be tamed and regulated for the good of all women, children, the poor, employees, microentrepreneurs, and even the investors themselves. Therefore, it is time for women to join with other sectors in demanding a financial system that is accountable and transparent and where speculators cannot divert the priorities of democratically elected governments: to maintain safety nets for children and other vulnerable populations; to invest in domestic priorities and civilian services; to regulate commercial activities and public interest; and to prevent exploitation of people and the natural environment.

Today's rampant, uncontrolled global financial system is a woman's issue. Minimally, we must begin by pressuring for the creation of a global Securities and Exchange Commission (SEC), similar to the US body which in the 1930s reduced fraud, speculation, and criminal abuse, thus saving Wall Street from its own excesses. Discussions at government and private sector levels are already occurring on how to harmonize all national securities regulations into such a global SEC. In commencing with such a global SEC to reduce excessive speculative financial flows, currency exchange fees should be levied to serve as "circuit breakers," like the circuit breaker instituted after the Wall Street crash of 1987 to dampen the effects of computerized "programmed trading."

Let us begin, then, by calling for these minimum approaches for taming the global casino. Even a fairly small .003 per cent currency exchange fee would raise approximately $9 billion a year on the trillion dollars traded daily, some of which could be diverted to more humane purposes.

Any uses or abuses of the global commons, such as cross-border pollution of the oceans

189

and atmosphere, arms and drug trafficking, and currency speculation, should be taxed. All commercial use of these common resources should be licensed, and fees should be collected so that prices of these products reflect their true social and environmental costs. Women everywhere can join in with other major grass-roots constituencies — including professional associations, unions, environmentalists, and advocates of human rights and the poor — to address the taming of this new level of the global financial system.

As the human family approaches six billion members, proposals and agreements for managing the global commons are emerging from many quarters. These global common heritage resources — the oceans, the atmosphere, and, the newest commons of all, the global economy — must be shepherded in equitable, transparent, democratic, and sustainable ways to ensure a future for our children and the next generations.

Hazel Henderson is an independent futurist and author of numerous books and articles including Paradigms in Progress (1991 and 1995) and Creating Alternative Futures (1978). She is an advisor to the Calvert Group Inc. (U.S.); a member of the Social Venture Network (U.S.); a fellow of the World Business Academy (U.S.); and a member of the Task Force on the Efficient Capital Markets of the World Business Council for Sustainable Development (Switzerland). From 1974 - 1980, Henderson served on the original Advisory Council of the U.S. Office of Technology Assessment.

This article draws upon the author's following publications: *Paradigms in Progress: Life Beyond Economics*, Indianapolis: Knowledge Systems, 1991, and San Francisco: Berrett-Koehler, 1995; "New Markets and New Commons: Opportunities in the Global Casino," *Futures* 27 (2), 1995; "Today's Rampant, Uncontrolled Global Financial System Is a Woman's Issue" (statement to the women going to the WCW), 1995.

Notes

1. World Bank. 1991. *World Development Report.* New York: Oxford University Press, p. 31.

2. Perez, Carlos Andres. 1990. "Redefining Wealth and Progress" (foreword), in The South Commission, *The Caracas Report: Toward a New Way of Measuring Development.* English version. New York: TOES Books/Bootstrap Press.

3. Henderson, Hazel. 1993. "Social Innovation and Citizen Movements," *Futures* 25 (3), p. 322.

4. Sachs, Jeffrey. 1994. "Beyond Bretton Woods," *The Economist* (1 October), pp. 23–27.

5. Sachs, cited in note 4.

6. Henderson, Hazel. 1994. "Information: The World's New Currency Isn't Scarce," in *World Business Academy Perspectives.* San Francisco.

ENGENDERING THE INTERNATIONAL REFORM AGENDA

RICHARD JOLLY

This year — 1995 — has marked many historical milestones. We have commemorated the 50th anniversary of World War II. We are celebrating the first 50 years in the life of the United Nations. It is a time of reflection.

Looking back over the last twenty years or so of development efforts — a period characterized by severe economic crises for some countries and unprecedented opportunities for others — we can identify the elements of an emerging consensus, now firmly in place, that development is about people. After decades of debate, we now have a comprehensive, multifaceted understanding of development, which views its economic, political, and social dimensions as part of one whole. In place of earlier definitions centered on GNP growth, the fulfillment of basic needs, and utilitarian notions of "human capital formation," human development — in the form of good quality basic services in health (including reproductive health), nutrition, education, water and sanitation — focuses on enabling people to live full and meaningful lives of their own choosing.

In turn, this human development consensus has helped to define a new agenda for international reform focusing on creative approaches to peace-making, conflict prevention, and humanitarian relief; comprehensive measures to eradicate poverty; human rights and democratic, participatory governance; environmental protection and sustainable development; the special needs of the poorest countries and poorest groups within countries; the need for a more comprehensive approach to structural adjustment; and the need to mobilize high-level political support for human development.

Each of the issues on this new agenda has benefited tremendously from the contribution of scores of women's groups, operating at all levels of society, from grass-roots women's cooperatives, to working women organized in unions, to the (still far too few) women who number among the world's political and business leaders. In this short paper, I would like to focus on the particular influence women have had in two key areas of the international agenda: the debate over structural adjustment and the effort to win high-level political support for human development. From these two sets of issues, I think it is possible to draw some important lessons regarding how to ensure that the voices and views of women exert ever greater influence over the great international debates of our time.

WOMEN AND STRUCTURAL ADJUSTMENT

In all societies, women have many roles. They may be farmers; home managers; care givers to children, the sick, and the elderly; workers in the formal and the informal economy; and, increasingly, community leaders. There is a growing body of evidence to support the assertion that structural adjustment has often made it much more difficult for women to perform these functions adequately.

In particular, adjustment has been associated with a contraction in formal-sector employment, at least in the short run, leading to reductions in family incomes, a decrease in the availability and quality of public services, and a consequent increase in the demands on women's time. In short, adjustment frequently forces women to do more with less: to provide home-based health care when the cost of visiting health centres rises too high, to step in when early childhood programmes are suspended, to spend even more time and energy hunting for ways to stretch the family's meagre income to cover the rising prices of food and other necessities. The growing uncertainty of daily life takes a further toll on women — especially those who are also heads of households — preventing them from planning for the long term and locking them into a desperate struggle to meet the growing needs of their families.

From this experience, we have learned to view adjustment within the broader context of human development. This approach, which the United Nations Children's Fund (UNICEF) has termed Adjustment with a Human Face, calls for the conscious incorporation of human concerns — and women's concerns in particular — into the objectives, content and monitoring of national and international policies of economic adjustment. It may be useful here to note briefly the main elements of this approach and to show their links to women's concerns.

First, we must make a change in the basic objectives of adjustment policy. There must be clear and explicit recognition of the importance of protecting the nutritional and other basic needs, especially of children and other vulnerable groups, like pregnant and nursing mothers, in the course of adjustment. Fortunately, over the years this has been increasingly recognized as an important element. But to give full expression to women's needs, one can and should, I believe, go further. Women's concerns, both in the household and in the workplace, need consciously to be made part of the analysis and formulation of adjustment policies. In turn, this means that women need to be involved directly in both the definition of adjustment programmes and their implementation and monitoring.

From UNICEF's perspective, there are six key policy components of Adjustment with a Human Face:

1. *More expansionary macro-economic policies which sustain levels of output and investment and allow for the satisfaction of basic needs over the adjustment period.* Structural adjustment of an economy normally takes much longer than conventional stabilization. A more gradual timing of adjustment and larger amounts of medium-term external finance is therefore necessary.

2. *The use of meso policies — within any given frame of macro policy — to reinforce the more expansionary macro approach and to secure the priority use of resources to fulfil the needs of the vulnerable.* Meso policies determine the impact of policies toward taxation, government expenditure, foreign exchange, and credit (among others) on the distribution of income and resources. Essential aspects of meso policies for Adjustment with a Human Face are using such policy instruments selectively for prioritizing and restructuring resources and activities in favour of the poor; for protecting the basic needs of the vulnerable; and for supporting economic growth.

3. *Sectoral policies which aim at restructuring within the productive sector to strengthen employment and income- generating activities and raise productivity in low-income activities,* focusing in particular on small farmers and informal sector producers in industry and services.

4. *Improving the equity and efficiency of the social sector* by restructuring public expenditure both between and within sectors (from high-cost areas toward low-cost basic services) by improving the targeting of interventions and their cost-effectiveness.

5. *Compensatory programmes (often of limited duration) to protect the basic health and nutrition of low-income families during adjustment before growth resumption,* enabling them to meet their minimum needs independently. Two major elements of such policies are public works employment schemes and nutritional interventions,

encompassing targeted food subsidies and direct feeding for the most vulnerable.

6. *Monitoring of the human situation*, especially the living standards, health, and nutrition of low-income groups during the adjustment process, so that needs may be identified and the effectiveness of adjustment programmes assessed and modified accordingly. Monitoring of human conditions, especially the health and nutritional status of the population, should be given as much weight in monitoring adjustment as monetary variables have in the conventional approach.

As someone who was deeply involved in the articulation of Adjustment with a Human Face, let me say clearly that our efforts have been informed by and have benefited greatly from the real-life experiences of women in all parts of the developing world. In this respect, UNICEF was particularly pleased, during the second meeting of the Preparatory Committee for the World Summit for Social Development, to help UNIFEM and the Women's Alliance for Economic Alternatives to bring together a group of women from developing countries and central and eastern Europe to relate their firsthand experience with structural adjustment.

MOBILIZING POLITICAL LEADERS: WOMEN'S GROUPS AND SUMMITS

The second area of international reform where I believe women have exercised tremendous leadership is that of mobilizing high-level political leaders around the twin causes of human development and gender equality.

In recent years, the international community has devoted considerable effort to using summits and global conferences to rally high-level political leaders around key aspects of the human development agenda. Each of these summits — the World Summit for Children (WSC, 1990), the United Nations Conference on the Environment and Development (UNCED, 1992), the World Conference on Human Rights (WCHR, 1993), the International Conference on Population and Development (ICPD, 1994), the World Summit for Social Development (WSSD, 1995) and now the Fourth World Conference on Women (WCW, 1995) — has produced a programme of action that commits world leaders to concrete, and in many cases time-bound, measurable goals for advancing human development.

While women's groups have played an important role in all these global conferences,

> *"International financial institutions, including the World Bank Group, the International Monetary Fund, the International Fund for Agricultural Development and the regional banks, should be invited to examine their grants and lending and to allocate loans and grants to programmes to implement the Platform for Action in developing countries..."*
>
> — *Platform for Action, UN Fourth World Conference on Women, Chapter VI, para. 355.*

193

it was the ICPD in Cairo and the WSSD in Copenhagen which demonstrated the extraordinary mobilizing power, tenacity, inspiration, and creativity of women's groups.

It was this creativity — and deft political manoeuvering — which allowed us at the ICPD to achieve an important shift in our thinking about population issues and policies, away from a narrow focus on family planning to a comprehensive, holistic view anchored in the reproductive health and the empowerment of women. This broader view recognizes that in order to manage the transition to lower fertility and sustainable population growth rates, we must improve the status of girls and women, secure their access to basic services — especially education — while increasing parents' confidence in the survival of their children.

At the WSSD in Copenhagen, the influence of women's groups was equally in evidence. Faced with the Summit's amorphous agenda of complex issues and a seeming lack of interest on the part of governments (at least until the final stages of the preparatory process), a coalition of women's groups led by Development Alternatives with Women for a New Era (DAWN) and Women's Environment and Development Organization (WEDO) used the opportunity to rally NGOs together to press a common agenda of economic fairness and gender equality.

In both Cairo and Copenhagen, women's groups made major contributions to the Declarations and Programmes of Action eventually adopted, challenging the free-market ideology that characterized early drafts and advocating instead a practical approach to (women's) development based on securing the reproductive health and literacy of women as well as their access to productive economic assets.

THE LONGER-TERM CHALLENGE: NEW PATTERNS OF DEVELOPMENT FOR THE 21ST CENTURY[1]

Having looked back on how far the international community has come in grappling with some of the urgent issues which crowd the international reform agenda, we should perhaps end by looking forward to some of the longer-term challenges still to be tackled. Three particular issues stand out.

First is the need to go beyond poverty reduction and human development to issues of greater global equity in lifestyles in both developing and industrial countries. The present gap between the richest and poorest groups globally is of the order of 150 to 1, exceeding many times the 26 to 1 gap in Brazil, where inequality within any one country is greatest. Addressing this vexing problem raises complex issues of ethics, equity, and political feasibility.

Second is the need to achieve reasonable standards of living and consumption, to achieve lifestyles of happiness and fulfillment while consuming far fewer of the world's resources than is typical of industrial countries today. This will be one way to moderate the ever-growing levels of inequality between the most industrialized countries and most of the developing countries. The very fact that the gaps in human welfare between developed and developing countries are so much less than the gaps in resource use is an indication of the economic inefficiency that needs to be addressed.

Third is the need to move to different patterns of growth and development, nationally and internationally. This in turn will require different mechanisms to influence and underpin this growth. The international institutions will need to devise ways to influence these patterns, certainly using the price mechanism but going beyond it.

INTERNATIONAL ROLES IN SUPPORT OF THIS AGENDA

What are the roles and comparative advantages of the various multilateral organizations in support of this agenda, both in its more immediate and in its long-run elements? In particular, what are the roles of the Bretton Woods institutions, the regional development banks, and the UN specialized and operating agencies?

At present there is in the industrial countries a tendency to underestimate the value and role of the UN agencies in contributing to economic policy-making and direct support of development in developing countries. True, the Bretton Woods institutions possess much more resources, provide each year more capital and more technical assistance to developing countries, and generally produce analyses of higher economic quality. By virtue of these characteristics (and of the voting control which the industrial countries possess over them), the Bretton Woods institutions also wield much more economic influence. Notwithstanding, the UN organizations also have important characteristics: much stronger field presence, a style of interaction with recipient governments characterized more by solidarity and political impartiality, and an approach to analysis which is, at its best, more technical and multidisciplinary. It is often forgotten that at least six Nobel prizewinners in economics have worked for the United Nations and that many of the basic innovations in Bretton Woods practices have grown out of analysis and recommendations first put forward by the United Nations and only later adopted by the World Bank or International Monetary Fund (IMF), often after a period of initial opposition.

Even in terms of resource flows, the UN operational agencies may be relatively more significant in relation to the World Bank and IMF than is often realized. In recent years, the net transfers to Africa by the United Nations have exceeded those of the World Bank and IMF together, and they have been made on grant terms rather than as loans.

But the basic point is that forceful, committed support is needed from all parts of the multilateral system if the goals of human development are to be achieved. All four pillars of the system must play their part, fully and together, if the goals of more balanced global development are to be realized — and realized within a time horizon which is politically and economically acceptable.

Basic leadership must be taken by each country. But supportive actions by the multilateral community will often be critical — in resources, in exchange of experience, in help with monitoring, and perhaps above all, in encouragement and focused catalytic support. Conditionality will be less important than assurances of long-term commitment and the avoidance of approaches or measures that may undercut what is being encouraged in poverty reduction, on the one hand, and human development, on the other.

With this as background, one can move to a final point: the need to provide strong and collaborative support, but not necessarily in total bureaucratic coordination. There is strength in diversity, especially of views and approaches in situations where it is not entirely clear what is needed to be done in the longer run. Recognition of the need for *diversity* would legitimize a measure of international debate on uncertain or controversial elements. This will be critical if the multilateral system is adequately to look forward and probe the longer-run actions required for further progress toward poverty reduction and human development in the 21st century.

As we forge ahead, building on the human development gains achieved to date and seizing these longer-term challenges, we must find ways to ensure that the voices and views of women — which proved so crucial in Rio, Vienna, Cairo, and Copenhagen — will continue to guide us, and, in ever greater numbers, to lead us forward.

Richard Jolly is Deputy Executive Director for Programmes in UNICEF, a position he has held since 1982. In this capacity, Dr. Jolly is concerned with all aspects of UNICEF's programmes in over 100 countries of the world, including the agency's strategy for support to countries in implementing the goals agreed at the 1990 World Summit for Children.

195

Notes

1. These two sections draw upon the author's "Poverty Eradication and Human Development: Issues for the Twenty-First Century," in Mahbub ul Haq et al. (eds.), *The UN and the Bretton Woods Institutions: New Challenges for the Twenty-First Century.* London: Macmillan, 1995.

FROM STABILIZATION TO GROWTH WITH EQUITY

ELLEN JOHNSON SIRLEAF

Women's centrality to economic production has always stood in stark contrast to the discrimination they face in accessing resources (financial, technical, and other) that would enable them to realize their full productive potential.

A recent study from Kenya makes a compelling case for investing in women farmers to raise overall productivity and growth. According to the study, "If women had the same human capital endowments and used the same amounts of factors and inputs as men, the value of their output would be increased by some 22 per cent. Thus, women are quite possibly better, more efficient, farm managers than men." The study further states that "simply raising the productivity of women to the same level as men could increase total production by 10 to 15 per cent." In addition to direct investment, an important tool for unleashing women's potential is devising effective gender-sensitive incentives that encourage women's full productivity.

One instrument that has been shown in some circumstances to release the potential of women is that of small-scale credit to the urban and rural poor, an area in which there was an early analysis and attempts to focus on the specific needs of poor women. Various supports to small-scale activities of the poor have been key mechanisms for strengthening productivity, facilitating the development of a cash economy, strengthening connections with the formal banking system, introducing formal financial and accounting procedures into the informal sector, and attaining similar finance-related goals. It has thus been a significant adjunct, albeit on a local scale, to the economic modernization that is the universal concomitant of development.

FINANCING FOR THE INFORMAL SECTOR

More than 500 million economically active people run small and micro-enterprises in the informal sector. Of these entrepreneurs, a significant proportion are women, as many as 50 per cent in a number of countries of sub-Saharan Africa. Fewer than 10 million of these enterprises have access to financial services other than moneylenders. Conventional banks concentrate only on the top 25 per cent of the economically active population, overwhelmingly in the formal sector. By contrast, such innovative ventures as the Grameen Bank in Bangladesh reach less than 2 per cent of low-income entrepreneurs; more than 80 per cent of these borrowers are women.

In sum, the available formal and informal loan resources are not reaching the informal sector, preventing many dynamic entrepreneurs from making their maximum potential contribution to economic growth. A significant proportion of those excluded are women, who have very good records as loan recipients and who have special financial needs.

We have long known the reasons for this worldwide mismatch. The vast majority of low-income women lack the collateral requirements of conventional banks. Their low levels of education also limit their ability to keep business accounts and records or to take advantage of conventional managerial and technical training. From the bank's point of view, it is too costly to make the very small loans — typically of US$100 or less and often only about US$20 — for which these women apply.

The exclusion of low-income female entrepreneurs from formal credit mechanisms is ironic. Their repayment rates average well over 90 per cent, even when the interest rates on the small sums they borrow soar to over 20 per cent at conventional banks and to 50 per cent or more through moneylenders. These women do not need subsidies. Provided banks can keep the overhead (administrative costs and allowances for bad debts) below 6 to 8 per cent, there is no reason why loans to female entrepreneurs could not be economically feasible. However, many small-scale credit institutions have overheads of 15 to 20 per cent. This is partly due to inefficiencies but also to the fact that the amount of administrative support required by illiterate borrowers is relatively high.

Women's famed low default rate is an important phenomenon. It is often cited as an indicator of the success of credit schemes. However, many of these schemes are providing loans to women under conditions of extremely limited demand for their products or services. They are unable to sell the buns that they bake, the bricks that they press, or the uniforms that they sew because the market is either flooded with similar products or local purchasing power is too low. Under such circumstances women divert funds from other sources, such as beer-brewing or remittances from wages, to repay loans, with the net result of a *reduction* in their disposable income.

However, in a dynamic economy, such small-scale enterprises can become an engine of growth that strengthens the formal sector: small and micro-entrepreneurs spend much of their turnover on purchasing inputs from formal businesses. In addition, groups of such entrepreneurs can and do increase social services by mounting self-help schemes for health and child care, home improvement, and the teaching of literacy and marketable skills — in short, the very social safety nets that debt-ridden governments find increasingly difficult to provide.

GIVING CREDIT WHERE CREDIT IS DUE

Structural reform must entail the reform of financial systems that now serve only the few. Neglecting the energy and ingenuity of the women whose unpaid work has subsidized all forms of society's wealth since prehistory is short-sighted — and dangerous. It risks reinforcing structures that perpetuate poverty, among them the structure of gender relations that exploits women's unpaid labour while denying the value of this labour and diminishes women's opportunities for gainful work outside the home.

By contrast, developing and strengthening institutions that give credit where credit is due both tackles poverty and, in appropriate circumstances, generates broad-based economic growth. If development is finally geared to enlarging human choice, financial reform must not only increase productivity but also enhance human dignity, a force whose creativity and strength has too long been ignored by development planners, public and private.

One such innovation could be to generalize mechanisms whereby the savings of small-scale producers could be invested in their own communities. Credit schemes are often accompanied by savings schemes: potential borrowers first have to demonstrate the capacity to save. It is precisely these savings that are loaned to group members, sometimes reinforced by funds provided by donors. However, to the extent that these funds are deposited in formal financial institutions, they are invested by these institutions in ventures that typically benefit the formal, more modern sectors of the economy.

Cooperative societies offer a model here, in which virtually all saved funds are locally loaned. However, cooperatives are riven by corruption, or suspicion of corruption, and are notoriously inefficient. Moreover, their loan policies tend to reflect the priorities of the more vocal members — principally men. Strengthening women's capacity to participate in, manage,

197

and direct cooperatives and other financial intermediaries could well be one way forward.

Another possibility would be to follow the example of the People's Bank of Nigeria (PBN), which was established in 1989 as part of concerted government and NGO efforts to integrate women into the socio-economic and political mainstream. The principal activity of the PBN is to make collateral-free loans to underprivileged women and the poor, who lack access to credit facilities available from commercial and merchant banks. Since its founding, 348 branches have been opened, of which 68 are mobile banks that take their services to the people, especially women, on weekly market days. Several focused schemes have been initiated to enhance the services offered by the PBN and to respond to the specific concerns of its clients. These include the Banking for Health Scheme, the Savings Scheme, the People's Emergency Deposit Scheme, and the Street Gangs Scheme. A total of about US$30 million has been disbursed to about 650,000 beneficiaries, and over 75 per cent of this amount has been given to women.

CHALLENGES FOR FINANCING WOMEN IN DEVELOPMENT PROGRAMMES

The prescription we know all too well. It is time that we set challenging targets for policy makers, decision makers, and bankers that will make a difference in the contribution women can make to advancing and sustaining human development. By the year 2000:

- Incentives should be created for banks to amend their lending policies regarding collateral required of women. Lending policies could be based instead on a proven track record in repayment of informal loans.
- Legislation should be created that would require banks and other lending institutions to eliminate practices requiring a husband's consent or co-signature.
- Gender-sensitive incentives should be designed to ensure that the full potential of women's work is unleashed as an engine of growth.
- Support should be given to women's active participation in all institutions of governance and civil society, including financial management institutions.

Ellen Johnson Sirleaf is the Assistant Administrator and Director of the Regional Bureau for Africa, United Nations Development Programme (UNDP), New York, and former Vice-President and Director of Equator Holdings Company, a member of Hong Kong Bank Group. She has served as Minister of Finance of Liberia; President of the Liberian Bank for Development and Investment; Vice-President of Citibank, Regional Office for Africa; Senior Loan Officer at the World Bank. Her most recent publication is "The Outlook for Commercial Bank Lending to Sub-Saharan Africa" with Francis Nyirjesy (1991).

This article draws upon the author's presentation "Women and the United Nations: Reflections and New Horizons," given at the Vienna International Centre, May 1995.

Toward a New Age of Equity

James Gustave Speth

There is little equity in today's world. On any given day in our world of plenty, 68,000 babies are born into families living on less than $1 a day, to begin their lives in a prison of poverty. A handful of countries have more food than they could ever consume, while many others have too little to meet even their minimum nutritional needs. Sadly, inequities like these are growing, not decreasing.

Some of the most appalling inequities occur between men and women. Women carry a disproportionately large share of the burden of global poverty. Among the 1.3 billion people around the world who can barely meet their basic survival needs, as many as 70 per cent are female. During the last two decades, the number of women in extreme poverty surged by 50 per cent, compared to a 30 per cent increase for men. The United Nations Development Programme (UNDP) has made a commitment to focus its resources on programmes that help eliminate these and other inequities by promoting "sustainable human development."

Sustainable human development does not merely generate growth but distributes the benefits of growth *equitably*. Sustainable human development is development that gives priority to the poor, that empowers people rather than marginalizing them; that regenerates the environment rather than destroying it; that promotes job-led growth, not job-less growth; and that enhances citizens' participation in decisions affecting their lives. It is development that is pro-poor, pro-jobs, pro-nature and pro-*women*.

Indeed, neither sustainable human development nor a more equitable world is possible without the advancement of women.

Within its overall objective of building developing countries' capacities for sustainable human development, UNDP has set the advancement of women as one of its main goals. Progress for women is essential for the achievement of UNDP's other main goals: poverty elimination, job creation, and environmental protection. UNDP, along with the rest of the international community, has come to realize that women are perhaps the most powerful force for development. Women's issues must therefore be part and parcel of any development strategy. We have come to realize that any effort to halt the growth of poverty in the developing world must take women's concerns into account. These efforts also require finding ways to unleash women's potential for contributing to development and economic growth.

Gender issues are central not only to poverty-reduction strategies but also to solving the world's worsening unemployment problem. UNDP is contributing to the search for ways to increase income-earning opportunities. Among other things, this means ensuring that women and men have equitable access to resources, training, and credit. It also means finding other ways to release women's economic and social potential. One sure way is ensuring their equitable participation in decision-making at all levels.

An essential point in the global employment debate is that the work performed by women at home is the foundation of every other kind of work. This work, including child-rearing, caring for the elderly and the sick, and participation in community affairs, has never been adequately measured. Development policies must be changed to reflect the fact that this unpaid work is productive.

Gender issues cannot be separated from broader social issues. For example, conflicts stemming from ethnic, racial, and religious hatreds has forced millions of people to flee their homes. The vast majority of these refugees are women and their dependent children, boys as

199

well as girls. The massive displacements create additional strains on national resources and trap refugees in a downward spiral that progressively strips them of dignity. Sustainable human development emphasizes the building of dignity and self-respect.

Natural resource depletion can also lead to further fragmentation of societies. We are now witnessing a swelling tide of environmental refugees from drought, desertification, deforestation, and the pollution of water, air, and soil. Sustainable development stresses what we call "intergenerational equity" — the need to conserve and manage the resources on which current and future generations depend.

Within the present generation, widespread gender inequities threaten sustainability. Indeed, the survival of entire ecosystems can be undermined by these inequities in the very near future. Regenerating the global resource base therefore involves righting the balance of gender responsibilities.

Women have traditionally managed fuel, fodder, and the soils used to grow food. But their views remain ignored in most critical policy decisions that affect these resources. Women have made major contributions to the environmental and developmental debates worldwide, but they have been denied a place at too many decision-making tables. This is not only unjust; it is unwise. When policy makers are deaf to women's voices, they deny themselves the benefits of women's invaluable knowledge, perspectives, and insights. It makes little sense for a government to formulate a policy to control deforestation if decision-makers fail to consult those largely responsible for gathering fuelwood.

The defining concern of international affairs in the decades ahead will be the struggle for equity — equity among nations, equity within nations, equity for future generations, and equity between the *sexes*.

As the Declaration of the World Summit for Social Development (WSSD) in Copenhagen recognized in March 1995, achieving equity requires an enabling environment: an environment that supports growth, gives priority to the poor and to jobs, and encourages participation, tolerance, and respect for human diversity and the rule of law. This enabling environment must promote justice and fundamental fairness among men *and* women. It must also promote justice among nations as well as within them. This means strong countries giving weaker countries access to their markets. It means sharing modern technology. And it means financial support for development assistance and debt relief.

The Declaration drawn up at the Copenhagen Summit also called upon all countries to formulate strategies and set time-bound targets for the eradication of poverty, especially among women. This commitment may be the most lasting accomplishment of that Summit. Now that we have the means to eliminate the worst aspects of world poverty, we have an ethical obligation to deploy these means.

Our world may be inequitable, but there is reason for optimism. We now have a better understanding of what is needed to create a more just world. Sustainable human development is central to that goal, and women are central to sustainable human development.

James Gustave Speth has served as Administrator of the United Nations Development Programme since 1993. Mr. Speth founded the World Resources Institute in 1982 and served as its President for the next ten years. He was a senior advisor to President-elect Clinton's transition team, heading the group that examined the US role in natural resources, energy and the environment.

Towards Ethical, Equitable, and Sustainable Livelihoods

Peggy Antrobus and Judithe Bizot

In 1992 more than 2,000 women — environmentalists, peasants, researchers, sociologists, writers, scientists, economists, and others — committed themselves to change, to a conviction that after 40 years of post-colonial development, a new world order based on other attitudes, values, and behaviours must emerge. Listening to their centuries of experiences and observation and seeking new involvement at all levels of society, women from North and South pooled their collective wisdom, hopes, and demands into the recommendations of *Agenda 21* that were presented and adopted at the United Nations Conference on Environment and Development (UNCED) in Rio. The following paper testifies to what these women have been thinking and doing about the crisis in development and the environment.

The difference between women's and men's perspectives lies in their different gender roles. Gender is a social construct which assigns certain attributes, behaviours, and attitudes to males and females. Unfortunately, most societies are constructed in such a way that those associated with females are devalued. From birth, socialization practices are constructed to enforce gender differences. To the extent that the feminine values of cooperation, caring, and compassion are important to achieving an ethical, equitable, just, and sustainable livelihood, understanding gender-power relations is critical to understanding how we might make the necessary changes.

In 1984, a network of Third World women researchers, activists, and those engaged in policy formation and communication came together to reflect on what they had learned from their experience of development during the Decade for Women (1976-1985). This network, Development Alternatives with Women for a New Era (DAWN), developed a feminist critique of the growth-oriented model of development and an analysis of the interlocking crises of food insecurity, environmental degradation, debt, deteriorating social services, militarism, and political conservatism.

Growth-oriented development is fundamentally flawed because, among other things, it (a) excludes women's unpaid work from calculations of Gross National Product (GNP), (b) does not recognize the link between economic production and social reproduction, and (c) does not acknowledge the existence of gender-based hierarchies in the household, the workplace, the community, and the society at large.

Women have brought a different perspective to the debate on the environment because of their different experience base: "Poor women's lives are not compartmentalized and their work is not seasonal. They therefore see the problem from a much broader and more holistic perspective" (Wiltshire, 1992: 19). They understand more clearly than policy makers that economics and the environment are compatible. Their experience makes this clear to them because the soil, water, and vegetation which the poor require for their basic livelihoods necessitates specific care and good management. Women from the South do not separate people from the natural resource base.

"Because women and the poor have the biggest stake in the natural resource base and the best knowledge of specific local conditions, problems and needs, solutions cannot be left up to even the most enlightened state, business, institution or representatives of local government" (Wiltshire, 1992: 19). These agencies and actors must be accountable to the community, which includes women. Because women's vantage point is different from that of men, and because women have been largely excluded from policy-making, their perspectives have to be specifically included and their involvement in decision-making institutionalized. According to Rosina Wiltshire,

> Women's importance to environmental policymaking, planning and programming derives from the roles that they play in many sectors central to environmental planning and management, and the fact that they play an important role socializing the young and shaping societal values and attitudes to the environment. Their perspective is therefore crucial to planning, conceptualizing and implementation of effective environmental management programmes which can help to maintain the quality of life in the 21st century (1992: 19).

An analysis from the perspective of grass-roots women illuminates, as does no other analysis, the linkages between the problems in development and those in environment, as no other analysis does. Starting with a focus on the health and livelihoods of the poor, women's analysis takes us directly to a consideration of the macro-economic policies which affect health and livelihoods. This, in turn, leads to an understanding of the patterns of production (including the arms trade) and finance, which also destroy the ecological system.

Internationally influenced policies of structural adjustment, adopted by governments to deal with the debt crisis of the 1980s, are a good example of the kinds of policies and programmes which emerge from the growth-oriented model of development. Cuts in social services, which are a prime consequence of these policies, emphasize economic production at the expense of the social sector (the separation of production from social reproduction), substitute women's unpaid work in the household for publicly-financed services in health and welfare, and underline the powerlessness of women to secure benefits for those dependent on their care — children, the elderly, and the sick. DAWN's vision is of "a world where inequality based on class, gender and race is absent from every country, and from the relationships among countries . . . [w]here basic needs become basic rights and where poverty and all forms of violence are eliminated . . ." (Sen and Grown, 1987: 80).

THE MYTHS

In its analysis of environment and development, DAWN's platform draws on local experiences of grass-roots women living in the economic South. These experiences explode several widely believed and oft-repeated myths of the environmental and development debate. The two myths most detrimental to the search for solutions are the following:

- The poor are destroying the environment.
- Population is responsible for environmental degradation.

On the contrary, research, case studies, and data reveal a very different reality:

- The poor have the biggest stake in protecting the natural resource base that provides water, food, fodder, and housing, which are the basis of their livelihood.
- The state, using its legal power in collusion with big business, contributes to damaging the environment, and this damage, in terms of both scale and quality, has been unsurpassed.
- The interaction between people and their natural environments has been broken

by forces external to the community. They include the globalization of capital and the incorporation of even the most remote areas into the global market. These factors, combined with debt and structural adjustment policies, have created major rifts within communities and between people and their natural environments. Material poverty is increasing and, both globally and nationally, the gap between the materially wealthy and the poor is increasing.

On the question of population, again the reality on the ground differs from the myth. Here are the facts:

- Areas of low population, falling population, and decreasing fertility rates are areas where there is extreme and growing environmental degradation.
- Extremes of wealth and poverty leading to overconsumption by some and the erosion of livelihoods of others, skewed distribution and use of resources, and patterns of human settlement have a stronger demonstrable relationship to environmental degradation than population size *per se*.
- Fertility rates decline when women have access to adequate reproductive health care and when their livelihoods and basic rights are respected. This is extremely difficult to achieve in the current global and national context.

Anticipating the pervasiveness of the belief that population is responsible for environmental degradation, DAWN worked with the Social Science Research Council and the International Social Science Council to examine the scientific evidence of the relationship between population growth and the environment. The conclusions reached at their consultation in early 1992 were that "population growth as a central variable in environmental degradation is not supported by reserach findings" and that "the focus on population growth as the key factor in degrading environment is thus misplaced."

DAWN's analysis of environment emphasizes

- the need for greater community control in environmental management;
- the need for women to have access to education and health care (including reproductive health care);
- the need for sustainable development to be grounded in sustainable livelihoods, defined to include socio-cultural, spiritual, and political elements along with material and ecological elements;
- the need for a new international order based on justice, equity, and respect for diversity of cultures, and for the identification of human development and sustainable livehoods as primary objectives of development; and
- the need to alter affluent lifestyles and eliminate overconsumption.

Some of the most serious environmental problems facing the planet today originate in the rich countries, and there is clearly a relationship between high levels of consumption caused by wealth and environmental degradation. It is also argued by some that profligate Northern consumption combined with unequal North-South political and economic power relations underlie poverty and environmental degradation in developing countries.

DAWN reflects the growing awareness of women for an alternative development paradigm, one which focuses on social-cultural needs of people rather than on unlimited economic growth. Within this paradigm, priority should be given to health, education, and

203

housing over military spending; ecology and conservation over unlimited economic growth; local over global management; survival over destruction; justice over profit; peace over war; accountability to communities over accountability to international markets; bio-cultural diversity over imposition of one culture; living in harmony with one's needs over "never enoughness"; women's rights to control their own bodies over intervention from governments and agencies.

Although in today's world these choices may seem to be unrealistic, they are increasingly the vision expressed by expanding networks of a variety of people, including academics, scientists, scholars, activists, and peoples' movements for peace, environment, and "alternative development." They include youth, women, indigenous people, and others, who essentially are all saying that no matter how powerless one feels, things could be different.

In 1960 the Northern societies were 20 times richer than the Southern countries. In 1980, it was 46 times. It is evident that the gap is widening. It is not so much a question of injustice as of having lured all countries into the same development mode. If all countries followed the industrial example, five or six planets would be necessary to serve as mines and waste dumps.

Vandana Shiva, an Indian physicist and feminist who works with community action groups fighting against the dominant model of development and environment destruction, made her position clear on this point when she said it should be recognized that scientists are as fallible as anyone else and that science and its institutions are, more often than not, prostituted to economic interests, since the structure of power is so closely married to the structure of knowledge. Many technologies are used to serve the economic interests of the powerful, not ecology or ethics. Women have already made their choices on these issues.

Today we are witnessing the collapse of both socialism and neoclassical liberalism. This collapse creates space for the emergence of new ethics and values. It raises questions of human and community development versus international aid and intervention, of quality of life versus unlimited growth.

For many, the major disappointment of the process leading to the Earth Summit was the failure to make connections between the crisis in our ecological system and the crisis in our economic system. In our view, the real differences at the events in Rio were not between the North and South (despite the clear differences between these two sets of governments), or between governments and NGOs, but between those, on the one hand, who believe that environmental crises can be solved by sustained growth, free trade, cleaner technologies, and better pricing of natural resources, and those, on the other, who believe that what is required is a fundamental shift in values and a different approach to development. This approach puts people at the centre and is therefore a new paradigm of development.

The essential issue, however, is that women's perspectives have still not been adequately taken into account or incorporated into other networks, thereby weakening the analysis. The call for a change in the balance between assertiveness/acquisitiveness and cooperation and for the recognition that this would more easily be achieved if feminine values were no longer subordinated to masculine ideas requires an understanding of the imbalance of gender-power relations.

In the call for fundamental social change, it is grass-roots women embedded in their cultures, marginalized outside the system, lacking inhibitions, and with nothing to lose, who have the greatest potential to see things differently and to help change the status quo. Why do they carry on when everyone else is cynical and hopeless? The reason is that they have a distinctive perception of what life is, a sense of what is really vital, that colours their view of what is at stake in the world.

If listened to and given self-confidence, these women can help us look more critically at ourselves and question our values. We must learn to shirk our smugness, to listen and search for the silenced voices. Bringing out the human values in all of us — women and men — is what is essential. At the center of these values must be caring, sharing, reciprocity. Money is not the only currency for women and the poor. Money cannot buy the human gestures which confer respect and dignity. Those seeking alternatives today say that when economics and maximimizing profits are put aside as central forces of existence, then we can find the seeds of change for the future.

Peggy Antrobus is the founder and the head of the Women and Development Unit (WAND) of the University of the West Indies. She is also the General Coordinator of the network of Third World women promoting Development Alternatives with Women for a New Era (DAWN).

Judithe Bizot is a free lance journalist and film maker, who works with UNESCO Courrier.

This article draws upon the authors' "Women's Perspectives: Towards an Ethical, Equitable, Just and Sustainable Livelihood in the 21st Century," *ISIS International/Women in Action*, April 1992 and January 1993. The inspiration for the original article was drawn from "Women Speak Out on the Environment," *UNESCO Courier*, March 1992; Rosina Wiltshire, "Environment and Development: Grass Roots Women's Perspective," Development Alternatives with Women for a New Era (DAWN) Platform for UNCED, 1992; and the Declaration by Women at the Global Forum, June 1992.

References

Sen, Gita, and Caren Grown. 1987. *Development, Crises, and Alternative Visions: Third World Women's Perspectives*. New York: Monthly Review Press.

Wiltshire, Rosina. 1992. "Environment and Development: Grass Roots Women's Perspective" in DAWN Platform for UNCED.

MOTHERING THE EARTH

MARGARITA ARIAS

One hundred and fifty years of struggle for women's equality have brought us to this moment in history. Had it not been for yesterday's struggles for universal sufferage, our voices would not be heard today. Were it not for the great battles waged for women's equality, the ethical dimension in the fight to protect our earth would be absent. There is thus no more appropriate place for women than as defenders of this planet.

No one speaks out for the protection of the environment with greater moral authority than women. Only those who have fought for the right to protect their own bodies from abuse can truly understand the rape and plunder of our forests, rivers, and soils.

It was a woman who first warned us about the silent spring. It was another woman worker who sacrificed her life to alert the world to the danger of nuclear reactors. The ills of our planet are now matters in the public domain. For some 20 years, we have been conscious that we are living in the present at the expense of the future. The contamination of the water, air, and land caused by uncontrolled waste disposal, the dramatic destruction of our forests, the erosion of our fertile soils, the disappearance of plant and animal species, the destruction of the ozone layer, the changes in our climate, and the extinction of non-renewable resources are all part of the anxieties of modern life.

NEW VISIONS, NEW ACTIONS

The bleak picture I have described is not, however, unalterably fatal. As awareness has grown, citizens have pressured their governments into implementing legislation regulating the use of natural resources. Innumerable laws have improved forest management, regulated the use of cultivable land, controlled factory and automobile emissions, and harnessed the indiscriminate dumping of human and industrial waste. Despite these gains, large-scale environmental destruction continues its course.

Environmental issues have become international concerns, the subject of multilateral treaties. Important land areas, such as Antarctica, have been declared off-limits for industrial development. New laws and treaties will aid in regulating emissions that threaten the ozone layer; others will protect many species in danger of extinction.

Despite the gains in defence of the earth, which have come about as a result of international collaboration, there is growing awareness that these efforts have not gone far enough. We need not await the latest rounds of international cooperation to verify that environmental deterioration continues apace. The global nature of environmental issues requires solutions that result from international cooperation. Still, there is more to the problems of the environment than merely the technical, legal, and administrative aspects, which are external to considerations of how we choose to live together on our planet.

CHANGING THE FLAWED VISION

We women want to call attention to the fact that environmental issues also have to do with human solidarity. It is not the absence of arable land in north-east Brazil that compels the peasants to migrate to urban slums or to destroy the jungle. In north-east Brazil there is plenty of fertile land, capable of sustaining a population that suffers in abject misery. But that land is owned by a handful of wealthy families.

We women want to remind the world that the problems of environment also have to do with the distribution of wealth and equity. We cannot compare the living conditions of citizens of the industrialized North with those of the impoverished South in their relationship to the land and to the environment. In Central America, where some 50 per cent of the population lives below the poverty line, 20,000 hectares of forest land are sacrificed each year to support cattle-raising. At the same time, children of Central America consume 52 times less meat than those of the North. The average citizen in the industrialized countries releases 27 times more carbon dioxide into the atmosphere, uses 115 times more paper, and consumes 35 times more commercial energy.

Consciousness about protection of the environment cannot coexist with poverty and hunger. The poor and indigent cannot be blamed for the destruction of the forests. A social order created by a culture lacking fundamental human values of solidarity gives rise to the conditions that perpetuate poverty. Both poverty and environmental deterioration are products of the same world view of how human beings should cohabit the earth.

The concept of sustainable development emerged out of this flawed vision. This concept, the importance of which cannot be underestimated, offers us the merest outline of a goal, an objective, the beginning of a different way of organizing human production and reproduction that aims to conserve resources for future generations. However, sustainable development itself is not the answer to the environmental dilemma we face, as it does not touch on the root of the problem. Nothing short of a transformation of our culture is needed to carry out the kind of development that we are proposing. No mere combination of technical measures will lead us to the goal of sustainable development.

Women are conscious of the fact that environmental problems are a measure of the ethical dimensions of our civilization. The governments of the world have not found it within their hearts to allocate the US$2.5 billion necessary to eradicate infant malnutrition. The cost of a worldwide vaccination programme is equivalent to one week of the interest payments on the Third World's foreign debt. But the industrialized world expects its payments on time, while demanding better environmental policies from governments of developing countries.

PEACE, EQUALITY, AND DEMOCRACY FOR A HEALTHY PLANET

All of the technological innovations, laws and international regulations will be worthless if we are unable to eliminate poverty, educate people, eradicate disease, and create better opportunities for human development everywhere. The problems of our planet will not be solved by merely allocating more funds, setting up programmes, or creating new bureaucracies. We will have to discover once again that fundamental values, such as peace, justice, equity among peoples, equality, and democracy, are necessary preconditions for the technical and legal measures to help us rebuild a healthy planet.

Given the multitude of problems facing our world today, our societies cannot continue to ignore the potential contributions of one-half of the world's human capital. We need the best and brightest minds to help us solve the problems that confront us. We need the unique perspectives that women bring to these problems, perspectives grounded in women's experiences.

WOMEN AS THE VOICE OF LEADERSHIP

Let us look beyond tradition and continuity to see the opportunities that an expanded role for women can bring. Women's role in the defence of the environment must not be limited to particular demands for gender-specific policy statements. Women must become leaders in shaping the way that future generations choose to live. Our collective efforts will transform the quality of our relationships across racial and cultural boundaries as well as the way we relate to our natural surroundings now and in the future.

We have made great strides. Our voices are being heard. But this is not enough. Now more than ever, nations everywhere are clamouring for strong leadership. History has shown the catastrophic consequences when leaders lack integrity, vision, and compassion. We have a historic opportunity to assert our leadership based on respect for the individual's right of choice, for divergent views, and especially, for life in all its forms.

The concerns and values of women have always been linked with the concepts of interdependence and harmony. Let us take these concerns to their logical conclusion and develop new models of global leadership. This is an excellent place to begin.

Margarita Arias is President of the Arias Foundation for Peace in Costa Rica.

This article draws upon the author's keynote speech at the World Women's Congress for a Healthy Planet, held in Miami, Florida, in 1991.

WOMEN AND SUSTAINABLE LIVELIHOODS

VIVIENNE WEE

The world is evolving in a way that is neither sustainable nor equitable. The environmental and social crises that confront us globally are worsening by the day. We are ourselves an endangered species because we are endangering our very basis of survival — the resource base on which our livelihoods are ultimately founded. Current development trajectories, left unaltered, will seriously threaten the survival of the human species and the many other species that co-exist with us.

The UN Conference on Environment and Development (UNCED) in Rio de Janeiro in 1992 was held in response to growing international awareness of environmental degradation and the need for sustainable development. But such awareness at the international level was late, relative to the awareness of the scientific community that has been monitoring ecological changes from multidisciplinary approaches and of the communities of ordinary people whose livelihoods have been endangered by an increasingly degraded natural environment. These include farmers who have had to deal with the loss of topsoil, drought and climatic change; indigenous people who have had to live with deforestation, polluted waters, and the loss of habitat and biodiversity; and women who have had to work harder and longer to obtain increasingly scarce food, fuel, water, and fodder for themselves, their families, and their communities.

There is an urban-rural gap in livelihood realities. Urban middle and upper classes are relatively insulated from the loss and degradation of livelihood resources. But rural and indigenous communities — especially women in these communities — are experiencing the direct impact of resource loss and degradation, livelihood difficulties, deprivation and displacement. Women are confronted by a crisis of survival on two related fronts, the ecological and the economic. They are more vulnerable to the loss of the household resource base because the livelihood activities under their management tend to be resource-based rather than money-based. On the one hand, the loss of land, food, water, shelter, fuel, and fodder means loss of livelihoods for women, more so than for men. On the other hand, women are constrained by traditional gender inequities from taking up economic alternatives.

THE ECOLOGICAL AND ECONOMIC CONTEXT
OF SUSTAINABLE LIVELIHOODS

For livelihoods to be sustainable, the ecological and economic context of such livelihoods must be stabilized and sustained. The allocation and use of land, for example, is of crucial importance to the sustainability of livelihoods. Some key questions that need to be asked are:

- Who needs the land and the resources for their survival?
- Who has access to the land and the resources?
- Who is barred from them?
- Who owns them?
- Who decides on their use and allocation?
- Who ensures their sustainable use and renewal?
- Who gains monetary benefits from them?

- Who extracts the resources and transfers them elsewhere?
- Who depletes the land and the resources?

Depending on their location in society, different individuals and groups relate to the environment very differently. For instance, all societies have a gender division of labour, as a result of which men and women have very different relationships to the environment. Ironically, while the gender hierarchy has discriminated against women in that they own only one per cent of the world's land and have fewer economic rights than men, the gender division of labour has allocated women a vital role as the primary managers of both environmental resources and community life. This was recognized in Principle 20 of the Rio Declaration: "Women have a vital role in environmental management and development. Their participation is therefore essential to achieve sustainable development."

Nevertheless, development planning and implementation generally does not focus on women as being of central importance. This is partly because of the discrepancy between women's vital role and their economic status, and partly because of a gender bias on the part of policy makers. Consequently, policies on environmental conservation are usually not gender-sensitive in the way they impact on women and therefore the livelihoods of communities that women manage. An example of this is the general failure of policy makers to recognize that deforestation has created a double crisis for women. While there is an awareness of the energy problem — for example, shortages of domestic fuel — the livestock feed problem has, for the most part, been invisible. Reforestation schemes have advocated the planting of trees, such as the eucalyptus, which do not provide women with the necessary sources of fodder for their livestock or food for their families. Similar observations can be made about the manner in which environmental problems are being dealt with regarding land, water resources, and crop varieties.

> *"We, the Women at the Global Forum held in Rio de Janeiro from 3 to 14 June 1992...Call upon the heads of government attending the Earth Summit...to commit themselves and their governments to...The empowerment of women by raising their economic, health, nutrition, education and social status as their inalienable right, and in recognition that their empowerment is a prerequisite to healing and sustaining the environment."*
>
> —From the Declaration by Women at the Global Forum, Rio de Janeiro, 1992.

The environment is not just a system of biological and physical resources; therefore, "environmental" issues cannot be addressed only in terms of protecting the physical environment through the conservation of forests, the protection of endangered species, and so on. On the contrary, the biophysical systems are in constant interaction with the human societies who live in them. Attempts to improve ecological management without integrating human behaviour and social forces deal only with symptomatic effects rather than causative processes and have, at best, been limited in their results. In the same way, attempts to engineer the environment for human benefit without considering ecological interactions and the relationship between different species have led to problems of long-term sustainablity. Such imbalance in favour of either the physical environment or human society derives from a dualistic worldview that is clearly inadequate for understanding and managing complex interactions between the ecosystem and the human social system. In order to achieve

209

sustainable development, the complex relationships between the ecological system and human society need to be clearly identified.

It is important to address not merely the physical environment, which is being steadily depleted, but more fundamentally, the human processes — social, cultural, religious, ideological, linguistic, economic, and technological — that have brought about the current crisis of sustainability. To address this urgent situation, it is necessary to work on the dynamic human-social-biological-inorganic linkages so that relationships of ecological equilibrium and renewability can be established as regular patterns of human existence. We have to draw lessons from those modes of livelihood that have survived the test of environmental sustainability, some for more than ten thousand years.

In particular, there is a need to focus on the livelihoods of rural and indigenous women because they are the primary users and managers of a diverse range of resources for daily human sustenance — including water, agricultural products, and forest and coastal resources. Most rural communities depend on nature for their livelihoods. And women are the key protectors of natural resources — managing soil, water, forests, and energy and making day-to-day decisions about the production and reproduction of biological and social life. These decisions are central to the use and protection of human habitats.

Women's firsthand knowledge of different natural resources — fruit, vegetables, herbs, spices, fuelwood, water, fodder, animals, and ecological processes — is rooted in their multiple roles and responsibilities. What is of particular value about women's knowledge is that

- it is indigenous to micro socio-ecological niches, and
- it is founded on everyday experiences, choices, and actions regarding the sustainable use of scarce resources at the micro-level.

Such knowledge is vital to the sustainability of biodiversity because the diversity of flora and fauna can be conserved only if their various micro-environmental niches are conserved. Again, ecological diversity is of greater importance to women than to men, precisely because they cannot depend on only one resource to meet their multiple responsibilities. For example, women tend not to focus only on one or two cash crops, because they have to ask what kind of food their money can buy to feed their families. Their everyday understanding of the survival value of biologically diverse resources at the micro-level is precisely what is needed for macro development planning and implementation.

Environmental degradation has resulted in the massive displacement and social disintegration of local communities. Such disintegration is often accompanied by male outmigration in search of waged employment, with women left behind to fend for themselves and to care for the young, the aged, and the disabled. When women and other vulnerable members of society are marginalized in their access to livelihood resources, they often have no choice but to overexploit increasingly scarce and increasingly depleted resources just to survive, even though they may have the knowledge for the maintenance of environmental sustainability within their earlier situation of ecological stability. This leads to the loss of vital indigenous knowledge concerning environmental management at the local level.

Women play a crucial role in maintaining livelihoods, cultural continuity, and community cohesiveness. Yet women's perspectives, significantly diferent from men's, have been invisible in the processes of change. Sustainability and equity are intrinsically related. There can be no sustainability if half the world's population is deprived and dispossessed of livelihood resources.

THE INTERNATIONAL CONSENSUS ON WOMEN'S LIVELIHOODS

The UN Conferences of the last few years have made it clear that women and the poor are essential elements of change. UNCED recognized the "critical role of women . . . in achieving sustainable development." There has been a growing recognition of the linkages between women, poverty, and environment. These linkages were discussed at UNCED and again at the 1995 World Summit on Social Development (WSSD) in Copenhagen. The Copenhagen Declaration states that "to ensure that the political framework supports the objectives of social development," it is essential to remove "all legal impediments to the ownership of all means of production and property by men and women" (Chapter I, para. 14).

These are important goals. It has become clear that their achievement is not just an ethical issue but a necessary survival strategy. While there is consensus on *why* it is necessary to eliminate poverty among women as a strategy toward sustainable development, there is insufficient attention on *how* this is to be done. Good intentions are not enough. Although these UN Conferences have identified many issues to be addressed, they have also been criticized by many NGOs for omitting from discussions the structural processes responsible for the global ecological and social crisis.

TOWARD A STRATEGY OF TRANSFORMATION

There is an urgent need for a fundamental rethinking of the development model and the global economic system. Attention must be given to the human consequences of the existing economic order based on rapid industrialization. There is a need to address the vicious circle that has emerged around international debt, enforced repayments, structural adjustments, the increased exports of natural resources, the destruction of the resource base of local communities, and widespread impoverishment.

Failure to do so will lead only to inadequate strategies that may even compound the problems. For example, the UN Conferences have repeatedly called for increased economic growth to finance strategies to bring about sustainability and equity, but there is no mention of the patterns and effects of growth, no questioning of who would enjoy the benefits and who would bear the costs of such growth. There is no analysis of the process of impoverishment, the creation of the new poor, the destruction of previously sustainable livelihoods, or the feminization of poverty.

To combat poverty, UNCED's *Agenda 21,* for example, recommends strategies that promote economic growth in developing countries by focusing on world trade, commodity prices, debt repayments, protectionism, and trade liberalization. There is no challenge to the global economic framework that has privatized natural and human resources on a massive scale, that has lowered livelihood safety nets as a result of export-led development, that has damaged environmental health (both ecological and human) through mega-development projects. Over the last four decades, the crisis of unsustainabilty and inequity has deepened. To call for an increase of the very same processes of economic growth as a solution to the problem would only exacerbate the problem.

An agenda for change designed to ensure sustainabilty must itself have a long-term reality. Such an agenda necessitates a comprehensive analysis and evaluation of the total range of livelihood options. Processes of production, consumption, and destruction that adversely affect environmental and human health — including warfare, deforestation, and nuclear testing — must be transformed. The foremost danger that confronts us is the unlimited extraction of

211

limited resources in a global economy that seeks to extract every possible resource as a commodity.

To address this devastating process of globalized resource extraction, an equally powerful global force must emerge as a counterweight. Women are half the world. This is more than a numerical statistic, because the overwhelming majority of women share the experience of gender inequity and, consequently, vulnerability to the loss of livelihood resources. Women want a different world — a world where all human lives matter, where the goal of development is universal human well-being and not the enrichment of a few people.

In the last 20 years, the women's movement has worked steadily to arrive at a new vision of a world founded on women's realities and women's rights. Women are not just asking for a larger portion of a fundamentally unsustainable and inequitable economy and polity. Women are seeking to transform the economic and political institutions and processes so that these would serve the needs and priorities of the poorest of the poor, most of whom are women. This is a key challenge for the women's development agenda for the 21st century.

Vivienne Wee is the Programme Director of ENGENDER (Centre for Environment, Gender and Development), a regional organization in Asia and the Pacific which she co-founded with Noeleen Heyzer. An anthrolopologist by training, she is working on critical issues that affect the sustainable livelihood of women and communities. She also coordinates research on Sustainable Development for Develoment Alternatives with Women for a New Era (DAWN).

WOMEN AND CONFLICT IN A CHANGING WORLD

LOURDES ARIZPE

Women's lives have expanded in our present world. In almost all regions women live longer and have fewer children, so that they now have greater periods of time to study, to train, and to work for pay both outside and inside the home. Women are also participating more visibly and in larger numbers in remunerated work, in research, in politics, and in social mobilization. As their spheres of action expand, so must their horizons of debate extend in order to encompass the major issues of today.

The women's movement has been shaped by analysis of the conflicts stemming from the oppression of women in gender structures, and such conflicts are now being appropriately framed in larger contexts. Women's access to and management of natural resources, as well as their competence in conservation, are now major issues in sustainable development. The recognition of women's social and political participation in human rights was made clear in 1993 at the World Conference on Human Rights (WCHR) in Vienna. Women's reproductive rights in population debates are recognized, as shown during the 1994 International Conference on Population and Development (ICPD) in Cairo. Women's political participation is already part of the debate on governance, and the issue of women and race has been intensely examined, especially in the United States. Another notable advance and one that will have far-reaching effects is that of women questioning theology and church structures in some religions.

As UNDP's *Human Development Report*s have demonstrated, the strategic importance of women's participation around issues of universal human rights, democracy, and sustainable development is no longer in doubt. In other areas, though, such as culture, ethnic strife, conflict resolution, media, and the information highway, women are just beginning to enter the debate. The women's movement must now reflect these expanding horizons while retaining the necessary concentration on fostering women's participation and gender awareness. Our contemporary world offers hitherto unimagined opportunities that can be taken up only if proliferating conflicts can be resolved or appropriately managed.

We live in a world in which economic and political restructuring is deepening inequalities, fuelling political and ethnic wars within and between countries. Accelerated technological and cultural change is fostering feelings of uncertainty as to place, identity, and meaning among many social groups. Therefore it is especially important that contemporary political, ethnic, and cultural conflicts be understood and analysed in the debates of the women's movement and those of the development community.

Can we women help the world face conflicts more rationally in today's turbulent situations? Our success at populating the earth has passed a turning point and has now turned against us. In this success, women's fertility was crucial. Now women's capacity to manage our reproductive behaviour is likewise crucial.

Much more should also be made of another, more recent success: men's remarkable skill at having averted a total, annihilating nuclear war. Yet low-intensity local and regional wars are proliferating. We know women can make a difference. Now the question we must ask ourselves is *how* we can make a difference.

No doubt we will make it by continuing to do what we are doing: curbing population growth, fighting for greater equity for all in the economy and in politics, helping manage natural resources more rationally, curbing conspicuous consumption, and safeguarding cultural heritage and diversity. More generally, we need to help match rights to responsibilities, production to sustainability, democracy to diversity, and culture to new meanings. This is not a tall order; rather, it is the only way out of dilemmas that will come to a head in 20 years' time.

The women's movement has grown exponentially in only two decades. Surely it can cope with the present and the future with the same determination and hope that made it one of humanity's greatest promises.

It is important to realize the power of women in all nations to reorient consumption toward more sustainable goals, to reflect on their possibilities for intervening in increasingly tragic ethnic wars and in the defense of human rights, to be aware of the vital role that women can play in helping check epidemics such as AIDS or the proliferation of new viral diseases. Their potential for training and educating human beings toward a more tolerant, democratic coexistence is simply waiting to be tapped. Women can indeed make a difference.

Lourdes Arizpe was one of the pioneering researchers on women's studies in Mexico and Latin America. A social anthropologist, she helped launch the first Mexican feminist journal and became the first woman president of the International Union of Anthropological Studies. She has organized a large number of international meetings on women and development and is at present Assistant Director-General for Culture in UNESCO.

GENDER ISSUES AND DISPLACED POPULATIONS

LAKETCH DIRASSE

Over the last 20 years, there has been a dramatic rise in the world's displaced populations. In Africa the magnitude and length of mass migrations are particularly alarming. The affected populations are usually fleeing from complex emergencies such as armed conflicts, economic deterioration, environmental degradation including drought and floods, systematic human rights abuse, and ethnic and religious strife. Unlike the postwar European refugees, displaced populations today are faced with a worldwide increase in generalized poverty, a widening gap between poor and rich nations, and increased restrictions on resettlement into the rich nations.

The aftermath of the cold war era also means the lessening of strategic interests and a concomitant decrease in the allocation of resources to many countries of the south. For Africa, burdened by external debt and structural adjustment programmes that have forced cuts in social services, the impact of displaced populations is an additional burden that even the most well-intentioned host government finds difficult to bear.

Currently 30 African countries are either producers of or hosts to refugees, and in many cases they are both. One-third of an estimated world refugee population of 20 million are African.[1] Fifteen African countries are mired in wars or civil strife and a severe drought is causing hardship in several countries. Democracy movements also are contributing to an uncertain future for many countries as previously repressed ethnic and community tensions become part of national debate.

The displaced populations who do not cross their national borders (i.e., the internally displaced) are more numerous than refugees. Since there is no special agency with a clear mandate for assistance to and protection of the internally displaced, their numbers are rough estimates. In 1991 the Centre for Policy Analysis and Research on Refugee Issues[2] estimated the population of internally displaced persons to be 16 million, including 4.5 million in Sudan; 300,000 in Chad, more than 1 million in Ethiopia, 825,000 in Angola, 2 million in Mozambique, at least 500,000 in Liberia, 2 million in Somalia, 4.2 million in South Africa, and 500,000 in Uganda. These figures do not include persons displaced as a result of natural disasters or environmental degradation.

The overwhelming majority of these internally displaced and refugee populations are women and children. Estimates range between 60 and 80 per cent of Africa's displaced population.[3] While international humanitarian relief and rehabilitation efforts are addressing the general survival and maintenance needs of displaced populations, the gender-specific impact of displacement and the gender-specific needs of displaced populations are not fully recognized or addressed. Many feel that gender issues are peripheral to the essential tasks of providing for the basic survival needs of the displaced. This is in spite of the considerable efforts made by the senior coordinator for women refugees at the office of the United Nations High Commissioner for Refugees (UNHCR) and numerous sensitization seminars and special guidelines that have been developed over the last few years.

This paper will discuss the critical gender concerns in assistance to internally displaced and refugee women. The paper starts with a discussion of the key challenges posed by the situation of displaced women and the potential that displaced women bring for durable solutions. After highlighting important lessons from UNIFEM's interventions in response to African Women in Crisis, some recommendations for policy makers, programme planners and gender equality advocates are outlined.

CHALLENGES OF DISPLACED WOMEN

Emergency and crisis situations often tend to exacerbate contradictions in normal societal relations and to telescope social inequities. Women's traditional gender inequality, their workload, and their vulnerability to various forms of violation are increased under displaced conditions. Yet amidst such difficult and traumatic situations, women courageously struggle to build a semblance of stability in the lives of their families and to promote reconciliation and peace.

Inequality and Workload

When women are forced to flee their homes, they must continue their traditional responsibilities as household managers and care providers in new and often traumatic situations.

Lack of food security is one of the basic problems women face. Women's critical role in household food security continues despite internal or external displacement. Clearly this responsibility places a great burden on women who have been forced to flee their homes and their source of food and livelihood. In the best of times food rations are inadequate, and when assistance is cut women must struggle to make up the difference.

Women and children are particularly susceptible to diet deficiencies and provide an early warning of nutritional deficiencies in the population at large. Pregnant and lactating mothers are especially at risk, as are infants and small children, whose cognitive development can be severely affected by an inadequate diet, as brain growth occurs in the first two years of life.

In some cases, distribution of food creates problems and inequities when it is carried out through a male network. It can, for instance, be difficult to reach the women-headed households. It has also been documented that most men sell the food ration in order to purchase cigarettes and other intoxicants, leaving their families without food. The need for a gender-sensitive food distribution system cannot be overemphasized. It is also rare to see women participating in any management committee where decisions about life in displaced and refugee camps are made. The Representative of the Secretary General on Internally Displaced Persons aptly points out this pervasive neglect:

> [W]omen are generally less consulted than men or not effectively included in the distribution of material assistance . . . In one camp in Burundi, for instance, where there were only 25 men out of several thousand displaced people, when the Representative asked to discuss the problems of the camp with several representatives, only men appeared.[4]

Violence

The vulnerability of women to physical and sexual violence is increased under crisis situations as traditional family support and protection mechanisms crumble. Rape as a crass and violent expression of dominance and power is increasingly being used in conflict situations.

Rape has featured prominently in the Liberian, Rwandan, Somali and Sudanese conflicts. Though it has yet to be fully documented many Rwandese women report that practically all the women who survived the genocide were raped, and most were raped repeatedly. Likewise, according to a 1993 Africa Watch report, the incidence of rape of Somali women in the refugee camps was reported to be extremely high:

> In the seven-month period from February 1993 through August 1993, the UNHCR documented 192 cases of rape. Of these cases, 187 involved women, four were against children and one was against a man. In the month of August 1993 alone, 42 additional rape cases came to light. While these figures are profoundly disturbing, they represent only the cases actually reported to UNHCR, who believes the actual incidence of rape could be as much as ten times higher.[5]

Most rapes occur during flight but continue after the women reach an asylum country or internal sanctuary. In displaced or refugee camps, women are further exposed to other forms of sexual abuse. Many women are usually forced into nonconsensual relationships in asylum countries in order to receive protection and food security for their children and themselves.

The violence against women in camp settings ranges from constant fear (of being raped, robbed or killed) to forced sexual/marital relations, beatings, and rape. Where an attempt has been made to provide some measure of social order and protection, the violence against women decreases, as evidenced by UNHCR's project for women victims of violence in Somali refugee camps in northern Kenya.

Health and Well-being

Health care is another important concern for displaced and refugee women. The importance of providing adequate health care to women is underscored by the vital roles they play in caring for their families, not only as the primary health-care providers but as food subsidizers, water collectors, fuel foragers, child-care providers, and generators of desperately needed additional income. While it is true that the health-care issue of internally displaced and refugee women is often the same as those of local women, in many cases they have particular problems associated with the experience of displacement. These women have special needs for gynaecological health care and mental health counselling to address the effects of sexual abuse, pregnancy complications, poor sanitary conditions, dislocation, and the loss of community support.

Most refugee health-care delivery programmes proceed from a care-and-maintenance approach, which fails to see gynaecological care as a basic need. Refugee women who have been raped, undergone female circumcision, or been forced into prostitution also have an increased vulnerability to AIDS and must be provided with health education and preventive care and counselling.

Another basic health need of women which is consistently ignored by humanitarian relief and rehabilitation agencies is the need for sanitary towels for menustration. It is important to recognize the stress and indignity caused uprooted women when they are not in a position to effectively manage their menstruation. A sixty-year-old grandmother at the Thessalia Displaced Persons Camp in Kenya poignantly illustrates the pain and shame experienced by women when emergency relief organizations fail to be sensitive to this kind of intimate and basic need of women:

> Can you imagine our shame as we helplessly watch the younger women struggle to cope with their monthly periods — with nothing to change into, and no privacy? Children watch the shame of their mothers, while fathers face a similar situation with their daughters.[6]

Following an expert consultation between UNIFEM's African Women in Crisis (AFWIC) programme and UNICEF on reproductive health issues of displaced women, UNICEF has proceeded to develop alternative sanitary materials that are cost-effective, culturally acceptable, and environmentally sound.

An increasingly important area of concern is the psychosocial health needs of displaced women. Uprooted women, like all displaced individuals, experience trauma resulting from flight, dislocation, loss of loved ones, and disruption of normal life. There are, however, a number of gender-specific factors that predispose women and girls to different mental health complications. These include the trauma of rape and other physical abuse and violence, stress resulting from role overload and increased responsibilities, guilt and shame resulting in loss of self-esteem because of their actual and perceived inability to care for the family.

Some insights into Rwandese women's psychosocial trauma come from a UNIFEM/AFWIC-sponsored study in two health centres in Rwanda (Tare, Kigali prefecture, and Kabarondo in Kibungo prefecture). The survey, conducted over a period of three weeks in November 1994, found that women as a group had been subjected to severe physical and psychological atrocities resulting in severe trauma. The study also found that by January 1995, eight months after the killings started in Rwanda, "at least four pregnant women were showing up daily at Kigali maternity hospital requesting abortion, which is illegal in Rwanda. These women had been raped during the war. Two women had by then given birth, prematurely, and did not want to see the babies. One of these women had been raped and impregnated by the very man who murdered her husband and four children."[7] Following on the survey, a UNIFEM/AFWIC consulting psychiatrist closely examined 100 women. These women were coming to the clinics to seek curative medical help. None had mentioned psychological problems, and yet the bulk of the complaints revealed the following symptoms:

217

- a feeling of "worms" in the head, chronic headache, generalized numbness, and abdominal discomfort, all indicating acute anxiety;
- tiredness, headache, body ache, dyspepsia, sleepless nights with nightmares, and loss of weight, all seen as malaria;
- low abdominal pain in rape victims and those with sexual problems;
- a feeling of generalized body heat or of the menopausal syndrome, worsened by trauma; and
- reactive psychoses attributed to cerebral malaria.

The psychiatrist diagnosed 70 per cent of these women as exhibiting severe post-traumatic stress disorders. The rest were suffering from reactive depression, grief reaction, and anxiety.

Another UNIFEM/AFWIC study conducted among displaced women in Kenya found that during the 1993 interethnic clashes over land, women were systematically raped and sexually abused: "the majority showed the rape trauma syndrome and individually and confidentially expressed their anxiety, anger, fear and disbelief that it had happened to them. As a group, they were tense, restless and withdrawn and showed complexes which were hidden behind a calm composed exterior . . ."[8]

Legal Status

The legal status of displaced and refugee women is another important area of concern. The UN Convention Regarding the Status of Refugees[9] defines a refugee as a person who has a well-founded fear of being persecuted for reasons of race, religion, nationality, membership in a particular social group, or political opinion and who is outside the country of nationality. People fleeing generalized armed conflicts are not considered refugees, because the persecution is not specific to the individual.

Africa, therefore, has the most progressive legal regime under the 1969 refugee treaty[10] of the Organization of African Unity (OAU). The OAU Convention includes within its ambit those who have fled civil strife and other events that seriously disturb public order. This treaty also establishes a right to receive asylum, declares the grant of asylum to be a peaceful and humanitarian act, and provides specific guarantees respecting the voluntary character of repatriation as a solution to the needs of refugees. In practice, however, African refugees and displaced persons are frequently subject to military attack, forced recruitment by insurgent or government forces, and periodic expulsions from countries of asylum.

For African women the broader provisions of the OAU Convention still fall short in providing needed protection. This is because the treaty makes no mention of gender and does not address the issue of women fleeing sexual torture or discrimination. Also, a woman fleeing harsh or inhuman treatment for having transgressed her society's mores will have great difficulty in establishing a claim for asylum. This is despite the fact that women are often deliberately targeted during a conflict. Women's dilemma is best articulated by one Somali woman:

> The war in Somalia is an anarchist war. It is a war on the woman. Any woman between the ages of 18 and 40 is not safe from being forcibly removed to the army camps to be raped and violated. And that's only the beginning. If her husband finds out, he kills her for the shame of it all; if they know that he has found out, they kill him too; if he goes into hiding instead and she won't tell where he is, they kill her.[11]

Beyond international conventions, it is important to note that the existence or absence of legislation and safeguards that protect women in the host country could also contribute to how abuses against refugee women are viewed. Internally displaced women also fall under the legal system of their own country, which is often discriminatory to women. Furthermore, in situations where protective legislation exists, enforcement mechanisms have not been successful, as evidenced by an extremely high incidence of gender-specific violence and violations of displaced women's rights.

A further area of concern is the fact that displaced African women, like most women in normal situations, are ignorant of their social and economic rights. Legal literacy is an important empowerment tool for displaced women.

Survival and Peace

Despite the traumatic lifestyle of displacement and their increased vulnerability, displaced women continue to anchor their shattered families and communities. Their skills and knowledge are critical in reconstructing family life, promoting healing, and resolving conflicts.

Whether a husband is present or, more likely, the woman heads the displaced household, displaced women take full charge of the survival of their children, the sick, the injured, and the elderly. Yet they are conveniently left out of all decision-making fora. Recognizing the skills displaced women do have, building on their initiatives, and introducing them to newer skills are the most cost-effective means of reducing long-term care-and-maintenance programmes and enhancing the self-reliance of displaced populations.

The critical role that displaced African women are playing in promoting healing and recovery among displaced communities is often unrecognized. Women also play critical mediation roles in conflict situations. For example, Somali women have taken a significant part in mediating the release of several hostages. Yet these important roles are never officially acknowledged or publicized. Neither are women included in official mainstream conflict resolution and peace negotiation teams.

"Refugee, displaced and migrant women in most cases display strength, endurance and resourcefulness and can contribute positively to countries of resettlement, or on return to their countries of origin, and they need to be appropriately involved in decisions affecting them."

— Platform for Action, UN Fourth World Conference on Women, Chapter IV, para. 138.

The situation of displaced African women clearly shows their resilience and ability to cope despite the trauma and tragedy that engulf their lives. It is women who have demonstrated their resourcefulness in applying their traditional knowledge and skills to develop more viable structures out of the shattered lives of their families and communities. International assistance efforts cannot continue to view women as mere victims and recipients of relief or charity. They need to be seen as a crucial resource and to be involved in all efforts to alleviate crisis situations.

Over the past two years, UNIFEM's work with AFWIC has enabled the Fund to learn important lessons which need serious attention by policy makers, programme planners, and gender equality advocates.

219

UNIFEM'S EXPERIENCE

UNIFEM's involvement in the area of assistance to displaced and refugee women is fairly recent. But the expertise gained in almost two decades of working with and supporting poor women around the world and in mainstreaming gender concerns has been indispensable in developing its interventions in support of displaced women.

In its development work, UNIFEM has been successful in supporting small innovative initiatives of women that have provided important lessons for mainstream development programmes; linking micro-level actions of women with the macro-policy level to influence changes nationally, regionally, and globally; facilitating women's social, economic, and legal empowerment; and mobilizing resources for women in need.

Beginning in 1990, UNIFEM has engaged in a number of activities related to displaced women. They include a project undertaken in collaboration with UNICEF to organize and sponsor the Planning and Afghan Women programme, which focuses attention within the UN system on the roles and situation of Afghan women and examines the possibility of including gender concerns in development planning, and participation in the UN Conference on Central American Refugees, Returnees and Displaced Persons, which advocates the necessity of incorporating women's concerns and needs in refugee relief and development programmes.

In Africa, UNIFEM's interest in the application of developmental approaches to addressing the needs of displaced women resulted in two UNIFEM missions — one to Guinea and Côte d'Ivoire in 1990, the other to Ghana and Côte d'Ivoire in 1991 — to assess the extent to which refugees are provided with the means to maintain a level of productivity and move from total dependence on relief to a level of partial self-reliance.

As a result of this assessment, two integrated projects for Liberian women refugees were designed and are being implemented. The projects in Côte d'Ivoire and Ghana have been designed to bridge the immediate trauma of dislocation while providing skills that would also be useful when the women are able to return home. The projects were formulated around needs identified by the women themselves; they have provided shelter, trauma counselling, health education, family planning services, a small-business management course, and training in housing construction. At the Buduburam camp in Ghana, trainees learned — in the process of building their own women's centre — to make bricks, lay foundations, put up roofs, and construct window and door frames. The centre is large enough to seat 220 people and has boosted morale in the camp by giving the women a space of their own. This on-the-job training enabled the women to then build a dormitory for female-headed households, and other construction projects are likely to follow. Bricklaying and carpentry skills will be invaluable to the women, not only as an immediate source of income but also in the future when returning families will need to rebuild housing and other infrastructure that were destroyed during Liberia's civil war.

UNIFEM's project for Liberian refugees was undertaken in close collaboration with the UNHCR and local NGOs and will serve as a gender-sensitive model for relief operations elsewhere in Africa. It is hoped that the longer-term development concepts will also be replicated as donors come to grips with the fact that relief operations alone simply restore communities to their pre-disaster level of vulnerability.

Based on such earlier initiatives, UNIFEM in 1992 developed a regional framework for assistance to AFWIC, which is designed to protect and empower African women who have been displaced by crises from their home communities. Its mission is to promote a gender-sensitive development strategy for *disaster prevention and mitigation* which ensures that women are viewed as both crucial resources and participants.

Through strategic analysis of the gender-specific implications of crisis situations in Africa and prioritization of critical issues and intervention measures, UNIFEM has been able to develop the AFWIC strategic plan and start an innovative regional programme. The programme strategy emphasizes development-oriented criteria in disaster prevention and mitigation to ensure that

- the needs of refugees, displaced, and returnee women are taken into account;
- women are seen as resources and fully participate in all efforts to alleviate their problems;
- activities are planned and implemented by local groups and local capacity is enhanced;
- project activities focus on the elimination of overall poverty; and
- interventions reduce future vulnerabilities and are sustainable.

AFWIC's mission and strategic direction are translated into action through three strategic objectives:

- *to support* innovative initiatives and strategies to ensure that refugee, displaced, and returnee women are full participants in efforts to find solutions to problems confronting them;
- *to promote* through catalytic action the gender sensitivity of UN agencies, governmental and non-governmental organizations in their ongoing efforts to assist women affected by emerging and ongoing crises;
- *to advocate* gender-specific national and regional legislation incorporating international refugee laws to provide increased protection for refugee and internally displaced women.

The programme is innovatively designed to enable UNIFEM to support quick responses and immediate assistance to women in crisis throughout Africa and to place African women at the centre of the search for solutions. It is particularly designed to enhance ongoing efforts to use the resources and skills of refugee and internally displaced women and to place UNIFEM in the role of a catalyst and advocate. Small amounts of funding are used to encourage a commitment of resources by partner organizations for gender-sensitive interventions that build on the capacities of the beneficiaries.

The strategy emphasizes close consultations with sister UN agencies, governmental and intergovernmental organizations, and the private sector in order to facilitate collaboration and avoid duplication of efforts.

AFWIC'S ACHIEVEMENTS

Highlights of AFWIC's activities are illustrative of the success of UNIFEM's innovative approach. The major achievements over the past two years include catalytic work, advocacy, promotion of peace, and direct support.

Catalytic Work

This work has several components. The first is a database of the major actors working with women in the emergency, rehabilitation, and development fields. This database is updated regularly, and information is shared with interested partners. AFWIC has also commissioned several baseline studies and needs assessments in order to generate data on refugee and internally displaced populations in Benin, Ethiopia, Kenya, Mauritania, Rwanda, Senegal, and South Sudan. A third component is organizing an expert consultation on reproductive and mental health issues of women and girls under situations of war and conflict in Africa, in close collaboration with UNICEF.

Advocacy and Peace-Building

To advocate for increased visibility of problems faced by displaced women, advocacy materials have been produced for wide distribution:

- *KIPOK,* a networking newsletter produced quarterly in English and French;
- a strategic plan;
- *Dignity: African Women in Crisis,* a 30-minute documentary film on women in crisis highlighting the varied coping strategies of Eritrean, Ethiopian, Mozambican, Liberian, Somali, and Sudanese women in emergency and crisis situations; and
- *Survival: African Women in Crisis,* a booklet featuring stories and poems of women in emergency situations.

To promote a gender-sensitive and gender-inclusive response to conflict resolution and peace in Africa, AFWIC initiated a small peace project in August 1994. The project works through the emerging African women's initiatives for reconciliation and peace. It promotes the exchange of ideas and experiences, leading toward the building of a strong African women-led coalition for peace and development. Activities thus far supported include:

- a series of 15 peace and reconciliation workshops for youths and women in the areas of western Kenya that have been affected by clashes;
- a September 1994 strategy workshop held in Kampala, at which participants included women ministers, peace movements leaders, and peace activists;
- an African women's peace mission to Rwanda and Burundi in November 1994, composed of leaders and activists in women's peace and human rights movements; the one-week mission was mounted in response to Burundi participants' appeal at the Kampala workshop for an outside demonstration of solidarity with their own efforts;
- support to the Sudanese Women's Voice for Peace for a two-day workshop to promote dialogue between South and North Sudanese women;
- support for inaugural meeting of the Association of Mozambican Women for Peace, which focused on developing strategies for community-level reconciliation and peace education in Mozambique;
- an African Women's Peace Tent at the Africa Regional Conference for Women in Dakar, which brought together peace leaders and activists from Angola, Burkina Faso, Burundi, Congo, Liberia, Mali, Mauritania, Mozambique, Rwanda, Somalia, South Africa, and South Sudan. Activities in the Tent included documentaries of women working in peace and conflict resolution, panel discussions, information and display stands, a petition and messages stand, free space for testimonies, small workshops, and performances by young African artists, including an Eritean women ex-combatants band and refugee artists from Mali and Ethiopia.

The AFWIC peace project is currently working at three reinforcing levels. First, it is beginning a documentary base for analysing traditional forms of conflict management and women's role in mediation. Second, it is continuing its advocacy and catalytic work in order to give visibility to the nascent African women's peace movements, promote networking, and facilitate their involvement in regional and worldwide dialogues on issues of peace, governance, and development ethics. Finally, it is planning a series of capacity-building activities to strengthen women's role in the peace process.

Direct Support

As part of its direct support activities, the AFWIC programme undertook several projects that addressed the critical needs and built the capacity of refugee and displaced women in Africa.

A resource centre for the South Sudanese Women's Association in Nairobi has been established in collaboration with the Royal Netherlands Embassy in Kenya. The centre, officially opened in July 1994, serves as a channel of communication, consolation, and interaction among and between Sudanese women of various linguistic, ethnic, and ideological groups living in Nairobi. The project has made provisions for psychosocial counselling of the war-traumatized women, a skills training programme, and a small revolving credit scheme.

In Rwanda there is a project on reproductive health care and trauma management complemented by training programmes in sustainable income-generating skills and techniques to increase the self-reliance of displaced and returnee Rwandese women and girls. This project, under the financial support of SIDA, is being implemented in collaboration with Africa Humanitarian Action at Tare and Kaborondo. In addition, a community centre, provided by the Government, is being renovated to serve as a women's centre where various training activities will be provided.

Support is also being provided to displaced ethnic clash victims in Kenya, in cooperation with UNDP Kenya. AFWIC has provided seed funds for selected activities of UNDP Kenya's Displaced Programme and has provided advice on mainstream gender-related issues.

LESSONS LEARNED

There is no doubt that UNIFEM's AFWIC programme provides important lessons to mainstream emergency relief and rehabilitation efforts. It has managed to use limited funds to catalyse considerable responses to issues critical to women in crisis situations.

The key success factors are to be found first in the programme's conceptualization, organization, and content. The programme is based on and addresses real needs. It has clearly laid out objectives and strategies that are development-oriented and that emphasize participation by the women in all initiatives. The call for emphasis on participation is not new. Over the years, relief agencies have began to realize that many of their best efforts yielded little return because they had neither consulted nor used the skills of the people whom the efforts were intended to benefit. Likewise, development agencies, after spending huge amounts of money, sometimes abandoned projects with little to show for their efforts. Unfortunately, the lessons are still being learned, and the rhetoric of participation is often greater than the practice. In mitigation of the failure to move from pronouncement to practice, however, it must be understood that the proportions of many disasters and their long-term nature, combined with limited resources, have meant that there is still a need for external assistance. This has often placed constraints on efforts to ensure indigenization of initiatives.

Perhaps the greatest lessons to be derived from UNIFEM's AFWIC programme is the benefit of a holistic approach that builds on the displaced and refugee women's own initiatives, upgrades their skills and know-how, and promotes their empowerment.

The devolved, autonomous, and nonbureaucratic structure of the programme further

223

enhanced innovation, flexibility in resetting goals in rapidly changing crisis situations, and speed of response.

In no small way, the competence, credibility, confidence and committment of the programme's advisory board and staff is an important ingredient of its success.

CONCLUSION

Displacement negatively impacts on the lives and well-being of uprooted individuals, families, and whole communities. But it is also true that this impact is gender-specific in character.

As discussed in this paper, the evidence shows that gender inequalities are exacerbated under emergency and crisis situations. Though women's responsibilities and workloads are increased and they are frequently exposed to various forms of violation and indignity, they courageously struggle to build a semblance of stability in the lives of their families. They feed and care for their children, the sick, and the elderly. They daily promote healing, reconciliation, and peace among family members, neighbours, and the wider community.

Women's resilience and resourcefulness under situations of displacement must be recognized and fully supported by international humanitarian relief and rehabilitation organizations. UNIFEM's catalytic and advocacy work is just a small demonstration of a gender-sensitive and gender-responsive approach to assistance for the displaced. Yet it is critical to note that gender issues cannot be viewed as mere subsidiary components of relief and rehabilitation efforts. The need to transform mainstream relief and rehabilitation work is apparent. The application of gender analysis to emergency response should be the rule rather than the exception.

Furthermore, the situation of internally displaced and refugee women calls for a holistic and integrated approach. Their health and well-being requirements — such as family-planning knowledge and services including information and treatment for sexually transmitted diseases and HIV/AIDS as well as the need for culturally sensitive psychosocial trauma-counselling services — should be combined with information, skills, and support services that reduce their vulnerability and workload, enhance their knowledge of their legal rights, and promote their self-reliance and empowerment.

A commitment to empowering displaced women further calls for recognizing the legitimacy of their concerns and their know-how and giving visibility to their actual and potential role in the survival of children, families, and communities. It also calls for the full participation of women in all efforts at preventing and mitigating crisis situations. Finally, it calls for a long-term vision and commitment to sustained support.

Laketch Dirasse is a Social Anthropologist with over 20 years of experience in managing women in development projects, teaching/training, research and consulting experience with international donors, governmental and non-governmental organizations and academic institutions. She has authored two books, several manuals and articles on women in management and socio-economic development. Currently Laketch Dirasse is Senior Manager of UNIFEM's Regional Programme for the African Women in Crisis (AFWIC).

Notes

1. United Nations High Commissioner for Refugees (UNHCR). 1993. *The State of the World's Refugees: The Challenge for Protection.* New York: Penguin Books.

2. Centre for Policy Analysis and Research on Refugee Issues. 1992. "Report on Internally Displaced Persons." Mimeo, p. 2.

3. Martin, S. F. 1992. *Refugee Women*. London: Zed Books. See also UNHCR, cited in note 1.

4. Economic and Social Council. 2 February 1995. "Report of the Representative of the Secretary General, Mr. Francis Deng, submitted pursuant to Commission on Human Rights resolutions 1993/95 and 1994/68." E/CN.4/1995/50, p. 9.

5. Women's Rights Project. October 1993. "Seeking Refuge, Finding Terror: The Widespread Rape of Somali Women Refugees in North Eastern Kenya" in *Africa Watch Report*, p. 3.

6. Kundu, M. Ayoti. "Kenya: A Place of Their Own" in AACC, *Survival: African Women in Crisis*, p. 20.

7. Hagengimana, A. Psycho-Social Trauma Management Consultancy Report to UNIFEM/AFWIC.

8. Gathirwa, N., and C. Mpaka. November 1994. "Report on Maela Camp in Kenya" in UNIFEM/AFWIC and UNICEF/ESARO, *Reproductive and Mental Health Issues of Women and Girls Under Situations of War and Conflict in Africa*. Proceedings of expert group consultation, p. 50.

9. UNHCR. 1979. *Collection of International Instruments Concerning Refugees*. Geneva: United Nations. See also Economic and Social Council. 9 November 1990. "Peace: Refugee and Displaced Women and Children." Report of the Secretary General E/CN.6/1991/4, p. 5.

10. Organization of African Unity. 10 September 1969. *Convention Governing the Specific Aspects of Refugee Problems in Africa*. Adopted by Assembly of Heads of States and Government, 6th Ordinary Session, Addis Ababa, Article 1(2). See also Economic and Social Council, cited in note 9, p. 5.

11. Martin, cited in note 3, p. 24.

ARMED CONFLICT AND CHILDREN: A RESPONSIVE MORALITY

JENNIFER F. KLOT

War is the saddest word that flows from my quivering lips. It is a wicked bird that never comes to rest. It is a deadly bird that destroys our homes, and deprives us of our childhood. War is the most evil of birds, turning the streets red with blood, and the world into an inferno.

— Maida, 12 years old, Skopje, former Yugoslavia

It is 1995, and the routine and systematic killing of children seems to have become acceptable — either acceptable or inoffensive enough to humanity's conscience to allow more than 1.5 million children to be killed in wars during the past decade. Its collective revulsion at the systematic targeting of civilians with acts of unspeakable brutality has not prevented the death of 20 million children and women and the injury of 60 million more since 1945. In conflict situations, women and children have become deliberate targets of mass slaughter, torture, rape and violent assaults. But even in non-conflict situations, significant numbers of women and children are routinely subject to torture, starvation, humiliation, mutilation, and murder. In times of so-called peace and war, these violations against women and children have not until recently been recognized as violations of human rights or obstacles to "development."

The physical and psychological toll of war on children and their families has been enormous. Children are particularly vulnerable to violence in conflict situations and require special interventions to ensure their physical, psychological, and social well-being. In hostile and volatile environments, children's need for security and stability is heightened. War has displaced millions of children within and outside their countries, leaving them without guardians or family. The growing phenomenon of child soldiers has also raised important protection and policy issues. Children have been instrumentalised as perpetrators of atrocities, and for the first time in history, will stand trial for genocide. From schooling to health care, community-based and family-centred programmes for children have proven essential to their development.

Recognizing the increasingly complex nature of armed conflicts and the catastrophic conditions to which children have been and continue to be exposed, in December 1993 the UN General Assembly passed a resolution calling on the Secretary General to appoint an expert to carry out a study on the impact of armed conflict on children. UNICEF and the Centre for Human Rights have been called upon to provide the main support to the study.

The following preliminary reflections about the impact of armed conflict on children are informed by the first six months of the two-year UN study. The first of its kind in the history of the United Nations, the study has set in place a process that aims to place the issues of children and war at the centre of political and development agendas worldwide. The study is actively engaging practitioners, experts, NGOs, agencies, regional bodies, policy makers and opinion formers, and women and children themselves in a wide range of consultations, seminars, studies, and field visits.

The study's inquiry into ways and means to better respond to the needs of the world's children has only just begun. While children are always the entry point, they inevitably become representative of larger and more fundamental questions about humanity and struggles for peace and justice. Not surprisingly, we have found that the situation of children in armed conflicts is intimately related to the way civil society, NGOs, governments, and the United Nations function or do not function. The root causes of conflict and the situation of women have tremendous bearing on a child's well-being. Children may not receive adequate care if their parents have been massacred, or shelter if their homes have been destroyed, or education if their teachers have been assassinated.

Excellent efforts to protect children from the horrors of war and genocide exist, and we have been encouraged by the creative use of human rights and humanitarian law as a basis for programming and advocacy in this area. The Convention on the Rights of the Child (CRC) and the Convention on the Elimination of All Forms of Discrimination Against Women (CEDAW) have been used effectively as a framework for broad-scale mobilization around a human rights agenda. Women's leadership in peacemaking and conflict resolution has made a significant impact on children's lives. And demands for the accountability of financial institutions, regional organizations, professional bodies, governments, agencies, and NGOs have attempted to set in place higher standards of conduct. This paper will not attempt to document the many promising efforts under way but rather to highlight some of the primary concerns that have guided them.

EVERYDAY WARS: EMERGING PATTERNS OF CONFLICT

In many developing countries, armed conflict is a persistent and chronic aspect of daily life. In societies plagued by inequity, poverty, and civil strife, conventional approaches to development have not worked. This has prompted an ongoing reassessment of the role of activists, policy makers, development professionals, and the international community in understanding and responding to the multiplicity of needs of civilians in conflict situations. While models of response have not yet changed significantly, it is interesting to note that the discourse in a small way has done so. It is impossible in 1995 to speak about sustainable human development without considering human rights, the situation of women and children, the role of humanitarian assistance, and the disintegration of human values. In an era when sovereignty places fewer limitations on the operation of the United Nations and NGOs, issues of accountability, neutrality, access, and responsibility have become paramount.

In 1993, 26 UN complex emergencies affected 59 million people. Thirty-two major and 15 minor armed conflicts are currently being waged throughout the world. More than 90 per cent of those affected — murdered, displaced, violated — are civilians, and most of these are women and children. The nature and pattern of conflicts have changed dramatically in recent years, as have the responses of the international community, governments, the media, and civil society. While the rules of war have not changed significantly, the battlefield, the players, and the victims certainly have.

Every few minutes on television screens across the globe, the international media depict brutal images of war, poverty, and destruction. The outbreak of violent conflict is often known and even predicted well in advance of the first violation of human life or strategic military advance. Even now, as UN peacekeepers withdraw from Rwanda, armed opposition is preparing to mount a major offensive from refugee camps outside the country. It is no secret that some of those who were empowered to protect civilians and to maintain peace in Rwanda during the throes of active conflict were the same people who provided arms and military training to the militia, or simply waited to act until it affected their so-called strategic interests. And in the post–cold war global economy, the wait can be very long. The strategic interest of western nations in many developing countries has waned — especially in those countries plagued by genocide and conflict.

The consolidation of new regional economic blocs in North America, western Europe, and South-East Asia is not unrelated to the systemic economic crisis affecting many marginalized developing countries in the Africa-Eurasia zone. In many of these countries, intrastate or so-called internal conflicts have superseded nationalist struggles of the 1960s and 1970s. Lacking any social or political programme, a "total war" is conducted in the absence of democratic processes, civil society, or functional state institutions and structures. Characterized by extreme violence and insecurity and by the manipulation of ethnicity, culture, and religion, the struggle for economic and political gains spares nothing.

How, then, does the discourse of prevention, protection, peacemaking, peacekeeping, and conflict resolution reflect and respond to these realities? How can governments, civil society, humanitarian organizations, and regional bodies best respond to the gross violations of international law that have become a routine and chronic aspect of life and death for millions? How within this moral vicissitude can priority concerns for the best interests of children be reasserted?

CHILDREN AS A ZONE OF PEACE

In many quarters, and particularly at the study's first consultations, the need for a UN declaration based on the principle of children as a zone of peace has been suggested. This would create an international obligation to allow access to children in situations of armed conflict through, for example, "corridors of peace" and "days of tranquillity." It could also stipulate that the provision of essential services for children, such as education and

227

psychological care, become an essential component of humanitarian assistance. It has been suggested that the principle be expanded to include preventive and long-term interventions that address the structural causes of violence.

Within the context of total war, however, the protection of specific groups has proven immensely difficult. Obstacles to effective enforcement reflect the limitations of the international relief apparatus as much as the complex conditions to which they attempt to respond. Their impact is often affected by the manipulation of aid by warring parties, limited access to vulnerable groups, and the sincere agreement by all parties to facilitate and prioritize such efforts.

But in some countries such as El Salvador and the Sudan, efforts to declare children as a zone of peace have had some success. These have provided essential relief to large numbers of needy children and brought about consensus among all warring parties that children must be spared the horrors of war. More fundamentally, they have demonstrated the principle that children's rights as guaranteed by international law must supersede all else.

Several important themes regarding the impact of armed conflict on children have recurred throughout the course of the study. The following summary reviews four majors concerns that require further inquiry and immediate attention.

Psychological Recovery and Social Reintegration

Programmes concerned with children's psychological recovery and social reintegration have been recognized increasingly as an essential component of all humanitarian relief and development interventions. While specific models of psychosocial care ranging from individual therapy to community-based mental health training are debated, the need for ongoing activities is not. The effectiveness of specific programmes is often related to the involvement of local communities, institutions, and families in their design and implementation. Other key elements include the incorporation of local traditions of coping, healing, and survival, a focus on the re-establishment of trust and self-esteem, a secure economic base, reunification with family or community, a safe environment, and a component that promotes peace and reconciliation. Appropriate training models and guidelines for programming have not been fully developed in this area. Without a code of conduct, many of the ethical issues connected with psychosocial programming have not been addressed.

Child Soldiers

Children have become weapons of war and are, for the first time in history, standing trial for genocide in Rwanda. While some children are coerced, forcibly recruited, or simply follow their brothers, fathers, or family to the front lines, others "choose" to become soldiers as a way to secure food, community, and protection. In some countries, governments and armed opposition groups justify the recruitment of children on the basis of culture, religion, and strategic necessity. In Southern Africa and Central America, highly politicized children and youth articulate with force and passion their motivation to take up arms.

As soldiers, children are more vulnerable to physical and sexual abuse and are more likely to commit atrocities. As soldiers, their rights as children are violated. Advocacy is essential to make the state responsible for the protection, rehabilitation, demobilization, and reintegration of child soldiers. Support for the creation of an optional protocol to the Convention on the Rights of the Child to raise the age of recruitment to 18 years is necessary, as is the application of other legal instruments to prevent their recruitment and to protect their rights as children.

Land-mines

In over 60 countries, there are an estimated 100 million land-mines — one for every 20 children. Land-mines do not distinguish between civilians and combatants and pose a major threat to the lives and well-being of children. Their use violates the provisions of the Convention on the Rights of the Child, which obliges the state to protect children in armed conflict. Social services in poor countries have minimal capacity to respond to the needs of children disabled and disfigured by land-mines. Child victims rarely receive medical care that is appropriate for their rapidly changing physical needs or resultant psychological trauma. Children who are no longer able to walk long distances often drop out of school and place additional pressure on already limited family resources. Girls and women victims are particularly vulnerable to abandonment and rejection and are even less likely to receive appropriate medical care or vocational training.

Once laid, anti-personnel mines can remain active for as long as 50 years and prevent the productive use of lands and roads. While only costing as little as US$3, land-mines can cost as much as US$1000 to remove and therefore impede any serious attempts to achieve sustainable development. While mine awareness and clearance programmes are essential, nothing short of a total ban on the production, use, stockpiling, sale, and export of anti-personnel land-mines is necessary.

Women and Girls

In conflict situations, parents, especially mothers, are critical to a child's survival and development. Yet motherhood is only one aspect of women's lives — they are also workers, heads of household, leaders, activists, sisters, daughters, wives, and widows. Women are often essential to the survival of their families and communities and have economic, reproductive, and mental health needs that extend well beyond their role as mothers.

In situations of armed conflict and even in times of so-called peace, gender violence has become a systematic weapon of war and an instrument of repression. Displaced and refugee women and girls have special gynaecological, maternal health-care, and mental health counselling needs that are related to the effects of rape, sexual abuse, pregnancy complications, poor sanitation conditions in camps, and the loss of traditional community supports. Health education, preventive care, and counselling are especially important for women and girls who have been raped, have undergone female genital mutilation (which appears amongst other realities of a different nature, and is not a result of war), or have been forced into prostitution and are more vulnerable to sexually transmitted diseases and AIDS.

THE HUMAN RIGHTS AGENDA

Two international treaties, the CRC and the CEDAW, provide a recognized legal basis for establishing and protecting the rights of women and children. These rights are also specified in other international instruments, notably the Geneva Conventions and their Additional Protocols. While these international standards could be strengthened — especially regarding their application to internal conflicts — they are most seriously limited by ineffective monitoring and enforcement.

Attempts to further state accountability for violations of children's rights through reporting procedures, treaty interpretation, and the use of regional instruments such as the African Charter have been made. Women's human rights activists are also attempting to test the legal obligation of other international agencies, such as the World Bank and the International Monetary Fund. To the extent that international humanitarian law is incorporated at the national level, the development of local jurisprudence can be an important strategy in countries with independent judicial systems. Redress for the violation of women's and children's human rights, often the "hidden" crimes of war, also requires the reinterpretation of humanitarian and human rights law, the demonstration of public or state responsibility for gender-based violations, and the establishment of remedies. This work could also help demonstrate the relevance of international instruments to another "hidden" crime — admittedly of smaller scale — that is, the complicity and participation of peacekeepers and humanitarian aid workers in trafficking, involuntary, and military-related prostitution and rape.

In many countries in conflict situations, the Convention on the Rights of the Child has been used by humanitarian organizations as a tool for programming and as a basis for advocacy. It has been used to develop national programmes of action in cooperation with governments and to create widespread awareness of the situation of women and children. Most important, it has helped to frame the fulfillment of basic needs as a fundamental issue of human rights.

THE HUMANITARIAN RESPONSE

No longer facing the same constraints of sovereignty, a growing number of NGOs, agencies, and international donors have established programmes in conflict areas in the absence or without the agreement of recognized governments, often outside their own policy and programme mandates. Many of these programmes have assisted large numbers of vulnerable people, especially when a state has relinquished its responsibility to protect the basic needs and fundamental human rights of its citizens, or have even become key agents of the expression of these rights. The so-called neutrality that has long guided the delivery of humanitarian assistance has given way to conduct on the basis of solidarity with affected groups and has resulted in new opportunities to engage non-state warring factions on humanitarian issues.

Yet as the battlefield opens to those who venture forth, lines of accountability have blurred and the control and manipulation of relief has become an important part of the political economy of conflicts. This new span of humanitarian activity has deflected attention away from the need to pursue political solutions. It has also highlighted the inadequacy of international guidelines and norms regarding the conduct and practice of those providing relief as well as the basis for their entry into and withdrawal from conflict situations.

Initially intending their interventions as temporary, emergency or ad hoc measures, humanitarian agencies have in many countries begun to assume responsibility for programmes that have been the traditional domain of the state, such as health, education, and human rights. This assistance may be taken for granted by newly emerged state institutions and structures and be used to justify spending priorities that emphasize structural or other strategic interests. As a result, foreign, NGO, donor, and other outside interests may not only find themselves with a significant say in how services will be delivered but also with long-term responsibility for their provision.

POST-CONFLICT RECONSTRUCTION

Although enduring characteristics of conflict have become endemic to many impoverished and embattled nations, some preliminary and general observations can be made about the needs of children in the post-conflict reconstruction period. While not limited to this period, the following brief considerations highlight key concerns that have been expressed over the course of the study's work, regarding the well-being of children during post-conflict reconstruction.

• In the aftermath of conflict, mechanisms for achieving national reconciliation as well as conflict prevention and conflict resolution must be established as an immediate priority. Women's central role in these efforts must be supported, as well as the importance of education in promoting peace and tolerance. The reconstruction of independent judicial systems, children's access to justice, fair investigations, tribunals, and reparations are essential to the establishment of democratic processes and civil society.

• The rapid withdrawal of international assistance in the wake of long-term conflicts often results in a sudden scarcity of resources. At the national level, capacity to meet basic needs, provide essential services, ensure security, and protect human rights is often limited. The role of regional institutions and neighbouring countries can be crucial — both by their support for fundamental reconstruction and also, notably, by their absence or continued interest in prolonging or abating conflict.

• Children are greatly affected by the militarization of their societies; many are born and raised in conflict situations. The re-emergence of civil society is critical to their well-being, physical and psychological recovery, and social reintegration. Local NGOs, service providers, human rights organizations, and women's groups are important in the stabilization and reconstruction of families and communities and the response to the special needs of women and girls. Activities and organizations working to demobilize militia and child soldiers are particularly important.

• In countries that have been heavily mined, immediate and rapid de-mining operations and mine-awareness programmes are essential to the restoration of civil society.

• Government spending in post-conflict reconstruction must prioritize human development and security. Psychological and social recovery programmes must not be sacrificed in the interest of physical reconstruction and military security.

ACCOUNTABILITY, MOBILIZATION, AND ACTION

We have begun to accept the incompatibility of conventional development models with the needs of those rendered most vulnerable by armed conflicts. We have even conceded that although relief is essential, it needs to be better construed and more effectively administered. But the most fundamental challenge remains elusive — to instill a sense of global and collective responsibility for the ongoing death, torture, and displacement of millions of children every day.

As a first response, many have turned to the traditional harbingers of human values: the family, community, popular culture, religious and educational institutions, and the state itself. But in recent decades, these historical gatekeepers of human morality have undergone dramatic reformulation. Pervasive social, political, and economic insecurity have contributed to a fundamental collapse of human values. Political inertia has impeded the adequate protection and care of the world's most valuable resource, our children.

Consensus exists on the need to protect the human rights of children victims of conflict. But making the issues of children and war a priority on the international political and development agendas worldwide has not yet happened. Toward this end, grass-roots constituencies are actively challenging the accountability, conduct and complicity of

231

governments, international institutions, regional bodies, agencies, the media, the humanitarian relief apparatus, and professional organizations. But this is only one part of a broader process of mobilization and structural reorganization that must take place in order to re-establish a culture of respect for human life.

Essential to this process is a guiding vision. As a first step toward building a comprehensive vision that takes as its starting point the safe keeping of our children, the study's Group of Eminent Persons offered the following thoughts at its first meeting in May 1995:

> We want to build a world where children will not become the victims of violent conflicts and will not be weapons of war, a world where children can live as children and adults can be more human, gentle, caring, and compassionate. To this end we must build and reinforce political, social, and economic institutions that safeguard against injustice and inequality and that provide mechanisms for grievances and redress. We believe that such institutions must be both locally grounded and nationally integrated. These institutions should be led by women and men who are socially responsible, nurturing, and committed to defending children against destruction. More women need to be included in these institutions so that their special talents and experiences can contribute to a redefinition of responsible and responsive leadership.

Jennifer F. Klot is the Programme Manager of the United Nations Study on the Impact of Armed Conflict on Children. The study is chaired by Ms. Graça Machel and is based in South Africa. Ms. Klot has worked with international non-governmental organizations, private foundations and multilateral agencies on projects focused on women's rights and youth development in Africa and in the U.S.

CHALLENGES FOR WOMEN'S EMPOWERMENT AND EDUCATION IN SOUTH ASIA

KAMLA BHASIN

The words *women's empowerment* mean very different things to different people. There are those who would like women to be empowered so that they can better serve the interests of economic growth and free markets. Their goal is freedom of the markets, not freedom of women.

There are, at the same time, a large number of women and their organizations as well as people's organizations and NGOs in South Asia and elsewhere who are convinced that the present paradigm of development can only further marginalize and disempower disadvantaged women and their families. For these individuals and organizations, women need to be empowered not to serve the present system but to challenge and change it.

An important question to explore at this critical juncture in history is whether women can be a major force in a movement to devalue power, domination, and consumerism so that it is the rich who feel ashamed not the poor, so that the rapists feel ashamed rather than those who are raped, so that those who always want to control feel ashamed rather than those who are controlled. Can women initiate and lead the process toward equity, justice, and sustainable livelihoods?

What has been derisively called feminine contains the key to our survival. What is feminine? Being nurturing, caring, selfless; being emotional, close to nature, creative; being non-violent, non-linear, non-specialized. These qualities have been labelled feminine and are therefore looked down upon, marginalized, or crushed. Imagine a world where these feminine values were affirmed and held in high esteem.

I am not talking specifically of women but rather of feminine principles and values. These are the values that philosophers and scientists have labelled feminine. They could, perhaps more accurately, be called human values. Today these human values are more often found in women than in men, not because the female body has special limbs or glands that produce these values but because of historical reasons.

Because we are at the bottom of all hierarchies, women know what harm inequality can do, how it can kill and destroy. Because we have been the victims of so many "isms," women have concentrated on exposing those "isms" that have obscured and undervalued large parts of humanity. Women are organizing against dualities like inside/outside, private/public, body/mind, nature/culture, emotional/rational. We are experimenting with ecological and integrated ways of thinking and being.

The 50 per cent of humanity which was rarely consulted in perpetuating the free market approach to development needs now to take the lead to create a humane world. Today, women face the challenge to find our own *dharma*, our own essential nature, to refine it and strengthen it. We have to participate in creating a new culture, a new civilization which is based on love and compassion, not on competition, a civilization which is not dying to be victorious but which is keen to live. We have to take men along and make them our partners in creating a new world. We have witnessed the feminization of poverty. Let us now feminize our politics and our governments.

233

EMPOWERMENT AS A DYNAMIC AND POLITICAL PROCESS

The main question which we face today — through all our projects and programmes to empower women — is what kind of power we want women to have. What is our definition of women's empowerment? Do we want women to compete with men in order to have better positions within the present system? Do we want women to head weapons industries? Do we want women to control corporations that produce junk foods or pornography?

Empowerment of women will make a difference only if our notion of power is different from the present notion. Power for us cannot mean power over others, power to exploit, power to control more than our share of resources and decision-making. For us, power should mean the power to be; the power to control one's own greed and avarice; the power to nurture, heal, and care for others; the power to fight for justice, ethics, and morality; the power to achieve inner growth leading to wisdom and compassion.

About ten years ago, I worked with a colleague to conduct a workshop for rural woman in Bihar, India. Most of the participants possessed few material goods. We asked them what they would request if some Goddess offered to make all their desires come true. Their answers baffled us, their wisdom challenged our narrow notions of development. Basic needs like food and shelter appeared toward the end of the long list. Their list of desires included:

- my own identity
- leisure and time to dream
- recognition and respect
- love
- affirmation
- freedom

Women's empowerment is an ongoing and dynamic process that enhances women's ability to change the structures and ideologies that keep them subordinate. This process enables them to gain more access to resources and decision-making, more control over their own lives, more autonomy. It is a process which enables women to gain self-respect and dignity and which improves their self-image and social image.

While talking about the empowerment of women, we must also recognize certain principles. We do not support all women regardless of their beliefs and practices. We are not working for the empowerment of women dictators or women patriarchs just because they are women. We recognize that women can also be patriarchal and dominating and that some men can be and are our partners in fighting patriarchy and other hierarchical systems. Our struggle is for certain principles and for a society where men and women have equal opportunities to live, to grow, to participate.

234

The process of empowerment is a political process, because it aims at changing existing power relationships. The goal of women's empowerment is not just to change hierarchical gender relations but to change all hierarchical relations in society: class, caste, race, ethnic, North-South relations. Because gender relations do not operate in a vacuum, because they are related to and influenced by all other economic, social and political systems, one cannot change gender hierarchies without changing other systems and hierarchies.

Women's struggles and movements, therefore, need to be closely linked to peace movements, ecology movements, worker and peasant movements, human rights movements, and movements for the democratization and decentralization of society. These different movements are different aspects of the same struggle, different segments of the same dream.

ISSUES THAT NEED MORE ATTENTION

The work of the women's movement in South Asia and globally has been responsible for some significant and positive changes for women. There is growing gender awareness, which translates into wider recognition of women's subordination and the need to challenge it. Violence against women is more visible and more loudly condemned. There have been improvements in some legal provisions and in educational and job opportunities for women. There is some increase in the number of women participating in government and in non-governmental development agencies and programmes. Many governments have established women's bureaus, commissions, departments, and/or ministries to look into gender issues.

While the groundwork for continued and effective action has been laid, there remain a variety of areas that are crucial to women's empowerment and that have not received adequate attention in the past. Some of the most important are women's lack of control over property and other productive resources; women's lack of access to gainful employment; the sharing of household and child-rearing work between men and women; women's ability to control their own sexuality; and an understanding of and response to those ideologies that justify and perpetuate practices and behaviours that discriminate against women.

THE ROLE OF FORMAL EDUCATION AND KNOWLEDGE IN WOMEN'S EMPOWERMENT

Education is a critical ingredient in women's empowerment. On the issue of education for women's empowerment, let us take a quick historical look at what education and knowledge have done to women in the past.

Because men from the leisured classes (and castes) have had exclusive control over the creation of knowledge, they have also had the power to define, to name. Male doctors have defined the female body and its illnesses. Male psychologists have been naming female neuroses and pathologies. Male historians have written primarily about the contributions and conquests of men, leaving most women without a sense of their own value to society. Male economists have defined work and its worth so that women's labour in caring for their families and homes is not recognized and has no official value.

This kind of patriarchal knowledge has done injustice to women by discounting women's knowledge, by marginalizing women's contribution, by first defining women as — and later turning them into — subordinates. These knowledge systems can only *domesticate women and not empower them*. Additionally, knowledge based on the experiences of half of humanity is only half-true, half-valid.

One of the most exciting and revolutionary changes of the recent past has been the work of significant numbers of women to begin creating knowledge. Women historians are now challenging male history, women theologians are challenging male religions and theologies. The same is being done by women scientists, sociologists, anthropologists, doctors, lawyers, and educators.

Women are combing textbooks and literacy primers to weed out sexism, they are scrutinizing colleges and universities to identify where sexist biases affect learning. This kind of work by our sisters and foremothers has empowered us, has enabled us to break our ignorance and silence and to stand tall.

235

EDUCATION FOR UNDERSTANDING

Education of women is indeed the most important component, the most important pathway to women's empowerment. We have to strengthen and multiply ongoing efforts to acquire information and knowledge which help us to challenge patriarchal norms, values, and behaviour patterns. We need education which will help us not only to read and understand *words* but to read, understand, and control our *worlds*. We need education which will help us not only *master the three Rs but to be masters of our lives* and makers of our destinies.

If we are involved with women's literacy, then literacy classes for women should become places for consciousness-raising. They should help women form strong groups so that they can gain more control over their lives. Literacy classes should create an atmosphere which allows women more freedom, which gives them more opportunities to realize their full human potential.

The methodology of women's education has to be participatory and non-hierarchical. Women must be involved in setting their own agenda and priorities, their own pace of learning. The educational process should build their confidence and self-respect, unleash their creativity, make them feel energetic and joyous. This is empowering education.

We need education which will not lead to more competition and ambition but which will create trust and solidarity among women. It should help women develop analytical and questioning minds and a scientific approach to understanding the realities around them. It should help them to see the connections between micro- and macro- policies, between the local and the global.

Finally, our educational efforts must provide to the participants some opportunity to clarify their *vision* of sustainable development and livelihoods, their vision of a safe society, and their vision of shared goals.

EMPOWERMENT TO TAKE ACTION FOR SUSTAINABLE DEVELOPMENT

The present form of development has marginalized and disempowered women. If the present system is to change, it is small people like you and me who will have to change it. Unless small people, small groups do experiments all over the world, sustainable development is not possible. So hopes lies in small experiments. All of us can try and do the following:

- Let us begin with ourselves. We women have to look after our bodies and our minds to feel strong and beautiful. We have to have *shakti* ("strength") and to radiate this *shakti*. Wherever we are, we should support other women, give them strength, tell them that they are important and that their knowledge is important. We begin with ourselves, our family, our daughters and mothers, and then within our organizations and in communities where we work.
- Wherever we are, whatever we are doing, we should empower people; tell people they are the subjects of their own development; treat them with respect; recognize their dignity, their wisdom, and their time-tested knowledge systems.
- Support people's organizations because empowerment of the poor or of women is not possible as individuals. Small groups have to become the training ground for grass-roots, participatory democracies.
- We have to practice democracy everywhere, in our families, in our organizations. We have to tell our male colleagues — or if we are the boss, to tell ourselves — to be more democratic so that democracy takes root in our NGOs and in the com-

munities we are working with. It is this practice which will create people and groups which are strong and autonomous and will allow no one to attack or rob their dignity, their economies.

• Wherever we are, let us talk about and insist on the values of justice, ethics, morality, beauty, love. Because people lost sight of these values, development lost its human face. We have to bring back these values into our private and public lives. Other values are reverence for all life, simple living in harmony with nature, respect for diversity. Wherever we find there is no justice, morality, ethics, we have to speak up. It is the joint efforts of all of us — women *and* men — that are leading to and will lead to women's empowerment.

Kamla Bhasin, *a social scientist by training, has been involved with development, education, gender, and media since 1972. Since 1976 she has been working with the FAO's Freedom from Hunger Campaign/Action for Development, supporting innovative NGO initiatives, and facilitating networking among NGOs, women's organizations and people's organizations in South Asia. Recently she has been writing songs for the women's movement and for children.*

This article draws upon a paper presented at the International Conference on Women's Empowerment and Education, organized by the Government of India in collaboration with the Royal Netherlands Embassy in India and held in New Delhi, 22–31 March 1995, as well as the article "Some Thoughts on Development and Sustainable Development," *Women in Action: ISIS International,* April 1992, January 1993.

A MOTHER DAUGHTER REVOLUTION

ELIZABETH DEBOLD, MARIE WILSON AND IDELISSE MALAVÉ

Resistance is the secret of joy!   — Alice Walker

What does it mean to love a daughter in a culture that is hostile to her integrity? In a culture where power equals dominance and superiority, men's control of public life — the world of political and economic power that shapes the desires of private life — places mothers in a double bind as their daughters approach womanhood. The common ways that mothers have of guiding daughters — what we call paths of least resistance — ask girls to make deep psychological sacrifices to straddle the cultural division of work, the "male" public world of politics and business, and love, the "female" world of home and family. As girls find that they cannot enter patriarchy fully and powerfully as themselves but must instead opt for one of these paths, they feel betrayed* by their mothers. But mothers did not create the separate spheres of public and private life. It is this cultural betrayal of human integrity, which divides our wholeness into separate spheres, that makes loving a daughter political work.

In countries where market-driven factory life in the Industrial Revolution usurped their traditional work of producing food, clothing, medicine, and crafts, women were suddenly stripped of their expertise and authority. Rather than adopting a rationalist solution of admitting women into modern society on an equal footing with men, male experts promoted the "romantic solution" of relegating women to the home, safe and separate from the capitalist forum of work.

In the US, the invention of motherhood as we know it, safely nestled in the nuclear family, ensured the increased consumption of goods necessary to a growing economy. Despite the reality that many women worked for pay on farms and in factories, it created the illusion that "true" women — and women who were truly loved — stayed at home with children.[1]

Since that time, girls have suffered an increasingly widespread crisis as they enter the culture as young women. They face the choiceless choices of denying themselves public power or dividing themselves internally to balance these separate dictates for living. And they *struggle* against making the devastating sacrifices called for by the separation of "male" public life from a "female" private world. As recent researchers have documented, young girls are clear-minded, courageous, and confident. At the edge of adolescence, though, girls see what is coming and fight. But without help, their courage is quickly turned into self-blame and self-doubt, which often turn into depression, eating disorders, suicide, and other forms of self-abuse. In the most simple terms, they lose their self-esteem.

Revolutionary mothering is the practice of encouraging girls' resistance. It rejects the myth of the perfect mother, who is all-nurturing, to encompass more of our personal and political heritage as women.

Transforming betrayal into power begins at home in the intimacy of the mother-daughter relationship and through the transformation of families. But the power of women's reclaimed voices must move into the public world. By reclaiming our connections with each other, as women, we transform mothering from an act of selfless nurturance confined to private life to a political act of solidarity through which we create a community of women for our daughters to join. A revolution of mothers joins all women in the political act of mothering the next generation of girls either as biological or adoptive mothers or as "othermothers," caring adults living outside the family story. By fully claiming and sharing the power of mothering, we radically change the role of mother from middle manager of patriarchy into visionary and activist.

When the dynamic of betrayal no longer haunts women's relationships with one another, women become free to lead powerfully and to support powerful leaders. The revolution begins on all fronts to claim the work of love and the love of work to be equally important and necessary to bring together. A revolution of mothers brings the separate spheres of work and love together so that daughters are not faced with choiceless choices, the either/ors that divide women from themselves and one another.

Transforming mother-daughter relationships begins with voice lessons that encourage resistance; a mother-daughter revolution begins with public speaking that resists cultural systems of separation and dominance. Naming for ourselves, speaking to each other about what we are not supposed to know or see is the first step.

---

* AUTHORS' NOTE: When we suggest that girls feel "betrayed" or a "betrayal" by their mothers, we are in no way implying that women are to blame. One of the most painful ironies in patriarchal cultures is that mothers, because they must enforce limits on daughters to protect them, end up taking the blame for a situation that is neither their fault nor their creation. Mothers grapple with the harrowing task of reconciling their overriding desire to keep their daughters safe with their desire to keep them strong and free in a world that insists on women's inferiority and subordination. While girls may feel frustrated or "betrayed" as they come to understand their mother's lack of control and power in the world, it is also important to recognize that the capacity of young girls to engage with others — learned in mother daughter relationships — is their deepest source of strength and resiliency.

There are no quick fixes to problems that are a part of the very fabric of patriarchal societies. The answer is continuing resistance: a process, first, of bringing into knowledge and, thus, power what has been unspoken and unnamed between mothers and daughters, among women, and between women and men; and, second, a resistance that brings mothering into public life by organizing at every level of society — from circles of mothers to politicized networks of women who love girls. What our daughters need to know is that women are serious about making the world a place where they can dare to be whole, true, and powerful.

We can create a community of women for them to join. This is leadership: taking responsibility to bring this vision into reality through our words and actions. A revolution of mothers calls all women into leadership on behalf of the next generation of women.

PUBLIC SPEAKING

What would it mean for women to speak the truth in public? Truth-telling mothers challenge the public world to be responsible to our daughters, ourselves, and one another. Like young girls, revolutionary mothers sound the alarm that life is not fair. Revolutionary mothers join daughters' voices to argue for fairness and compassion in public policy and the world of work. These women talk their talk in community centres, at school meetings, in the halls of legislatures, on television, and with their votes. The call to revolutionary mothering invites women to tell the truths of their lives and to redefine the purpose of public life. The boundary between public and private, work and love, disappears as mothers speak and lead from home to capitol. Only then can girls join the culture without giving up part of themselves.

When women speak in public, separations in the culture get caught in women's throats. The most common routes for women into patriarchy — the paths of least resistance — provide the options for public speaking: either to embrace traditional feminine roles and speak a language of nurturance or to adopt the "girls will be boys" or "one of the guys" approach and to think, and speak, "like a man." Feminist public speakers have different voices, but these voices are also distorted in a male-voiced culture. Women in public life are simply in a bind: if they speak like a "man," they are charged by other women with selling out; if they speak for "women," their concerns are marginalized because these discussions take place at the edges — the margins — of public life, not at its centre.

In the recent past, women leaders in the US have struggled to articulate women's concerns and perspectives and be taken seriously. Through the 1970s, women spoke in two predominant voices: the *voice of equality* and the *voice of victimization.* The voice of equality is a demand for rights spoken in a language understood by male culture. Equality speaks of contractual exchange — this equals that — which is the foundation of market relations and the legal system.

Speaking in this voice has had the unintentional effect of legitimizing the legal system created by privileged men to protect their interests. The call for women's right to equality with men in the US was made and answered predominantly by white, middle-class women. As social critic bell hooks asks, since all men are not equal to each other in this country, "which men do women want to be equal to?"[2] For the women who dominated the women's movement, the answer was fairly clear: privileged white men. These women, in effect, asked to compete with men on the terms that men had defined. As these women protested to be able to move from the world of love to the world of work, their goals, at best, idealized work and, at worst, sought to give white women the privileges of upper-class white men. This approach inadvertently continued the race and class divisions among women that were created in the middle-class ideal of "true" womanhood.

239

As many women in the women's movement of the 1970s began speaking with the voice of equality, another voice could be heard in its echo. The voice of victimization attempted to bring the personal plight of many women's pain and powerlessness into public light. This voice has broken the silence around rape, battering, poverty, and the sexual and physical abuse of children. It has caused a deep shift in public awareness. Yet it also distorts women's reality. This voice presents a simplistic polarization of human beings as victims or victimizers. Women's strength and resilience were left out of the equation. For women whose lives were hard but who lived bravely, being cast in the role of victim felt like a betrayal.

By the early 1980s, these voices were joined by a different voice, the *voice of care*. By listening to women describe their experience and ways of understanding themselves and the world, the feminists who first articulated this voice in public speaking attempted to name women's strengths and vulnerabilities *in their own terms* rather than in comparison with men. This voice spoke of the primacy of relationship in women's lives as a virtue that becomes entwined with women's intimate subordination. The voice of care asked for a re-ordering of cultural values; it broke a silence in public discourse around issues of human connection and interdependence. The voice of care asserts that the values assigned to private life are *also* values for public life. These values, speakers of the voice argued, were critical to the future of civilization itself.

To some women, the voice of care sounded very similar to the romantic, traditionalist voice — the voice of the patriarchal woman. This traditional voice argues that women are different from men because women are specially called to nurturance. Women are viewed as special and better than men, not simply different because their life experiences are different from men's. Naming differences between men and women has historically been dangerous to women. In the 19th century, women in the United States insisted that their moral superiority as nurturers should give them the right to vote. After the vote was granted, women almost summarily were sent back home — where they had said they belonged. Women's current status as the voting majority has yet to be translated into political power.

The feminist voice of care has not been able to articulate a way of public speaking that addresses the political concerns of women. It does not speak to the system-wide betrayal of women in discriminatory laws and practices. In cultures divided between public and private life, this voice is rarely heard as the critique of public life that it is. While it is a voice that transgresses the boundary line between public and private life by raising "private" concerns in "public," it is often considered to be a voice that keeps women out of public life because it doesn't sound like the public speaking voices we are used to hearing, and so, it can be too easily subverted by traditionalists.

What would new public voices for the revolution of mothers sound like? We cannot say exactly. We do know that the voices of equality and care must be brought together with a recognition of our different experiences of oppression and exploitation and our extraordinary capacities for joy, resistance, and power.[3] The voice of equality that insisted on women's equal treatment with men must be revolutionized by caring about the particulars of women's situations. Equality of outcome, not equal treatment under the law, is what is fair to redress historical discrimination.[4] Equal rights may have been an important strategic demand in the first phase of the contemporary women's movement. But our issues and concerns are far more complicated than those allowed by a blanket insistence on rights.

By holding together the complexity of our lives and our experiences, we, and what we care about, are not split into pieces that then fragment our unity as women. Within a revolution of mothers, the new voice for public speaking forges a radical — meaning, literally, *to the root* — consciousness of the divisions that we have accepted in our lives. Only through our commitment to a radical solidarity of women can we speak in ways that move women, and their allies, to meet the challenge of leadership.

PERSONAL AND POLITICAL CHANGE

"Change is what people want most, and fear most desperately," says activist Catlin Fullwood. "That's what accounts for the forward mobility and backtracking that all change efforts experience." Whether personal or political change, the route is at best more of a spiral than a straight line. Those of us who have struggled to create new selves from troubling pasts have learned how often we remember and then lose the insights we have gained through our hard work. We disintegrate under stress. Our stories about ourselves and who we are constantly evolve. We dance through our lives doing the two-step: two steps forward, two steps back, side to side, in an energized but ambivalent set of movements.

The dance of social change is also the two-step. Both in psychological and political change, when we are on the verge of transformation, we feel a strong pull, like a dangerous undertow, to stay as we were. But backlash itself is a sign of progress, a signal that at a personal, relational, or societal level, we are changing enough to cause alarm. It also tells us that we can expect more pressure to turn back with each step forward.

With each step, each change we make in how we mother, we will experience discomfort or the feeling that we just can't do it. To oppose the status quo, to betray the culture that expects us to raise daughters who hold men at the centre of their lives, to confront the myths of perfection, self-sacrifice, and separation that hold sway for mothering a daughter will not be comfortable. While it is important that we acknowledge and experience these feelings, they are not always our best guide to action. If we listened to them, we would never move forward. A circle of mothers and a community of women is essential to test strategies and behaviours, to sort out feelings, to find confirmation for our authority and to make choices about where and when to act differently. At a societal level, only true solidarity — ever larger circles of mothers — can claim the power of mothering and begin to build communities where girls' losses are truly unnecessary.

Each generation of women has wanted a better life for their daughters. The changes that have already been made for women have been dearly paid for at both a personal and political level. If these changes were easy, life would be different right now. The proliferation of mother-blame and women-blame assures us that our daughters will not love or trust us for our compliance or for demanding theirs at the cost of the life force of their deepest desires. By engaging in continuing resistance to oppression and commitment to solidarity for liberation, we mother a revolution in life as we know it.

Through practices of resistance, we free our hearts and minds from traditional betrayals. Leadership begins by laying claim to the important questions, by beginning a public discourse that erases the divisive boundaries in our lives, by seeking partners who challenge our assumptions. Every woman can mother a revolution in her own life and join in mothering a revolution in the world for the next generation. The power of a mother-daughter revolution waits to be born.

Elizabeth Debold is a member of the Harvard Project on Women's Psychology and Girls' Development. She has consulted with a variety of organizations, such as the Ms. Foundation for Women and the Children's Television Workshop.

Marie C. Wilson has been President of the Ms. Foundation for Women for ten years. While at Ms., she founded the National Girls Initiative, a grant-making and public education campaign *for pre-adolescent and adolescent girls and sponsored the annual "Take Our Daughters to Work" day in which 25 million people participated in 1994.*

Idelisse Malavé *joined the Ms. Foundation for Women as Vice President in 1990. She was previously a civil rights litigator with the Puerto Rican Legal Defense and Education Fund and practiced family law.*

This article draws from the final chapter of the authors' book: Mother Daughter Revolution: From Good Girls to Great Women, New York: Bantam Books, 1993.

Notes

1 See Barbara Ehrenreich & Deirdre English, *For Her Own Good: 150 Years of the Experts' Advice to Women.* New York: Anchor/Doubleday, 1978.

2 hooks, bell. *Feminist Theory: From Margin to Center.* Boston: Southend Press, 1984, p. 18.

3 In the last chapter of *In a Different Voice: Psychological Theory and Women's Development,* Cambridge, Mass.: Harvard University Press, 1982, Carol Gilligan suggested that maturity in adulthood would combine the moral voices that she identified — the voice of justice and the voice of care.

4 See, for example, Martha Albertson Fineman, *The Illusion of Equality: The Rhetoric and Reality of Divorce Reform.* Chicago: University of Chicago Press, 1991.

REFLECTIONS ON FEMINIST LEADERSHIP

DEVAKI JAIN

The first UN world conference on women, held in Mexico in 1975, provided a space for the women of the world to meet and discuss their ideas and concerns. For those who attended the conference, it did something more. It affirmed the existence of a worldwide identity and became the first step in the development of a worldwide women's movement (WWM) and international feminism.

This is not to suggest that the women's movement or feminism was born out of the UN conference. Women have been meeting locally, nationally and internationally throughout this century — as revolutionaries, as professionals, and under many other political and religious banners. What the conference in Mexico and its follow-up conferences in Copenhagen (1980) and Nairobi (1985) added was a worldwide identity and the evolution of formal and informal communications structures and organizations.

The WWM has evolved in many ways since 1975. It has often been marked by internal differences and equally often with a united voice. Most of the global platforms that have emerged from women's organizing efforts respond to the WWM's recognition of discrimination against women in all aspects of their lives, regardless of class, colour, or culture. Its platforms focus, as well, on a wide range of locales, from the United Nations to the family, and including all the stops along the way: national governments; farms, firms, and other workplaces, including the home; legislatures; and finally, the mind. In fact, the critique of inherent discrimination against women — in the very premises of theories, in the evolution of knowledge, in the understanding of evolution itself — has been one of the most important sources of unity within the WWM.

In the recent processes which have called on the WWM to appear as a global force or, minimally, as a lobby — the UN Conference on Environment and Development (UNCED, Rio de Janeiro, 1992), the World Conference on Human Rights (WCHR, Vienna, 1993), the International Conference on Population and Development (ICPD, Cairo, 1994), and the World Summit on Social Development (WSSD, Copenhagen, 1995) — the WWM has established itself as a major force for influencing international policy. It has flagged the perspectives of women, their capabilities, and most of all, the importance of taking note of their views in the political battlegrounds that these global issues have become.

On the other hand, when the women's movement has to address itself, as it has on the road to the Fourth World Conference on Women (WCW, Beijing, 1995), many differences appear and often dissipate the sense of unity and common purpose. It is always easier to form a solid front against an outside agency than when the subject is self.

International feminism, as distinguished from the WWM, has had a smoother passage. The ideological base of feminism, which gives those who identify with it some common language and beliefs, bridges the distance and distress of difference. International feminism, however vaguely defined and ostensibly in disarray, is still the thread that holds together the WWM. But it has yet to re-construct the structures and processes dominating the globe. It has yet to be recognized for the ethical leadership it infuses into the international landscape.

The underlying assumption of this essay is that the principles of feminist leadership are precisely the principles required to replace the forces of injustice and violence with the forces of peace and justice. But first we must ask: What are the diverse tracings or sets of elements that define women's leadership and feminist leadership? How can the unique power or quality of women's leadership influence governance, whether in the family or at international decision-making levels? Is it possible to attribute specific qualities to feminist leadership, as distinguished from men's leadership?

TRACING THE SOURCE OF WOMEN'S LEADERSHIP QUALITIES

Women's special strengths have been traced in several ways and to several sources or root phenomena. Traditional and religious texts and beliefs provide some particular insights.

Amongst some social groups, like the one I belong to, it is customary to bless a girl or woman every time she sits for a ritual bath (which used to be quite often) with the names of Indian heroines known for their unflinching devotion to their spouses — Ahalya, Sita, Draupadi, Tara, Mandodari-Panchakalnya. These names can be replaced by other equally venerated heroines who are known for intellectual strength and rebellious spirits — Ambapalli, Gargi, Savithri, Avaiyar. We can argue that whichever set of "virtues" are chosen are not necessarily women's attributes, but are forced on women by a patriarchal culture. This heterogeneity or plurality of images is common to many traditions and "cultures," whether Islamic, Christian, Judaic, Hindu, or another. A second type of imagery comes from the poetry of women and from folk tales. These are totally different archetypes, derived from the context of lives which are not bound into marriage and family syndromes but rather are based on women involved in livelihood activities, demonstrating strength and leadership.

Tracings come as well from looking at women's struggles. A review of women's collective affirmative action in India reveals their strength and courage. Spontaneous mass-based resistance in India — Chipko in the Himalayas, Arrack in Andhra, vending space in

243

Ahmedabad, drinking in Manipur, land in Assam — reveal that when there is a threat to livelihood or social peace, or when there is household violence, women rise like a wave, mobilized through their individual experience.

Another tracing is from women's roles that arise out of a biological construct, that is, women as bearers of children and, somewhat consequently, the nurturers of the weak and vulnerable. Here, too, there are cultural and moral derivatives. The symbol of mother is an image which has been presented in a myriad of ways. Notions of altruism, sacrifice, and responsibility are some of the psychological attributes derived from these images.

This reproductive capability is a key tracing — whether we are examining patriarchy or women's ways and strengths. It is this beginning that I think often determines the path of other tracings. As those who are responsible for the continuation of life, women learn to plunge quickly into collective struggle when there is a threat to survival or peace. Whether in a household or a wandering family, girls and women become mediators and managers with multiple skills. As those who are almost always excluded from formal structures, they are neither groomed in the styles of communication that men often indulge in nor are they hampered by the bloated self-images that many men suffer when they are wearing their public faces.

The late Indian modern poet Ramanujan has offered beautiful imagery on this notion in his juxtaposition of "mother's tongue" and "father's language." From Ramanujan we get vivid images of father in the sitting room talking pompously about politics in the "official" language, while mother remains in the kitchen talking in dialect, cooking, and telling stories and parables which leave a lasting impression on the mind.

Finally, tracings can be found in women's stories. Much feminist knowledge is derived from seeing and listening. It is largely experiential. Anecdotes and personal stories are not only enriching personally but reveal identity beyond the divides of class, race, and locale and are the basis of feminist solidarity.

In telling what we see to one another, we reveal much about women's leadership. Once in Bangalore on an International Women's Day platform, a woman psychologist was describing the difference between a boy and girl in dealing with a hedge over which a ball had flown. She was trying to illustrate the old stereotype — men are aggressive, women inhibited. The boy jumps over the hedge to get the ball; the girl walks around the hedge. The psychologist implied that as feminists, we must teach girls to be aggressive and jump over rather than walk around.

This set me thinking how much nicer it was to walk around. Maybe the hedge would have been damaged by jumping over. How often women "walk around" an issue, not only to avoid confrontation, but to understand it better and sometimes to acknowledge that there is no perfect answer.

I once wrote about the way my late mother appeared passive, unclear, tentative, often tongue-tied in relation to "male talk" and questioning in public arenas. I argued that silence was essential for listening and that listening was necessary for learning. I argued that to be tentative was a higher level of intellectual ability than to be clear and self-assured.

THE DILEMMA OF LEADERSHIP IN FEMINIST PRACTICE

The attempt here is to identify some attributes that affect women's leadership and that cut across the usual boundaries of class, religion, race, and caste. The tracings suggest various perspectives on this. Avoiding conflict, pre-empting injustice, protecting the basic needs of the family, learning through doing, being tentative, consulting, sharing, caring, undoing

244

hierarchies, and rebuilding informality are some aspects of these qualities.

Writing about this is entering into disputed territory. Words like *sacrifice* and *altruism* do not sit well with many feminists because these qualities have been abused by society. Even though many feminists have been vocal supporters of environmental activism that promotes reducing wastefulness and consumption — which in turn requires a certain amount of sacrifice and austerity — we feel uncomfortable when these "values" of sacrifice or austerity are mentioned as a quality that women have shown through the ages. We find the praising of women's self-denial running counter to our liberty and seeking of happiness — our reading, our dancing, our visions of a just society. It reminds us of nutritional deprivation, of sequential feeding, and of all the other unjust uses of sacrifice and self-denial.

As feminists become more involved in mainstream policy negotiations, we see the blossoming of mistrust and suspicion in the womens' movement. For many feminists, the State and the men who control it — their ideas, methods, and structures — are adversaries. Increasingly, trust and dialogue are viewed as co-optation. There is little valuing of the power of persuasion. Isolation is the trend. We cannot quote anyone. We cannot refer to any visionary. We are exemplars unto ourselves.

COMING TO TERMS WITH A FEMINIST APPROACH TO LEADERSHIP

The challenge for feminists is whether we can create an environment where women's qualities of leadership — those that have emerged from our tracings — gain dominance.

Why not suggest that leaders are those who can lead communities to well-being and peaceful living? Why not value leaders who make sacrifices, who are altruistic and look after others? Unless we promote a feminist ethic of leadership — and raise our own consciousness about the quality and content of feminist leadership — there is no point in struggling to put ourselves in the political and cultural spaces that men have defined and designed.

This paper argues that the missing link in governance — whether it is governance at the level of the family/household, the village, or the global arena — is an explicitly stated feminist consciousness and its articulation of leadership.

An Indian experience of grass-roots politics, which includes an element of positive discrimination in favour of women, offers an encounter which is evocative and inspiring. The Indian attempt at deepening women's representation was ushered into the political system by an amendment to the Indian Constitution in 1993 which mandated the establishment of administrative councils at the village and municipality levels to be composed of persons elected through universal adult franchise, which was to occur every five years. The same amendment required that 33 per cent of the seats on the councils be reserved for women, and it included funds for social and economic development programmes. It also mandated that district planning committees be set up so that planning and implementation would be done at the district and subdistrict levels.

245

One million women are now in place in this system of local self-government. Research, as well as listening and seeing, reveals that women are enjoying their seats of power. These women, elected through rough-and-tumble party-based politics and campaigns, want it all. They see the medium of politics as a negotiation for power, and they are clear that they want to use this instrument to negotiate for their power and often to retaliate.

Women's entry into political participation in such large numbers — often more than the required 33 per cent — and their success in campaigning and defeating male candidates shattered the myth that women are not interested in politics, that women have no time to go to meetings and do all the other work that is required in political party processes. Women did not need to be thrust into the space — they were ready and waiting to occupy it.

These one million women are already revealing the difference between men and women in governance. To the surprise of all those who believed that rural women — especially those who entered politics without previous experience with women's organizations — lack any consciousness of gender-based solidarity, the first item on the agenda of these women has been to redress gender relations.

Most of the new women politicians are illiterate and have never been in public office. But instead of being overwhelmed by this, they are exhibiting a kind of bravado, intervening in all areas of local governance with informality and spontaneity. By ignoring protocol and valuing their power as a responsibility, these women are changing the "culture" of development management in rural areas.

There is a possibility here for women to transform the State from within. The local councils on which these women sit have administrative and financial powers to raise and expend funds and to decide priorities.

Few are happy with these changes. The men of the villages, the officials, the educated women extension workers, the whole system is revolting against the entry of these untrained "outsiders" into the serious business of development. Many elements of the Indian women's movement were also skeptical, initially, about the real value of this "revolution." They were concerned that these women were often fielded as proxies by men, which called into question their ability to represent women's interests. Feminists were also uncomfortable with the process of localization and decentralization, since there is always the accompanying possibility of deepening conservatism and regional imbalances.

But as their encounters with these elected women politicians increased, many Indian feminists learned to appreciate their vitality, awareness, and determination. This has been an important vehicle for learning within the Indian feminist movement. It has also been humbling and, at the same time, has infused a renewed sense of vitality into the women's movement. In some ways, it has provided a rallying point around which to unite: feminists are growing to understand the need to facilitate the work of the local women politicians and to safeguard them from waiting enemies.

To sustain the colour and light of this "natural" feminist leadership that is emerging in local governance in India, we still need to develop a better definition and articulation of the special qualities of women's leadership. Women in grass-roots politics in India are proving the difference every day. There is a need to grasp and convert this experience into theory, into a widespread political ideology. There is a need to nurture these shoots so that they may blossom into a global feminist ethic for global governance.

Devaki Jain has written and spoken extensively in the broad field of women, development and social change. She is the former Director of the Institute of Social Studies Trust, a research centre in Delhi, India. From 1987-1990, Jain served as a member of the South Commission headed by Julius Nyerere. Currently she holds several national and international positions as trustee or member of advisory bodies working primarily on public policy and justice.

From Cairo to Beijing

Nafis Sadik

The International Conference on Population and Development (ICPD) in 1994 was one of a series of United Nations conferences that will set the world's social development agenda for the 21st century. It signalled international acceptance of a broad approach to population issues and confirmed that no single solution will slow population growth and mitigate the effects of rapid population growth on society. The ICPD Programme of Action places population within the context of sustainable development and improvements in individual health and well-being.

The historic new thinking endorsed by the ICPD is that the advancement of women is critical for all efforts in the area of population and development. The broader policies outlined in the ICPD Programme of Action include sustainable economic development, high quality health care and—critically important—specific recommendations to educate and empower women. Its emphasis on reproductive rights and the centrality of women in development were reaffirmed by the World Summit for Social Development in Copenhagen in March 1995 and have paved the way for the Fourth World Conference on Women in Beijing in September 1995.

Women themselves have played a major role in shaping this emerging global consensus on the importance of women's empowerment. Women from all over the world came to Rio to participate in and influence the drafting of *Agenda 21*. Building upon this momentum, women and women's NGOs participated in unprecedented numbers in all the successive events, most notably in the ICPD preparatory process and the Cairo conference itself. The Women's Caucus at the ICPD in Cairo reportedly comprised more than 400 organizations from 62 countries. The consistent voice of women's groups was largely responsible for the strong language in the ICPD Programme of Action promoting women's health, rights, and opportunities.

The ICPD Programme of Action, the landmark agreement reached at the conference, goes beyond human numbers and demographic targets and explicitly places people at the centre of all population and development activities. It recognizes that without the full and equal participation of women, there can be no sustainable human development. The Programme of Action focuses on one goal: improving the quality of life of all people. It also affirms forcefully that to achieve sustainable development, population issues such as population growth, distribution, structure, composition, mortality, fertility, and migration should be considered.

The Programme of Action reaffirms the basic human right of all couples and individuals to decide freely and responsibly the number and spacing of their children and to have the information, education, and means to make these decisions. The Programme's premise is that development objectives—including early stabilization of population growth—can be achieved only by basing policies and programmes on the human rights, needs, and aspirations of individual women and men.

In affirming human-centred development, the ICPD has called for increased investments in health and education as well as efforts to build gender equality and equity. For the first time, the empowerment of women is acknowledged as a cornerstone of national and international population and development policies. The Programme of Action emphasizes that men have a key role to play in bringing about gender equality, in fostering women's full participation in development, and in improving women's reproductive health. The Programme's goals are focused on three related areas: expanded access to education, particularly for girls; reduced mortality rates; and increased access to quality reproductive health services, including family planning.

Many recommendations are aimed at strengthening and supporting families. The Programme recognizes that both married and unmarried adolescents need sex education and counselling services to protect them from unwanted pregnancies and sexually transmitted diseases and that these efforts should involve parents. Special attention is paid to internally displaced persons and international migrants and to easing the pressure that rapid urbanization puts on social infrastructure and local environments.

Comprehensive and forward-looking, the Programme of Action is grounded in a human rights framework that underscores the need to reconcile the aspirations of individuals with macro-economic development objectives. It reaffirms the lesson of experience from the past four development decades: one of the surest ways to achieve socio-economic advances is to take into account the perspective of the individual and to invest in people. The Programme of Action is notable for its action-oriented recommendations, which are directed not only at governments but also at the international community, NGOs and, indeed, all members of society.

The ICPD Programme of Action urges all countries to make reproductive health-care and family planning accessible through the primary health care system to all individuals of appropriate ages no later than 2015; the financial resources required for this effort in developing countries and those with economies in transition is estimated at US$17 billion for the year 2000, increasing to US$21.7 billion by 2015. Developing countries will continue to meet up to two-thirds of the costs themselves; approximately one third—$5.7 billion in 2000 and $7.2 billion in 2015—will have to come from external sources.

The international community is responding to the recommendations made in Cairo. A large number of activities have already been started to raise awareness of issues addressed by the Programme of Action. In addition, numerous countries are reviewing their policies and programmes to ensure that they conform with the ICPD recommendations. National committees have begun to delineate country implementation strategies.

In a number of countries, discussions are under way and institutions are being restructured in response to the Programme of Action. These include recommendations to integrate and expand maternal and child health and family planning services into more comprehensive reproductive health programmes, and to increase the role of NGOs and community groups in formulating population and development initiatives. Financial, political, institutional, and personal resources are being mobilized.

Within the United Nations system, many of the specialized agencies and organizations are formulating and implementing strategies in response to the ICPD Programme of Action. An Inter-Agency Task Force will focus on policy development and inter-agency coordination in this regard. The Population Commission of the United Nations is being revitalized as a Population and Development Commission.

The United Nations Population Fund (UNFPA) is committed to the widest possible dissemination of the Programme of Action, ensuring that the messages and goals of Cairo are amplified in both developed and developing countries and reflected and built upon in the draft Platform for Action to be adopted at the Beijing Conference. The Fund's commitment extends to governments, to other United Nations agencies and organizations, and especially, to NGOs to build broad-based support throughout society for the realization of the ICPD's goals and recommendations. The aim is to increase and focus assistance in order to improve national capacity to implement programmes in population and reproductive health. The Fund is supporting a wide variety of global, regional, and national initiatives to put the Programme of Action into operation.

It is evident that as a result of the ICPD and the other recent international conferences, major gains have been made for women and, thus, for development. But enormous challenges remain: to reinforce these successes at the Fourth World Conference for Women and especially to turn paper agreements into tangible and effective action. These challenges can be met, but it will take the concerted efforts of all parties.

The conferences in Cairo or Beijing are not isolated events but, rather, critical stepping-stones in the process of promoting gender equality. Speaking as one of the world's women, I would urge that we fashion a strategic agenda and forge the solidarity necessary to achieve it. We must recognize that the realization of our agenda requires that we find mechanisms for working effectively with decision makers—most of whom, at this time, are men.

The empowerment of women is not a zero-sum game in which women's gains are men's losses. It is the rising tide which will raise all ships.

Nafis Sadik is the Executive Director of the United Nations Population Fund (UNFPA) and holds the rank of Under-Secretary-General. On her appointment in 1987, she became the first woman to head one of the United Nations' major voluntary-funded programmes. As chief executive of UNFPA, the world's largest source of multilateral assistance to population programmes with a programme level of approximately US$300 million in 1995, Dr. Sadik directs about 800 staff members worldwide.

AFTER CAIRO:
CHALLENGES TO WOMEN'S ORGANIZATIONS

GITA SEN AND CARMEN BARROSO

A decade ago, issues of reproductive health and sexuality were considered either irrelevant or divisive by important sectors of the women's movement in many countries. Today these issues have galvanized the energies of a rapidly growing women's health movement that has become an active and respected player in policy-making at the international level. In countries as varied as Brazil and India, Nigeria and the Philippines, the same is true at the national level.

In these countries, the women's health movement usually includes grassroots organizations of all sizes and mandates as well as more formalized national networks with clearly articulated feminist agendas.[1] Reproductive health has entered the agenda of groups traditionally impervious to such concerns.[2] A recent essay by C. García-Moreno and A. Claro documents the size and dynamism of the movement: "The Women's Global Network for Reproductive Rights doubled from 800 members and newsletter subscribers in 1988 to 1,655 in 1992. Its membership spans 113 countries . . . The Latin American and Caribbean Women's Health Network, created in 1984 by approximately 30 groups and individuals, now has a contact list of 2,000 . . . The International Women's Health Coalition, working with about 30 groups in 1984, now has contact with over 2,000 individuals and groups in Southern

249

countries. About 150 organizations in Asia include women's health in their agenda."[3]

The emergence of reproductive health as a priority within the women's movement had a different history in each country. But in all of them it was the result of a complex process that involved both the internal dynamics of the women's movement and the role played by other political actors.[4] In this process, two factors were prominent: the growing awareness about the dramatic impact that poverty, powerlessness, and lack of access to information and health services were having on the lives of women; and the increasing mobilization of pronatalist and antinatalist forces, both of which may have profoundly deleterious effects on the policies and allocation of resources to programmes that affect women's access to the means of controlling their own reproduction.

The awareness within the women's movement about the devastating "conditions of reproduction" came about as a result of the growing participation of grass-roots women. These women brought the complex texture of their daily lives to a movement that in attempting to prioritize the issues that affected the majority of the world's women — who are poor — had been limited in many instances to the most obvious concerns of survival and livelihoods. The voices of grass-roots women gave life to statistics that were the staple of demographers but had not really caught feminists' attention.

Five hundred thousand deaths due to maternity-related causes every year is a worldwide catastrophe. The dimensions of this scandal reach the unspeakable when we realize that the majority of these deaths are easily preventable. An estimated 100 million married women want to avoid a pregnancy and have no access to contraceptives. Uncounted millions more who are unmarried face the same problem every time they have a sexual encounter with a man. Many of them — married and unmarried — become the casualties reflected in the maternal mortality statistics when, in desperation, they resort to illegal abortion in unsafe conditions. Those who die are only a fraction of the enormous number of women (an estimated 20 million annually) who are victims of legal and health systems that deny women the much needed services of safe abortion.

Grass-roots women also voiced their distress about the poor quality of services when they are available and reported cases of abuse and even coercion by service providers. They presented a wide range of concerns — of which the above examples are just the most common — making it possible for the women's movement to incorporate reproductive health and rights as an integral part of a broad agenda for structural change. The movement then developed its expertise in the area through the creation of self-help groups, alternative services that demonstrated the kind of attention women needed, and a rich variety of educational materials that promoted health education using participatory methodologies.

The second factor that prompted the emergence of an integrated agenda of reproductive health and women's empowerment within the women's movement in many countries was the attempt to affect the way resources allocated to population policies were being used and the need to counteract the growing mobilization of antiwomen forces. In some countries, population policies command a relatively large share of the portion of the national budgets devoted to social services. Data is very precarious, but estimates of total family planning expenditures in the Third World range from US$3.5 billion to US$7.1 billion, or from about 4 to 9 per cent of the total government health and family planning expenditures. This average figure camouflages diversity across countries. In India, for instance, family planning makes up 15 per cent and maternal and child health only 1 per cent of total health expenditures. Foreign aid may account for up to one-quarter of resources spent on family planning in the public sector. Population assistance in 1990 was estimated to be US$936 million, of which 60 per cent is provided by bilateral donors, 36 per cent by multilateral donors, and 4 per cent by private foundations and NGOs. While the absolute amounts are pitiful when compared with military expenditures, for instance, they are quite large when viewed from the perspective of women whose share of national resources are even more paltry.

Traditionally these resources have funded programmes inspired by demographic goals in which a woman's role was only that of an "acceptor" of contraceptives. When the women's movement started to criticize the inadequate attention given to contraceptive safety, the poor quality of services that ignored women's multiple reproductive health needs, the limited range of contraceptives available, the preference for sterilization, and the barriers to safe abortion, the population policy makers initially saw women activists as irritants, to be silenced and ignored as much as possible.

However, during the last decade, population policies had to face a barrage of attacks coming from the opposite direction: the conservative forces that see the provision of contraceptive services as undermining their traditional control over women's sexuality and reproduction. These attacks were more evident when the Catholic Church became very active in the International Conference on Population and Development (ICPD), held in 1994 in Cairo, with the Vatican enlisting the support of the Islamic fundamentalists. More covert manoeuvring in that direction had been going on since at least 1984, in the previous international population conference held in Mexico City. It is important to note that the conservative forces are by no means restricted to Catholics and Muslims but encompass a broad range of religious and non-religious trends. Under fire from that side, and in search of new allies, the population policy makers re-examined their assessment of the women's criticisms and found some validity in them, opening the opportunity for a new dialogue.

At the beginning, women activists were skeptical about the motives and possible consequences of these exchanges. Many feared the risk of co-optation and doubted the possibility of radical policy changes. Others welcomed the challenge and felt that even incremental changes were worth the effort, given the immense immediate needs of women worldwide. Moreover, they believed that the decision not to participate in the shaping of population policies would mean leaving the control of power in the hands of others. The tension persists, but as García-Moreno and Claro point out, "There is increasing recognition that dialogue with the establishment is a critical strategy for change."

WOMEN'S IMPACT ON THE INTERNATIONAL CONFERENCE ON POPULATION AND DEVELOPMENT[6]

The growing capacity of women's organizations and networks to act together as subjects and agents of change in international policy-making has been demonstrated recently at two major events: the first World Conference on Human Rights (WCHR), held in Vienna in 1993, and ICPD, mentioned above. At both conferences, women's organizations successfully strategized, negotiated, and lobbied governments and agencies in order to achieve major gains. Women's rights were recognized as part of universal human rights in Vienna, while the substance and language of population policies were transformed from demographic imperatives to critical aspects of women's health and rights in Cairo.

ICPD was a major political marker for the international women's movement. In the processes leading up to and at Cairo, women had to marshal arguments, evidence, and political support for a major policy transformation in the presence of two formidable sets of actors. The first was a population-policy establishment that had defined its mandate and received considerable public funds over four decades, largely on demographic grounds. Women have long been critical of the traditional population establishment, which has had control over resources and the directions of policies and programmes (including reproductive technologies) but has been wedded far too long to an approach that has subordinated women's reproductive and sexual health needs and rights to the control of numbers. For over a decade, many women's organizations and networks have also been critical of the directions of contraceptive research and development and of abuses within family planning programmes. At the same time, women's health organizations strongly affirm women's rights to plan and manage their own fertility, to have access to decent health services, and to secure livelihoods and productive resources. An ongoing challenge for women's organizations has been to work out how to be effective in their critique of existing programmes without falling into the game of those who criticize family planning programmes from an entirely different perspective — one that denies women's rights.

The second set of actors at ICPD used religion as a weapon in their mission to keep women in their "proper," subordinate place. The attempt by these forces to wrap themselves in the mantle of cultural sovereignty and anti-imperialism came to the surface during ICPD. At a conceptual level and in open public debate, it is quite easy for women to address the challenge of fundamentalists, since the representation of culture in their discourse is so unabashedly patriarchal, as became obvious during the ICPD debates. But at the national level in many countries, it is the most dangerous and difficult force for women to contend with, since it unleashes political powers and processes that operate outside the realm of rational discourse.

The above actors are still present and vocal in the policy arena. The ability of women's organizations to prevail in their transformative agenda during ICPD does not, therefore, signal a final victory. There is an effort to obtain the resources needed by the Cairo agenda for reproductive and sexual health and rights, to shape programmes and services to empower and strengthen women in different countries, and to ensure that women are present when critical decisions are being made. This is especially difficult as not everyone within the traditional population establishment fully accepts the new directions. Even more difficult are the fundamentalists with whom there is little possibility of negotiation, since they appear intent on waging an all-out war on the world's women.

ICPD has been crucial for women's organizations, not only in testing their ability and resolve *vis-à-vis* powerful external agents. Equally important was the ability of organizations and networks with widely differing histories and experiences to work together for a common agenda.

Both prior to and during ICPD there were sections of the women's movement that were reluctant to address reproductive health and rights, and some continue to question the gains of Cairo. This reluctance does not stem from a fundamental disagreement about their substantive importance. Rather, it reflects a fear that other pressing issues (the problems of macro-economic policies, especially structural adjustment, or the poor quality of primary health services, for example) will be neglected. For some groups, there is a fear of being co-opted by powerful economic and political forces and seeing the sharpness of their critique of existing systems diluted. And some fear being misunderstood and misinterpreted by their political constituencies. These fears are legitimate, and women's organizations worked to address them prior to ICPD. Women's strategies became increasingly sophisticated and careful during the two years leading up to the Cairo conference. These strategies have had four aspects.

1. To clarify positions and bottom-line non-negotiables. It is necessary to affirm reproductive health and rights in the context of equitable development strategies and to be critical of past population policies and programmes, including technologies, without throwing the baby out with the bath water. Soon after the United Nations

Conference on Environment and Development (UNCED, Rio de Janeiro, 1992), there was an early attempt by a number of women's organizations and networks to define a bottom line. This endeavour ran into criticism as being unclear about the broader development context. A clearer statement, one that affirmed common ground across a range of women's organizations while acknowledging the existence of differences, was negotiated at the "Reproductive Health and Justice: Cairo 1994" meeting, which brought together members of over 200 organizations in Rio de Janeiro in 1994.

2. To acknowledge the multiple roles of women's organizations at this juncture. North-South and ideological divisions (as well as personality clashes and ego problems) have been as present in the international women's movement as in any other social movements. Furthermore, global politics is itself in flux. Some of this is strongly positive, since spaces are opening up for new methods of citizen action, as well as ways of linking international and national politics. Women have had to learn, sometimes painfully, how to move between positions of pure opposition and positions of negotiation with those in power. How to negotiate without compromising on fundamental positions and with transparency and accountability and how to criticize with a degree of responsibility and without holier-than-thou posturing have been difficult lessons, but many women's organizations are learning them. As a result, women were able to be extraordinarily effective in their advocacy both during the third Preparatory Committee meeting for the Cairo conference (PrepCom III) and under the logistically more challenging conditions of ICPD itself.

3. To increase information flow, communication, and planning. Advocacy networks exchanged a great deal of information, sometimes faster than governments, during the process leading up to ICPD. Their ability to mobilize women's energies during the negotiations for the draft of the Programme of Action during PrepCom III was critical. Women were thereby able to influence the draft to make it stronger in terms of the right to development, reproductive health and rights, and resources. New skills of working together across national boundaries under intense pressure, of negotiating and lobbying with governments and international agencies, and of working inside delegations and in the corridors have been learned.

4. To produce carefully researched materials that could be the basis of the new paradigm. A wealth of new material has begun to be published, and new research agendas as well as new material for popular communication[7] are being defined.

These strategies, developed during the preparations for the ICPD, have had to be re-shaped to respond to the post-Cairo scenario in a flexible manner.

IMPLEMENTATION AND ACCOUNTABILITY AFTER CAIRO: INDIA AS AN ILLUSTRATION

India was one of the first countries in the world to implement an official family planning programme in the early 1950s. Since that time, the programme has expanded and gained considerable experience. After a brief and unhappy experiment with coercive sterilization in the mid-1970s, the programme changed its name to "family welfare," became more low-key in its advertising campaigns, and attempted to forge stronger links among birth control services, safe motherhood, and primary health care. Despite these attempts, the Indian programme

253

continues to be criticized by women's organizations on a number of grounds.

First, the programme operates under a vertical, bureaucratic chain of command and is funded and monitored directly by the central government, although state departments of health and family welfare do the actual implementation. This excessively top-down structure has all the problems of insensitivity to people's needs, inflexibility, and weak accountability that are the usual hallmarks of such structures.

Second, the performance of all the different levels of service providers is evaluated on the basis of their ability to meet annual contraceptive method-specific targets. Heavy emphasis on such targets, as well as the use of monetary and other incentives and disincentives, have become emblematic of the programme. Between January and March, which is the end of each financial year, there is a desperate scramble in most states to fulfill their targets. Sterilization camps occur largely during this period, and the numbers game becomes paramount. The use of incentives and disincentives within the family planning programme has also distorted the incentive structure for village-level workers (such as auxiliary nurse-midwives who are the actual providers of services) away from safe motherhood and toward contraception.

Third, as a result, the quality of services provided under the programme is poor, and services rarely meet the criteria[8] that have now come to be generally accepted as appropriate quality indicators in family planning programmes. Indeed, minimal criteria of hygiene and sanitation, as well as pain management, are often breached.

Fourth, although the Indian programme started out emphasizing condoms and vasectomy and even provided diaphragms in its early years, female sterilization now accounts for over 90 per cent of the services provided. This excessive emphasis on an irreversible method makes service provision a one-time affair. It becomes only too easy for service providers to ignore women's health needs, including prior check-ups and follow-up care, let alone broader reproductive and general health needs. Consequently, women have few options and little ability to plan their reproductive lives healthfully and effectively.

Fifth, women's organizations in India have been especially concerned about the conditions under which some of the newer hormonal contraceptives are being tested and introduced into the country. Formally the system of clinical testing and approval is an elaborate one, but many feel that it lacks both transparency and accountability in practice. Women's health activists are also very concerned about the potential long-term effects of hormonal contraceptives on Indian women, the majority of whom are under- and malnourished and suffer from iron-deficiency anemia, as well as a high incidence of reproductive tract infections.

Although abortion laws have been liberalized since the early 1970s, the actual services provided by the public system are poor in both quality and coverage. Most Indian women seeking abortions are married and have two or more living children but are forced to take recourse to illegal, expensive, and unsafe services.

Along with some health organizations, social scientists, and demographers in India, women's organizations have been critical of the government's family planning programme for at least two decades. Although some gains have been made (largely through the courts), these criticisms have not been able to effect any significant changes in the programme's functioning. Indeed, in recent years it has appeared to many that the bureaucracy has become increasingly impervious to criticism. In the year prior to ICPD, a number of women's organizations decided to work together to attempt to reopen the dialogue. Their purpose was to use the opportunities provided by a global conference to make an impact on the national programme. To do this, it was necessary to start a process of dialogue before the conference and to continue it during the conference, so as to be in a position to raise issues of implementation and accountability in the period after.

Accordingly, a series of meetings were held before ICPD[9] in which women's organizations began to agree on common positions and to show the government that they had both knowledge of and access to key actors in the international arena. The government in turn responded by continuing the process of information-sharing and discussion during the conference itself. (The senior Indian civil servant at the conference met with almost 70 NGO representatives in daily briefing sessions.) It also drew upon the advice of NGO representatives at pivotal moments during the official ICPD debates. Further, it was agreed that the dialogue would continue after the conference.

In the months following Cairo, many organizations at multiple levels have been exploring methods of ensuring implementation. Some of the organizations that have been engaged in this process have come together to form a network, HealthWatch, one of whose principal objectives is to ensure implementation of the ICPD programme. HealthWatch is now in the process of expanding its membership beyond the initiators. At this stage, it has defined its priorities as

- the replacement of method-specific contraceptive targets, incentives, and disincentives in the family planning programme by a system of monitoring and performance evaluation that would be more consonant with the ICPD programme of action;
- expansion of services to better meet people's reproductive health needs and improve service quality;
- increasing resource allocation for primary health care; and
- regular dialogue among NGOs and between NGOs and government.

Clearly, the post-ICPD process of implementation and accountability has a long way to go in India. The way forward will depend on the willingness of government to live up to its international agreements; the tenacity, patience, and skill of the organizations of civil society; and the support of key international agencies. Some positive pointers can be seen. Agencies such as the United Nations Population Fund appear to be seriously reorienting their approaches and are far more open to NGOs than they have been in the past, both at the international and at the country level. Partly as a result of all the NGO efforts, state governments in the country have recently been mandated for the first time to experiment without targets in one or two districts in each state. How successful this experiment will be will depend on the extent to which network members and other NGOs are able to work with state governments to replace the target-based system with a more comprehensive, need-sensitive, and high-quality programme.

255

CHANGES FOR THE FUTURE

The process of engagement between states and civil society that ICPD represents has created a number of challenges for women's organizations. These include both immediate needs related to holding governments and agencies accountable for implementing the Cairo agenda and ongoing strategies to strengthen the capacity of the women's movement to engage in the next phase.

The most important immediate challenge is to mobilize resources and gain political clout to affect policies at national and international levels without losing a critical stance. To do this well, women's organizations will have to further develop their capacity to construct and articulate policies and programmes that will support women's health and rights. Many organizations already have considerable ability to do this at both national and international levels; their knowledge and experience, particularly in empowering women to demand and access health services and in providing more holistic health care, are invaluable and need to be brought centre stage. This is the necessary antidote to temptations within the population establishment to go back to business as usual under the new rubric of reproductive health or to exclude women's organizations, the main stake-holders of the Cairo agenda, from the implementation stage of the policy debate.

The longer-term, more strategic challenge for women's organizations is to come to terms with access to power at the policy level. After two decades of experience criticizing existing political, economic, legal, and cultural systems and the practices of those who wield power within those systems, women themselves are now poised to access power. Access to power for those who have previously been powerless can be both heady and intimidating. For the women's movement, the diversity and heterogeneity that are the source of its strength and richness also add to the complexity of this challenge. Three types of activities are essential for the movement to build on its achievements to date. The first is to strengthen the movement by establishing a constructive dialogue within its diverse constituencies, building bridges across different cultures and classes and responding more meaningfully to the concerns of the younger generation. The second is to develop a conceptual framework that offers a comprehensive critique of current culture and macro-economic trends and policies and provides an inspiring and realistic vision of an equitable society free from poverty, violence, and gender discrimination. The third is to permeate different levels of civil society in order to achieve a transformation of values by establishing a presence in the media and in education systems.

Gita Sen is Professor of Economics at the Indian Institute of Management, Bangalore, and an Adjunct Professor of Development Economics at the Harvard Centre for Population and Development Studies. A leading researcher on women in development, Dr. Sen is pursuing policy research on women, development, health and population, and the environment. She is a founding member of DAWN (Development Alternatives with Women for a New Era).

Carmen Barroso is the Director of the Population Programme of the John D. and Catherine T. MacArthur Foundation. She has published numerous books and articles, mostly in Brazil where she taught in the Sociology Department of the University of São Paulo and did research at the Carlos Chagas Foundation. She has been active in the women's movement in Brazil and was one of the founding members of DAWN.

Notes

1. Examples of national networks are the Brazilian Feminist Network on Health and Reproductive Rights, created in 1991, which incorporates more than 50 regional groups and has a representative on the National Health Council, a board advising the president of the country; and the Women's Health Organization of Nigeria, a group of NGOs aimed at strengthening the capacity of Nigerians, particularly women's groups at the grass-roots level, to respond collectively to their identified health needs.

2. For instance, the first Latin American and Caribbean conference on rural women, scheduled for late 1995 in northeastern Brazil (one of the poorest regions of the world), has planned sessions on self-help and sexuality.

3. C. García-Moreno and A. Claro. "Challenges from the Women's Health Movement: Women's Rights versus Population Control," in G. Sen, A. Germain, and L. Chen (eds.), *Population Policies Reconsidered: Health, Empowerment, and Rights*. Cambridge, MA: Harvard University Press, 1994, pp. 47–61.

4. For detailed accounts of the interplay between feminists, the left, the Catholic Church and the State in Brazil, see C. Barroso, "The Women's Movement, the State and Health Policies in Brazil," in G. L. Nijeholt (ed.), *Towards Women's Strategies for the 1990's: Challenging Government and the State*. The Hague: Macmillan and Institute of Social Studies, The Hague, 1991, pp. 51–70. See also J. Pitanguy, "Feminist Politics and Reproductive Rights: The Case of Brazil," in G. Sen and R. C. Snow (eds.), *Power and Decision: The Social Control of Reproduction*. Cambridge, MA: Harvard University Press, 1994.

5. J. Zeitlin, R. Govindaraj, and L. Chen. "Financing Reproductive and Sexual Health Services" in G. Sen, A. Germain, and L. Chen (eds.), *Population Policies Reconsidered: Health, Empowerment, and Rights*. Cambridge, MA: Harvard University Press, 1994, pp. 235–48.

6. This section draws upon G. Sen, "The World Program of Action, A New Paradigm for Population Policy." *Environment* 37 (1) (Jan/Feb 1994), pp. 10–15, 34–37.

7. An example is the summary of the DAWN platform document (Correa, 1994) which is already available in English, French, Spanish, Portuguese, and Arabic.

8. J. Bruce. "Fundamental Elements of the Quality of Care: A Simple Framework." *Studies in Family Planning* 21 (2) (1990), pp. 61–91.

9. UNFPA and the Ford Foundation jointly supported a number of these consultations.

SIGNPOSTS ON THE ROAD TO BEIJING

ROSISKA DARCY DE OLIVEIRA

The banality of the day-to-day does nothing to disguise the distinctive future of a generation. It took us a thousand years to recognize this time of ours, the moment of our peculiar destiny at the close of the century (worse still, or better, the close of the millennium). This is our lot and our luck: it is we who are to prepare the New Year's Eve festivities for the year 2000, we who live this mix of anguish at the past, perplexity at the present, and obstinate infatuation with the future.

The 1992 Earth Summit in Rio de Janeiro — the UN Conference on Environment and Development (UNCED) — was a conference of planetary afflictions. That is how the millennium started to end, on the shores of Guanabara Bay, and on its sands came the realization of an immense fiasco, the failure not just of a regime, nor of any society in particular, but of a whole project of civilization. A failure that can be seen in global imbalances, in the disruption of the seasons, in the dust that pollutes the wind, in the desolation of amputated forests and in the drifting of the Poles. We suffer it as disharmony among peoples, as the isolation of forgotten continents, the humiliation of human beings treated as expendable, in the ruthlessness of the Market, the silence of Meaning. It is tangible as life thrown off course, the forced sterilization of women's wombs, the delirium of Science, the exile of Ethics.

As the 20th century draws to a close, we face the disturbing realization that, to date, thinking has been a man's job. So far, it is only one of the sexes that has thought out the world and culture on behalf of men and women. Now, coming from the whole world over, slogging

257

their way across male territory, women have begun to set foot in the forbidden halls of Knowledge and Power, bringing creative disorder into the Order of Failure. In opposition to the order that has failed, women are raising the Order of Life.

WOMEN ORGANIZING GLOBALLY FOR A NEW ACTION AGENDA

As we move toward the Fourth World Conference on Women (WCW) in Beijing in September 1995, women have an appointment with their history and inspiration as a global movement striving for democracy and for the recognition of the right of half of humankind to emerge from their centuries-old political exclusion. Women's voices and concerns have gained unprecedented visibility in UN global conferences as women have created international linkages and networks to promote their own action agenda.

Women's Rights Are Human Rights

The 1993 World Conference on Human Rights (WCHR) in Vienna confronted women with a twofold challenge: to ensure, at last, their full inclusion in humankind through the recognition of their inalienable rights and to exercise their duty toward the whole of humankind through their refusal to condone an inequitable and unethical world order which exiles one out of three human beings from freedom and human dignity.

These two challenges gave rise to a new and inescapable task for women. The elimination of all forms of discrimination against women inaugurates for them the possibility of a radical critique of our present mode of civilization, putting an end to the use of violence to rule relationships among persons and nations.

Civilization or barbarism: humankind stands today at this crossroads. The full safeguard of women's rights is evidently one of the basic preconditions of democracy. The refusal of apartheid at the global scale and the reshaping of the world order to overcome the exclusion and expendability of the poor are the preconditions of a truly common future for all. For us women, our rights are also our duties and responsibilities.

On the eve of the 21st century, the eruption of the voice of women is a vital contribution to the discourse and praxis of human rights. It questions and reshapes the prevailing world view, based on the negation of the Other, of all others. Women's aspiration is not for inclusion in a sexually undifferentiated society. Women's task and responsibility is to give full expression to their own history, culture, and life experience, thus enabling humankind to regain its constituent and irrepressible richness.

The new awareness of women's rights will affect all fundamental political, economic, social, cultural, and civil rights. These basic changes in human rights will in turn have far-reaching effects on democracy and development. Democracy will no longer be able to conceal the existence of women and men behind abstract universal principles, nor will development be able to disregard in its planning, implementation, and evaluation women's needs, values, and inputs.

In today's world, the safeguarding of human rights is the permanent responsibility not only of States and international institutions but, more than ever before, of the citizens of the Earth. Only people's awareness and involvement, both at the local and the global level, can really ensure the strength of this emerging human consensus which underlies the cause of human rights. Following the compass of ethical values and daily practices which enabled them to ensure the permanence of love and the quest for happiness as the matrix of human life, women are called upon today to invent, together with men, a new and more compassionate common future for humankind.

Women's Influence on the Population Debate

To include women in humankind and, therefore, in human rights: this was the cornerstone of the debates at the WCHR. The recognition of women's reproductive rights, women's bodies as the battleground between humanists and fundamentalists: these are our memories of Cairo.

The International Conference on Population and Development (ICPD, 1994) in Cairo represented yet another major turning point. It took 20 years for the international community to realize that the question of global population transcended the narrow confines of demography. Over and above the numbers — how many are we, how many shall we be — there is a whole universe of crucial moments and events of human experience.

The demand that women defended forcefully in Cairo is that human development policies be aimed at improving people's quality of life. Let us do what is ethical and needed, and as a result, the population growth rate will decelerate. Policies and programmes aimed at fulfilling basic social needs — such as basic education, preventing deaths from lack of nutrition and health services and ensuring the full exercise of reproductive rights — are preconditions for a standard of quality of life that in turn will be a factor in stabilizing the world's population.

I remember the distressing fact that throughout the preparatory process leading up to Cairo, it was as if the poor themselves, wherever they were, North or South, had become a problem, if not a threat. They were the ones to blame for overpopulation, environmental pollution, illegal immigration, narcotics trafficking, and religious fanaticism. Their migration to the rich neighbourhoods of the world had to be prevented. Their economy was to be structurally adjusted and monitored to ensure that they did not mismanage resources and did pay their debts. Even their sexuality was considered too exuberant and, as such, a threat to the fragile limits of the Earth.

Our global village has an expanding slum area. And many of those who live in the world's affluent neighbourhoods are either indifferent to or afraid of the poor. Poverty is certainly not a new phenomenon, but the discardability of human beings is something unprecedented. Never before has the idea been so cynically accepted that the solution to poverty is to reduce the numbers of the poor rather than eliminating poverty itself. Development means satisfying the basic needs and securing the conditions of a fully human life for all. Development must be thought of in terms of population and not population in terms of development.

> *"At Nairobi women outlined a comprehensive plan of Forward Looking Strategies for the Advancement of Women. At Rio women were recognized as managers of natural resources and the moving force for sustainable development. At Vienna women's rights were acknowledged as universal, inalienable and indivisible human rights. At Cairo women's health, empowerment and reproductive rights were placed at the centre of population-related development policies. At Copenhagen the political, economic and social empowerment of women were recognized as key to eradicating poverty, unemployment and social disintegration. But too many of these promises remain unfulfilled."*
>
> *— From "A Pledge to Gender Justice" (1995), developed by a working group of NGOs at the third Preparatory Committee meeting for the Fourth World Conference on Women and now endorsed by over 100 organizations worldwide.*

Women's Insistence on Poverty Elimination

The fight against global poverty and social apartheid is not an economic problem; it is a non-negotiable ethical and moral imperative. The constant restatement of this commitment, without, however, any tangible results being achieved, is giving rise to a very perverse twist: the shame one feels by insisting on something which is increasingly perceived as hollow rhetoric. Instead of fighting poverty, we now talk about poverty alleviation, as if it were a kind of pain whose causes cannot be cured but only alleviated.

Fortunately, some voices remain faithful to this most basic human commitment and keep calling for the elimination of global poverty. In Copenhagen, Ambassador Juan Somov_a of Chile, Chairperson of the Preparatory Committee of the 1995 World Summit on Social Development (WSSD), made an eloquent plea reaffirming that the elimination of poverty was an objective within the reach of the present resources of humankind and as necessary as had been the abolition of slavery.

Women's struggle to defend their own rights would be meaningless without their unwavering commitment to safeguard the freedom and dignity of the poor. I choose here to use deliberately the word *poor*. In the entire history of Western culture, the poor have been the ones to whom all the members of a given community were expected to show mercy, compassion, solidarity. These age-old values are at risk today. If they perish, it is our civilization which will fall into barbarism. On the other hand, the restoration of these permanent values represents a new challenge: how to transcend the barrier of national frontiers in order to envision democracy and well-being as the heritage of all citizens of the planet.

ON THE ROAD TO BEIJING

Women's voices have moved on from the modest ambition of being heard on public matters to the far more subversive endeavour of plotting a different course for Civilization. As we approach the WCW, the achievements of Vienna and of Cairo are arriving in Beijing "in brackets." The bracket is the signpost of what is still in doubt, of how hard and delicate is women's negotiating position. The world is not yet used to our existence and, even less, our freedom to participate and influence. And yet women will truly be peacemakers only when they have smoothed conflicts among men as well as erased the millennial violence that has struck women themselves.

It is both women's existence and women's freedom which has to be acknowledged. Human destiny hinges on our capacity to grasp the magnitude of our contribution to the future and the risk inherent in any renunciation. We will arrive in Beijing not as an army, driven by warrior-like metaphors. Rather, we will come by a variety of pathways, guided by the labyrinths of trial and error, guided by an ever-winding Ariadne thread.

Along this road we have been shedding our quarrels and bickerings, all that divides and drive us apart. In a number of years, hopefully, we will be able to look back at our disputes in the same way as forgotten passions are remembered. What will remain is the remembrance of a common adventure, in which we will all have played an active role.

Seen from too close, revolutions may look prosaic. Seen from my office in Brasilia, where I preside over the Brazilian National Council on Women, they seem far-fetched and outlandish. All seems contingent, banal . . . seems but isn't. We are living through a change of seismic proportions. Women are on the move all over the world to proclaim that they are alive and that the world will not be the same as before.

Rosiska Darcy de Oliveira is a Brazilian writer and coordinator of the International Women's Task Force/Terra Femina. She serves as President of Brazil's National Council on Women.

WOMEN AND HUMAN SETTLEMENTS DEVELOPMENT

WALLY N'DOW

The development and maintenance of human settlements, our human habitat, is an essential part of the struggle for equality, development and peace. Women within the subsistence economy in both urban and rural contexts — especially in the developing countries of the world but increasingly so also in the developed countries — struggle daily to eke out an existence for their families. The lack of humanly adequate housing and infrastructure (especially safe water, adequate sewerage, schools, health-care and child-care facilities, economically feasible and timely transport, and street illumination) makes women's roles more burdensome and often dangerous. Housing is a *basic human right* that is, however, not adequately recognized or enforced.

In the last two decades, women have suffered even more because of the prevailing model of economic growth. They have new leadership roles in both rural and urban human settlements, but these roles are not recognized and are often openly opposed by private industry and governments.

Women are not equitably involved in deciding on the design of the home, the choice of the area to live in, the planning and development of the neighbourhood, or even more important, the planning, development, and maintenance of our villages, towns, and cities. This makes their struggle even more difficult.

These are the main priorities as stated by women themselves — in women's groups, NGOs, and community-based organizations (CBOs) as well as women and men in government in the developing regions of Africa, Asia, Latin America, and the Caribbean:

- to review the whole model of economic development, seeing economic growth in relation to environmental sustainability and the sustenance of human life;
- to promote equal access to and control of land and property for women and men, including inheritance rights;
- to offer equal access to credit for housing, infrastructure, and income-generating activities for women and men;
- to promote specific training and job development for women in both formal construction skills and managerial and advocacy skills;
- to undertake capacity-building in gender awareness through the training of both women and men trainers capable of communicating a clear gender perspective, in order to build up "gender competence" among government officials, CBOs, and NGOs directly involved in human settlements development;
- to continue to research and develop concrete "gender-sensitive tools" for use among human settlements development practitioners; and
- to build and strengthen networks to make women and women's groups more active and more visible within the human settlements development process.

Looking toward Beijing and the Fourth World Conference on Women (WCW), we dream of the creation of countries, cities, towns, and villages where all of us — women, men, girls, and boys, conscious of our differences and respecting those differences, can feel part of, responsible for, and participants in the building of our common future. The development and maintenance of the human habitat will not be possible without the participation of all of us.

It is not enough to have services, houses, and so on; we must also be the builders of our own destinies and the destinies of our communities, cities, and countries. Women must be designers of their own future — a future without constraints and without domination.

These common goals can be achieved with some of the following essential ingredients: a government which is *of, for,* and *by* the citizens, both women and men; an active, conscious, vibrant civil society of women and men; committed communities composed of women and men; homes where all members, women and men, boys and girls, have equal opportunities and equal responsibilities.

Currently we are at a crisis point with the urban explosion — a crisis that must be addressed as we all move into an existence of global urbanization in the next millennium — which is a major, though not yet insurmountable, deterrent to our achievement of the aforementioned goals. As the rural poor, predominantly women and children, flood into the megacities at the end of the century — seeking often nonexistent food, shelter, jobs, and opportunities — they become, along with the youth and the elderly, the new urban poor. Going hand in hand with the urbanization of poverty is the great strain — almost to the breaking point — on home and family, further exacerbated by the feminization of poverty. More and more, we see that it is the women who suffer the most and who have the worst shelter. And that is true for cities in both developing and industrialized countries. It is to raise the dominant issues of women and human settlements development that the United Nations Centre for Human Settlements (UNCHS) is organizing Habitat II, the second global conference on human settlements, to be held in 1996. The UNCHS Women in Human Settlements Development Programme is also contributing to the WCW in Beijing in 1995.

Our challenge, at both these conferences and beyond, is to enfranchise the dispossessed, who so often are women and the children dependent on them. It is to create homes and communities with citizen participation by all. The world's cities should be revitalized and restored, with women playing a key role in this reconstruction. We must begin by supplying a holistic human environment for all, the vital basis from which to surmount all other ills plaguing our urban areas. Housing must be recognized as a human right, a fundamental right for all.

Wally N'Dow *was named the Secretary-General of HABITAT II (the United Nations Conference on Human Settlements to be held in Turkey in June 1996) in February 1994, a few weeks after his appointment as Assistant Secretary-General of the UN Centre for Human Settlements in Nairobi, Kenya. Dr. N'Dow served as UNDP Resident Representative to the Central African Republic and the United Republic of Tanzania.*

This article draws upon the author's "Women and Human Settlements Development," UNCHS *Habitat News* 16 (2), August 1994.

FIVE YEARS AFTER BEIJING: TOWARDS A JUST AND ENABLING GLOBAL ECONOMY

WENDY HARCOURT

Let us imagine that we are now in 2000, five years after the historic UN Fourth World Conference on Women in Beijing, where all the world's governments met together on equal terms with women representing civil society and signed a binding charter fully endorsing justice and equity for all people regardless of gender, economic class, race, religion, and caste. And on their return home, all the chauvinists (men and women) in the governments and the businesses resigned and opened up the way for women and men committed to social justice to put into practice all the promises in the document.

What would our world look like if gender relations were not merely an interesting footnote to our understanding of history and societies, but were as central to how a society operates as the power battles betweeen classes and nations? What would happen to our society and culture if women were not subordinated to men and if the needs of women and nature were not excluded from economic development?

THE OLD WORLD ORDER

Let me take you through a fantasy of an ideal, gender-balanced, socially and economically just world. The first premise of this new world would be that we should recognize our differences. Let us imagine how this world would seem from the point of view of six different actors: Gillian, who in September 1995 was a committed peace activist in Australia, working for a small women's NGO campaigning to end nuclear testing in the Pacific; Lourdes, a government-employed family planning doctor who was working in Mexico City with sex workers; Anita, a Sri Lankan domestic worker who was employed by a rich Saudi Arabian family; Leo, a young Kenyan who was living on the streets with other homeless and parentless children in Nairobi; Henry, a successful executive who ran a profitable London-based firm which invested in rubber plantations in Latin America; and Manfred, a retired teacher in Germany who lived in a hospice for the aged.

Let us look at their key economic, environment, and gender issues in the years prior to September 1995.

Gillian (the committed peace activist) was deeply concerned with the local environment. She cycled to work, recycled waste, and tried to conserve energy use in her household and office. She had been involved in a number of international campaigns primarily around women's rights in Pacific islands where there had been nuclear testing and where numerous

263

women suffered from reproductive diseases. She wrote for community newspapers distributed throughout Asia and the Pacific and led public education campaigns to lobby governments to stop nuclear testing and to provide more appropriate medical care for these women. She also worked in the local shelter for battered women and did counselling for unemployed migrant women. In between she cared for her family: her partner, who taught at the university, her two children and her infirm mother who had been widowed. She had a major problem juggling her political interests, organizing child care, keeping the household running smoothly, serving the needs of the women at the shelter and the immigrant community, and trying to find money to keep the education campaign going while finding the governments unresponsive. She felt committed but tired and unsure of how all these efforts were improving the lives of the people around her, saving the environment or the world.

Lourdes (the family planning doctor in Mexico) came from a small village and had been the only one in her village to go to university. She had trained in Mexico City as a gynaecologist. She was concerned with the alarming increase of HIV-AIDS among sex workers and lack of education on sexually transmitted diseases among these women — many of whom were very vulnerable migrant workers who had returned to prostitution to survive. Her problem was that having trained locally, she was not given the decision-making jobs (they went to overseas-trained experts or those working in international agencies), and she found that the funds were assigned to research on prevention among men being serviced by the prostitutes, and not to education for these women nor to research on female reproductive diseases triggered by HIV-AIDS. Whenever she tried to raise gender-related issues, she found a strong bureaucratic resistance, and the other doctors were not interested in working in her community development programme when she tried to involve the sex workers. Her husband, who was also a doctor, was not supportive because he felt that she could be making more money in a private practice. The pollution in Mexico City meant that Lourdes often felt ill, especially working long hours in a small, badly staffed office. Under the circumstances she had decided not to have children, because she saw no possibility of child care and her husband expected her to take on all domestic responsibilities.

Anita, (the Sri Lankan domestic worker in Saudia Arabia) had attended school until she was 12 but had to help her mother with her younger brothers and sisters and so had left school. When her father lost his job when she was 16, her family had decided that she should train as a domestic worker and were very pleased that she had found a place in Saudi Arabia through an agency. She had been taught at a three week course run by the local government how to iron, work an electric stove and a vacuum (all new technologies to her), and then she had been put on a plane with 20 other young Sri Lankans and sent to Saudi Arabia. At the airport she was met by her employer, who took her passport, and she began immediately a heavy schedule of domestic work with three hours off every week, time spent in her room as it was not safe to go outside alone. She learned to communicate in English to the family, but they spoke Arabic among themselves and she had no contact with anyone else. Every year she came home with duty-free goods and money for her family, who relied on her income to pay the newly reintroduced school fees and health expenses for her father. She wondered if she would ever marry, as at 22 she was getting too old. Each time she went back, the village had changed. Roads had been cut into the forest; her brothers too had left for Colombo and never visited. With her father ill, her mother had to spend a lot of time trying to sell the spices she grew in the garden while trying to keep the house in good repair. Anita would have liked to go to work in London or return home, help her mother, and find a husband.

Leo (the Kenyan street child) was located in Nairobi, with no home and no parents. At 11 years old he had become very adept at picking which people were best to ask for coins, and he knew which areas were the best to scrounge for food. He slept where he ended up at night and stayed clear of anybody who looked important and asked him questions. He was unsure where his parents originated, but he knew that it was outside Nairobi. He and his little brother sometimes joined up with other boys their age when it was cold so that they could sleep together. He did not trust the church people but sometimes went there for the night and for soup. He did not like to be bullied by the older boys but was becoming by now strong enough to fight back. He was sometimes given a piece of clothing by a market stall owner when he was lucky (or he could pinch it). He was not often hungry but his little brother was becoming thinner every day.

Henry (the business executive) lived an eventful life flying to his export outlets in Latin America three or four times a year, where he was entertained by men in government and the business community. He was a member of an exclusive London club where he could return such hospitality and confirm the deal; he found his Oxbridge connections very useful in that regard and the Tory government most encouraging of his business. His bank account was growing, and he had a good stockbroker. His personal flair for finding new ventures in the many market openings in the South was paying off well. He hoped to be buying a little country property soon. He had a loyal office and an excellent secretary. Though he was divorced, he saw his son once a month for a film and a meal at McDonald's (if he was not travelling). He enjoyed weekend trips to the country with his British girlfriend, and he found that his Spanish had improved considerably through pillow talk with the women discreetly introduced to him on his travels by his business contacts. Once or twice he had been annoyed by thefts in his house, and the ecological extremists irritated him with their talk about the Amazon forests, as did the growing numbers of beggars in the underground (why didn't they find themselves decent jobs?). His wife's lawyers tended to harp on about alimony, and he regretted the long scratch down one side of his Mercedes, which happened when he thoughtlessly left it in a "bad" area. In general, though, he had no complaints.

> *"It is relatively easy to pay lip service to the importance of women's empowerment during conferences and seminars; it is less simple to ensure that it takes place on the ground and, equally importantly, to accept the consequences of enabling the development of an enlightened and empowered citizenry."*
>
> — *Ammu Joseph in Dawn Informs, 1/95.*

Manfred (the retired teacher from Germany) had devoted all his adult life to teaching biology and history at a secondary school in rural Germany. He had lived through two world wars, seen the German reunification, and was a keen peace activist. He had not married but was very fond of his nieces and nephews and still liked to hear news of his pupils. After retirement, he had kept a careful garden and cottage, but he became too old and was forced to leave and to move into an old-age hospice. Sometimes one or two of his students or nieces would visit him, but he was lonely with the company of old people who seemed to be waiting for the end, and none of whom shared his interests in the peace movement or gardening. He felt that he had nothing to complain about and the administrators of the hospice were nice, but his pension did not allow him to rent much more than a small room and shared bathroom with a television for company.

So, in my fantasy, we have Gillian in Australia, Lourdes in Mexico, Anita in Saudia Arabia, Leo in Kenya, Henry in Britain, and Manfred in Germany, suddenly finding that after September 1995, women's voices and views on the health of our planet have been heard.

Governments were now to note the prevalence of global poverty, question and disregard the blind pursuit of economic growth at the cost of human disruption and environmental degradation, aim to end increasing quality-of-life disparities, racism, and military conflict. And in an immediate transformation of values, they were to decide to enable women and men committed to a healthy environment, peace, basic human rights, participatory democracy, self-determination of peoples, and the protection of all species to put into practice a global economy which would protect the earth for future generations.

A GLOBAL ECONOMY TO ENABLE AND CONSERVE

In 2000 we have, instead of a growth-oriented "free market" system, a people-centred economics which ensures that a nation's wealth is managed and distributed for the benefit of people in relation to long-term global and human ecological security. Economics is now understood as part of a complex set of social, ecological, and cultural interplays which have a direct impact on human and natural resources. The concept of development now embraces quality-of-life issues and determines policies which actually do rid us of environmental degradation and poverty and encourage political participation of people everywhere.

The global economy does not focus on profit, rather on balancing the needs of peoples, nations, and nature. Policies are determined by local communities which take into account women's experience, perspectives, and approaches based on their understanding of the social, ecological, and ethical dimensions of real life processes. Gender bias has been removed. Instead of constantly defining women in relation to men and in terms of dual division of public/private, work/home, rational/emotional, and mind/body, which privilege men's productive activity over women's work and make women's productive activity and contribution to the economy and environmental care invisible, an enabling and conserving economy based on holistic principles is in its place.

Building self-reliance and the empowerment of people through a wider distribution of unearned income, greater access to the physical means of production, and more home-based work have become the principles of development. The assumption that self-interest is the driving force of the economy has been replaced by people being rewarded for intrinsically useful, interesting community-based work. The informal and household sectors are recognized as major economic activities which can meet people's economic needs as global systems are designed to build up from the local to the global. Women's productive and reproductive activities are valued, and the houseworker is seen, along with other professions, as a producer, investor, and worker. There are no distinctions between the formal and the informal economy, and men take their share of responsibility and work with child care and domestic arrangements.

The principle of investment is no longer based on economic growth but on enabling the productive capacities of people. Food production, household provisions, health, education, and appropriate technology are key aims of economic investment. Instead of a dependence of the South on the North, the world economy is determined by local community needs for technological innovations, food imports, financial transfers, and the conservation of natural resources. The global economy is characterized by a cooperative self-reliance where the productive associations between people are based on local food security, decentralized and efficient energy production, access to resources, healthier living conditions and environments, and a holistic world view which respects differences. The dismantling of the military, the cessation of all polluting and nuclear industries, the restructuring of the United Nations, the inclusion of women in all decision-making bodies, the democratization of all institutions and communications channels have released enough funds and facilities to allow for new education schemes, health care, communal domestic arrangements, fair trading, cultural exchanges, and leisure time for all world communities organized in locally autonomous, self-reliant, and democratically run units.

So let us return to the citizens of the new world: Gillian, Lourdes, Anita, Leo, Henry, and Manfred. What does life look like for them in the new global economy in the year 2000?

THE POST-1995 WORLD

Gillian is still living in Australia with her family, but she has free child care and a communal system for cooking, and the new schools have been relocated close by so that she no longer has a problem with ferrying her children to and fro. Her mother goes to the day centre around the corner. The refuge centre has been closed as the women are now relocated in large houses which have been vacated by former politicians. Gillian is now involved in training these women and the migrants in skills management and attending language and cultural exchange classes to learn more about Pacific livelihood systems. Her former NGO is now in the process of transferring high-quality medical equipment and technology to women in the Pacific, who are selecting education or employment training courses they would like to attend. They are producing a video of their previous lives for the historical record and for use in the new adult education centres. The funds released from the end of nuclear testing and military expenditure are now being given to NGOs that are part of the global project to redistribute money to all people living in once-affected areas and to design courses to rehabilitate the old power brokers. The money is now being used to generate jobs of people's choice and to redesign the production processes to remove the problem of waste. Gillian's partner now only teaches a few hours a week at the local centre — lessons which he puts on E-mail for public use — and spends the rest of the time at home or in the local trading centre where he and other members of the community are designing their ideas for a local trading system. While organizing community input into the new local-global trade, governments are now promoting an education campaign to explain exactly where any product comes from, how it has been manufactured, and who has profited from it to enable people to choose more carefully. Gillian and her partner have joined this project (as can anyone) and send in information on their public modem. Her children are now learning Pijinjara and Maori and tease her about her poor knowledge of koorie culture.

Lourdes has joined many workers in the move from Mexico City to rural areas in the regional decentralization programme. She has returned to her village, where she has been paid the standard international rates to run the education exchange program where village women teach her about the local environment and she explains to them about reproductive rights. Due to the new communications systems paid for by the funds released from the closure of all military bases, she is now also able to do research on different medical conditions of women by using the satellite computer link-up with medical practitioners and researchers all over the world. Many of the former sex workers have also chosen to move back to their villages through the decentralization programme. They were given a fixed income from the government to enable them to retrain in the employment or education area they are interested in (including the arts and entertainment industry). Those who have HIV-AIDS are now being counselled and encouraged to choose activities which will improve their quality of life. The locally based economy is being supplemented by goods once only available in the West, which can be ordered, but no one is required to work more than a few hours each day to allow time for the education exchange programmes. The dismantling of the slums of Mexico City is a major

267

project, and all Mexicans are encouraged to send in their ideas about which type of recreation centres should be installed, and former military researchers are looking at ways to solve the environmental degradation in the area. Now that Lourdes is out of the city environs and is not required to commute or work long hours under stressful conditions, she is considering having a child, especially as her husband has more time for domestic activities.

Anita has returned to Sri Lanka and is studying English so that she can qualify for a study trip to Britain in the new cultural exchange programme for students. Her Arab family has been required to pay her back wages equivalent to 30 per cent of their income, which, as with all unpaid and unrecognized house workers, was placed in a bank account in Anita's name shortly after September 1995. With free medical care and education now available and community eating houses, her family no longer relies on Anita's wages. Her mother is now running the local trade centre and her spices are doing well on the national market, which has enabled them to purchase one of the houses left by the expatriate businessmen no longer able to operate in Sri Lanka. Her father is at a good clinic in Colombo, and his health is improving. Anita's brothers visit him regularly and ensure that their mother is kept informed of improvements in his health. The reforestation programme and habitat redesign of their village is now under way, and the whole family is considering how they would prefer their local habitat to look when the new communications centre, school, and hospital are finished. Anita is no longer sure whether she wishes to be married but will consider the question again after her study trip.

Leo is now in school in Nairobi, and the new local administration has made it a priority to trace his origins and see which lands he could eventually return to if he wishes. He and his brother are now part of a large urban community living in the former military quarters, where all the children are being educated or trained for a community job. They have elected to watch television and films not only for fun but also to understand about other areas in Kenya and the rest of the world. They work in a community garden where they are learning about all the different local foods they could grow. Leo, it turns out, is quite good at mechanical things and so is part of the group in charge of the community car pool. He is saving his state allowance to travel around Kenya, possibly in a car of his own.

Henry no longer has his house and has been grounded from international travel. He attends educational courses in domestic duties and civic responsibilities. His house is now being used as a child-care centre, and he hopes to be allocated a cottage somewhere near the catering centre where he will be working after his two-year course. The profits from his firm have been redistributed to the Latin American firms, and the profits from the plastic goods companies (since the introduction of consumer-friendly explanation programmes of products in place of advertising) have plummeted, with the new environmentally friendly products replacing them almost entirely. Some of his Oxbridge connections have ended up in similar centres, and they are encouraged to meet to discuss the problems they find in the new world. Counselling is also available. His ex-wife has invited him to contribute to her new community centre — he does the bookkeeping and his son calls him every so often to check how he is. His secretary is running the national trading centre and is a member of the new parliament — or so he gathers from newspapers; members of his former office never did contact him again. His Mercedes was donated to a car pool in Brixton, but Henry can travel cheaply on the buses and trains with his training centre pass. He is going to night class to learn about Amazonian plants.

Manfred is now living in a community of mixed ages and is in charge of the local communications link-up. He devotes most of his time to sending messages to other communities and is enjoying a very stimulating discussion on German history after Bismarck with other teachers in Chile and Venezuela. He and another E-mail user from Kenya are suggesting course directions for a biology class for 12-year-olds in a rural town in Canada. Through the modem he has located some of his former students and they now update him regularly on their lives. Swimming every day has improved his health — and a very interesting community in Scandinavia has suggested he use his next free ticket (issued by the government every six months to pensioners) to visit them for a swim in the Nordic sea, but he is tempted more by the invitation of a biologist working in Vanuatu. In his spare time he supervises the community garden and has agreed to take part in a video project by some of the younger people who are doing local histories.

BACK TO REALITY

My fantasy is not full-fledged — and begs many unanswered questions, even if we could reverse world values, dismantle the military and unfair economic procedures, and start again. What institutions could we devise to ensure democratic rights, diversity, and solidarity? What would be the mechanisms to ensure environmental ethics and accountability of the world's governments? Could local trading, better communications, people's political participation, and the recognition of people's needs reverse the disastrous social, environmental, and economic consequences of international lending practises and the current terms of trade between industrialized and non-industrialized nations? How could we dismantle unfair protective trade measures and reverse the overexploitation of land and unsustainable agricultural practices? Just how much damage have heavy industrialization, colonization of people's knowledge and culture, and policies such as structural adjustment done — could we ever reclaim the lost knowledge and social community vision? All these questions remain. But one hope held out by my story of these fictional people is that if we were to recognize women as a powerful catalyst for creating a healthier planet, we could begin to change the policies responsible for economic, social, and political inequalities through tools such as *Agenda 21,* the foundation for much of my fantasy.

As women working in environment and development prepare for the UN Conference in Beijing, we will have a chance to draw up workable strategies to meet our vision, based on people's different realities, which could collectively unsettle the understanding of development as economic growth. Women in alliance with other groups in civil society contributed to the sustainable development debate in UNCED the vision of a new productive ethic at the heart of development which, if put into practice, would value the quality of human relations with each other and with nature. At Beijing we now have to consider the strategic activities which will transform the many useful documents and critiques of the current economic development model to include women and nature and together challenge the gender blindness of the dominant power structures of development.

Wendy Harcourt is the Director of Research, Information and Communications Editor of Development at the Society for International Development (SID) headquartered in Rome, Italy. She joined SID in 1988 after completing her Ph.D. at the Australian National University and since then has coordinated the Society's women in development programmes (SID-WID). She has written widely on gender and development, population, alternative economics and environment and recently edited Feminist Perspectives on Sustainable Development published in 1994 with Zed Books.

This article draws upon the author's "Five Years After Beijing: A Fantasy for a Just and Enabling Global Economy," *Development: Journal of the Society for International Development* (1994:4).